92083

D0932277

Political Parties and Democracy

A *Journal of Democracy* Book

•

BOOKS IN THE SERIES

Edited by Larry Diamond and Marc F. Plattner

Globalization, Power, and Democracy (2000)
(Edited by Marc F. Plattner and Aleksander Smolar)

The Democratic Invention (2000)
(Edited by Marc F. Plattner and João Carlos Espada)

Democratization in Africa (1999)

Democracy in East Asia (1998)

Consolidating the Third Wave Democracies (1997)
(with Yun-han Chu and Hung-mao Tien)

Civil-Military Relations and Democracy (1996)

The Global Resurgence of Democracy, 2nd ed. (1996)

Economic Reform and Democracy (1995)

Nationalism, Ethnic Conflict, and Democracy (1994)

Capitalism, Socialism, and Democracy Revisited (1993)

Published under the auspices of
the International Forum for Democratic Studies

Political Parties and Democracy

Edited by Larry Diamond
and Richard Gunther

The Johns Hopkins University Press
Baltimore and London

© 2001 The Johns Hopkins University Press and the National Endowment for Democracy
All rights reserved. Published 2001
Printed in the United States of America on acid-free paper

9 8 7 6 5 4 3 2 1

Chapter 3 of this volume appeared in the April 2001 issue of the *Journal of Democracy.*

The Johns Hopkins University Press
2715 North Charles Street
Baltimore, Maryland 21218-4363
www.press.jhu.edu

Library of Congress Cataloging-in-Publication Data

Political Parties and Democracy/ edited by Larry Diamond and Richard Gunther.
    p.   cm. — (A Journal of Democracy book)
    Includes bibliographical references and index.
    ISBN 0-8018-6863-7 (pbk.: alk. paper)
    1. Political parties. 2. Democracy. 3. Political science. I. Diamond, Larry Jay. II.
Gunther, Richard. III. Series.

    JF2051 .P5675 2001
324.2--dc21
                                        2001038464

A catalog record for this book is available from the British Library.

CONTENTS

IV. Conclusion

ACKNOWLEDGMENTS

Like many of the previous volumes published under the auspices of the International Forum for Democratic Studies and the *Journal of Democracy,* this book originated in a conference organized by the International Forum. More than was the case with most of our previous volumes, the essays published here (most of which were initially presented only as brief sketches) have been extensively developed, researched, and revised since the conference. Held in Washington, D.C., on 18–19 November 1996, the conference was funded by a grant from the Carnegie Corporation of New York, whom we would like to thank for its support. We are particularly grateful to the codirector of the International Forum, Marc F. Plattner, who worked closely with Larry Diamond and Richard Gunther in organizing the conference and conceptualizing the book volume that would grow out of it. We also thank the National Endowment for Democracy, especially its president Carl Gershman and its board chairman during this period, John Brademas, for their strong support of the International Forum and this project. We owe a special intellectual and personal debt to Juan Linz for his innovative thinking on the questions addressed by this book and for his encouragement of our individual and collaborative work on this and related themes. For their early contributions, we thank Debra Liang-Fenton, who assisted with the organization of the conference and production of the report, and Neovi Karakatsanis, who prepared the conference report (available online at *www.ned.org*). At the Hoover Institution, Alice Carter ably and cheerfully supported our efforts in her role as assistant to Larry Diamond.

This book has been a truly collaborative project, not only between the two editors but also among all the participants. We are grateful to the authors for their responsiveness to our research agenda and to the critical comments and editorial suggestions they received, as well as for the candid and challenging comments they offered us on our theoretical framework. Once again, we thank Henry Tom and the staff of the Johns Hopkins University Press for their wise counsel and enthusiastic support of our books and the *Journal of Democracy*. Most of all, we thank the staff of the *Journal of Democracy* for their outstanding work in editing and producing this volume. Zerxes Spencer managed these stages of our work with unfailing efficiency, thoroughness, grace, and good humor. Stephanie Lewis brought the same impressive creativity, passion, and precision to the production of these pages that she brings to the quarterly publication of the *Journal of Democracy*. In editing the manuscripts as they reached their final form, Zerxes and Stephanie were joined by Jordan Branch and Kristin Helz. All four performed with skill, care, enthusiasm, and equanimity, even as our book deadlines approached and overlapped with those of the *Journal*. Kristin also prepared the index scrupulously and intelligently, without wilting under the usual last-minute pressure of this final step. It has been a great pleasure and a redeeming relief to work with this enormously talented, devoted, and generous staff.

INTRODUCTION

Larry Diamond and Richard Gunther

There is an ironic and worrisome twist to the third wave of global democratization. In the past quarter-century, democracy has spread around the world to an unprecedented degree. Levels of civil and political freedom are the highest, on average, in history. Authoritarian ideologies have waned, and no form of government other than democracy has any significant legitimacy. Yet there is substantial and growing disaffection with many of the specific institutions of democracy, and no single institution is held in greater disrepute than the political party.

Throughout the established Trilateral democracies—Japan, North America, and Europe—confidence in government is in decline. Citizens are cynical about their representative institutions, political parties, and, most of all, their politicians. Trust or confidence in these institutions is almost everywhere low (with more than half the public cynical or distrusting) and it has been steadily declining. Indeed, Robert Putnam, Susan Pharr, and Russell Dalton conclude, *"there is evidence of some decline in confidence in politicians in 12 out of 13 countries for which systematic data are available."*[1]

Even more "clear and striking" has been the erosion of partisan attachments among contemporary publics. In almost all the advanced industrial democracies (including 17 of 19 for which time-series data are available), the proportion of the population identifying with a political party has declined in the past quarter-century, as has the strength of party attachments.[2] This appears to have been driven not only by objective political developments but also by generational trends, as younger, better-educated citizens have lower levels of party loyalty, even though they have *higher* levels of political interest and engagement.

In the developing and "third-wave" democracies, the attachment to political parties is even weaker, and cynicism about parties and politicians is more ominous in its implications for democratic stability. Only one in five Latin Americans (across 17 democracies in the region) expresses "a lot" or "some" confidence in political parties, while 45 percent have no confidence at all in parties.[3] Only one in five Koreans trusts political parties, while across 11 postcommunist states the proportion is only one in eight,[4] reflecting the diffuse communist legacy of distrust of parties and state institutions.

Outside the Trilateral democracies in particular, political skepticism extends well beyond parties. In both Korea and the postcommunist states, levels of trust or confidence in national legislatures stand at a mere 22 percent, and in Latin America they average only 28 percent. Confidence in the judiciary is much higher in Korea (57 percent), but not in Latin America (34 percent) or the postcommunist states (29 percent). In these countries, disaffection is a broader phenomenon, encompassing detachment and even alienation. Both individual political efficacy and system efficacy (belief that the system is capable of solving the country's problems) appear to be declining. And satisfaction with the way democracy works is well under 50 percent.[5]

In consolidated democracies (including, for example, India and Costa Rica), disaffection does not translate into delegitimation, because the *values* of democracy are so deeply rooted. However, the implications of disaffection are much more serious in countries where democracy is not consolidated—most of the third-wave democracies of Asia, Latin America, Africa, and the postcommunist world. Where the legitimacy of democracy is not deeply rooted at all levels of society, dissatisfaction and disaffection with democracy are much more likely over the long term to give rise to preferences for, or diminished resistance to, the return of some form of authoritarian rule.[6] It would be too much to argue that institutionally strong political parties are a *necessary* condition for consolidating democracy or maintaining its vitality. Even in the absence of stable and institutionally strong parties, Poland, Hungary, and the Czech Republic consolidated their new democracies fairly rapidly during the 1990s because of other overwhelmingly favorable factors (including close proximity to Western Europe and political cultures that generated strong initial commitments to democracy).[7] Where democracy is not rapidly legitimated by other means, however, weak political institutions, poor political performance, and the consequent cynicism about parties and politicians obstruct the consolidation—and even risk undermining the viability—of democracy.

Why Has Support for Parties Declined?

As we have seen, survey data collected in both new and established democracies reveal low and declining levels of support for parties among the general public. Why have these negative attitudes become so widespread? A wide variety of explanatory factors have emerged from the literature in recent years. Juan Linz has recently speculated that the fault may not lie with the parties per se, but rather may be rooted in the values and beliefs of the mass public. His empirical evidence suggests that many of the criticisms of parties by ordinary citizens may derive from attitudes that are inherently contradictory, or from unreasonable expectations of party performance that are impossible to meet, particularly in light of the increasing number of demanding roles that parties must perform in democratic systems.[8] Richard Gunther and Anthony Mughan speculate that negative attitudes toward partisan politics in the United States (and increasingly in some other countries as well) may be at least partly the product of a pervasive cynicism toward politics and politicians on the part of journalists, especially those who cover political news on television. In the aftermath of Watergate and the Vietnam War, journalists have increasingly exhibited disdain for politicians as a class, questioned their motives, and portrayed their policy proposals as little more than manipulations in a cynical game whose objective is nothing more than self-perpetuation in office.[9]

Still other studies attribute declining support to the inability of political parties to adapt to social and cultural changes and thereby satisfy new demands and expectations of citizens. Ronald Inglehart traces declining party loyalty to deep currents of normative and social change, to which most political parties have only weakly adapted. The major parties were established in eras defined by class conflict and the preeminence of economic issues, whereas the more recent, "postmaterialist" generations are concerned more with "cultural and quality of life issues" that cut across the established party divisions. In addition, postmaterialist publics do not take well to the "hierarchical, oligarchical" structures of old-style, centralized political parties.[10] In some new democracies, low support for contemporary parties may result from the inheritance of antidemocratic attitudes explicitly disseminated by the previous regime,[11] popular revulsion against the previous all-encompassing domination by a single totalitarian or authoritarian party, or the "flattened landscape" left behind by communist rule.[12] In short, mass public detachment from political parties may be generated by social, cultural, or historical factors having little to do with the current performance of parties in contemporary democracies.

Our concern in this volume, however, is with the actual roles that parties play in contemporary democracies and with how well they are meeting both citizens' performance expectations and the functional demands implicit in the concept of representative democracy. Accordingly, a different set of explanatory factors assumes greater relevance. One of these factors involves the extent of misconduct by parties and politicians in many countries. Susan Pharr's analysis of Japan suggests that declining or persistently low levels of trust in public institutions are driven much less by economic or policy performance than by "conduct in office." Perceptions of official misconduct—generated by the interaction between actual misconduct and media exposure of it—are significantly correlated with declines in public confidence in political institutions.[13] And entrenched corruption generates gross maladministration that interacts in a vicious circle with public disaffection and distrust. The Italian experience of pervasive, institutionalized misuse of public resources for party and personal enrichment (and the ultimate instability of this system) is particularly important for its generalizability to so many African, Latin American, and other developing democracies.[14]

Another potentially powerful explanation is the general sense that politicians and government officials are a privileged class unto themselves. The mass media feed with frenzy on this cynical view, pouncing on any story that substantiates it. But to some extent, it is grounded in reality. Perceptions of self-serving, unresponsive, and unaccountable governance may derive from the change in the nature of political parties in many advanced democracies. It has been widely argued that parties have evolved over the past century from ideologically distinctive and compelling mass-membership organizations that touched and even enveloped a large proportion of the citizenry toward more generic "catch-all" parties. In this volume, Seymour Martin Lipset documents substantial ideological change among West European "socialist" parties, which have progressively abandoned traditional commitments to public ownership of the means of production and regulation of the economy, in favor of the free-market, smaller government policies of the American Democratic Party in the 1990s. Insofar as party supporters and activists remain committed to traditional ideological and programmatic stands, this shift may contribute to disillusionment and distance. (This may be particularly true of cases like Britain under Tony Blair and Germany under Gerhard Schröder, where the party leadership has moved decisively toward the center of the political spectrum.) The tensions between party leaders and followers arising from a sense of betrayal of a party's ideological commitment were identified in the early twentieth century by Robert Michels. However, the notion of a self-interested, unprincipled, power-seeking party elite finds its most extensive elaboration in Richard Katz and Peter Mair's concept of the "cartel party."[15] As the latter term implies, the new model of party appears more separated than ever from society, as party leaders use public financing and expanded state functions to restrain competition and perpetuate themselves in power for power's sake.

Disaffection may also spring from a much broader accumulation of institutional deficiencies in the functioning of democracy that inhibit public accountability and good governance. Systems of party and campaign finance are deeply flawed in many democracies—old and new—permitting the raw (and often secret) purchase of power and influence by privileged interests. Many of our case studies show how the need for large and ever-growing amounts of political finance has become particularly acute in an era when television has become the principal medium of communication between parties and citizens, and in systems that permit the purchase of airtime for commercial campaign advertisements. Ironically, the problem has intensified with the rupture of the state's monopoly over the electronic media, generating a market for political advertising. Citizens seem powerless to change this system, but the media are certainly not powerless to expose it and rail against it (even as they profit enormously from the sale of political advertising time). The combination of a more or less corrupt system of party and campaign finance with a stream of blatant scandals and a backlog of public aspirations for more responsive government that go unmet (while being amplified by a cynical media) generate growing public disillusionment with democratic politics and government. In short, parties may be the lightning rod for criticisms growing out of dissatisfaction with the broader functioning of democracy.

But the more fundamental questions that have served as a recurring theme in this volume involve the extent to which parties have simply ceased to perform their core representational and governmental roles in contemporary democracies. Is the decline in popular support for parties a reflection of a "decline of parties?" To what extent have parties ceased to perform the functions traditionally assigned to them both in democratic theory and in traditional democratic practice? Are other groups or institutions in society stepping in to perform services that were once the responsibility of parties, as Philippe Schmitter implies in chapter 4 of this volume? Or are the changes in the scope of their organizations, in their penetration into society, in their recruitment of citizen activists, or in the tasks performed by parties merely indicative of an evolution from one type of political party to another over the course of the twentieth century? It is to this broader set of issues that we turn our attention.

Before doing so, however, a word about the scope of this volume is in order. The design of this book has grown from a conviction about the urgent need to expand the comparative breadth of research on democracy. In particular, understanding how parties are evolving and changing as political institutions requires examining parties within a wide variety of democratic regimes, in different cultural and historical settings and levels of development. The literature on political parties is enormous: One survey of the field since 1945 has found approximately 11,500 published articles, monographs, and books dealing with parties and party systems in Western Europe alone![16] But the overwhelming majority of previous publications have been of three kinds: 1) noncomparative, monographic studies of individual parties or of parties within a single country;[17] 2) crossnational comparative studies of parties that focus exclusively on one region;[18] and 3) more rigorous comparative analyses of specific sets of party-related themes, but restricted to the advanced industrial democracies (usually of Western Europe and North America).[19]

In many respects, this is a rich literature that has contributed much, empirically and theoretically, to comparative politics. Yet with few exceptions, its limited geographical focus has impeded the kind of broadly comparative empirical research necessary to identify truly general patterns and ultimately to develop theories regarding parties in general—in all varieties of democratic regimes, both new and long-established. One of the strengths of this volume is that it includes empirical studies of parties in a wide array of democratic systems, in Western Europe, Eastern Europe, Latin America, Japan, India, Turkey, and Taiwan, as well as more theoretically oriented pieces with no specific geographical focus.

Evolution and Change in the Nature of Parties

As we note in our own opening chapter, the pervasive erosion in party membership, loyalty, and social ties can be read in different ways. Where some analysts perceive a decline in the central role of political parties in democracy, others see an evolution in the nature and, to some extent, the functions of parties. A systematic analysis of whether political parties are truly declining or merely evolving must therefore begin by delineating the functions that parties perform, and then relating these functions to different types of parties. These are the two essential tasks of chapter 1. We begin by identifying seven functions that parties commonly perform in democracies. First, they recruit and nominate candidates for elective office. Second, they mobilize electoral support for these candidates and stimulate electoral participation. Third, they structure the choices among competing groups of candidates along different issue dimensions. Fourth, they represent different social groups, either symbolically or in advancing different specific interests. Fifth, they aggregate specific interests into broader electoral and governing coalitions. Sixth, they form and sustain governments. Seventh, they integrate citizens more broadly into the nation-state and its political process. Different parties and parties in different political systems perform these seven functions to different degrees and with varying levels of effectiveness.

One value of identifying such a core list of functions is that it permits us to explore hypotheses that parties may be changing in the mix of functions that they perform. For example, the electoral functions of parties, in nominating candidates, waging campaigns, and mobilizing support, remain core functions of parties, and ones that parties are uniquely well equipped to perform. However, as interests grow more diverse with modernization (and "postmodernization"), and as increasingly numerous and diverse organizations and movements in civil society gain in resources, sophistication, and popular involvement, parties appear to be losing the dominant roles they once played in structuring issues, and particularly in representing and aggregating interests. The decline of parties relative to civil society in the latter two functions is a major theme of Schmitter's chapter 4. Civil society may also be eclipsing parties in the "social integration" function, even as parties retain the dominant role in forming and sustaining governments.

The framework we present in chapter 1 is distinctive and perhaps controversial for its conscious decision to eschew the parsimony of existing typologies. The latter, we argue, suffer two major deficiencies. First, having been derived from studies of West European parties over more than a century, they fail to capture crucial features of parties in other parts of the world. One reason why the previous typologies may have been so parsimonious is that they were derived from and applied to only one geographical region, within which there was a small range of variation among the existing political parties. For the purposes of this volume—whose cases range across both old and new democracies and include all regions of democratic experience except Africa—the sharply restricted number and range of party models in the traditional typologies proved to be wholly inadequate. Second, by selecting only one criterion as the basis of the typology, earlier frameworks have not adequately captured the real-world variation in party types. By contrast, our typology is constructed on the basis of three criteria: the size of the party's formal organization and scope of its functions, whether the party is pluralistic or hegemonic in its aspirations, and the level of commitment to an ideology or program. These criteria yield a typology with 15 different "species" of party, each belonging to one of five broader party types (elite parties, mass-based parties, ethnicity-based parties, electoralist parties, and movement parties). These 15 party types are then distinguished by their goals, their electoral strategy, their organizational structure and linkages, and their social bases. (For a summary of these features, see Table 2 of chapter 1.)

A major implication of our framework in chapter 1 is that political parties have evolved over the past century toward leaner, more organizationally "thin" structures that perform a more limited set of functions, focused principally around elections. Yet while the function of parties in structuring issues, particularly in coherent, sharply ideological terms, has generally declined, we do not discern a universal trend toward less ideological or programmatic parties (as was anticipated by Otto Kirchheimer's widely influential model of the "catch-all" party). In fact, we find that the degree of issue structuration by parties may shift back and forth over time. Clearly, the historical model of the centralized, hierarchical, mass-based party (such as the European socialist, social democratic, and denominational parties) is waning, with only religious fundamentalist parties (among new or recently formed ones) still manifesting this character. With socioeconomic modernization (and the value transformations associated with "postmodernization"), and with the spread of mass communications (particularly television and now the Internet), the ways that party organizations and elites relate to citizens and social groups have fundamentally changed. But changes in party organizational forms, electoral strategies, and programmatic goals are not driven merely by broad social changes. Any typology of parties must leave room for political choice and innovation. This is why change is not always linear, with old types reviving and mutating even as new ones emerge.

The rise and historical evolution of parties is the subject of Hans Daalder's study in chapter 2. Political parties emerged in Western societies through a number of different paths to inclusive democracy (polyarchy). In the United States, parties developed early alongside the early introduction of responsible government and a wide franchise, but well before the onset of industrialization. As a result, parties were relatively loose organizationally and localized in scope. In Great Britain, where industrialization came earlier but the franchise was extended later, parties developed early on a more elitist but cohesive nature, and only later did they develop broader mobilizational capacities. In Germany, where industrialization occurred early, along with universal suffrage but well before responsible government, "the socialist movement developed into a prototype of a mass party," but parties were retarded by the long history of autocratic rule. Elsewhere in Europe, Daalder shows how the timing of industrialization in relation to the development of electoral institutions shaped the emerging structure of political cleavages and hence the nature of political parties. The variety of parties that emerged in Western societies is then analyzed along five dimensions. One of these dimensions concerns legitimacy. In countries with a long tradition of representative government, parties generally developed slowly, but developed strong legitimacy. By contrast, where democracy followed or was interrupted by a long period of authoritarian rule, parties struggled for legitimacy or became radicalized. Parties can also be distinguished by whether they were "internally created" (by elites) or "externally created" from social groups mobilizing a mass base; by their success in integrating large swaths of the population; by their geographical scope (national versus local); and by the extent of their reach into various arenas of the state. Each of these five dimensions has also generated characteristic criticisms of parties, for their divisiveness, their populism, their denial to voters of truly free choice, their patronage and corruption, and their parochialism—or instead their excessive centralization. Daalder's conclusion corresponds with our own analysis in chapter 1: While parties face increasing competition from a variety of other actors "in the expression and articulation of policy demands," they remain, "almost by definition . . . the decisive agents of political recruitment."

In chapter 3, Seymour Martin Lipset identifies "the Americanization of the European left" as a striking trend in the recent evolution of parties globally. Marxist thinkers theorized in the nineteenth and early twentieth centuries that the United States, as the most industrialized capitalist country, would lead the world into socialism. Yet, Lipset notes with irony, Marx's dictum—that the more developed country "shows to the less developed the image of their future"—has been realized in reverse fashion. The United States has led other countries not into socialism but into the abandonment of it, as "the left in other Western democracies has become increasingly like the American nonsocialist left." Like the U.S. Democratic party, other Western parties of the left have eroded or rejected the interventionist social democratic state and moved toward or embraced "the free-market, smaller-government policies of Bill Clinton." In Australia, New Zealand, and most of Western Europe, social democratic and labor governments have pushed deregulation, privatization, tax cuts, wage restraint, and fiscal responsibility. This gravitation of left parties toward a much more ideologically moderate agenda, particularly on economic issues, "heralds an end to class as the dominant feature structuring party politics," and is in fact driven by profound changes in class structure. The historic rigidities and inequalities of European societies have been substantially leveled by economic growth and expanding access to education. As a result, not simply in the United States but throughout the Western democracies left political parties must "appeal more to the growing middle strata than to industrial workers and the impoverished," as the latter two groups account for declining proportions of the population. Both the proportion of workers in manufacturing and union membership rates have declined sharply in recent decades, greatly weakening the class basis of voting, while globalization has diminished the policy scope of all governments (a point echoed in the following chapter by Schmitter, and in the conclusion by Stefano Bartolini and Peter Mair). In a growing climate of affluence, ideological conflict over the role of the state has increasingly given way to concern with "postmaterialist" quality-of-life issues, such as health, the environment, and gender equality. And the parties of the left have increasingly emphasized these types of social and cultural issues. The distinction between "left" and "right" persists, Lipset observes, but it "will never again be defined by the contest between socialism and capitalism." Rather, ideological differences between parties have narrowed and become more fluid as "party systems float in search of a new grand line of cleavage."

For Schmitter, the most crucial historical change is that parties have lost their preeminent role in the representation and aggregation of interests. Citizens have acquired a much more diverse array of interests and skills, and interest associations and social movements have become much more vigorous competitors to parties for the opportunity to represent and mobilize citizens outside of the electoral arena. In the effort to consolidate new or recent democracies (which are the focus of his study), parties remain dominant in structuring the electoral process, governing, and perhaps even in "symbolic integration" of citizens into the democratic process, but they perform these functions much less effectively than they once did. In these democracies, electoral turnout is low or declining, partisan alignments are notoriously volatile, and nonparty or "antiparty" candidates have enjoyed growing success. As for "symbolic integration," the low rates of party membership and identification (by historical standards) suggest that parties do "not seem to be providing much of a diffuse political identity for citizens." To be sure, parties still form governments, but these are thrown out of office more frequently than in the past. And once in power, parties find their independent scope to set broad policy courses constrained by various supranational actors.

Schmitter speculates that parties are losing their capacity to control governing elites. For as they become less connected to society, and more professionalized and dependent on the state for revenue, their claims to represent "the interests and passions of civil society and individual citizens" become ever more implausible. Their capacity to aggregate interests, Schmitter argues, has been weakened, not enhanced, by the evaporation of distinctive partisan ideologies, in that parties no longer "aggregate 'actively' by asserting a higher public purpose." The erosion of linkages to other types of organizations and of direct channels of communication with citizens has also undermined parties' ability to aggregate interests. All of these trends lead Schmitter to question "whether or not political parties are really so indispensable for the consolidation or even the simple perpetuation of democracy." Indeed, he suggests that democracies new and old will probably have to live with "a great deal less electoral structuration, symbolic identification, party governance, and interest aggregation" than were produced in earlier historical eras.

The first section of the book concludes with an essay in chapter 5 by Giovanni Sartori on the consequences of electoral systems for political parties and party systems. In offering several rules and hypotheses, Sartori challenges several misconceptions about electoral systems and their effects. Electoral systems shape party systems by constraining (manipulating) voters. If they do so with some effect, then they reduce the number of parties. But Sartori cautions strongly against the tendency to "count" parties at face value by purely mathematical formulas. Reviving a major theme of his earlier work, he insists that parties should only be counted if they are "relevant," and this depends on their coalition potential and their blackmail potential (and hence their ability to affect other parties and the party system as a whole). Among the misconceptions Sartori shatters is the notion that a plurality system inevitably produces two predominant parties. A plurality system will help to maintain an existing two-party system, but it will only *produce* a two-party format where there are nationwide parties, and where politically cohesive, "incoercible minorities" are dispersed throughout the constituencies in proportions below those necessary to win a plurality of the vote. Otherwise, third parties can take hold based on support from these "incoercible minorities" (be they racial, linguistic, or ideological). More generally, the distribution of such minorities territorially across districts is crucial for understanding whether and how electoral systems (including ones of moderate proportional representation) will restrain the number of parties.

Most change in electoral systems has been toward greater proportionality, but Sartori ponders the question of why the switch toward a more majoritarian formula worked in France (after 1959) but not in Italy (after the reforms of the mid-1990s). The answer, he argues, lies in France's choice of the double-ballot plurality system, along with heightened thresholds of exclusion and a direct-majoritarian presidential election. Italy had none of these three additional tools to reduce the number of parties and suffered in particular from its failure to adopt the double-ballot system. As Italy switched to single-member-district, plurality elections (for three-quarters of the seats in parliament), small parties actually acquired greater "blackmail leverage" in the new districts, where victory or defeat could be decided by very small margins. This leverage could have been neutralized by a second ballot, but without that crucial institution, electoral alliances have had to grant small parties some seats in order to keep them from drawing away votes in other districts. Thus, ironically, in post-reform Italy, "it is not PR but the winner-take-all system that multiplies parties (by extending and facilitating their relevance)."

Sartori also criticizes the common confusion over "mixed" electoral systems. Many observers treat the German electoral system as "mixed" but it is in fact an entirely proportional system that is "mixed" only in that half of the members are elected in individual districts (with the remainder of the house drawn from party lists to achieve proportionality). Truly mixed systems, such as the Japanese, Russian, and Italian, "are objectionable in that they confuse voters" with two contradictory logics ("sincere" versus "strategic" voting) and similarly prompt parties "to engage in schizophrenic behavior" (coalescing in plurality district contests while fighting one another for the PR vote). The ultimate end of PR, Sartori reminds us, is "representative justice" while that of majoritarian elections is "governing capacity." In his view, "One of the two ends . . . must have clear priority and prevail over the other."

Less clear is the impact of electoral systems on the nature of parties. Single-member-district systems tend to generate more "personalized" and locality-based politics, and PR more "party-based" politics with centralized parties. But many other factors bear on these features of parties and politics, including who controls the financing of parties.

Parties and Party Systems After Reform

In the advanced industrial democracies, two-party systems experienced significant upheaval during the 1990s as a result of scandals, pressures for reform, and the altered political and ideological context that followed the end of the Cold War. These two cases, Italy and Japan, are explored in chapters 6 and 7. As Leonardo Morlino shows in chapter 6, the transformation of Italy's parties and party system has been particularly striking. Established in 1948, the postwar Italian republic featured organizationally strong and complex parties that deeply penetrated society. As a result of the variety of strong social and political (including ideological) cleavages and Italy's highly proportional electoral law, the Italian system has also featured a large number of parties. Three of these were classic mass parties with a strong ideological or programmatic definition and very extensive organization. The long-time dominant force in postwar ruling coalitions, the Christian Democratic party (DC), was in many ways the model of a denominational party, heavily dependent on the support of Catholic organizations (but with a rather diffuse agenda and a low level of internal institutionalization). The communists (PCI) epitomized the classic party of mass integration (based on class identity). For much of its postwar history, the party had a Leninist style of organization with strong leadership domination, no trace of the factions that riddled the DC, and a widespread network of cells composed of devoted followers. Over time, however, as Italy developed economically and any prospect of social revolution faded, the PCI evolved into a more pragmatic, less mobilizational party. The third mass party, the Socialists (PSI), strived for but never attained the communists' scope and intensity of mobilization. Yet until it imploded in the 1990s, the PSI averaged around half a million members (one-third the level of the other two mass parties). The other principal parties of the postwar era were elite or opinion parties with much smaller memberships and less extensive alliances in society, but still important enough to serve as recurring coalition partners for the Christian Democrats.

The parties of the postwar era and especially the 1950s heavily pene-trated and dominated Italian civil society, not only through ideological and organizational ties but also through extensive clientelistic networks that drew heavily on parties' control of the booming public sector to distribute patronage. Morlino shows how increasing competition among governing parties intensified the need for material and political resources after the early 1960s, and especially after the mid-1970s, with the growth of private television broadcasting and new communication technologies. This not only reinforced the dependence of interest groups and other civil society actors on the parties but also led to growing levels of political corruption, as governing parties came increasingly to rely on kickbacks to finance increasingly expensive campaigns. It was the systematic exposure of these practices in the *mani pulite* ("clean hands") investigation of 1992–94 that brought the postwar party system crashing down and essentially wiped out the Christian Democrats and Socialists (while the communists renamed and transformed themselves after the fall of the Berlin Wall).

The parties of the new era in Italian democracy are considerably weaker institutionally and less ideological, and have been partially eclipsed by political movements or electoral campaigns based on single issues or personalities. Party membership and political participation have sharply declined, apathy and alienation have mushroomed, and parties have largely lost the pervasive, hierarchical ties they once had to interest groups and ancillary organizations in civil society. The transition toward more shallow, "electoral" parties has been paralleled by the striking rise of personalistic politics, particularly as waged by Silvio Berlusconi, the billionaire founder of Forza Italia who won a stunning victory in 2001 to recover the prime ministerial post he had briefly held in 1994. To some extent, these developments accelerate trends that were already underway during the 1980s. However, they have put a decisive end to the era of mass parties in Italy. The ghost of that party model survives in the form of the "modern cadre party," but with greatly reduced membership and greater prominence of electoral and movement parties. In Italy, as elsewhere, Morlino concludes that parties no longer monopolize key functions the way they once did, particularly the representation and aggregation of interests.

As Bradley Richardson explains in chapter 7, Japan had an even more remarkably stable (and clientelistic) party system that also suffered major shocks and pressures for reform in the 1990s (triggered, as in Italy, by corruption scandals and an associated loss of leadership credibility). These did topple the "1955 system," under which the conservative Liberal Democratic Party (LDP) had held sway over the society and all other parties for nearly four decades. But they did not obliterate the long-ruling party, as happened in Italy. Instead, after the defection of nearly a fifth of the party's MPs and its 1993 electoral setback and loss of power, the party soon returned to power, albeit without the institutional strength, self-confidence, and sociopolitical hegemony it had enjoyed for nearly four decades.

The most striking features of the LDP, as Japan's prototypical political party, have been a highly factionalized structure and the pervasive salience of personal networks. Factions are in fact networks—"groups of followers of a particular politician" who over time evolved into more the role of manager than that of pure patron. However, factions are themselves composed of more localized and personalized networks of support for individual candidates. Together, factionalism and networking substantially negate the formal centralization of party organization and in fact so thoroughly characterize the actual operation of the LDP that Richardson terms it a "mass personalized-network party." Factionalism produces "multiple party hierarchies," which generate a multiplicity of influence flows within the party, some of which move from the bottom up. Richardson's highly informed account of the LDP substantiates Angelo Panebianco's argument that parties are ultimately coalitions, not unitary organizations. Japanese parties in particular, he shows, are "political systems with enormous amounts of internal conflict," and their need to evolve informal as well as formal rules and structures to regulate these conflicts has been an important determinant of their nature. The coalitional nature of the LDP, functioning internally "much like a multiparty system," has been particularly apparent when it has had to make leadership choices, though it is also visible in the party's considerable policy cleavages (expressed in different policy groups). The latter divisions have been exacerbated by the party's very breadth of domination, encompassing a much wider range of interest-group ties than those of any single Italian party. The strength of the LDP—its huge coalitional breadth—has thus also been its vulnerability, bringing the party repeatedly near the brink of collapse. Other Japanese parties, such as the Socialist (now Social Democratic) Party, have suffered from the same fragmenting potential of factionalism, but without anything like the LDP's power or base of support.

The prominence of clientelistic ties, and the importance of government positions in helping to fill the mounting need for political finance, are two significant similarities between the Italian and Japanese postwar party systems. Factions, Richardson shows, have rested on "an exchange of political resources" between the members and the leader. Within the long-ruling LDP factions, members supported their leaders in contests for overall party leadership, and in exchange they received political funding and access to party and government positions. Factional ties also helped Diet members to service the needs of their districts (notably through a seemingly endless flow of public works projects). In these ways, factions have been important resources for election and reelection. But no less crucial have been the personal support associations (koenkai) of LDP politicians. These local electoral machines have been crucial mechanisms for exchanging favors with voters, representing local interests, and so maintaining MPs' bases of electoral support. At the same time, these political machines of Diet members are a principal means for the "strong upward flow of pressure" on behalf of local and regional interests to the national party councils. It is these informal structures that give the party an active local base, even though the formal structures of individual membership and local party branches may be largely nominal. In fact, it appears from Richardson's analysis that if factionalism and informal personal networks have contributed much to the LDP's institutional fragility and recurrent crises, they may also account for its remarkable resilience.

Developing and Postcommunist Systems

The third section of our book begins with an examination of party evolution in Latin America, then moves on to three illuminating individual country cases—India, Turkey, and Taiwan—before concluding with an analysis of the divergent paths that party systems have taken in postcommunist democracies.

Next to Europe and North America, Latin America is the region with the longest democratic experience and therefore some of the oldest political parties and party systems. Yet as Michael Coppedge demonstrates in chapter 8, most Latin American political parties have not lasted long. Indeed, of the 1,200 parties that competed in 166 twentieth-century legislative elections, only 15 (barely 1 percent) contested all the elections held in their countries, and 80 percent contested only once before disappearing! Most of these parties—especially those that endured, and even the more ideological ones—have been strongly clientelistic in nature. European-style class-mass parties have fared much more poorly in Latin America, in part "because industrialization came late to Latin America and never transformed society to the same degree that it did in Europe." Treating the same variables as Daalder does in chapter 2, Coppedge shows that a rapid expansion of the suffrage and electoral politics in advance of industrialization led in most of Latin America to "national revolutionary" parties that sought to mobilize broad cross-class coalitions behind diffuse nationalistic and anti-oligarchical platforms. These parties epitomized the eclectic features that would continue to characterize Latin American parties and make them, in Coppedge's view, difficult to fit neatly within the typology in chapter 1. To a considerable extent, these parties sought to mobilize mass followings, and in some cases heavily penetrated society with strongly hierarchical (and in the case of Venezuela's AD, even Leninist) organization. However, their political methods were heavily clientelistic, and their lack of any coherent ideology or consistent program resembles the "catch-all" party type. Seemingly denominational parties were also more clientelistic and often personalistic, as well as less closely tied to the church, than their European counterparts. In general, the nature of Latin American parties has changed in recent decades. As in Europe, interpersonal methods of mobilizing mass constituencies have greatly declined with economic development and technological change, focusing election campaigns around polling and mass-media advertising, and making parties increasingly dependent on large amounts of public and private funding. But more so than in Europe, "new techniques often

supplement the old ones," for the persistent poverty and huge inequalities of Latin America continue to provide fertile soil for clientelism.

Coppedge's main concern is to explain the change in the nature of
parties and party systems during Latin America's economically trying
period of structural adjustment, from 1982–95. He finds that change
came more from the rise of new parties and the fall of old ones than from
adaptation by longstanding parties. His Table 3 shows that among the
biggest winners of this period were a long list of newly emerging parties,
while governing parties—which were held responsible for economic
performance—typically suffered large and even devastating losses. Not
all parties were equally vulnerable to this harsh, Darwinian process of
selection, however. The impact of economic performance on the vote
was mediated by the strength of party identification, as parties with a
solid support base weathered stresses much better than those with a
fluid base. Among the latter, governing parties that presided over raging
inflation suffered especially large losses.

Coppedge's case studies of three established, left-of-center governing
parties show how important policy adaptation was to political survival.
Peru's APRA and Venezuela's AD failed to reposition themselves
ideologically by consistently implementing and embracing market-
friendly stabilization and structural adjustment measures. By contrast,
under Carlos Menem, Argentina's Peronist party did make this
"wrenching adaptation," liberalizing trade, privatizing state enterprises,
and cutting budgets in a manner reminiscent of what Lipset describes in
the "Americanization" of Europe's left-of-center parties. As a result, the
Peronists thrived under Menem (and Argentina conquered inflation),
while APRA nearly went extinct following the economic disarray of
Alan García's presidency, and AD lost 40 percent of its voters. Coppedge
concludes that the Darwinian reality of this period involved a Faustian
bargain for leftist parties: "Surrender your soul and you can live forever;
otherwise, you will die." Most of the ruling left-of-center parties in this
period "either would not or could not keep such a bargain" and thus
were replaced by right-of-center or highly personalistic and opportunistic
political alternatives.

In its first half-century, India's democracy has also witnessed the rise
and fall, as well as transformation, of many parties. But as E. Sridharan
and Ashutosh Varshney demonstrate in chapter 9, the evolution of parties
and the party system in India has been constrained by three key factors.
Two of these are institutional: a majoritarian, first-past-the-post (FPTP)
electoral system and federalism. The other is India's extraordinarily
complex web of multiple, cross-cutting cleavages (including religion,
language, and caste), each containing to some extent the nationwide
mobilizational potential of the other. This combination of intricate social
diversity and two powerful institutional arrangements has "created an
increasingly *plural*—but not sharply *polarized*—party system at the

national level," while pressing the "wide and often confusing array of political parties" toward moderate, centrist, coalition-building postures. The Indian case demonstrates one of Sartori's arguments in chapter 5: that a plurality electoral system will only produce a two-party framework where there are nationwide parties, and where politically cohesive, "incoercible minorities" are not sufficiently concentrated to win pluralities in single-member districts. In India, neither of these conditions obtains. As Sridharan and Varshney show, numerous regional and sectional parties arose to contest the long-running dominance of the Congress Party (the only truly national party), and they benefited precisely from the ability to win in constituencies as well as entire states dominated by more peripheral linguistic and caste groupings. Together, the two institutions of federalism and FPTP have produced an interesting hybrid of "multiple polarities": a highly fragmented party system nationally, straddling a collection of mainly two-party (or two-alliance) systems at the state level.

Sridharan and Varshney document two quite striking features of this party landscape in India. First, even though one might expect the presence of so many parties (with 24 in the BJP's 1999 pre-election coalition alone) to produce polarizing, centrifugal tendencies, the logic of Indian party politics has been centripetal. Parties like the BJP have had to attenuate militant ideological tendencies if they are to have any hope of leading a national governing coalition. The moderation over time of the right-wing, Hindu nationalist ideology of the BJP has been particularly striking, as the party has had to forge alliances with a welter of different regional, caste, and religious interests. Even in the linguistically homogeneous states, parties have had to reach somewhat broadly across caste and other social divisions in order to prevail. Second, although religion and ideology (still often leftist or socialist) appear to figure strongly in the substantive appeals of many parties, Sridharan and Varshney argue persuasively that most of India's parties are better viewed as ethnic in nature. The Congress party, we argue in chapter 1, has been the quintessential model of a broad ethnic alliance party resting on a vast network of regional elites and local notables (although Sridharan and Varshney view it as having evolved into a catch-all party). The many state-based, linguistic parties are, by definition, ethnic. The BJP's program appears centered around its elevation of Hinduism, but given the religion's doctrinal diversity and lack of an organized church, and given the party's promotion of "a broad Hindu identity" rather than religion per se, the BJP is better labeled an "ethno-nationalist party." Its overarching ideological goal has been to mold Hindus as a people with a common culture into a "consciously Hindu nation" that transcends linguistic and caste lines.

The powerful social and institutional incentives toward "moderate pluralism," Sridharan and Varshney suggest, keep India's democracy stable, even while the party system fragments nationally and individual parties wax and wane. The stable persistence of Indian democracy is especially impressive given the "long-term deinstitutionalization" of what was once thought to be the anchor of the system: the Congress as a dominant ruling party. For over two decades, the Congress party ruled a succession of stable majority governments (regularly manufactured by FPTP from a mere plurality of the vote). However, beginning in the late 1960s under Indira Gandhi, the party's organizational depth, pluralism, tolerance, and ability to resolve conflict and maintain coalitions all crumbled, while the party failed to respond to the demands of "newly mobilized interests and identity groups." The party has never fully recovered from this long institutional decline. Corresponding with this rising electoral uncertainty and competitiveness over the past three decades have been globally familiar trends: the increasing use of mass-media advertising and centralized, professional campaigning, and parties' growing need for large-scale campaign finance, often generated by kickbacks on government licenses and contracts. In this respect, India confronts a problem that increasingly vexes many democracies, new and old, around the world.

Institutional decline has been even steeper and more sweeping in Turkey, afflicting virtually all the established parties as well as the party system, in the judgement of Ergun Özbudun in chapter 10. Competitive party politics have been developing in Turkey for about as long as in independent India, but several factors have made the Turkish experience much less successful. First, as Özbudun shows, Turkey's party system has been prone to severe ideological polarization (and more recently, polarization around the cleavage of religious versus secular). This has led to the second huge difference: repeated military intervention, with the suspension of political parties in 1971 and then their complete liquidation following the 1980 military coup. These military interventions have interrupted the institutional development of parties and other political structures. But, third, the institutional decline of parties in Turkey has also been heavily of their own making. Virtually all of Turkey's parties have fallen dramatically in public esteem and organizational capacity over the past three decades, owing in no small measure to their own failings of leadership, performance, and strategy. As a result, parties' linkages to civil society and to individual voters have shrunk, producing a fickle and cynical electorate that has swung sharply and unexpectedly in party support from one election to the next. Shortly before the 1983 elections, the military tried to immunize the system against such volatility and polarization by imposing very high national and constituency thresholds. But this has had no lasting effect, as "the Turkish party system is more fragmented than ever." In the context of increasing personalization of politics and factional strife, the center-right and center-left political tendencies each fractured into two political parties, and their collective share of the national vote steadily declined throughout the 1990s. Correspondingly, more extreme parties—ethnic, ultranationalist, and Islamist—have rushed in to mobilize voter disenchantment and occupy the floating political space, increasing the polarization and instability of Turkish politics.

Accentuating the institutional dilemma of Turkish party politics has been the strict secularism of the Constitution. The only Turkish party that has approached the model of a mass party, by building an active, grassroots base—the Welfare Party (WP)—was shut down and banned by Turkey's Constitutional Court for violating the mandate against religious parties. Its successor, the Virtue Party, tried to pursue a more careful and elliptical advocacy of religious themes, but it, too, was banned in June 2001.[20] Hovering between ideology and pragmatism, and between formal commitment to democracy and more ambiguously antipluralist sentiments, the Welfare Party (reborn in 1984 from a more modest predecessor) combined Islamic religious appeals with others based on honesty and social justice. The WP surged to electoral prominence (and briefly to the leadership of government) during the 1990s by appealing on both religious and class grounds to voters discontented with economic problems, social pressures, and widespread corruption on the part of the established parties. With its Islamist agenda, mass mobilization, deep ancillary structure, strictly hierarchical organization, and base among the lower classes and the strongly religious, the WP partially fit the model of a religious fundamentalist party. Two parties mobilize Turkish nationalist and Kurdish ethnic identity. All others are catch-all parties "with strong clientelistic features" but with little of the grassroots structure and local branch activity that they once had. Since 1971, parties have received sizable state subsidies, but this has not quenched their thirst for money to finance increasingly expensive, media-based campaigns, with the help of professional public-relations experts. As in Italy, but with more recent effect, the legalization of private radio and television broadcasting and the general trend of urbanization and economic development have helped drive profound changes in the nature of campaigning and of parties as organizations.

Among our five country cases, Taiwan stands out as the most recent democracy and the one with the longest period of hegemony by a single, party, the Kuomintang (KMT). As Yun-han Chu shows in chapter 11, the KMT was in many respects a classic Leninist (but not Marxist) party, heavily merging party and state and penetrating virtually every aspect of Taiwan's society. The KMT dominated Taiwan politics not only through nearly four decades of authoritarian rule but also for almost 15 years following the inception of democratic transition until its stunning defeat in the 2000 presidential election. During this period of democratization and democracy, the KMT's hegemony (including top-down control of interest mediation and a huge financial empire) and its quasi-Leninist nature shaped and constrained the party system and the character of political and ideological competition. For one thing, the system of the single nontransferable vote (SNTV, initially implemented to "divide and rule" during the authoritarian era) entrenched factionalism in both the ruling and opposition party (as it had done for several decades in Japan). The fragmenting impact of SNTV and the long shadow of KMT hegemony shaped the opposition Democratic Progressive Party (DPP) as a weak, decentralized party lacking strong leadership, while also preempting the DPP's ability to forge strong links with civil society organizations. But the KMT ultimately suffered from two "fatal institutional flaws" that derived from its very (quasi-Leninist) hegemony: weak mechanisms of leadership accountability to the party and the absence of institutionalized means to resolve intraparty conflicts.

As Chu demonstrates, the "ubiquitous presence of partisan politics in all organized sectors of the society" and related features of politicization endowed the party system with "many superficial signs of maturity." These included high levels of party membership and partisan identification, low levels of electoral volatility, and the continued pervasive presence of parties in almost all organized sectors of society. But the institutional strength of the KMT rested heavily on its control of the state, and when this was lost in March 2000, the party entered a new era of struggle and decline. The DPP had been gradually improving its electoral competitiveness during the 1990s, evolving from an ethnic into a more programmatic party, while benefiting from the introduction of public subsidies and free media time for major parties. However, the DPP had difficulty adapting to the responsibilities of governance in a system "crafted by the KMT for the purpose of its own continued dominance." Unwilling to form an interparty coalition despite its minority status in parliament, and unable to transcend its factional and ideological divisions, the DPP floundered in its first year in office, although it did dismantle some structural legacies of ruling party hegemony over state and society (while simply taking over others).

Democratization (and Taiwan's continuing rapid economic development) transformed the context of parties and elections, especially for the KMT. The traditional means of mobilizing votes—through patron-client networks, lineage and communal ties, and vote buying—lost their iron reliability. Party membership and identification dropped sharply from their hegemonic levels, and local factions became more restless and independent (often challenging the KMT's formal nominees). Ideological and leadership divisions intensified, twice driving KMT defectors to form new parties and mount rival presidential campaigns. Partisan electoral competition became more vigorous. As in every other country and region in our study, the mass media became much more important in waging campaigns, and the erosion of the state (and thus KMT) monopoly over the media added to the competitiveness of elections. The initiation in 1996 of direct election for the presidency heightened trends toward the personalization of politics and the use of more direct mechanisms for mobilizing votes while deepening divisions within the ruling party. All of this (in a context where vote-buying and vote-brokering still counted in many local constituencies, and where SNTV necessitated highly personalized campaigns) made elections hugely expensive in Taiwan.

A major theme of Chu's analysis is the distinctiveness of the Taiwan case for the absence of class cleavage in structuring partisan issues and identification. Rather, the principal line of cleavage has involved national identity, democratic reform, and the related issue of the ethnic power balance between Taiwanese and mainlanders. While President Lee Teng-hui narrowed the distance on these issues between his KMT and the historically pro-independence DPP, he also split his party in the process. The DPP countered by raising issues of the environment and social justice, and by campaigning against the deepening corruption of politics, with some success at the subnational level. However, the KMT, evolving rapidly toward a catch-all party, adapted its platform to compete on these issues as well, and thus to "retain its broad appeal to all classes and social groups." Ultimately, the DPP won the presidency in 2000 by greatly moderating its position on national identity (essentially abandoning its pro-independence stance) while continuing to push its clean-government and social-justice themes.

This section of the book closes, as it begins, with a comparative treatment of parties and party systems in a major—albeit much more recent—region of democratic experience, postcommunist Europe. In chapter 12, Herbert Kitschelt uncovers a striking degree of path dependence in explaining the diverse development of these systems. His particular concern is to understand why the dominant mode of linkage between citizens and parties in a country takes one of three different forms—clientelist, charismatic, and programmatic—and the differing strategies of party competition that result from this distinction. He finds that, across different types of postcommunist countries, market-liberal parties are most likely to be programmatic and least likely to build mass-party organizations on the basis of clientelism. In the aftermath of the communist collapse, socialist ideology was too discredited to provide the basis for a programmatic appeal. Thus communist-successor parties were only able to become programmatic if they lost the founding elections, prompting them to abandon their old ideology in favor of a more viable one—democracy and capitalism, albeit with social democratic leanings. By contrast, where communist-successor parties managed to retain control over the state apparatus, they used state resources to reconstitute support through the clientelist distribution of material benefits, such as insider privatization deals, cheap credits, and subsidies.

Clientelist politics have also been favored by what Kitschelt terms "particularist sociocultural parties," that is, those appealing to some religious, ethnic, cultural, or nationalist section of the country. Such sectional constituencies are clearly identifiable (for distributive purposes) and lack coherent policy commitments.

Kitschelt traces the three different paths of political development to the structural legacies of the communist and even precommunist political eras. East Germany and what became the Czech Republic had interwar experiences of democracy with strong working and urban middleclass political mobilization. They then developed a bureaucraticauthoritarian form of communism that was harsh in its repressiveness but brittle, imploding very suddenly in 1989 and leaving the former communists no real role in institutional choice. Consequently (following a general rule by which Kitschelt associates institutions to depersonalize electoral competition with the strength of liberal democratic forces), these countries chose proportional representation with closed party lists, giving rise to programmatic party competition. A second path was taken by several countries (Hungary, Poland, Slovenia, and the Baltics) with partially democratic interwar experiences, small working classes, and party mobilization of middle-class and rural peasant constituencies. These countries experienced a less repressive, more coopting form of "national-accommodative communism," with more flexible communist parties that negotiated transitions to democracy. With negotiating power often finely balanced, mixed electoral systems tended to be chosen (combining "both personalist and programmatic principles of interest aggregation"), and these were also relatively favorable to the development of programmatic parties. The third, sharply differing path (in countries such as Romania, Bulgaria, Albania, and Russia) began prior to communism in the absence of democracy, with mass mobilization occurring only around the poor peasantry. Communism took a "patrimonial-statist" form that was intensely repressive and coopting. When communism began collapsing in the region, these ruling communist parties engaged in preemptive reform to try to hang on to power. They were often able to steer the new institutions away from programmatic incentives (by choosing strong presidentialism and more personalist electoral laws) and, in the face of weak, divided liberal opponents, they clung to power by using patronage and personal (charismatic) appeals.

These paths have had obvious consequences, although, as Kitschelt concedes, it is difficult to untangle their impact from that of other related factors, such as geographic distance from the European Union. Where programmatic parties and politics took root, in the first two groups of countries, progress toward democracy and the market has been relatively rapid. The legacy of patrimonial communism, by contrast, has been deep cumulative divisions, "with populist appeals to rally the losers of the economic liberalization," and stunted progress toward democracy and the market.

Parties Under Challenge

In their conclusion, Stefano Bartolini and Peter Mair ponder the implications of the chapters in this volume for the questions we raised earlier. Weighing the evidence of party performance from the various countries and regions examined in this book, they find that in no instance "is the diagnosis clearly benign; problems of performance and legitimacy appear to impact parties in all these settings with varying degrees of intensity." They consider three possible interpretations of the trends. One is evolutionary, that parties in every democracy evolve through similar stages (for example, from elite to mass to catch-all parties). But this clearly does not square with the evidence that parties in new democracies now appear to be largely passing over the stage of mass organization and mobilization. A second "generational" interpretation would expect the roles and importance of parties to reflect the social and political circumstances (such as globalization, individualization, and mass communication) in which they now compete. There is some considerable evidence for this approach, in that—no matter their age or the age of their democracy—parties in vastly different democratic countries seem to be grappling with similar challenges. A third, genetic interpretation posits that parties "will tend to vary according to the circumstances of their initial formation and development." By this logic, parties in the third-wave democracies would remain quite different from those of the established, postindustrial democracies. It may still be too early to reject this hypothesis, but one conclusion Bartolini and Mair come to is that the "golden age" of the mass party is now over. This is why they caution against putting too much weight on what a party *does* when trying to figure out what it *is*. Some of "the functions classically ascribed to political parties" appear unique to the era of the mass party, but these functions should not be confused with the definition of a party (which, at a minimum, is an organization that presents groups of candidates for election).

Bartolini and Mair group the numerous possible functions of parties into two broad categories: *representative* (interest articulation and aggregation and policy formulation) and *institutional* (recruitment of political leaders and organization of parliament and of government). Social and technological changes have undermined the representative functions of parties, as citizens have acquired "an apparent capacity for direct action, and no longer [seem] reliant on political mediation." Along with parties' representative functions, their social bases and linkages have also faded. These changes challenge party *organizations,* but not necessarily parties as such, which "could quite easily learn to live with" rival or parallel agencies of representation and even "to take advantage of their presence to learn of new interests and demands." Bartolini and Mair envision a new era in which party and societal channels of representation will coexist and "may well feed off one another." Meanwhile, the institutional functions of parties not only persist, they may even have been enhanced as parties are more and more subsidized, recognized, and regulated by the state.

The shift of parties "from society to the state" may be a necessary "survival strategy," but for Bartolini and Mair, it threatens to undermine parties' legitimacy in the long run. Indeed, they speculate that the present widespread malaise of parties may well derive from the "ever more pronounced separation" between "their enhanced and increasingly well-protected institutional role" and the "seeming erosion of their relevance within the wider society." As their representative capacity declines, so does the ability of parties to control individual and group behavior and so foster "political integration." If parties cannot mediate and restrain societal demands, Bartolini and Mair wonder, can they continue to provide institutional integration (by harmonizing the working of different political institutions)? This is the question they leave unanswered. But they do underscore the institutional danger to parties of their excessive regulation by public law. Parties, they insist, must "recover their autonomy and coherence." This means not only less legal regulation and intervention, but a renewed emphasis on the authority of party politicians (as opposed to technical experts or popular referenda). At the same time, parties must clean up their own corruption and lack of transparency while finding ways to bridge "the sense of growing 'insulation' of the political class from popular concerns and grievances."

The evidence in this book demonstrates that, across a widely varying range of democracies, political parties are losing the support and involvement of citizens, even as they remain essential for structuring electoral competition and organizing governance. In our view, this growing breach is not healthy for democracy, but neither is it entirely beyond the scope of intelligent policy and institutional renovation to repair.

NOTES

1. Robert D. Putnam, Susan J. Pharr, and Russell J. Dalton, "Introduction: What's Troubling the Trilateral Democracies," in Susan J. Pharr and Robert D. Putnam, eds., *Disaffected Democracies: What's Troubling the Trilateral Countries* (Princeton, N.J.: Princeton University Press, 2000), 14 (emphasis in the original); see also Susan J. Pharr, Robert D. Putnam, and Russell J. Dalton, "Trouble in the Advanced Democracies? A Quarter-Century of Declining Confidence," *Journal of Democracy* 11 (April 2000): 5–25.

2. Russell J. Dalton, "Political Support in Advanced Industrial Democracies," in Pippa Norris, ed., *Critical Citizens: Global Support for Democratic Governance* (Oxford: Oxford University Press, 1999), 65–66. In fact, the strength of party attachment declined in all countries for which time-series data are available.

3. Marta Lagos, "How People View Democracy: Between Stability and Crisis in Latin America," *Journal of Democracy* 12 (January 2001): Table 3, and Latinobarometro data provided by Lagos. The data is for 2000, but the lack of confidence in parties has been remarkably stable since the survey first began to be conducted in 1995.

4. Yun-han Chu, Larry Diamond, and Doh Chull Shin, "Growth and Equivocation in Support for Democracy in Korea and Taiwan," *Studies in Public Policy* 345 (Glasgow: Centre for the Study of Public Policy, University of Strathclyde, 2001), 19 (Table 5); and Richard Rose and Christian Haerpfer, "New Democracies Barometer V: A 12-Nation Survey," *Studies in Public Policy* 206 (Glasgow: University of Strathclyde, Centre for the Study of Public Policy, 1999), 59–62.

5. Yun-han Chu, Larry Diamond, and Doh Chull Shin, "Growth and Equivocation in Support for Democracy," Table 7; and Hans-Dieter Klingemann, "Mapping Political Support in the 1990s: A Global Analysis," in Pippa Norris, ed., *Critical Citizens: Global Support for Democratic Governance* (Oxford: Oxford University Press, 1999), 53.

6. For a discussion of this linkage, see Larry Diamond, *Developing Democracy: Toward Consolidation* (Baltimore: Johns Hopkins University Press, 2000), ch. 5.

7. Gábor Tóka, "Political Parties in East Central Europe," in Larry Diamond, Marc F. Plattner, Yun-han Chu, and Hung-mao Tien, eds., *Consolidating the Third Wave Democracies: Themes and Perspectives* (Baltimore: Johns Hopkins University Press, 1997), 93–134.

8. See Juan J. Linz, "Parties in Contemporary Democracies: Problems and Paradoxes," in Richard Gunther, José Ramón Montero, and Juan J. Linz, eds., *Political Parties: Old Concepts and New Challenges* (Oxford: Oxford University Press, forthcoming).

9. See Richard Gunther and Anthony Mughan, "Conclusion" (especially pp. 425–29), and Thomas E. Patterson, "The United States: News in a Free-Market Society," in Richard Gunther and Anthony Mughan, eds., *Democracy and the Media: A Comparative Perspective* (Cambridge: Cambridge University Press, 2000).

10. Ronald Inglehart, *Modernization and Postmodernization: Cultural, Economic, and Political Change in 43 Societies* (Princeton, N.J.: Princeton University Press, 1997), 311.

11. See Mariano Torcal, Richard Gunther, and José Ramón Montero, "Antiparty Sentiments in Southern Europe," in Richard Gunther, José Ramón Montero, and Juan Linz, eds., *Political Parties*.

12. See Juan J. Linz and Alfred Stepan, *Problems of Democratic Transition and Consolidation* (Baltimore: Johns Hopkins University Press, 1996).

13. Susan J. Pharr, "Officials' Misconduct and Public Distrust: Japan and the Trilateral Democracies," in Susan J. Pharr and Robert D. Putnam, eds., *Disaffected Democracies*, 173–201.

14. Donatella della Porta, "Social Capital, Beliefs in Government, and Political Corruption," in Susan J. Pharr and Robert D. Putnam, eds., *Disaffected Democracies*, 202–28.

15. See Robert Michels, *Zur Soziologie des Parteiwesens in der modernen Demokratie* [1911] (Stuttgart: Alfred Kröner Verlag, 1970); and Richard S. Katz and Peter Mair, "Changing Models of Party Organization and Party Democracy: The Emergence of the Cartel Party," *Party Politics* 1 (January 1995): 5–28.

16. Stefano Bartolini, Daniele Caramani, and Simon Hug, *Parties and Party Systems: A Bibliographical Guide to the Literature on Parties and Party Systems in Europe since 1945* (CD ROM) (London: Sage Publications, 1998).

17. See, for example, Samuel H. Barnes, *Party Democracy: Politics in an Italian Socialist Federation* (New Haven: Yale University Press, 1967); and Paul Allen Beck, *Party Politics in America*, 8th ed. (New York: Longman, 1997).

18. Ruth Schachter Morgenthau, *Political Parties in French-Speaking West Africa* (Oxford: Clarendon Press, 1964); Stefano Bartolini and Peter Mair, eds., *Party Politics in Contemporary Western Europe* (London: Frank Cass, 1984); and Klaus von Beyme, *Political Parties in Western Democracies* (Aldershot: Gower, 1985). The latter focuses almost exclusively on Western Europe.

19. See, for example, Russell J. Dalton, Scott C. Flanagan, and Paul Allen Beck, *Electoral Change in Advanced Industrial Democracies* (Princeton, N.J.: Princeton University Press, 1984); Mark N. Franklin, Thomas T. Mackie, Henry Valen, et al., *Electoral Change* (Cambridge: Cambridge University Press); and Stefano Bartolini and Peter Mair, eds., *Identity, Competition and Electoral Availability* (Cambridge: Cambridge University Press, 1990).

20. The decision to ban the Virtue Party occurred after Özbudun completed his chapter and just before this book went to press.

I

Theoretical and Historical Perspectives

1

TYPES AND FUNCTIONS
OF PARTIES

Richard Gunther and Larry Diamond

Richard Gunther *is professor of political science at Ohio State University. Among his recent publications are* The Politics of Democratic Consolidation *(1995),* Democracy and the Media *(2000),* Parties, Politics and Democracy in the New Southern Europe *(2001), and* Political Parties: Old Concepts and New Challenges *(forthcoming 2001).* **Larry Diamond** *is a senior fellow at the Hoover Institution, coeditor of the* Journal of Democracy, *and author of* Developing Democracy: Toward Consolidation *(1999).*

Political parties are not what they used to be. In the longstanding, established democracies in particular, they lack the depth of involvement and emotional and ideological attachment that they commanded a century, even two or three decades, ago.[1] In many democracies, in both developed and less developed countries, there is growing evidence that membership in political parties is declining,[2] that parties' ties with allied secondary associations are loosening or breaking, that their representation of specific social groups is less consistent, and that public opinion toward parties is waning in commitment and trust. Does this mean, as some have argued, that parties as institutions are declining, that they are ceasing to play a crucial role in modern democracies, and that their former functions may be performed as well or better by other kinds of organizations—social movements or interest groups, for example?

This is the overarching question that motivates this book. Are political parties in modern democracies losing their importance, even their relevance, as vehicles for the articulation and aggregation of interests and the waging of election campaigns? Or have we entered an era, more keenly felt in the advanced industrial democracies but increasingly apparent in the less developed ones as well, where technological and social change is transforming the nature of the political party without diminishing its importance for the health and vigor of democracy?

While the empirical evidence for the "decline of parties" thesis may be strong in many countries, these data may be interpreted in very different ways. One might contend that the manifestations of party decline reflect more a shift from one *type* of party to another.[3] By this logic, the declining levels of affiliation with political parties may simply be due to the progressive displacement of mass-based parties by party organizations that are structured in different ways, pursuing different objectives, or pursuing the same objectives through different means. Similarly, the fact that parties emerging in new democracies may depart substantially from party models that emerged in Western Europe in the early twentieth century may imply that newly emerging organizational forms are more quickly adapting to dominant features of the contemporary socioeconomic and technological environments than are older parties that institutionalized in an earlier era.

Even if this "evolution of party" explanation is valid, however, it would not necessarily imply that all of the functions performed by older types of parties are being adequately fulfilled by new types of parties. Conversely, it is possible that new types of parties are better suited to meet the demands and expectations of today's citizens than those that were established by previous generations of political elites. In either case, the performance capabilities of different types of parties have important implications for the quality of democracy in new and old democracies alike.

Given these substantial questions concerning the interpretation of these findings, it is important to systematically survey the types of parties that exist in today's democracies, and to examine the kinds of functions that are performed or privileged by each party type. It is not unreasonable to expect that no single party type can simultaneously achieve a number of often incompatible political and social objectives, and that the displacement of one party type by another may have a substantial impact on the character and quality of democracy in the world today.

A Typology of Parties

Some students of political parties may not welcome the introduction of yet another typology of parties. Indeed, the literature is already rich with various categories of party types that have been in use for decades. However, we have not found the existing models of parties sufficient to capture all of the important characteristics of parties dealt with in this volume. This is for several reasons.

First, all of the existing typologies of political parties were derived from studies of West European parties over the past century-and-a-half. Accordingly, they fail to capture important distinguishing features of parties in other parts of the world. This is certainly true of parties that have emerged in developing countries whose populations exhibit considerable ethnic, religious, or linguistic diversity, upon which competitive parties have most commonly been based. It is even true of the United States, whose two highly decentralized parties fit uneasily with most existing party typologies.[4] Thus while we acknowledge the many contributions of empirical studies of parties that have been based upon these traditional West European party models, we believe that the study of parties in other world regions would be greatly enhanced by a reassessment and broadening of these typologies.

Second, the existing party types have been based on a wide variety of criteria, and little or no effort has been invested in an attempt to make the resulting party types consistent with one another. Some typologies are *functionalist,* classifying parties on the basis of some specific goal or organizational *raison d'être* that they pursue. Sigmund Neumann, for example, distinguishes between three types of parties: "Parties of individual representation" articulate the demands of specific social groups. "Parties of social integration" have well-developed organizations and provide a wide variety of services to members, encapsulating them within a partisan community, in exchange for which they count on financial contributions and volunteered services of members during election campaigns. "Parties of total integration" have more ambitious goals of seizing power and radically transforming societies, demanding the full commitment and unquestioning obedience of members.[5] Herbert Kitschelt differentiates parties that emphasize the "logic of electoral competition" from those (such as his "left libertarian" type) that place much greater stress on the "logic of constituency representation."[6] And Richard Katz and Peter Mair implicitly advance a functionalist logic in setting forth the model of the "cartel party," in which public financing of parties and the expanded role of the state induce party leaders to restrain competition and seek primarily to perpetuate themselves in power in order to avail themselves of these new resources.[7]

Other classification schemes are *organizational,* distinguishing between parties that have thin organizational structures and those that have developed large infrastructures and complex networks of collaborative relationships with other secondary organizations. The classic statement of this kind was by Maurice Duverger, who advanced a two-and-a-half-category scheme separating "cadre" parties (most commonly led by individuals with high socioeconomic status) from "mass" parties (which mobilize broad segments of the electorate through the development of a large and complex organization), with the Leninist "devotee" party alluded to but dismissed as "too vague to constitute a separate category."[8] Kitschelt posits a four-part classification system distinguishing between "centralist clubs," "Leninist cadre" parties, "decentralized clubs," and "decentralized mass" parties.[9] And Angelo Panebianco, in the most elaborate articulation of an organizational typology, contrasts "mass-bureaucratic" parties with "electoral-professional" parties.[10]

Some scholars of party politics implicitly or explicitly base their work on the notion that parties are the products of (and ought to represent the interests of) various social groups. This *sociological* orientation characterizes the analysis of parties set forth by Samuel Eldersveld and Robert Michels, as Panebianco points out.[11] Finally, there are some prominent scholars who indiscriminately mix all three of these sets of criteria, such as Otto Kirchheimer, who posits four party models: "bourgeois parties of individual representation," "class-mass parties," "denominational-mass parties," and "catch-all people's parties."[12]

We do not object to the notion that several different criteria may be employed to differentiate one type of party from another. (Indeed, as is apparent below, we use three criteria as the basis of our own integrative schema.) Instead, we regard the current status of the literature on parties as unsatisfactory for several reasons: First, this typologizing has not been sufficiently "cumulative," as proponents of the various typologies based on differing criteria "talk past" one another, and do not systematically assess the overlap or distinctiveness, not to mention the relative merits of the various classification schemes.[13] Second, by selecting just one criterion as the basis of a typology (be it organizational structure, principal organizational objective, or social basis of representation), the focus of analysis is narrowed excessively, and much variation within each party type is not systematically analyzed. What is gained in terms of parsimony is lost in terms of the ability to capture theoretically significant variation among real-world parties. This weakness is compounded insofar as these typologies were based almost exclusively on the West European experience, and thus ignore important features of parties that have emerged elsewhere. Third, many of these studies are excessively deductive, positing at the outset that one particular criterion is of paramount importance without sustaining that assertion through a careful assessment of relevant evidence. Finally, in attempting to build theory on the basis of these thin, deductive schema, some studies fall victim to reductionist argumentation. Duverger, for example, sets forth an organization-based typology, but also acknowledges the great importance of social class—linking cadre parties with the middle and upper strata, and the working class with mass-based parties. He explains this relationship by contending that these organizational forms are dictated by varying levels of resources and constraints faced by party-builders in their efforts to secure the funding necessary to support their activities.

We believe that it is premature to attempt to build elaborate theories on the basis of what may be inadequate typologies, and that a more open and ultimately productive line of empirical analysis should begin with a theoretically more modest but empirically comprehensive and accurate set of party types that are better reflective of real-world variations among parties.[14] This is particularly necessary in an effort (as represented

by this volume) to include countries outside of Western Europe within
a preliminary comparative analysis. Thus we shall increase the number
of party types, building on models and terminology previously advanced
by other scholars, while at the same time imposing some semblance of
order on some of the criteria most commonly used as the basis of party
typologies. Specifically, we will try to avoid the common temptation to
introduce a new party type on ad hoc grounds, simply on the basis of a
conclusion that a particular case cannot be adequately explained using
the existing typologies. Instead, we will systematically place all of our
party models within a comprehensive framework constructed on the
basis of three criteria: 1) the size of formal organization of the party and
the extent of the functions they perform (ranging from thin, elite-based
parties to extensive mass-based party organizations); 2) whether the
party is tolerant and pluralistic or proto-hegemonic in its objectives
and behavioral style; and 3) its distinguishing programmatic or ideological commitments.

It is important to note that the models of political parties that we will
describe below are *ideal types,* in the strictest Weberian sense of that
term. As such, they are heuristically useful insofar as they give easily
understandable labels that will help the reader better comprehend otherwise complex, multidimensional concepts. Moreover, they facilitate
analysis insofar as they serve as baselines for comparisons involving
real-world cases, or as extreme end-points of evolutionary processes
that might never be fully attained. But like all ideal types, there will be
no real-world cases that fully conform to all of the criteria that define
each party model, and some parties may include elements of more than
one ideal type.

Seven Functions of Parties

In order to achieve this objective and explore some of the implications
of different party types for the character and quality of electoral
democracy, it is first necessary to identify the various functions
performed by political parties. While the following is not an exhaustive
list of the functions performed by all parties (particularly in nondemocratic regimes, where a party-state may play a dominant role in the
economy or in regulating the lives of individual citizens), the functions
outlined below appear to represent a reasonable "common denominator"
that will assist in the comparison of parties crossnationally.

Clearly, the core function played by parties involves elite recruitment.
This, in turn, involves two distinct phases of the electoral process: 1)
candidate nomination, in which the contestants representing each party
in the following interparty election are designated; and 2) *electoral
mobilization,* in which parties motivate their respective electoral
clienteles to support their candidates and, in some instances, facilitate

their active participation in the electoral process. Over the short term, electoral outcomes may be dependent on a number of factors, some of them quite transient. Over the long term, however, depending on the electoral-mobilization strategy adopted by the party, repeated iterations of electoral campaigns may structure the vote in a relatively durable manner, as social groups may "freeze" their attachments to parties, or as individuals may come to "identify" with political parties. Whether they adopt electoral mobilization strategies primarily stressing questions of only transient relevance, or focusing on the more durable interests of various social groups, parties play a crucial role in structuring the choices and alternatives along different issue dimensions. We call this function 3) *issue structuring*.

Parties also 4) represent various social groups, either symbolically or in advancing specific interests. This *societal representation* function can be performed in the course of electoral competition, as parties bid for the support of various groups. Societal representation also takes place in the legislative arena, following the election, when bills are drafted and deliberated upon. This often, if not invariably, involves calculations of gain or loss on behalf of various social groups, whether parties openly acknowledge that fact or, according to their calculations of self-interest, downplay or completely conceal the potential impact of legislative proposals on social groups. 5) *Interest aggregation* is another function performed by political parties. Democratic systems vary in the extent to and the means by which they meld the separate interests of individual groups into broader, if not more universalistic, appeals. In the two-party presidential system of the United States, for example, parties perform the interest aggregation function during the electoral process itself (either formally, in drafting platforms at party conventions, or informally, as appeals are made to different groups in the course of the campaign). In parliamentary systems with fragmented multiparty systems, this aggregation process occurs after the election, when a governing coalition is negotiated and formed. Success in the performance of this interest-aggregation process has important implications for the coherence of public policy and for "policy stability"[15] over the long term. Similarly, the parties' success in 6) *forming and sustaining governments* in office represents a key performance dimension. Finally 7), parties may play a crucial *social integration* role, as they enable citizens to participate effectively in the political process and, if successful in that task, to feel that they have a vested interest in its perpetuation.[16] In the following section, we identify the different ways in which and degrees to which our different types of parties perform these seven functions.

This listing of functions does *not* imply that all parties perform all of these functions, nor that they perform them equally well. Quite the contrary, the following discussion of various party types will make it

TABLE 1—SUMMARY TYPOLOGY OF PARTY TYPES

	PLURALISTIC	PROTO-HEGEMONIC
ELITE PARTIES	Local Notable	
	Clientelistic	
MASS-BASED PARTIES		
IDEOLOGICAL/SOCIALIST	Class-mass	Leninist
IDEOLOGICAL/NATIONALIST	Pluralist Nationalist	Ultranationalist
RELIGIOUS	Denominational-mass	Religious Fundamentalist
ETHNICITY-BASED PARTIES	Ethnic	
	Congress	
ELECTORALIST PARTIES	Catch-all	
	Programmatic	
	Personalistic	
MOVEMENT PARTIES	Left-Libertarian	
	Post-Industrial Extreme Right	

clear that a particular party type will stress one or a set of these functions over others. Thus we suggest that the character of electoral democracy may by substantially affected by the differential performance of these functions as one party type comes to prevail over the others.

Types of Political Parties

A typology of parties should explicitly deal with several different dimensions of party life involving the varying electoral strategies, social representation, principal objectives, and organizational capacities of parties. Some parties are organizationally thin while others are large and complex; some parties are exclusively based in a particular ethnic, religious, or socioeconomic group, while others are heterogeneous if not promiscuously eclectic. Some parties are clearly programmatic or ideological, while others are pragmatic or even unprincipled. Some parties are intensely committed to securing some specific social objective, while others merely want to win elections. Our typology (summarized in Tables 1 and 2, and in Figure 1, with "organizationally thin" parties toward the left and "organizationally thick" parties towards the right side of the diagram) identifies 15 different "species" of party, each of which, in turn, belongs to a broader "genus" of party types: elite-based parties, mass-based parties, ethnicity-based parties, electoralist parties, and movement parties. Several of these genera are, in turn, separated into subcategories of "pluralistic" versus "proto-hegemonic" parties (separating loyal, democratic parties from semiloyal or antisystem parties within democratic regimes), or into subcategories based on their level of commitment to an ideology or program.

We must stress at the outset that, although we shall order our presentation of party types in rough accord with the timing of their respective initial appearances on the scene, we do not assert or imply

TABLE 2—TYPES OF PARTIES AND THEIR FEATURES

TYPES OF PARTIES	GOALS	ELECTORAL STRATEGY	ORGANIZATIONAL STRUCTURE & LINKAGES	SOCIAL BASE
ELITE PARTIES				
LOCAL NOTABLE	Traditional elite representing geographically defined constituency	Gain votes through appeals to local interests and authority of local notables	None, except for the personal resources of the candidate and the symbolic appeal of the party label	Local and heterogeneous
CLIENTELISTIC	Defense of particularistic interests and status quo	Gain votes through hierarchical structure linking local to national leaders and through exchange of particularistic benefits	Vertical networks of loyalty and exchange between voters and local party elites; factional ties and shared material interests between local and national elites	Rural constituencies, lower classes, less well educated, urban migrants
MASS-BASED *Ideologically based, pluralist:*				
CLASS-MASS	Social change for benefit of working class	Mobilize working class and build political identity with universalistic appeals and provision of group benefits	Mass membership organization with ties to trade unions and sometimes with ancillary social organizations	Working and lower classes, state employees, and the liberal professions
NATIONALIST	Defend national popular classes			Working and middle classes
Ideologically based, proto-hegemonic:				
LENINIST AND ULTRANATIONALIST	To seize power and implement its ideologically defined program	Recruit, socialize, and mobilize core constituency for electoral and extraparliamentary struggle for power	Strongly hierarchical and disciplined, with highly selective recruitment and intense indoctrination of militants; and domination of ancillary social organizations	Working class or nationalists, depending on ideology
Religious-based:				
DENOMINATIONAL (PLURALIST)	Programmatic: Defense of core interests of religious adherents	Use of religious organizations and themes, and distribution of benefits, to mobilize religious adherents	Overlap between party support and religious-community membership, often with explicit linkage to lay organizations	Cuts across class; religious and socially conservative
FUNDAMENTALIST (PROTO-HEGEMONIC)	Ideological: Reorganizing state and society around religious, doctrinal principles	Mobilize religious believers and build religious political identity through invocation of religious doctrine and distribution of benefits	Hierarchical organization based on religious authority with extensive party and ancillary organizations established throughout society	Religious, and lower (to lower-middle) classes

TABLE 2—TYPES OF PARTIES AND THEIR FEATURES (CONT'D)

TYPES OF PARTIES	GOALS	ELECTORAL STRATEGY	ORGANIZATIONAL STRUCTURE & LINKAGES	SOCIAL BASE
ETHNICITY-BASED				
ETHNIC	*PARTICULARISTIC:* Defense and advance of ethnic group interests	Mobilize ethnic group with appeals to ethnic group benefit and threat and through clientelism	Varies from weak organization based on traditional community ties and loyalties to well-established mass personal organizations with ancillary social and cultural organizations	A single ethnic, regional, religious, or national group
CONGRESS	*PARTICULARISTIC:* Contain social conflict through sharing of power and resources among ethnic groups	Gain votes through clientelistic loyalties and exchanges among constituent groups, and through appeals to national integration	Coalitional or federative organization, based on regional elites and local notables	Coalition of distinct ethnic, religious, and regional groups
ELECTORALIST				
CATCH-ALL	Maximize electoral support through broad aggregation of interests	Gain votes through broad and eclectic issue appeals and candidate image	Organization primarily around election campaigns, otherwise weak party organization; weak and shifting linkages with civil society organizations	De facto core social groups supplemented by shifting constituencies
PROGRAMMATIC	Advancement of programmatic or ideological agenda	Gain votes through articulation of programmatic (and/or ideological) appeals	Same as catch-all	May be as heterogeneous as catch-all (or may have somewhat more defined bases)
PERSONALISTIC	Acquisition or retention of power by party leader	Gain votes through emphasis on the personal charisma of the party leader, particularistic benefits, and activation of clientelistic linkages	Shallow and temporary organization focused dominated around the election campaign and by the national party leader	Diffuse but broader appeal within lower classes
MOVEMENT PARTIES				
LEFT-LIBERTARIAN	Advancement of postmaterialist agenda	Combine protest activities with periodic voter mobilization	Open "membership," weak leadership, "assembly" style of deliberation	Well-educated postmaterialists
POSTINDUSTRIAL, EXTREME RIGHT	Advancement of anti-immigrant, anti-social welfare-state agenda	Gain votes through appeals emphasizing program and leader's charisma	Strong leader, but weak organization	Traditionalist conservatives and anti-immigrant groups

that any one type of party was, is, or will be dominant within any particular period of time. Instead, we are impressed with the diversity of party types that exist today, even when many of the social or cultural circumstances that gave birth to them have long since disappeared. Neither do we assert that one party type is likely to follow a predictable trajectory, evolving into another type. At the same time, however, it is clear that there is a general trend (noted in several chapters of this book and elsewhere in the literature on parties) away from organizationally thick parties, be they mass-based or ethnicity-based, and towards organizationally thin "electoralist" parties. This is in part because socioeconomic modernization and technological development, such as the spread of mass communications, and particularly television, have fundamentally transformed the channels linking party organizations and elites to citizens, interests, and organized groups. This has tended to make the survival of some archaic party types (for example, the traditional local notable and clientelistic parties) much more problematic, while at the same time laying the groundwork for the emergence of new party types (for example, electoralist and left-libertarian parties) that may require a certain type of communications medium or a relatively high level of citizen education.

Elite parties. "Elite-based" parties are those whose principal organizational structures are minimal and based upon established elites within a specific geographic area. Deference to the authority of these elites is a feature shared by the two species of parties that fall within this genus. Whatever national-level party structure exists is based upon an alliance among locally based elites.

Historically, as Hans Daalder points out in this volume, the first party type to emerge was the *traditional local notable* party.[17] This early-to-mid nineteenth century development emerged at a time of sharply limited suffrage in semidemocratic regimes.[18] Given that the right to vote and hold office was restricted in most of these countries to males owning substantial property, this competitive game was limited to the upper socioeconomic strata. And given that election to office required appeals to a small number of enfranchised voters, campaigns did not require an extensive organizational effort. Local notables could often count on their traditionally based prestige or personal relationships with their few and socially homogeneous constituents to secure office. Central party bureaucracies did not exist, and national-level "party" organizations consisted of relatively loose alliances or cliques linking elected members of parliament on the basis of shared interests or bonds of mutual respect. The parliamentary factions that dominated the British House of Commons in the first half of the nineteenth century, French conservative parties in the nineteenth century and the first half of the twentieth century, and several conservative parties in Brazil today are

FIGURE—EXTENT OF ORGANIZATION

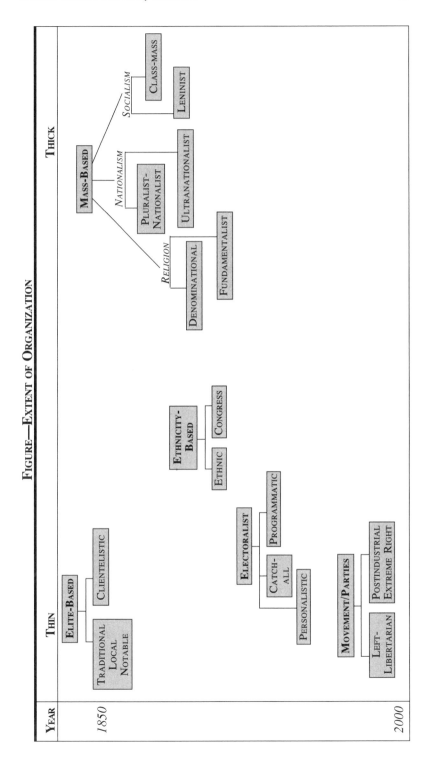

examples of this variety of elite party. Expansion of the suffrage and socioeconomic modernization (which entailed the political mobilization of formerly excluded sectors of society) progressively limited the electoral effectiveness of such poorly institutionalized and resource-poor parties, while urbanization made the predominantly rural traditional notables increasingly irrelevant to most voters.

The *clientelistic party* began to emerge just as the traditional local notable party was subjected to challenges from newly enfranchised segments of the electorate within societies undergoing industrialization and urbanization. Indeed, it is reasonable to hypothesize that the emergence of the clientelistic party was a direct response by local elites to the challenges posed by the political mobilization of formerly "subject" populations: As traditional deference to local elites began to break down, electoral mobilization relied increasingly on an exchange of favors or overt coercion. The clientelistic party, as we shall define it, is a confederation of notables (either traditional or of the newly emerging liberal-professional or economic elite), each with his own geographically, functionally, or personalistically based support, organized internally as particularistic factions. Such a party typically has a weak organization and places little or no stress on program or ideology. Its principal function is to coordinate the individual campaign efforts of notables, usually indirectly or loosely, for the purpose of securing power at the national level. Their campaign activities, in turn, are based on hierarchical chains of interpersonal relationships of a quasi-feudal variety, in which relatively durable patterns of loyalty are linked with the exchange of services and obligations.

While all clientelistic parties are characterized by particularistic factional organization, in their heyday in the late nineteenth and early twentieth century—in Southern Europe,[19] Latin America,[20] and North American big-city machines and southern rural politics[21]—the exchange of personalistic favors also served as a principal tool for electoral mobilization at the mass level. Such relationships are most common in rural, premodern societies: Under conditions of geographical isolation from a dominant center of government, coupled with low levels of functional literacy and poorly developed transportation and communications media, a localized patron-client relationship can be mutually beneficial to both the patron and the client. (In the United States this variety of politics focused on immigrant populations,[22] otherwise vulnerable and without political resources, particularly among those without adequate English-language skills.) As a party official in a socioeconomically lagging, rural part of Spain described it, "The citizen who is worried about resolving problems with the doctor or the school, or the problem of an unjust accusation before the courts, or of delinquency in paying his taxes to the state, etc., . . . has recourse to an intermediary . . . who can intercede on his behalf, but in exchange for pledging his very conscience and his vote."[23] As socioeconomic modernization proceeds—as shrinking rural populations became increasingly literate, exposed to mass communications media, and "mobilized" politically (or as immigrant populations in the United States learned English and became educated and assimilated into American society)—the utility of the patron to the citizen declines, and the patron's attempts to influence voting decisions are increasingly perceived as objectionable interference. Under these circumstances, more coercive forms of patron-client exchanges tended to emerge, often involving the threat to withhold economic benefits from the client unless his or her political support is pledged, or overt vote-buying displaces the exchange of favors. Over the long run, however, socioeconomic modernization and the increasing "cognitive mobilization" of the mass public greatly reduce the utility of clientelism as a vehicle for electoral mobilization.[24]

Once institutionalized and embedded within the structure of political parties, however, these patron-client relationships may take on a life of their own, independent of the socioeconomic conditions that had given rise to them originally. It would appear that in both Italy and Japan, whose postwar party systems were established in less modernized societies (particularly in the south of Italy and rural parts of Japan), clientelism was embedded into the very structure of the dominant parties (the Christian Democrats and the Liberal Democratic Party, respectively). Once established, these factional networks became the principal bases of elite recruitment within the governing parties of both party systems, and were perpetuated well beyond the time when the socioeconomic conditions that had given birth to them had largely disappeared. While these organizations survived for decades, it is interesting to note that the clientelistic exchanges on which they were based may contain the seeds of their own eventual destruction. Particularism and the distribution of rewards based upon faction membership easily evolve into overt corruption. Not surprisingly, clientelistic parties in both of these systems ultimately suffered serious (and in the case of the Italian parties, fatal) electoral setbacks as part of a popular reaction against corruption scandals. (The same has happened more recently in Thailand and the Philippines, although some parties in each of these countries retain features of the clientelistic model.) Since social change had made these kinds of exchanges increasingly repugnant to ever larger numbers of voters, when high-level scandals were exposed, a series of defections from the once dominant governing parties drastically undermined their organizational unity and strength.

With regard to the basic functions of these elite-based parties, and especially clientelistic parties, 1) candidate nomination is based largely or entirely on loyalty to faction leaders and bargaining among the principal faction leaders; 2) electoral mobilization is based upon the mobilization of vertical social networks; 3) the issues that are most salient are particularistic rewards and payoffs that are offered to citizens at the bottom of these hierarchical networks; 4) local interests are paramount, with regard to the societal representation dimension; and 5) interests are aggregated de facto, as the almost inadvertent by-product of deals among faction leaders over 6) the formation of governments. 7) Limited social integration of isolated, rural citizens, seriously lacking "social capital," is privileged, at the expense of the functional representation of the interests and programmatic preferences of the more modern sectors of society.

Mass-based parties. The second genus of party has deep roots in the literature, as well as in the nineteenth- and early-twentieth-century history of Europe. The quintessential "externally created party," the mass-based party, emerged as a manifestation of the political mobilization of the working class in many European polities.[25] It is characterized by a large base of dues-paying members who remain active in party affairs even during periods between elections. In an effort to disseminate the party's ideology and establish an active membership base, the party seeks to penetrate a number of spheres of social life. Affiliated trade unions, religious, and other social organizations serve not only as political allies, helping to mobilize supporters at election time, but for the projection of the programmatic objectives of the party from the electoral-parliamentary arena into a variety of spheres of social life. Networks of local party branches are established nationwide, as well as extensive arrays of supportive organizations, including party newspapers and recreational clubs. These organizational networks not only serve as a framework for mobilization at election time but also provide side-benefits for party members, such as by providing opportunities for fraternization and recreation.[26]

Two types of distinctions further divide this genus into six different species of party. The first involves the basic thrust of the party's ideology or unifying belief system. Most commonly, these have involved varying types of commitment to 1) socialism, 2) nationalism, or 3) religion. The second dimension involves the extent to which each of these is either tolerant and pluralistic, on the one hand, or is committed to securing a hegemonic position within the political system and imposing its radical programmatic commitments on society. Pluralist parties assume that they will always be functioning within a democratic system; they therefore accept its institutions and rules of the game. Proto-hegemonic parties, in contrast, strive over the long term toward the replacement of the existing pluralist society and democratic system with one that is better suited for the achievement of their radical transformative objectives. Accordingly, they accept existing institutions and rules only insofar as they are expedient and cannot be replaced over the short run, and their behavior is, at best, semiloyal in its willingness to link up with antisystem parties.[27] Pluralist parties seek to win elections as the principal avenue toward achieving their programmatic objectives, and their vote-mobilizational strategy relies heavily on the development and activation of a mass-membership base. Consequently, recruitment of militants to the party is open, although some resocialization of new party members is required. Proto-hegemonic parties, by contrast, place greater emphasis on discipline, constant active commitment, and loyalty on the part of party members for the conduct of political conflict in both electoral and extraparliamentary arenas. Thus recruitment is highly selective, indoctrination is intensive, and acceptance of the ideology and short-term party line is demanded of all members. In some instances (particularly when the proto-hegemonic party exists clandestinely), a secret, conspiratorial cell structure is adopted, in contrast with the open "branch" organization noted by Maurice Duverger. In the aggregate, the distinction between pluralist and proto-hegemonic comes close to Duverger's differentiation between branch-based mass parties and cell-based "devotee" parties,[28] as well as Neumann's separation of parties of "social integration" from parties of "total integration."

With regard to the basic functions performed by parties, the characteristics of the ideal-type mass-based party are these: 1) Candidate nomination is under the control of the party's leadership or professional bureaucracy, although this often involves struggles with local branches of the party dominated by party militants. Loyalty to the party and its ideology, and previous work on behalf of the party are important criteria for nomination. 2) The party's electoral mobilization strategy is focused on the optimal use of its formidable organizational resources. Party militants perform a variety of tasks, ranging from proselytizing to distribution of printed propaganda to escorting voters to the polls. The party's allied secondary organizations urge its members to support the party, and its newspaper is flooded with partisan messages. 3) The most salient issues do not change much from election to election, and tend to revolve around programmatic commitments in keeping with the party's ideology. 4) The interests to be represented are those of the working class, of fellow religious believers, or of fellow nationalists, depending on the party's ideology. 5) The advancement of this broad swath of society implies that the interests advocated would be highly aggregated rather than narrow. 6) Insofar as the party seeks to implement the maximalist interpretation of its ideological and programmatic commitments, it may not be regarded as an acceptable coalition partner by parties of a centrist or sharply opposed ideological orientation. If the mass-based party is "proto-hegemonic"—undemocratic in its beliefs and basic goals—it will be eschewed as a coalition partner by democratically "loyal" parties of every ideological stripe. 7) Even if the party fails to come to power at the national level, its parliamentary representation of otherwise disenfranchised sectors of the working class,

religious believers, or fellow nationals can play an important social integration role, particularly if this limited opposition role is augmented by control of local or regional levels of government.[29]

Parties with socialist ideological commitments have taken the form of either democratic socialist (or social-democratic) "class" parties,[30] or have adopted the proto-hegemonic stance of the "Leninist" party. In the typical *class-mass party* (to use Otto Kirchheimer's terminology), the center of power and authority in the party is located in the executive committee of its secretariat, although formally the ultimate source of legitimate authority is the full party congress. In addition, the parliamentary leadership of the party occasionally challenges the party secretariat for control of the programmatic agenda and the nomination of candidates. Invariably, the open, tolerant stance of these parties has made possible considerable intraparty conflict, particularly between pragmatists whose primary concern is electoral victory and ideologues who place much higher value on "constituency representation" and ideological consistency with a more orthodox reading of the party's ideology.[31] In some cases—such as the former Italian Social Democratic Party and Italian Socialist Party—of Italy's "first republic"), this may give rise to a split of the party into two separate organizations. Much more commonly, this has culminated in the gradual conversion of more maximalist socialist parties into more moderate and pragmatic parties.

Class-mass parties establish bases within their class constituency through groups organized both geographically (the local "branch") and functionally (trade unions). While they seek to proselytize prospective members or voters, indoctrination and the demand for ideological conformity are minimal. While social integration through the activities of party and trade union allies is a significant objective, the party is primarily concerned with winning elections and taking part in the formation of governments. Recruitment of members is quite open, and the larger the party's mass base, the better, given the party's primary concern with securing electoral majorities and its traditional reliance on electoral mobilization through the activities of members. The social democratic parties of Germany, Sweden, and Chile are good examples of this party type.

Leninist parties (as we define them, based on a class ideology and proto-hegemonic) have as their objective the overthrow of the existing political system and the implementation of revolutionary change in society. Given that their revolutionary goals are likely to be vigorously opposed if not repressed by their opponents, the party adopts a closed structure based on the semi-secret cell (rather than the open branch, which characterizes pluralist class-mass parties). Membership is highly selective, and the party demands strict loyalty and obedience on the part of members. Ideological indoctrination of party members is intense and uncompromising, and the party penetrates into key sectors of society (especially trade unions and the intellectual middle class in Western countries and the peasantry in Asia) in an effort to secure tactical allies over the short term and converts over the long term. Decision making within the party is highly centralized and authoritarian, even if "democratic centralism" often allows for open debate prior to the taking of an official stand.[32] The party sees itself as the "vanguard" of the proletariat, and even though the party portrays itself as representing the working class, it performs an explicitly directive and top-down role of leading the class that it represents and defining its interests. While the initial stand of the prototypical Leninist parties—those belonging to the Comintern—was to reject "bourgeois" representative institutions and parliaments, most communist parties participated as antisystem or semiloyal contenders in electoral politics in Western democracies. The ultimate objective of the party is the seizure of power, by force if necessary. In Western democracies, parties that were originally Leninist have either undergone gradual transformations—generally in the direction of becoming pluralist class-mass parties—or schisms, such as that which separated the former Italian Communist Party into a moderate party (the Democratic Party of the Left, now Democrats of the Left) and a more orthodox rump (the Communist Refoundation).

If the party succeeds in coming to power, as it did in Central and Eastern Europe and Asia, it modifies its self-defined role and its behavior toward other social and political groups. It sees itself as nothing less than the "organized expression of the will of society." In the former Soviet Union "it [was] the expression 'of the interests of the entire nation,' for the Chinese it represents 'the interests of the people.'"[33] As such, it establishes hegemonic control over the political and economic system, abolishing or taking over established secondary organizations, and using virtually all organized social groups as arenas for the social integration of individuals into the new society which it hopes to create. The party will direct the activities of the state and preside over the recruitment of governing elites.

While the classic Leninist parties were those belonging to the Comintern and embracing Lenin's 21 Points (which differentiated communist parties from other Marxist parties), some noncommunist parties—such as the Kuomintang (KMT) prior to Taiwan's democratization in the 1980s and 1990s—conformed to many of these organizational and operational characteristics.

Pluralist nationalist parties, such as Spain's Basque Nationalist Party and, until the late 1990s, Taiwan's Democratic Progressive Party, have assumed a variety of forms. Most of these involve mass-membership bases, extensive party organizations and collaboration with ancillary secondary groups usually including cultural organizations and sometimes trade unions. The electoral clientele of these parties will be those individuals who subjectively define themselves as belonging to a distinct national group. While most commonly these national identities will revolve around some objective social characteristic (especially involving language and culture), the boundaries of the electoral clientele will be quite malleable. Indeed, one of the key functions of nationalist parties is not only to convince citizens to cast ballots for the party but also to use the party's election campaign and its affiliated secondary organizations to foster and intensify their identification with the national group and its aspirations. Moreover, those aspirations, by definition, involve a demand for some level of territorial self-governance, ranging from autonomy within a multinational state to outright independence or the re-drawing of international boundaries in response to an irredentist claim. Accordingly, even though these parties may be moderate in their policy preferences concerning economic, religious, and most other issues on the left-right continuum, they may assume a semi-loyal or anti-system stand regarding issues of territorial governance. Internally, moreover, there will often be tension between those demanding a more militant stance in defense of the group's nationalist demands, on the one hand, and those stressing gains that can be secured by cooperating with other parties in forming government coalitions and pressing for the enactment of incrementally beneficial legislation.

Ultranationalist (proto-hegemonic) parties, particularly fascist or neofascist, are organized around the personality of a charismatic leader and an ideology that exalts the nation or race above the individual, detests minorities, and openly admires the use of force by a strong, quasi-military party often relying on a uniformed militia.[34] The striking coincidence of this party type with the domination by a charismatic leader suggests there is something about the social and historical circumstances giving rise to ultranationalist and fascist parties, and something about the personalities drawn to such parties,[35] that generate intense and submissive devotion to an exceptional, all-powerful leader. In some respects, they may share many organizational and behavioral characteristics with Leninist parties, especially the highly selective recruitment process, intensive indoctrination of members, strict internal discipline, the overriding objective of seizing power through force if necessary, and antisystem or semiloyal participation in parliament. Also, if they come to power, the ultranationalist parties are similar to the Leninist parties in their establishment of hegemonic domination of polity and society through repression or cooptation of existing secondary organizations, coupled with a broad penetration into society in an effort to resocialize all persons to actively support the regime. They differ, however, not only with regard to the content of their ideologies but also insofar as these ideologies are less precisely stated and subject to reinterpretation by a charismatic national leader.[36] In addition, the national leader will be the ultimate source of power and authority, and the party's bureaucracy will be supportive if not servile. Hitler's Nazi party and Mussolini's fascists are good examples of such parties. However, there have been more contemporary manifestations, such as Aleksandr Barkashov's Russian National Unity party and the Croatian Democratic Union under Franjo Tudjman.

A third ideological basis for mass-based parties is religion. Again, two different variants can be identified. The first is pluralist, democratic, and tolerant. In the aftermath of World War II, particularly in Italy and Germany, where the previous nondemocratic regime had either destroyed or "tainted" a number of secondary organizations that might have served as the basis for partisan mobilization, and where the advent of the Cold War was perceived as threatening the very existence of the Western way of life, the Church emerged as a powerful organization whose infrastructure served as the basis for the development of another model of political party. While the origins of the *denominational-mass party* (again, using Kirchheimer's terminology) can be traced back to the late nineteenth century, this type of party reached its maximum ascendancy in the aftermath of World War II.[37] Examples of denominational parties include numerous Christian democratic parties in Western Europe that have played important political roles since World War II (in Italy, Germany, Belgium, the Netherlands, and elsewhere), as well as Christian Democracy in Poland and the Christian and Democratic Union in the Czech Republic more recently. They share many of the organizational characteristics of the mass-based party, including the existence of a large base of dues-paying members, hierarchically structured party organizations linking the national and local levels, party newspapers and broadcasting outlets, allied secondary organizations (generally religious, but in some instances trade unions). Nonetheless, they differ in one important respect from parties based on secular ideologies: Since the basis of the party's programs is a set of religious beliefs that are determined by a combination of tradition and interpretation by clerics or a religious institution outside of the party itself, the party is not fully in control of its core ideological precepts whenever they are directly linked to religious values—such as those relating to abortion, divorce, sexual preference, or some manifestations of artistic expression. This can lead to intraparty tensions whenever party leaders choose to modify the party's electoral appeals or programmatic commitments in such a manner as to conflict with those values. The Italian Christian Democratic Party, for example, experienced serious internal tensions in dealing with legalization of divorce, which was stoutly opposed by the Catholic Church hierarchy. Insofar as religious beliefs may be subject to varying interpretations, considerable heterogeneity may exist within denominational-mass parties that can periodically give rise to such conflicts.

The final mass-based party is the proto-hegemonic religious party, or *religious fundamentalist* party. The principal difference between this and the denominational-mass party is that the fundamentalist parties seek to reorganize state and society around a strict reading of religious doctrinal principles, while denominational-mass parties are pluralist and incremental in their agenda. For fundamentalist parties, there is little or no room for conflicting interpretations of the religious norms and scriptures that serve as the basis of the party's program and of the laws that it seeks to impose on all of society. The authority of religious leaders to interpret that text and translate it into politically and socially relevant terms is unequivocally acknowledged. In this theocratic party model, there is no separation between religion and the state, and religious norms are imposed on all citizens within the polity irrespective of their own personal religious beliefs. Given the far-reaching objectives of these parties (which may verge on the totalitarian), the organizational development of these parties and the scope of their activities are extensive. Member involvement and identification is substantial and even intense, and ancillary organizations establish a presence at the local level throughout society. Given the religious fundamentalist nature of these parties and their strict reading of religious texts, authority relations within the party are hierarchical, undemocratic, and even absolutist, and members are disciplined and devoted. Religious fundamentalist parties mobilize support not only by invoking religious doctrine and identity, and by proposing policies derived from those principles, but also through selective incentives; they often perform a wide range of social welfare functions which aid in recruiting and solidifying the loyalty of members. This web of organized activities and services encapsulates members within a distinct subculture. Although these are not class-based parties, they disproportionately attract support from the poor and downtrodden, as well as the marginalized middle class—groups in which denunciations of injustice and corruption have a particular resonance. Algeria's Islamic Salvation Front is the most extreme example of this kind of party, with Turkey's now-banned Welfare Party sharing some of these characteristics.

Ethnicity-based parties. Parties based on ethnicity typically lack the extensive and elaborate organization of mass-based parties. What most distinguishes them, however, are their political and electoral logics. Unlike most mass-based parties, they do not advance a program (whether incremental or transformative) for all of society. Their goals and strategies are more narrow: to promote the interests of a particular ethnic group, or coalition of groups. And unlike nationalist parties, their programmatic objectives do not typically include secession or even a high level of decision making and administrative autonomy from the existing state. Instead, they are content to use existing state structure to channel benefits toward their particularistically defined electoral clientele.

The purely *ethnic party* seeks only to mobilize the votes of its own ethnic group. Some such parties of this type are the Northern People's Congress and the Action Group of Nigeria's First Republic (1960–66); South Africa's Inkatha Freedom Party; Bulgaria's Turkish minority party, Movement for Rights and Freedoms; the Hungarian Democratic Union of Romania; and the (Sikh) Akali Religious Party in India's Punjab state. Although the ethnic party may run candidates in other geographic constituencies, or raise larger national or even ideological issues, these actions only thinly mask its true ethnic or regional purpose. As Herbert Kitschelt argues in chapter 12 of this volume, the defining feature of ethnic parties (which he refers to as "particularistic sociocultural parties") is that they limit their appeal to a particular sectional constituency, and "explicitly seek to draw boundaries" between ethnic "friends" and "foes." The principal goal of the ethnic party is not any universalistic program or platform, but rather to secure material, cultural, and political benefits and protections for the ethnic group in its competition with other groups. As such, ethnic parties have an extremely low level of ideological or programmatic commitment and coherence, and they typically lack a highly developed organizational structure and formal membership base. Absent any functional interests or ideological agenda, the ethnic party tends to mobilize preexisting clientelistic relations, and therefore its structure and internal authority relations resemble those of the clientelistic party. Given the fact that ethnic parties mobilize powerfully emotive symbolic issues of identity and even cultural survival, they are prone to be dominated by and even organized around a single charismatic leader. The electoral logic of the ethnic party is to harden and mobilize its ethnic base with exclusive, often polarizing appeals to ethnic group opportunity and threat, and unlike virtually all other political parties (including nationalistic parties[38]), electoral mobilization is not intended to attract additional sectors of society to support it. Thus, even more than the religious fundamentalist party, the potential electoral clientele of the party is strictly defined and limited by ethnicity, although within that definitional category cross-class electoral appeals may lead to the adoption of eclectic programmatic objectives.

As Donald Horowitz explains, what distinguishes an ethnic party is not necessarily that most of its votes come from one ethnic group or that a party affiliation can be predicted by ethnicity.[39] In fact, "it is perfectly possible for a single ethnic group in a deeply divided society to split its support equally among two or more ethnically based parties."[40] What marks a party as "ethnic" is that, however broad its support within the ethnic group, its only real appeal is to members of that group, and its only real mission is to advance the interests of members of that group. There is no effort to aggregate interests beyond the ethnic group; instead, the party's rationale, at least implicitly, is that the group's interests are intrinsically in conflict with those of other ethnic groups.

Ethnic parties may be highly centralized around the personal leadership of a single leader, or may be more decentralized and federative in their structures. This feature of organization may affect how they perform some party functions. 1) Candidate nomination may be determined by the hierarchical ethnic party leadership or by more localized ethnic elites. Often, however, the nomination to run for parliament, regional or state governor, or premier may be the subject of intense intraparty competition, because in ethnicized polities it is virtually tantamount to victory. 2) Electoral mobilization resembles more the clientelistic pattern of reliance on vertical social networks than the mass-based pattern of organization and programmatic communication. 3) Again, like the clientelistic party, the ethnic party stresses particularistic issues—both the narrow particularism of specific benefits that ethnic patrons promise to deliver to their clients and the wider particularism of competitive gains for the entire ethnic group. By definition, 4) the ethnic party represents only the interests of a particular ethnic group and 5) is, at best, aggregative only of the interests of subgroups encompassed by the wider ethnic identity. 6) If the ethnic group is a majority, or nearly so, the ethnic party may aspire to form a government unilaterally, though (as was the case in Sri Lanka) it may have to face a rival ethnic party and a potentially ugly process of ethnic outbidding.[41] Otherwise, the ethnic party is available to form a coalition with parties of other ethnic groups in order to distribute the spoils of power and manage their competition in some kind of consociational fashion. In fact, its principal aim is often to win material benefits for the ethnic group or region through the log-rolling of coalition politics (an increasingly prominent feature of India's politics). Except insofar as their ethnic objectives may be seen as threatening by other groups, ethnic parties may be regarded as acceptable coalition partners by other parties. 7) Finally, the more purely a party is ethnic, the less it will integrate the citizen into a nationwide polity and breed identification with it. The ethnic party's particularistic, exclusivist, and often polarizing political appeals make its overall contribution to society divisive and even disintegrative.

A *congress party* is a coalition, alliance, or federation of ethnic parties or political machines, although it may take the form of a single, unified party structure. Hence, it may share some organizational features with the ethnic party at the local level (such as the distribution of benefits through a vast array of patron-client networks), but within the national political system it behaves dramatically differently. Its electoral appeal is to national unity and integration rather than division, to ethnic sharing and coexistence rather than domination and threat. Where the consociational system tries to share power and resources among and assure the mutual security of all groups within a coalition government formed *after* the election, a congress party constructs the coalitional guarantees in advance, within the broad tent of its party organization. If the tent it builds is broad enough, it can become a dominant party, like the archetype of this model, the Congress Party during India's first two decades of independence, or even more so (but less democratically), the National Front coalition of Malaysia in the past quarter-century. If the coverage of the multiethnic tent is incomplete, the congress party may merely be the first among equals, as with the National Party of Nigeria during the Second Republic (1979–83) or Nigeria's current ruling party, the People's Democratic Party. In either case, the congress party allocates party posts and government offices, and distributes patronage and other benefits, with proportional or other quasi-consociational formulas. Its social base is broad and heterogeneous, and the party's goal is to make it as inclusive as possible. Its very breadth, however, renders it vulnerable to fracture along ethnic or regional lines.

Like the purely ethnic party, the congress party tends to 1) rely heavily on regional and local ethnic elites, as well as clientelistic ties for its electoral mobilization, but with emphasis on themes of national integration rather than division. Because it is less subject to hierarchical control from the national level, 2) the nomination process tends to be more competitive and decentralized. Because of its coalitional nature, the congress party is more effective at performing other party functions than its narrower ethnic cousin. 3) The issues it emphasizes are much more broadly national (even if these may shift markedly from one election to the next, like the catch-all party); in particular, they cut across ethnic, class, and even caste divisions. The party's very inclusiveness, however, blurs rather than structures issues. 4) By definition, the representation of social groups is broad and inclusive, and 5) no type of party is more aggregative of diverse class and functional interests. 6) Government formation and stability is greatly facilitated as a result of its breadth, programmatic heterodoxy, and the sizeable electoral base (even an outright parliamentary majority) that it is likely to secure. 7) Finally, social integration is the very objective of this type of party.

Electoralist parties. There are three party types in the broader genus of "electoralist parties." A general evolutionary trend toward these kinds of parties has been frequently noted.[42] Although there are differences between these three party types (as well as between the "catch-all," "electoral-professional," and "modern cadre" parties of Otto Kirchheimer, Angelo Panebianco, and Ruud Koole, respectively), they are all organizationally thin, maintaining a relatively skeletal existence (the offices and staffs supporting their parliamentary groups not-withstanding). The one exception to this thinness comes at election time, when they spring into action to perform what is unequivocally their primary function, the conduct of the campaign. They utilize "modern" campaign techniques (stressing television and the mass-communications media over the mobilization of party members and affiliated organizations), and they rely heavily on professionals who can skillfully carry out such campaigns.[43] But they differ in some other regards, and these differences lead us to three different types of electoralist parties.

As Kirchheimer and others noted, many parties substantially soften their ideological commitments and loosen their ties to specific clienteles in pursuit of votes, thereby evolving into *catch-all parties*.[44] These parties are distinguished by their shallow organization, superficial and vague ideology, and overwhelmingly electoral orientation. The overriding, if not sole, purpose of catch-all parties is to maximize votes, win elections, and govern. To do so, they seek to aggregate as wide a variety of social interests as possible. In societies where the distribution of public opinion (on a left-right continuum) is unimodal and centrist, catch-all parties strive to capture the median voter by appearing moderate in their policy preferences as well as behavior. In an effort to expand their electoral appeal to a wide variety of groups, their policy orientations are eclectic and shift with the public mood. Lacking an explicit ideology, catch-all parties tend to emphasize the attractive personal attributes of their candidates, and nominations are largely determined by the electoral resources of the candidates rather than by such organizational criteria as years of experience in, or service to, the party. The Democratic Party of the United States, Labour under Tony Blair, the Hungarian Democratic Forum, Spain's Popular Party, and the Spanish Socialist Workers' Party (PSOE) are clear examples of this party type; Taiwan's KMT is completing its long-term transformation from a Leninist to a catch-all party. Korea's principal parties manifest many features of the catch-all party but remain heavily regional in their electoral bases and identities and dominated by individual leaders, giving them some of the flavor of ethnic parties.[45]

It should be noted that our conceptualization of the catch-all party departs from the classic party type described by Kirchheimer insofar as he posited that, as the importance of party militants as vote mobilizers declines, control over the party and its nomination of candidates would increasingly fall into the hands of dominant national-level party leaders (obviously basing his analysis on the experience of centralized West European socialist parties). The experience of American catch-all parties clearly indicates that this is not an essential component of the model: Indeed, the increase in television-dominated, issue- or personality-oriented campaigns and the shifting or weakening of party alliances with the social groups serving as their traditional electoral clienteles have gone hand in hand with the spread of primary elections as the principal form of candidate nomination and the commensurate decline of party bosses. By relaxing the organizational determinism inherent in Kirchheimer's model, eliminating this redundant feature, its applicability to a broader array of real-world cases is strengthened, and some other typologies in the comparative parties literature can be more easily subsumed within this species of party.[46]

With regard to the seven functions of political parties outlined above, catch-all parties are characterized as follows: 1) Nomination is based largely on the personal electoral appeal of the candidate (either as perceived by a party nominating committee or on the actual support received by a candidate in a primary election), rather than on such considerations as length of service to the party or formal institutional position within the party. 2) Electoral mobilization is based not upon face-to-face efforts by party militants or allied secondary organizations, but on direct, unmediated appeals by the candidate to voters through the mass media, especially television. 3) Campaign appeals tend to focus on relatively transient issues (or on the personal abilities of the candidate and the weaknesses of his or her opponent), and are not clearly linked to established programmatic or ideological commitments. 4) In an effort to maximize the breadth of electoral appeal, the catch-all party and its candidates avoid defending the interests of specific social groups during election campaigns and eschew institutionalized links with specific social groups. 5) Given the lack of standing commitments to specific interests, the party and its candidates have considerable discretion in aggregating interests. Given the candidate-centered personalism of the party's electoral campaigns, however, it may be less overtly involved with the formulation of programmatic commitments. 6) The party has wide latitude to form or join governments, given the lack of ideological or programmatic commitments; and the low salience of such concerns makes it easier for such parties to remain within governing coalitions. 7) Low levels of citizen involvement and identification with such parties limits their potential for social integration.

Like the catch-all party, the *programmatic party* is a modern-day, thinly organized political party, mainly focused around election campaigns.[47] However, the programmatic party is somewhat closer to the classic model of a mass-based, ideological party in three respects. First, it has much more of a distinct, consistent, and coherent programmatic or ideological agenda than does the ideal-type catch-all party, and it clearly incorporates those ideological or programmatic appeals in its electoral campaigns and its legislative and government agenda. If it operates within a majoritarian electoral system, as in Britain, the United States, or Mexico (the Conservatives under Margaret Thatcher, the Republicans since 1980, and the National Action Party [PAN], respectively), it must still broadly aggregate interests, but its issue appeals are less diffuse, vague, and eclectic than those of the catch-all party. Thus, second, it seeks to win control of government, or at least a place in it, precisely through this sharper definition of a party platform or vision. Third, while its organization and social base may, in a majoritarian system, resemble that of the catch-all party, in a highly proportional system (such as Israel's), the programmatic party has a narrower, more clearly defined social base, and possibly some firmer linkages to like-minded organizations in civil society. In this case its electoral strategy is to mobilize its core constituency rather than to enlarge it through interest aggregation. For example, as Taiwan's Democratic Progressive Party seeks to establish itself as a viable ruling party, it is rapidly evolving from a nationalist party into a programmatic party based around issues of social justice or equity, good governance, and quality of life. And as Kitschelt argues in this book, a significant number of programmatic parties have emerged in postcommunist Eastern and Central Europe. These include the Democratic Union in Poland; the Hungarian Socialist Party, and the Federation of Young Democrats–Hungarian Civic Party (formerly known simply as the Federation of Young Democrats, or by its acronym FiDeSz), also of Hungary; as well as the Czech Republic's Communist Party of Bohemia and Moravia, the Czech Social Democratic Party, and the Civic Democratic Party of Václav Klaus.

The most purely electoralist party is what we call the *personalistic* party (named the "non-partisan party" by Piero Ignazi),[48] since its *only* rationale is to provide a vehicle for the leader to win an election and exercise power. It is not derived from the traditional structure of local notable elites, but rather is an organization constructed or converted by an incumbent or aspiring national leader exclusively to advance his or her national political ambitions. Its electoral appeal is not based on any program or ideology, but rather on the personal charisma of the leader or candidate, who is portrayed as indispensable to the resolution of the country's problems or crisis. While it may make heavy use of clientelistic networks and broadly distribute particularistic benefits to party supporters, its organization is weak, shallow, and opportunistic. Indeed, it may be so temporary that, even in the service of an incumbent president, such as Alberto Fujimori in Peru, it may change its name and structure with every election. Numerous other twentieth-century examples abound, including Silvio Berlusconi's Forza Italia, the Congress-I rump which defected from the rest of the Congress party in support of Indira Gandhi, and the Pakistan People's Party that Benazir Bhutto inherited from her father (hence with deeper roots than some personalistic parties). Clear examples also include the hastily established electoral vehicles created to bring to power Hugo Chávez Frias in Venezuela, Fernando Collor de Mello in Brazil, Joseph Estrada in the Philippines, and Vladimir Putin in Russia. A recent classic example is the Thai Rak Thai party of the Thai business tycoon Thaksin Shinawatra, whose personality and vast personal fortune gained his party an unprecedented absolute majority of parliament even though it was formed only a few months before the November 2000 elections.

The personalistic party only weakly performs the functions of parties: 1) Nominations are determined or sanctioned by the party leader, but in a presidential system with legislative districts, the "party" may be so shallow that it hardly bothers to field candidates for parliament or other offices. 2) Electoral mobilization is around the personality and indispensable leadership of the party leader. 3) Campaign issues are candidate-centered and eclectic. 4) The effort to mobilize a catch-all or populist, anti-establishment electoral base, and the tendency to equate the election of the party leader with the welfare and destiny of the entire nation, preclude representation of distinct social groups. 5) Thus interests are not so much aggregated into a political coalition as they are blurred or reduced before the candidate's political juggernaut. 6) With an election victory, the personalistic party may form a government, but its institutional weakness and complete dependence on the political skills and personal popularity of the leader (which may fluctuate over time) makes it difficult to sustain an effective government. 7) The hyper-centralization of the party organization and mission around the personality of the leader does little to draw citizens actively into politics or advance social integration. At the same time, some marginalized groups may feel better integrated into politics and society to the extent that the candidate is seen as a representative of their identity group or stratum of society.[49] It is more likely, however, that when the candidate loses popularity and trust in office, political alienation increases.

Movement parties. Finally, there is a type of partisan organization that straddles the conceptual space between "party" and "movement." The prominent examples of the German Greens and the Austrian Freedom Movement make it clear that these types of organizations must be included in this comprehensive typology since they regularly field candidates, have been successful in electing members of parliament, and, in Germany in 1999, were able to form part of a coalition government at the national level and in several Länder (states). These movement parties are of two types: *left-libertarian parties* and *postindustrial extreme right parties.*

   Herbert Kitschelt presents the most detailed analysis of the "left libertarian" variety of the movement party. These he contrasts with "conventional parties" in Western Europe, which are principally oriented toward winning government power through elected office; have a professional staff of party functionaries, and an extensive party organization; represent economic interest groups (labor or business); and are mainly concerned with economic distributive issues.[50] Instead, "left libertarian" parties are quintessentially "post-materialist" in their attitudinal orientation and behavior. They reject the paramount status of economic issues, and are characterized by "a negative consensus that the predominance of markets and bureaucracies must be rolled back in favor of social solidarity relations and participatory institutions."[51] Since there is no consensus in support of a single comprehensive ideology or set of programmatic preferences, this "negative consensus" functions as the very lowest common denominator shared by an otherwise heterogeneous clientele, and the party's agenda revolves around a multiplicity of issues not limited to a single arena. There are no barriers to membership in the group, which is open to all who wish to participate, making the social base and attitudinal orientation of activists even more diverse. The strong commitment to direct participation leads to the weakness or even rejection of centralized organization and leadership, and a sometimes chaotic "assembly" organizational style (as best illustrated by the water-balloon attack on the foreign minister Joschka Fischer at the 1999 congress of the German Greens). Organizationally, the movement party is based on "loose networks of grassroots support with little formal structure, hierarchy and central control."[52] Finally, the left-libertarian movement party stresses "constituency representation" over the logic of electoral competition, making it a sometimes unpragmatic and unreliable coalition partner.

Ignazi presents a succinct overview of the *postindustrial extreme right* party, which he regards as a different kind of reaction against the conditions of postindustrial society.[53] As he points out, where the left-libertarians place greatest emphasis on self-affirmation, informality and libertarianism in their reaction against modern society and state institutions, supporters of the extreme right have been driven by their atomization and alienation to search for more order, tradition, identity and security, at the same time as they attack the state for its intervention in the economy and for its social welfare policies.[54] Like their fascist predecessors, they embrace the "leadership principle" and do not question the directives of the party's paramount leader (as is the case with the National Front's Jean-Marie Le Pen in France or the Freedom Movement's Jörg Haider in Austria). However, they differ from fascists—who supported a strong, disciplined, and militant party as a weapon to be used against their enemies, especially socialist and communist parties— in that they are hostile to the notion of "party" and, more generally, "the establishment." Instead, xenophobic, racist hostility toward migrants is a highly salient line of conflict. In addition, where fascists favored the construction of a strong state, neoconservative anti-state rhetoric and attacks on the social-welfare state permeate the speeches and program proposals of party leaders and candidates.[55]

Fifteen Ideal-Type "Species" of Parties and Theory Building

The typology developed here is certainly less parsimonious than the two-, three-, or four-category frameworks that have dominated the comparative literature on political parties to date. Scholars who prefer styles of theory building based upon deduction from a simpler set of one-dimensional criteria may not welcome this contribution on the grounds that its complexity may hinder theory building. We respect-fully disagree. We believe that all good theories in the social sciences that purport to explain human behavior or institutional performance must accurately reflect real-world conditions. As stated earlier, we have found most of the previously dominant typologies lacking insofar as they were based upon the historical experience of Western Europe from the nineteenth through mid-twentieth centuries. Accordingly, they do not adequately reflect the much more diverse reality of political parties in other parts of the world: As we have suggested, the deep ethnic clea-vages that divide many societies in Africa and Asia have no counterpart in the much more ethnically, linguistically, religiously, and culturally homogeneous context of Western Europe. Hence, in order for a typology of parties to be useful for broad, crossregional comparative analysis it must allow for the emergence of distinct types in greatly different kinds of social contexts, such as the ethnic, congress, and religious-fundamentalist parties described above.

Similarly, it cannot be assumed that typologies based on characteristics of West European parties in the late nineteenth or early twentieth centuries will be valid for all time even within that single region. The socioeconomic context and communication technologies continue to evolve, and these have important implications for the structure, resources, objectives, and behavioral styles of political parties. Consequently, a dichotomous division of cadre versus mass parties, or parties of individual representation versus parties of social- or total integration may have accurately reflected the reality of Western Europe throughout the first half of the twentieth century, but by the second half of that century, these classic party models had become increasingly incapable of capturing the diversity of party type in established democracies. Kirchheimer's catch-all model certainly helped to address this shortcoming by identifying ways in which many parties were tending to deviate from the mass-based party model.[56] Over the following decades, however, the catch-all label has been used to describe an excessively wide variety of parties whose electoral strategies and programmatic commitments differed substantially. In large measure, we believe that this is because the evolution of parties or the emergence of new types of parties may be the product of several fundamentally distinct causal processes, not all of which would move the transformation of the party in the same direction, and not all of which are unilinear in their evolutionary implications.

Hypothesis testing and theory building are facilitated by ideal types that capture all of the defining elements of a concept, but at the same time do not "overaggregate" by including elements that do not con-ceptually or empirically belong together. For example, as Peter Mair has pointed out, the catch-all party model as elaborated by Kirchheimer includes both an ideological and an organizational component: The downgrading of a party's ideological commitment is integrally linked to the "thinning" of the party's organizational structure and an increased emphasis both electorally and organizationally on the party's national-level leadership.[57] With Steven Wolinetz we believe that it is necessary to separate the ideological and organizational dimensions (as we have in elaborating our catch-all, programmatic, and personalistic party models) both in order to reflect reality more accurately, and to facilitate analysis of the causes of party change.[58] With regard to the organizational dimension, Kirchheimer's prediction (actually, lament) regarding the decline of mass parties and their replacement by or evolution into what we have called electoralist parties has certainly come true. Numerous empirical studies have documented a decline in party membership[59] and the loosening or rupture of ties linking parties to communications media and secondary associations in most West European countries,[60] as well as the emergence of organizationally thin parties in the new democracies of the former Soviet Bloc.[61] Indeed, since Kirchheimer was writing at a time that predated the emergence of television as by far the dominant medium of campaign communication throughout the world,[62] he actually understated the extent to which electoral politics would be personalized and would cease to be dependent on a mass base of party militants.

But Kirchheimer's prognosis that these organizational changes would be accompanied by a progressive downgrading of parties' ideological commitments has not come true, at least in countries like the United States and Britain. Some electoralist parties, such as the British Conservatives under Margaret Thatcher and the U.S. Republicans at the national level since 1980,[63] have adopted a much more intense ideological commitment and confrontational style, at the same time as they have mastered "the new campaign politics." Others, such as the Dutch socialists, have come full circle over the past three decades, sharply shifting towards a more radical leftist posture in the late 1960s,[64] then returning to the political center two decades later.[65] Thus it is necessary to separate the organizational from the ideological and programmatic dimensions both in order to describe these diverging evolutionary tendencies accurately and to try to account for them.

Accordingly, we think it desirable to break down overaggregated party models into the leaner and more theoretically modest types proposed here in order to analyze the separate impacts of distinct causal processes which may be moving parties in different directions simultaneously. To be sure, much of the variation in party organizational forms and campaign modalities may be explained largely by long-term processes of socioeconomic development, altering the society within which campaigns will be conducted, and by technological advances. For example, technological change—especially the emergence of tele-vision as the dominant medium of political communication in nearly all democracies (and more recently, the Internet as a new form of "narrowcasting")—has opened up more direct channels of party-elite access to voters, rendering unnecessary older and less efficient vehicles for voter mobilization based on door-to-door campaigning by party militants.[66] But while these socioeconomic and technological developments may create circumstances favorable to the development and progressive dominance of organizationally thin parties, they cannot predict precisely what kind of party is likely to emerge, let alone become a dominant model. Elite decisions to pursue different strategies of voter mobilization or different goals altogether (like, constituency representation instead of vote maximization) can lead to the adoption of a much more sharply defined ideological or programmatic stand. These latter decisions may be influenced by, but are not solely determined by, socioeconomic or technological factors,[67] and thus cannot be assumed to evolve in a unilinear fashion.

Party ideologies, philosophies of representation, and, to some extent, organizational styles may be affected by other societal trends that may have little to do with socioeconomic or technological change. Rather than evolving in a unilinear manner, the defining characteristics of some partisan political subcultures appear to emerge, instead, through a dialectical process in reaction against certain features of the status quo. Indeed, one could hypothesize a chain of reactive changes in party ideologies whose temporal origins can be traced back to the earliest period covered in our survey of political parties, with the emergence of elite-based parties of individual representation in the early nineteenth century in Western Europe. These tended to be either traditionalist conservative or liberal in their ideological orientations. Traditionalist conservative parties defended various aspects of the *ancien régime* that were threatened by political and socioeconomic change, while classical liberalism emerged as a reaction against that old order. Since the traditional, predemocratic social and political order in Western Europe was characterized by mercantilism, monarchy, aristocratic privilege, and established state religions, it was not surprising that classical liberalism would stress free-market capitalism, individualism, and religious freedom or anticlericalism. In the second half of the nineteenth century it was free-market capitalism that defined the status quo, with social polarization between economically privileged and working classes fueling the emergence of socialist parties, stressing class solidarity and economic equality. By the early twentieth century, conflict between free-market capitalism and socialist alternatives largely defined the parameters of political conflict, leading to the articulation of a corporatist "third way" as an alternative (the classic statement of which may be found in the 1891 Papal encyclical *Rerum Novarum*), involving a view of society upon which both denominational and ultranationalist parties could be based. And by the late twentieth century, widespread affluence, Keynesian interventionism, and a large social welfare state defined a status quo against which both left-libertarian and postindustrial extreme-right parties would react.[68] Accordingly, we can see that the defining features of important political ideologies emerged not as the product of a unilinear evolutionary processes— such as long-term, continuous processes of socioeconomic moderni- zation—but through a discontinuous reactive process that was driven by political and social elites. While this dialectical interpretation of the emergence of ideologies and parties is speculative, it is an example of the kind of hypothesis that can be empirically tested using a more fine-grained differentiation among political parties, such as we have proposed.

Political parties have not emerged or evolved in a continuous, unilinear manner, and neither have they converged on a single model of party. Instead, we believe that changes in the organizational forms, electoral strategies, programmatic objectives, and ideological orientations of parties are the products of multiple causal processes—some of them related to broader, long-term processes of social or technological change, others involving the less predictable innovative behavior of political and social elites. If this is true, then it would be a mistake to rely on an excessively restricted number of party types. This would lead scholars to attempt to cram new parties into inappropriate models, or to abort the theory-building process by concluding in frustration that existing theories and models simply do not fit with established party types. Therefore, we believe that the typology presented here—less parsimonious but more fully reflective of the real variation in party types around the world—should facilitate the testing of numerous hypotheses about the origins, functions, and evolutionary trajectories of political parties in widely varying social, political, technological, and cultural contexts.

NOTES

We gratefully acknowledge the comments and criticisms of earlier drafts of this paper by Hans Daalder, Peter Mair, Herbert Kitschelt, Jakub Zielinski, Bradley Richardson, and Anthony Mughan.

1. Juan J. Linz, "Change and Continuity in the Nature of Contemporary Democracies," in Gary Marks and Larry Diamond, eds., *Reexamining Democracy: Essays in Honor of Seymour Martin Lipset* (Newbury Park, Calif.: Sage Publications, 1992), 182–90.

2. Peter Mair and Ingrid van Biezen, "Party Membership in Twenty European Democracies, 1980–2000," *Party Politics* 7 (January 2001): 5–21.

3. Peter Mair, "Party Organizations: From Civil Society to the State," in Richard S. Katz and Peter Mair, eds., *How Parties Organize: Change and Adaptation in Party Organization in Western Democracies* (London: Sage Publications, 1994); and Piero Ignazi, "The Crisis of Parties and the Rise of New Political Parties," *Party Politics* 2 (October 1996): 569–85.

4. See Paul Allen Beck, *Party Politics in America* (New York: Longman, 1997).

5. Sigmund Neumann, "Towards a Comparative Study of Political Parties," in Sigmund Neumann, ed., *Modern Political Parties* (Chicago: University of Chicago Press, 1956).

6. Herbert Kitschelt, *The Logics of Party Formation* (Ithaca, N.Y.: Cornell University Press, 1989).

7. Richard S. Katz and Peter Mair, "Changing Models of Party Organization and Party Democracy: The Emergence of the Cartel Party," *Party Politics* 1 (January 1995): 5–28.

8. Maurice Duverger, *Political Parties* (London: Meuthen, 1954), 71.

9. Herbert Kitschelt, *The Transformation of European Social Democracy* (New York: Cambridge University Press, 1994).

10. Angelo Panebianco, *Political Parties: Organization and Power* (New York: Cambridge University Press, 1988).

11. Samuel Eldersveld, *Political Parties: A Behavioral Analysis* (Chicago: Rand McNally, 1964); Robert Michels, *Political Parties: A Sociological Study of the Oligarchical Tendencies of Modern Democracy* (New York: Hearst's International Library, 1915); and Angelo Panebianco, *Political Parties: Organization and Power* (New York: Cambridge University Press, 1988), 3.

12. Otto Kirchheimer, "The Transformation of the Western European Party Systems," in Joseph LaPalombara and Myron Weiner, eds., *Political Parties and Political Development* (Princeton, N.J.: Princeton University Press, 1966).

13. Alan Ware, *Political Parties and Party Systems* (Oxford: Oxford University Press, 1996).

14. See Ruud Koole, "The Vulnerability of the Modern Cadre Party in the Netherlands," in Richard S. Katz and Peter Mair, eds., *How Parties Organize: Change and Adaptation in Party Organization in Western Democracies* (London: Sage Publications, 1994).

15. R. Kent Weaver and Bert A. Rockman, "When and How Do Institutions Matter?" in R. Kent Weaver and Bert A. Rockman, eds., *Do Institutions Matter? Government Capabilities in the United States and Abroad* (Washington, D.C.: The Brookings Institution, 1993), 445–61.

16. It should be noted that this list of functions of political parties closely corresponds with those identified by Anthony King and Leon D. Epstein. See Anthony King, "Political Parties in Western Democracies: Some Skeptical Reflections," *Polity* 2 (1969); and Leon D. Epstein, *Political Parties in Western Democracies* (New York: Praeger, 1967).

17. See also Joseph LaPalombara and Myron Weiner, "The Origin and Development of Political Parties," in Joseph LaPalombara and Myron Weiner, eds., *Political Parties and Political Development;* and William Nisbet Chambers and Walter Dean Burnham, *The American Party Systems: States of Political Development* (New York: Oxford University Press, 1967).

18. Michael Burton, Richard Gunther, and John Higley, "Introduction: Elite Transformations and Democratic Regimes," in John Higley and Richard Gunther, eds., *Elites and Democratic Consolidation in Latin America and Southern Europe* (Cambridge: Cambridge University Press, 1992).

19. A classic description of this appears in Raymond Carr, *Spain: 1808–1939* (Oxford: Clarendon Press, 1966), ch. 9.

20. See, for example, Frances Hagopian, *Traditional Politics and Regime Change in Brazil* (Cambridge: Cambridge University Press, 1996).

21. Harold Foote Gosnell, *Machine Politics: Chicago Style* (Chicago: University of Chicago Press, 1939); Paul Allen Beck, *Party Politics in America*, 8th ed. (New York: Longman Beck, 1997), 73–77; and V.O. Key, *Southern Politics* (New York: Vintage, 1949).

22. Steven P. Erie, *Rainbow's End: Irish-Americans and the Dilemmas of Urban Machine Politics, 1840–1985* (Berkeley: University of California Press, 1988).

23. Richard Gunther, Giacomo Sani, and Goldie Shabad, *Spain After Franco: The Making of a Competitive Party System* (Berkeley: University of California Press, 1986), 84–85.

24. This change in the nature of mass-level politics is captured by Huntington and Nelson's model of the transition from "mobilized" to "autonomous" participation. Samuel P. Huntington and Joan M. Nelson, *No Easy Choice: Political Participation in Developing Countries* (Cambridge, Mass.: Harvard University Press, 1976).

25. It should be noted that some peasant parties shared many characteristics with the working-class-mass party, including many organizational features and similar historical origins. We are restricting our attention here to the more widespread working-class variant of the mass-based party, which provides a fuller manifestation of the various characteristics of this model.

26. Samuel H. Barnes and Samuel P. Huntington, *Party Democracy: Politics in an Italian Socialist Federation* (New Haven: Yale University Press, 1967).

27. Juan J. Linz and Alfred Stepan, *The Breakdown of Democratic Regimes: Crisis, Breakdown and Reequilibration* (Baltimore: Johns Hopkins University Press, 1978).

28. Maurice Duverger, *Political Parties*, 63–71.

29. Anna Bosco, "Four Actors in Search of a Role: The Southern European Communist Parties," in P. Nikiforos Diamandouros and Richard Gunther, eds., *Parties, Politics, and Democracy in the New Southern Europe* (Baltimore: Johns Hopkins University Press, 2001).

30. For excellent descriptions and analyses of these kinds of parties, see Samuel Barnes, *Party Democracy;* and Leon D. Epstein, "The Socialist Working-Class Party," in Leon D. Epstein, *Political Parties in Western Democracies*, ch. 6.

31. See Robert Michels, *Political Parties.*

32. It is in these organizational respects that the KMT has often been labeled a "Leninist" party, from its founding on the Chinese mainland in the early twentieth century until its democratization in the 1990s and particularly following its defeat in the 2000 presidential election. However, the KMT in power (on the mainland and in Taiwan) shed the revolutionary aspects of its ideology and became only "quasi-Leninist" in nature.

33. Franz Schurmann, *Ideology and Organization in Communist China* (Berkeley: University of California Press, 1966), 100.

34. Dietrich Orlow, *The History of the Nazi Party: Vols. 1 and 2* (Pittsburgh: University of Pittsburgh Press, 1969 and 1973).

35. T.W. Adorno, Else Frenkel-Bruns, D.J. Levinson, and R.N. Sanford, *The Authoritarian Personality* (New York: Harper, 1950).

36. As Mussolini once stated: "We allow ourselves the luxury of being aristocrats and democrats; conservatives and progressives; reactionaries and revolutionaries; legitimists and illegitimists; according to conditions of time, place and circumstance." Quoted in Carl T. Schmidt, *The Corporate State in Action* (London: Victor Gollanz, 1939), 97.

37. See Michael Patrick Fogarty, *Christian Democracy in Western Europe, 1820–1953* (Notre Dame: University of Notre Dame Press, 1957); and Stathis Kalyvas, *The Rise of Christian Democracy in Europe* (Ithaca, N.Y.: Cornell University Press, 1996).

38. This is the key factor that separates the ethnic party from nationalist parties. The latter seek to expand their electoral base by convincing every larger number of citizens that they should identify with the national group and its mission, and often define the "nation" in a flexible manner that facilitates this objective. The ethnic party takes the demographically defined boundaries of the group as "given," and seeks to represent its interests exclusively.

39. Donald L. Horowitz, *Ethnic Groups in Conflict* (Berkeley: University of California Press, 1985), 294–97.

40. Donald L. Horowitz, *Ethnic Groups in Conflict*, 295.

41. Donald L. Horowitz, *Ethnic Groups in Conflict*, 354–59.

42. Otto Kirchheimer, "The Transformation of the Western European Party Systems"; and Angelo Panebianco, *Political Parties;* and Ruud Koole, "The Vulnerability of the Modern Cadre Party in the Netherlands."

43. David M. Farrell and Paul Webb, "Political Parties as Campaign Organizations," in Russell J. Dalton and Martin P. Wattenberg, eds., *Parties Without Partisans: Political Change in Advanced Industrial Democracies* (Oxford: Oxford University Press, 2000).

44. Otto Kirchheimer, "The Transformation of the Western European Party Systems." With Steven Wolinetz, we have disaggregated Kirchheimer's catch-all party into two distinct types, based on their differing levels of commitment to an ideology or generally stable set of programmatic commitments. What we call the catch-all party is referred to by Steven Wolinetz as the "issue/opportunistic" party. Steven Wolinetz, "Party System Change: the Catch-all Thesis Revisited," *West European Politics* 14 (January 1991): 113–28. We share his use of the term "programmatic party" to refer to organizationally thin electoral parties that have reasonably strong ideological or programmatic commitments.

45. Byung-Kook Kim, "Party Politics in South Korea's Democracy: The Crisis of Success," in Larry Diamond and Byung-Kook Kim, eds., *Consolidating Democracy in South Korea* (Boulder, Colo.: Lynne Rienner, 2000), 53–86; and Hoon Jaung, "Electoral Politics and Political Parties," in Larry Diamond and Doh Chull Shin, eds., *Institutional Reform and Democratic Consolidation in Korea* (Stanford, Calif.: Hoover Institution, 2000), 43–71.

46. Koole's modern cadre party, for example, is quite similar to our catch-all model: It is defined by highly professionalized leadership groups, a low member/voter ratio; a weakening, or break, in ties to a *classe gardée;* and an increasing personalization of television-dominated election campaigns. Consistent with our catch-all model (but sharply diverging from Kirchheimer's), it points out that party leadership has not become so dominant as to crush out internal democracy,

particularly with regard to the nomination of candidates. It differs from our model insofar as its electoral appeals are somewhat more stable and focused than the more eclectic and shifting electoral appeals of catch-all parties. Thus, although Koole is not sufficiently precise regarding this point, his model may also apply to what we call "programmatic" parties. It also differs insofar as a mass-based organizational structure is retained. This, we believe, may reflect the transitional status of the Dutch parties studied by Koole, and may therefore not be a relevant defining feature of an ideal-type of political party.

47. See also Steven Wolinetz, "Party System Change."

48. Piero Ignazi, "The Crisis of Parties and the Rise of New Political Parties," *Party Politics* 2 (October 1996): 569–85.

49. For example, in South Korea, Kim Dae-Jung is the political leader and symbol of the historically disadvantaged and politically marginalized Cholla region of the southwest, and his victory did much to reduce this area's sense of political exclusion.

50. Herbert Kitschelt, *The Logics of Party Formation* (Ithaca, N.Y.: Cornell University Press, 1989), 62.

51. Ibid., 64.

52. Ibid., 66.

53. Piero Ignazi, "The Crisis of Parties and the Rise of New Political Parties."

54. Ibid., 557.

55. See Hans-Georg Betz, and Stefan Immerfall, eds., *The New Politics of the Right: Neo-Populist Parties and Movements in Established Democracies* (New York: St. Martin's, 1998). One is tempted to speculate that this fundamental difference is the product of differences in the social and political status quo that the party is reacting against. In the 1920s, the state was "thin," and the principal threat to the social order came from militant parties of the Marxist left. In the 1930s, the depression made the call for a more activist state a reasonable response to widespread unemployment and poverty. By the 1980s and 1990s, however, the social-welfare state had been fully developed in most West European countries (especially Austria and France, where these extreme-right parties have had greatest political impact), so attack on the interventionist state represented the obvious "reaction" in this dialectical process of ideology formation. In addition, the decline of militant Marxism and the mass-based class party, coupled with massive migration into many West European countries from Third World and post-Soviet countries effectively created a new minority to be detested by these xenophobic parties.

56. Otto Kirchheimer, "The Transformation of the Western European Party Systems."

57. Peter Mair, "Continuity, Change and the Vulnerability of Party," *West European Politics* 12 (October 1989): 169–87; Otto Kirchheimer, "The Transformation of the Western European Party Systems."

58. Steven Wolinetz, "Party System Change: The Catch-all Thesis Revisited."

59. For example, Susan E. Scarrow, "Parties Without Members? Party Organization in a Changing Electoral Environment," in Russell J. Dalton and Martin P. Wattenberg, eds., *Parties Without Partisans;* Peter Mair and Ingrid van Biezen, "Party Membership in Twenty European Democracies, 1980–2000," *Party Politics* 7 (January 2001): 5–21.

60. Ruud Koole, "The Vulnerability of the Modern Cadre Party in the Netherlands"; and Cees van der Eijk, "The Netherlands: Media and Politics Between Segmented Pluralism and Market Forces," in Richard Gunther and Anthony Mughan, eds., *Democracy and the Media: A Comparative Perspective* (Cambridge: Cambridge University Press, 2000).

61. Petr Kopecký, "Developing Party Organizations in East-Central Europe," *Party Politics* 1 (October 1995): 515–34.

62. Richard Gunther and Anthony Mughan, eds., *Democracy and the Media: A Comparative Perspective* (Cambridge: Cambridge University Press, 2000); and Gianfranco Pasquino, "The New Campaign Politics in Southern Europe," in P. Nikiforos Diamandouros and Richard Gunther, eds., *Parties, Politics and Democracy in the New Southern Europe* (Baltimore: Johns Hopkins University Press, 2000).

63. It is exceedingly difficult to categorize American parties according to a single party type since parties in the United States are really confederations of state parties, which may vary quite considerably (some approximating the catch-all or programmatic models, while others may still include strong clientelistic elements). See Paul Allen Beck, *Party Politics in America.* Thus, at the same time as the Republican party in the U.S. Congress has become increasingly programmatic, many state governors and their supportive parties have remained centrist and pragmatic practitioners of catch-all politics.

64. Steven Wolinetz, "Party System Change: the Catch-all Thesis Revisited," 121.

65. Ruud Koole, "The Vulnerability of the Modern Cadre Party in the Netherlands," 281.

66. See David M. Farrell and Paul Webb, "Political Parties as Campaign Organizations."

67. Increased affluence and the growth of a sizable middle class, for example, may undercut the credibility and attractiveness of ideologies or programs calling for radical socioeconomic change.

68. For an excellent overview of the emergence of European political parties in conjunction with these ideological trends, see Klaus von Beyme, *Political Parties in Western Democracies* (Aldershot: Gower, 1985), 29–158. Von Beyme's classification scheme bears some resemblance to ours, but it is based primarily on the ideological or programmatic orientations of parties. See Alan Ware, *Political Parties and Party Systems* (New York: Oxford University Press, 1996), 21–49. Accordingly, it overlooks some of the organizational features and behavioral characteristics that we regard as of considerable importance.

2

THE RISE OF PARTIES
IN WESTERN DEMOCRACIES

Hans Daalder

*Hans Daalder was professor of political science at Leiden University
from 1963 to 1993. He is one of the founders of the European Consortium
for Political Research and was the first head of the department of
political and social sciences at the European University Institute in
Florence. He has contributed chapters to several books on comparative
politics, including* Political Parties and Political Development *(1966)
and* Political Oppositions in Western Democracies *(1966). He is the
editor of* Comparative European Politics: The Story of a Profession
(1997).

When did political parties first form in the history of democracy?
Some have seen them as early as ancient Athens, when different groups
sought actively to influence debates and decisions in the large popular
assembly, based on a variety of familiar criteria: social status, locality,
occupation, favorite leaders. Others have referred to the Guelphs and
the Ghibellines, the Protestants and the Catholics, Church and Chapel,
Court and Country—opposing groups locked in long-term partisan
conflict and seeking to attain political power. A case has been made
recently that the Jacobins meet all the characteristics of Maurice
Duverger's *parti de masse,* which is usually thought to have arisen
much later.[1]

The title of such early groupings to the term party has been denied,
however, by those who stipulate the need for a stricter definition: In
their view, only an organization linking rulers and ruled, which seeks to
ensure representation and to capture power by nominating candidates
in elections, can be a party.[2] Others see the origin of political parties in
eighteenth-century Britain, when the organization of parliamentary
support and attempts to influence the outcome of elections became
questions of vital concern for the powers that were; when Bolingbroke
provided the first articulate defense of institutionalized opposition;
when David Hume spoke of "factions from interest," "factions from
affection," and "that most unaccountable phenomenon that has yet

appeared in human affairs, factions from principle"; and when Edmund Burke made a clear case for party as being "a body of men united upon a particular principle to promote the common good of men." Yet in a sophisticated analysis of these writers and political developments in their time, Giovanni Sartori found that even then the notion of party was neither fully developed nor accepted.[3] He concluded that parties properly understood were phenomena that arrived only after both constitutional government and genuine elections had come to stay.

Modern political parties, from that perspective, formed as part of the democratization process, which Robert A. Dahl has analyzed along two fundamental dimensions: 1) the legitimation of opposition, and 2) a process of "inclusion" of more and more groups in the political system.[4] Or, to borrow from the richest of all schemata of comparative European political developments, Stein Rokkan's macromodel of Europe, one can speak of the development of mass democracy in terms of four thresholds that mobilizing or mobilized groups must pass to become fully integrated into a political system:

1) Legitimation: "From which point in the history of state-formation and nation building was there effective the right to petition, criticism, demonstration against the regime . . . and regular protection of the rights of assembly, expression and publication?"

2) Incorporation: "How long did it take before the potential supporters of rising movements of opposition were given formal rights of participation in the choice of representatives on a par with the established strata?"

3) Representation: "How high were the original barriers against the representation of new movements and when and in what ways were the barriers lowered to make it easier to gain seats in the legislature?"

4) Executive power: "How immune were the executive organs against legislative pressures and how long did it take before parliamentary strength could be translated into direct influence on executive decision-making, whether under some form of *Proporz* rule of access for minority parties or though the institutionalization of cabinet responsibility to legislative majorities?"[5]

Three Roads to Democracy

If one inspects the actual crossing of these thresholds, one can see that developments in different societies were far from linear. There were clear differences in both the timing and the sequence in which responsible government arrived and the franchise was extended in Western societies. These had important consequences for the rise and character of political parties. This may be illustrated by a scheme elaborated in the 1960s within the seminal project on *Political Oppositions in Western Democracies* by Robert A. Dahl, Stein Rokkan, Otto Kirchheimer, and others, in terms of three major variables: the establishment

TABLE—THREE ROADS TOWARD INCLUSIVE POLYARCHY

	USA	UK	GERMANY
ARRIVAL OF RESPONSIBLE GOVERNMENT	early	early	late
INTRODUCTION OF GENERAL SUFFRAGE	early	gradually	early
MODERN INDUSTRIALIZATION AND URBANIZATION	later	early	early

of responsible government, the extension of the franchise, and the processes of urbanization and industrialization.[6]

The bare outline of the scheme is given in the Table above. On the left is the United States, which knew representative government as early as the end of the eighteenth century, and which instituted a wide franchise very soon after, long before the onset of mass immigration, urbanization, and industrialization. In America, political parties developed early, as relatively loose organizations that sought to organize voters locally and regionally to support candidates. They came together ad hoc for presidential elections every four years, but otherwise barely had an enduring national existence. The importance of such organizations was sufficient, however, to weather the later advent of urban and industrial growth: "Political machines" did much to mobilize and integrate immigrant and native lower-class groups in preexisting formations. Labor became an important social and political actor, but although many small socialist organizations or looser leagues sprang up, a durable and powerful socialist party never developed. What are now called "Democrats" and "Republicans" remained relatively loose associations, and for all the party identification that grew, the highly localized nature of electoral processes and practices made political parties far from cohesive political actors.

Great Britain, represented in the second column, also developed representative government early, but industrialization came earlier than in the United States, while the franchise was extended later and more gradually. Thus the early development of parties was more elitist: Tories and Whigs first organized within Parliament for or against a sitting Cabinet. They only slowly developed organizations for electoral purposes, which became more important with the abolition of rotten boroughs and electoral reform. From time to time, the "official" political system was faced by widespread social unrest, which led to some extraparliamentary movements, such as the Chartists. But from the Reform Bill of 1832 onward, Conservatives and Liberals both began to build up political organizations, particularly after the franchise extensions of 1867 and 1882. The Conservatives successfully mobilized what eventually came to be known as the "working-class Tories," becoming an enduring mass movement. Liberals developed a "Lib-Lab" wing, which sought to tie trade unions to the Liberal Party, but proved eventually unable to stem the development of a separate Labour Representation Committee (1900), the precursor of the Labour Party, which eventually displaced the Liberals as the major party in a predominantly two-party system. The strength of parliamentary politics remained such, however, that this new movement came to respect fully the rules of democratic politics, including the practice that the political leadership should rest first and foremost with the front benchers in the House of Commons.[7]

The third course of political development was that taken by Germany. That country, too, knew a relatively early process of industrialization. Responsible parliamentary government, on the other hand, came very late. In fact, universal suffrage was granted in the *Kaisserreich* long before governments became accountable to the *Reichstag.* Universal suffrage and early social insurance were twin instruments in attempts to integrate a newly developing working class *within* an autocratic political system. If the new central government wavered between banning and insulating a socialist movement, that movement itself hesitated between adaptation to a Bismarckian state and its eschatological revolutionary beliefs. The socialist movement developed into the prototype of a mass party, which served as a prestigious example to budding socialist parties elsewhere. The long persistence of autocratic government remained a substantial handicap, however. Even when world war and revolution had resulted in Weimar, parties were far from being universally accepted as legitimate political actors: Parties that accepted the legitimacy of the new Weimar Constitution had to compete with lingering resistance from older parties seeking to salvage the older political order and from movements that did not accept a democratic order, but were a harbinger of a new totalitarian nationalism or an allegedly internationalist proletarian revolution.

Other Roads to Party and Democracy

Can all European democracies be fitted into the three patterns of political development presented in the Table? The answer is no, for three reasons: First, there are the countries that developed responsible government relatively early, extended the franchise gradually, but industrialized rather late. If the presence of early responsible government and a limited franchise resembled the British case, the late arrival of industrialization led to the politicization of cleavages and the incorporation of voters in mass organizations before a new working-class politics made itself fully felt. Thus controversies between secular and more religious elements of the population preceded and limited the later growth of socialist movements in countries like the Netherlands and Belgium, as did the mobilization of agrarian parties and counterculture protests in Scandinavia against the modern urban centers and the official establishment. At a minimum, then, attention should be paid to the special character of religious parties and *Venstre* parties, which forestalled a bipolar opposition of conservatives and Labor. The

late arrival of industrialization and modernization also caused clear
splits between reformist and radical socialist groupings, which led to
what Rokkan called "split working-class systems" of socialists and
communists in some countries.[8]

Second, even when so amended, the scheme gives insufficient place
to countries that extended the franchise early and underwent reversals
from democratic to autocratic regimes. Thus France had its revolutionary
experience and elections on a very wide franchise. The French Revolution and reactions to it, however, created persistent divisions in French
political development, burdening the legitimacy of successive regimes,
complicating the formation of strong, nationwide political parties, and
leading to alternative *rassemblements,* plebiscitary adventures, and
repeated institutional tinkering rather than stable party politics. Spain,
too, had early party divisions and democratic constitutions alternating
with repressive regimes. So did Italy, where the new unitary state was
faced, after 1870, with a long-term boycott of parliamentary and electoral
politics by Catholics hankering for the restoration of the Papal States,
knew for long a system of elite politics (which became the classic
example for elitist theorists[9]), and proved unable to stem the development of a new totalitarian fascism.

Third, Europe has an increasing number of cases of postauthoritarian
(or even post-totalitarian) democratic restorations. Of course, the scheme
of the Table does not really hold in these cases. A renewed responsible
government and universal suffrage arrived together, possibly after the
process of urbanization and industrialization had already come in full
force. One might note the changed attitude in Germany toward
democratic political parties: If fears of Nazism or communism could
lead on the one hand to a constitutional banning of nondemocratic
parties, then on the other, legal and financial provisions deliberately
strengthened the role of democratic parties to such an extent that German
parties have been active agents in the promotion of like-minded parties
elsewhere. Parties were also given a new lease on life and very much
extended means of leverage in Italy, Spain, Portugal, and Greece. To
what extent their deliberate strengthening contributed, in turn, to an
increased resentment of their role in societies that have historical reasons
to regard the state and political power as repressive agencies seems a
relevant question. Loaded terms like the German *Parteienstaat* and
Politikverdrossenheit or the Italian *partitocrazia* have no clear
equivalents elsewhere, for all the recurrent discussions about (the lack
of) political participation and a "crisis of parties."

The Varied World of Parties

This (admittedly simplified) sketch of some possible routes toward
fully inclusive democracy throws light on the great variety of parties

that emerged in Western societies. One can review these along a number of important dimensions:

1) Legitimacy. In countries with a long tradition of representative government, parties developed slowly and generally came to be regarded as legitimate players. This is not the case, or less so, in countries where democracy developed against long-term authoritarian rule, especially in countries where clear reversals to autocratic or totalitarian politics occurred. In such cases, adherents of former regimes and advocates of a more revolutionary politics might question the legitimacy of the new democratic politics. This might give rise to specific "antisystem" parties, as well as to antisystem activities beyond party politics, which threaten democratic party governance.

2) The elite-mass dimension. Whenever democratization came gradually, parties were more likely to develop from traditions of legitimate elite competition. Parties, as Duverger has argued, may be "internally created."[10] Groups were formed within a representative assembly around particular leaders and common interests. They established organizations in local constituencies to ensure the election and reelection of particular representatives. The typical initial form of party, outside a parliamentary caucus, was therefore the *parti-comité*—a loosely organized group of local notables who became active at election time in support of favored candidates. Only when the franchise was extended were tighter forms needed to organize mass support, which is also a reason for organization across constituencies. Yet the parliamentary origin remained visible. Generally speaking, leadership of such parties continued to rest squarely in the hands of the parliamentary leadership.

In addition to these looser movements, there were "externally created" parties—social groups hitherto excluded from existing elite politics that were organized outside parliaments in pursuit of particular principles and interests. Seeking a clear mass base, they were active not only at election time but also between elections. The balance of power lay, at least initially, much more outside than inside parliaments. From an organizational point of view, they were superior to the older *partis-comités*. Duverger expected that this would lead to a "contagion from the left" as older elite parties had to assume tighter organizational forms to avoid being outdone by the superior organizational skills of newly arriving competitors. Hence, he postulated a natural process from *partis de cadre* to *partis de masse*.

3) Integration. Parties have differed greatly in the extent to which they have succeeded in integrating particular sections of a given population. There is a considerable range from what Sigmund Neumann called older "parties of individual representation," to "parties of social integration," to the ultimate logic of "parties of total integration."[11] In parties of individual representation, both leaders and voters may move relatively freely over a political space (as is somewhat true to this day of

American parties). This is not the case for parties of integration, where both leaders and followers remain within specific bonds of class, religion, or ethnicity, having to operate in relatively closed electoral markets with lasting divides, in relatively tightly organized party universes buttressed by all kinds of ancillary organizations.

4) The nationalization of parties. Parties differ markedly in the extent to which they have become effective national actors. Thus, in the United States, party activities remain highly localized, oriented toward the nomination and election of local officers, and as far as the federal level is concerned, that of congressmen and perhaps senators, with the presidency forcing only intermittent "national" action. In France, too, local factors remain very strong in both nominations and elections, which has tended to prevent the development of truly cohesive parties. In other countries, the politicization of social cleavages has led to the formation of truly national parties that integrated sections of the population into national politics.

5) The "reach" or "permeation" of parties. There are also considerable differences in the extent to which parties penetrate beyond what has been called the "partisan-electoral arena": the structuring of elections, the formation of groups within representative assemblies, and the formation and support of political executives. There are differences in the extent to which party organizations outside parliament effectively control the actions of representatives and ministers. Beyond that, parties also differ substantially in the degree to which they reach beyond these "sites" of decision making to control bureaucratic appointments, to determine the composition of the judiciary, and to become decisive players in the possibly lucrative sectors of parastatal administrative bodies and enterprises.

The Criticism of Parties

The development of political parties has been accompanied by strident criticism.[12] These criticisms can be analyzed along the five dimensions in the preceding paragraph:

1) The questioning of legitimacy. The rise of parties has been resisted by those who had an interest in the traditional order, who feared that the organization of parties would lead to a sharpening of divisions, if not to a revolutionary attempt to change existing power divisions. Parties have been attacked in the name of authoritarian values—the monarch, the state, the nation—that should not fall prey to "special interests." And they have been held to be illegitimate by those "democrats" who believe in the possibility of "direct democracy" and the existence of a general will and decry both representation and *associations partielles* in their name.

2) The role of the masses. Again and again, the claims of social groups

not yet included in the polity were denied. They were held to threaten
property and freedom, to lack the intelligence and judgment for good
government, and to be vulnerable to demagogues, vulgar tastes, and
group egoism. Against a world of mass organizations, a fictitious ideal
of elite politics was held up: an ideal parliament populated by free-
speaking and free-judging deputies unfettered by unwanted mass
organizations. Such sentiments were mixed with views that the coming
of mass democracy was inevitable, not least because elites themselves
came to organize new entrants into mutual competition. Yet then also,
one can trace an element of continued rejection, as in the aristocrat
Moisei Ostrogorski's portrayal of mass parties that he wanted to replace
with ad hoc issue groups,[13] or in the "iron law of oligarchy" analyzed by
Robert Michels, who started out as a leftist intellectual but ended up
embracing fascism.[14] There is a constant undercurrent of doubt and
distrust, which leads to the regulation of the role of parties: attempts to
regulate internal party processes by party statutes or the American reform
movement's successful drive to take nomination decisions out of the
hands of parties through primaries.

   3) Integration. Here, too, there have been ambivalent attitudes. The
right of groups to organize was granted in the name of "voice" and "fair
representation." Parties have been praised as vehicles of emancipation
and social learning. They have been hailed for their role in structuring
opinions and interests, in securing cohesion, in providing the basis for
stable representative government and in forestalling the dangers of an
undifferentiated mass society. In the well-known "responsible party
government" literature,[15] the underlying thesis was that (American)
parties should offer more durable and specific integration of groups
than they did, to make choices clearer and governments more accountable. At the same time, however, there was an equally consistent counter-
tune. Parties were held to encapsulate groups and to deprive voters of
their natural freedoms. Frozen alignments were thought to make for
immobility, preventing the expression of new issues and interests, and
hindering new choices.

   4) The nationalization of politics. Here, parties have been criticized
on two grounds. Some argue that representatives elected solely on local
criteria are likely to be both parochial and too little disciplined for the
good of national decision making. Others inveigh against overly
centralized power within parties in matters like nominations and the
enforcement of parliamentary discipline. It is no accident that the latter
have argued for a greater say by local forces in such matters as party
nominations and electoral reform, whereas the former have pleaded for
reforms in opposite directions. Witness the differences between reform
movements in the United States that have successfully taken the power
of nominations from parties to primaries and those that have advocated
a strengthening of "responsible parties."

5) The hold of parties. Critics of Weimar have argued that democratic parties proved insufficiently capable of controlling the authoritarian remnants of the army, the bureaucracy, and possibly the judiciary as, paradoxically, the Nazi party was to do much more successfully in the short-lived Third Reich. Older sentiments against a *Parteienstaat* became somewhat discredited in Germany in the process, which opened the way to a much stronger organization and penetration by parties into various sectors of government and society after World War II. In fact, patronage and political appointments seem to have gained legitimacy in many systems. They are defended in the name of accountability and control, the primacy of politics becoming all the more important as the scope and variety of state intervention increase. But here again sentiments against parties linger. There are cries about spoils and corruption. Certain reforms seek to take choices out of the hands of parties, by the deliberate introduction of direct choice of political executives and the introduction or greater use of referenda. There are attempts to block the role of parties in judicial and bureaucratic appointments through a stronger insistence on competitive examinations and achievement criteria. There is a widespread call for the services of presumably "independent" experts and a desire to replace "politics," "government," and "administration" with market forces.

Sequences in the Development of Party Types

There have been various attempts to portray a definite sequence in the development of particular party types.

As we saw, Duverger suggested a typical movement from the older category of *partis-comité* to more modern *partis de masse*. In his view, the latter were bound to get the upper hand in an age of mass democratization: The superior organization of mass parties in a time of mass electorates would inevitably force elite parties to follow suit in self-defense. Similarly, Neumann foresaw that parties of social integration would supplant older types of parties of individual representation, with the ever-present danger that parties of total integration would take over next.

With the new evidence of the post-1945 world in hand, later authors criticized these predictions. With the admitted chagrin of a disillusioned left-wing socialist, Otto Kirchheimer diagnosed a replacement of older mass parties by "catch-all parties." According to his analysis, such parties showed the following features:

a) Drastic reduction of the party's ideological baggage . . .
b) Further strengthening of top leadership groups, whose actions and omissions are now judged from the viewpoint of their contribution to the efficiency of the entire social system rather than identification with the goals of their particular organization.

c) Downgrading the role of the individual party member, a role considered a historical relic which may obscure the newly built-up catch-all
image.
d) De-emphasis of the *classe gardée,* specific social class of denominational clientele in favour of recruiting voters among the population at large.
e) Securing access to a variety of interest groups.[16]

Attempts to test Kirchheimer's forecast against empirical data have
resulted in somewhat ambiguous findings. There seems little doubt that
the bonds of social class and religion have tended to weaken in modern
societies. Traditional organizational links between political leaders and
voters have loosened concurrently. A deemphasis of the ordinary party
member and a greater role for political leaders, bolstered by professional
electioneering support, are characteristic of most modern parties. There
is less agreement, however, on Kirchheimer's prediction that ideologies
will wither away. This might not be true for all parties, and does insufficient justice to the possibility that new ideologies are replacing older
ones (as in the argument that new "postmaterialist values" are replacing
more traditional ideological bonds). And his assumption that interest
groups would begin to play a greater role within parties seems less certain than that interest groups bypass parties in their attempt to influence
decision makers.

Doubts about a wholesale replacement of older elite and mass parties
by mere catch-all parties have led other observers to develop alternative
models of parties. Thus Angelo Panebianco has spoken of an "electoral-
professional party"[17] and Ruud Koole of the "modern cadre party."[18] The
most challenging proposition comes from Richard Katz and Peter Mair,
who have suggested the existence of a definite trend in time and in kind:
from the nineteenth century "elite party," to the mass party (which was
characteristic for the period of political mobilization and democratization
between 1880 and 1960), which, after 1945, was followed by "catch-all
parties," only to be replaced increasingly since about 1970 by a new
type called "cartel parties."[19] This type of party is the result, in their
view, of "the interpenetration of party and state, and . . . a pattern of
interparty collusion,"[20] which makes parties privileged agents of the
state, at the expense of earlier roles of representation, articulation and
aggregation, and democratic participation by ordinary members.
Although the process is still at an early stage and is true for countries to
different degrees, Katz and Mair foresee an unmistakable trend to turn
politics increasingly into a managerial and professional game.

Whether or not one agrees with this forecast, there is considerable
agreement on the relevant forces at work: the expansion of the state
deep into society; the rapid increase in the number of "sites" where
political and administrative decisions are taken; the very considerable
expansion of specialized interest groups and ad hoc action groups; the

rise of the electronic media, which has brought about substantial change in the older mass media as well; the rise in the standards of living; the revolution in mass education; increased geographical and social mobility; the partial breakup of family and other primary groups; strong processes of social individualization in society; and the like. But if some see a clear shift in party types as a result of such phenomena, others suggest that different types of party are likely to persist in different countries and settings, and possibly to coexist in particular systems.[21] They emphasize less the dynamic changes in party *types* than shifts in party *functions,* some of these becoming weaker and others possibly stronger. In modern society, parties face increased competition from the media, interest groups, and action groups, and even bureaucracies have become strong rivals to parties in the expression and articulation of policy demands. Both the programmatic and representational roles of parties have tended to suffer in the process. Yet almost by definition, parties have remained the decisive agents of political recruitment and often seem to have become stronger, rather than weaker, in extending their hold on formerly less accessible social and political arenas.

NOTES

1. George Th. Mavrogordatos, "Duverger and the Jacobins," *European Journal of Political Research* 30 (July 1996): 1–17.

2. The more specific definition is intended to differentiate the notion of a political party from other political groups, such as factions on the one hand and promotional and interest groups on the other.

3. Giovanni Sartori, *Parties and Party Systems: A Framework for Analysis* (New York: Cambridge University Press, 1976), ch. 1.

4. See notably Robert A. Dahl, *Polyarchy: Participation and Opposition* (New Haven: Yale University Press, 1971).

5. Stein Rokkan, *Citizens, Elections, Parties: Approaches to the Comparative Study of the Process of Development* (Oslo: Universitetsforlaget, 1970), 79.

6. There are elements of the scheme in the concluding chapter "Some Explanations," in Robert A. Dahl, ed., *Political Oppositions in Western Democracies* (New Haven: Yale University Press, 1966), 348–86, and it was elaborated upon in much greater detail by Stein Rokkan, *Citizens, Elections, Parties,* 72–144.

7. See the classic analysis by R.T. McKenzie, *British Political Parties: The Distribution of Power Within the Conservative and Labour Parties* (London: Heinemann, 1955).

8. Stein Rokkan, *Citizens, Elections, Parties,* 93.

9. Witness the work of Vilfredo Pareto, Gaetano Mosca, and Robert Michels.

10. See Maurice Duverger, *Les Partis Politiques* (Paris: Armand Colin, 1951), 1–16.

11. Sigmund Neumann, "Toward a Comparative Study of Political Parties," in Sigmund Neumann, ed., *Modern Political Parties: Approaches to Comparative Politics* (Chicago: University of Chicago Press, 1956), 395–421.

12. For a more complete exposition, see Hans Daalder, "A Crisis of Party," *Scandinavian Political Studies* 15 (December 1992), 269–88.

13. Moisei Ostrogorski, *Democracy and the Organisation of Political Parties,* Frederick Clarke, trans. (New York: Macmillan, 1902).

14. Robert Michels, *Zur Soziologie des Parteiwesens in der Modernen Demokratie: Untersuchungen über die oligarchischen Tendenzen des Gruppenlebens* (Leipzig: Klinkhardt, 1911). See also Juan J. Linz, "Introduzione," in Robert Michels, *La Sociologia del Partito Politico* (Bologna: Il Mulino, 1965), vii–cxix.

15. The *locus classicus* was the APSA Report *Towards a Responsible Party System, Supplement to The American Political Science Review* 44 (1950). See also Austin Ranney, *The Doctrine of Responsible Party Government: Its Origin and Present State* (Urbana: University of Illinois Press, 1954).

16. Otto Kirchheimer, "The Transformation of the Western European Party System," in Joseph LaPalombara and Myron Weiner, eds., *Political Parties and Political Development* (Princeton, N.J.: Princeton University Press, 1966), 177–200. For valuable critiques of Kirchheimer, see notably Steven B. Wolinetz, "The Transformation of the Western European Party Systems Revisited," *West European Politics* 2 (January 1979): 4–28; and Steven B. Wolinetz, "Party System Change: The Catch-All Thesis Revisited," *West European Politics* 14 (January 1991): 113–28.

17. Angelo Panebianco, *Political Parties: Organization and Power,* Marc Silver, trans. (Cambridge: Cambridge University Press, 1988).

18. Ruud Koole, *De Opkomst van de Moderne Kaderpatij: Veranderende Partij-organisatie in Nederland 1960–1990* (Utrecht: Het Spectrum, 1992).

19. Richard S. Katz and Peter Mair, "Changing Modes of Party Organization and Party Democracy: The Emergence of the Cartel Party," *Party Politics* 1 (January 1995): 5–28. This essay is now reprinted in Peter Mair, *Party System Change: Approaches and Interpretations* (Oxford: Clarendon Press, 1997), 93–119. See in particular the concise summary of the argument in Table 5.1, on pp. 110–11.

20. See Peter Mair, *Party System Change: Approaches and Interpretations,* 108.

21. See Ruud Koole, "Cadre, Catch-All or Cartel? A Comment on the Notion of the Cartel Party," *Party Politics* 2 (October 1996): 507–23, followed by a rejoinder by Richard S. Katz and Peter Mair, 525–33.

3

THE AMERICANIZATION OF THE EUROPEAN LEFT

Seymour Martin Lipset

Seymour Martin Lipset is Hazel Professor of Public Policy at George Mason University and senior fellow at the Hoover Institution, the Progressive Policy Institute, and the Woodrow Wilson Center. His many books include Political Man: The Social Bases of Politics *(1960),* American Exceptionalism: A Double-Edged Sword *(1996), and* It Didn't Happen Here: Why Socialism Failed in the United States *(2000).*

In a book published in 1998, a distinguished sociologist asserted, "No one any longer has any alternatives to capitalism—the arguments that remain concern how far and in what ways capitalism should be governed and regulated." What makes these words especially noteworthy is that the man who wrote them, Anthony Giddens, was also widely known as the intellectual guru to British prime minister and Labour Party leader Tony Blair. By embracing "The Third Way" (the title of Giddens's book), explicitly understood as a middle path that avoided both the anti-capitalism of the left and the conservatism of the right, Blair helped bring to an end a century-long period in which the European left had been dominated by socialists. By so doing, he and his counterparts on the continent have also furthered the process of making political party divisions in Europe resemble more closely those of the United States, where socialism never gained a serious foothold.

Socialist theorists from the late nineteenth century on have been bedeviled by the question of why the United States, alone among industrial societies, has lacked a significant socialist movement or labor party. Friedrich Engels tried to answer it in the last decade of his life. In 1906, the German sociologist Werner Sombart published a major book on this theme, *Why Is There No Socialism in the United States?* That same year, the Fabian H.G. Wells also addressed the question in *The Future in America.* Both Lenin and Trotsky were deeply concerned with the phenomenon, for it questioned the inner logic of Marxist historical materialism, as expressed by Marx himself in *Das Kapital,* where he stated that "the country that is more developed [economically] shows to the less developed the image of their future."[1] From the last quarter of the nineteenth century on, the United States has been that country.

Given Marx's dictum, leading pre–World War I Marxists believed that the most industrialized capitalist country would lead the world into socialism. This position became entrenched in Marxism. While still an orthodox Marxist (before he became the most influential revisionist of Marxist ideas), Edward Bernstein noted, "We see modern socialism enter and take root in the United States in direct relation to the spreading of capitalism and the appearance of a modern proletariat." In 1902, Karl Kautsky, considered the German Social Democratic Party's leading theoretician, wrote that "America shows us our future, in so far as one country can reveal it at all to another." He elaborated this view in 1910, anticipating that the "overdue sharpening of class conflict" would develop "more strongly" in America than anywhere else. August Bebel, the political leader of the German Social Democrats, stated unequivocally in 1907 that "Americans will be the first to usher in a Socialist republic."[2] This belief—at a time when the German party was already a mass movement with many elected members of the Reichstag, while the American Socialist Party had secured less than 2 percent of the vote— was based on the fact that the United States was far ahead of Germany in industrial development.

The continued inability of socialists to create a viable movement in the United States was a major embarrassment to Marxist theorists who assumed that the "superstructure" of a society, which encompasses political behavior, is a function of the underlying economic and technological systems. Max Beer, whose 50-year career in international socialism included participation in the Austrian, German, and British parties, and who worked for the Socialist International, described the anxiety voiced in private discussions by European Marxist leaders regarding the weakness of socialism in America. They knew that it was a "living contradiction of . . . Marxian theory" and that it raised questions about the validity of Marxism itself.[3]

In a 1939 publication intended for a popular American audience, Leon Trotsky reprinted the sentence from *Das Kapital* quoted above, only to dismiss it with the comment, "under no circumstances can this . . . be taken literally."[4] Trotsky, of course, knew his Marxism and was well aware that the theory demanded that the United States should have been the first on the path to socialism. His comment suggests that the contradiction was much on his mind. His effort to dismiss it as a figurative statement indicates that he had no answer to the conundrum it posed.

Yet in spite of the sorry record of organized socialism in America, it may be argued that, in a sense, Karl Marx was right in saying that the most developed country "shows to the less developed the image of their future." American political culture—as it actually developed, not as

Marxists hoped it would—reflects the logic of an economically and technologically advanced society. The never-feudal United States has been the prototypical bourgeois society. As Max Weber understood, the United States could become the world's most productive economy precisely because its culture thoroughly encompassed capitalist values. The ideal-typical capitalist man was an American—Benjamin Franklin. For Weber, "the spirit of capitalism" was best expressed in the Pennsylvanian's writings.[5]

The argument that American nonsocialist politics would prove to be the model for the European left was presented in full flower in 1940 by Lewis Corey (Louis Fraina), an early leader of the American Communist Party, in a series of articles in the Lovestoneite organ *Workers Age*. Corey's insight is summarized by Harvey Klehr as follows:

> Rather than being an exception, America was actually the model for capitalist countries. Only the positions in the race had been changed; European socialists could see in America the image of their own unhappy future. Far from being a unique or even only slightly different case, America was the prototype for capitalism. In a curious reversal of roles, it was now the European socialists who could look across the ocean to see the future of their own movement. American development was not different than Europe's; it was merely at a more advanced stage.[6]

Changing Societies, Changing Politics

As Corey anticipated, the left in the other Western democracies has become increasingly like the American nonsocialist left. To a greater or lesser degree, all major parties of the left now reject statist economies and accept competitive markets as the way to achieve economic growth and raise standards of living. Social-democratic and labor parties are now socially and ideologically pluralistic. The Socialist International has effectively been recast into a new grouping of progressive parties, dubbed the "third way," in which the Democratic Party represents the United States.

This change in the character of the European parties reflects a transformation of economic and class structures that has made them resemble those of the United States. The emphasis on fixed, explicitly hierarchical social classes derived from a feudal and monarchical past has declined greatly. The growth in the European economies, together with the consequent increase in consumption goods and a more equitable allocation of education, has greatly reduced the differences in style of life, including accents and dress, among social classes. The distribution of income and occupational skills has changed from the pyramidal shape that characterized the late nineteenth and early twentieth centuries to one that resembles a diamond, bulging in the middle.

Political parties on the left now seek to appeal more to the growing middle strata than to industrial workers and the impoverished, who constitute a declining proportion of the population. In the United States—the prototype of industrialized societies—the proportion of those employed in nonmanual pursuits increased from 43 percent in 1960 to 58 at the end of the century, while the proportion of workers employed in manufacturing fell from 26 to 16 percent. The corresponding dropoff for the United Kingdom was from 36 percent to 19 percent; for Sweden, from 32 percent to 19 percent; for the Netherlands, from 30 percent to 19 percent; and for Australia, from 26 percent to 13.5 percent. The declines have been less dramatic but still pronounced for France (28 to 20 percent) and Germany (34 to 29 percent).

America has always placed a lesser emphasis on class awareness and organization than European societies; in any case, these have been declining on both sides of the Atlantic. Union membership, the predominant base of parties on the left, has fallen in proportional terms in four-fifths of the 92 countries surveyed by the International Labor Organization. Between 1985 and 1995, union membership rates declined by 21 percent in the United States. As of 2000, only 13.5 percent of employed American workers—and less than 10 percent of those in private employment—were members of trade unions. These declines have been even greater in France and Britain (37 and 28 percent, respectively), while Germany fell off by 18 percent.[7] The European and Australasian social-democratic parties, like the Democrats in the United States, have become more socially heterogeneous in membership and support. The correlations between class and voting, which are lower in the United States than elsewhere in the industrialized world, have been falling in most developed nations in recent decades as the distribution of economic classes and consumption levels have changed.

Some of the underlying forces giving rise to these developments have been specified by a number of neo-Marxist social scientists in discussing the emergence of "postindustrial society," "postmaterialism," and the "scientific-technological revolution." Daniel Bell, a lifelong social democrat, has been the central figure in conceptualizing these changes in the West. Radovon Richta and his associates in the Czechoslovak Academy of Sciences projected similar developments in Eastern Europe and the Soviet Union.[8]

The consequent changes in class and political relations within industrially developed societies, much like the shifts in left-wing politics in the United States and Europe, may be analyzed within the framework of an "apolitical" Marxism—that is, by accepting the proposition that technological advances and the distribution of economic classes determine the political and cultural "superstructures," but without assuming that socialism will succeed capitalism. Many of the trends anticipated by Marx—the growth of factories, a steady increase in the industrial proletariat, a decline in self-employment—have ended. The proportion of people employed in tertiary technological and service occupations has been increasing rapidly. The number of university graduates and students in higher education has grown sharply. Alain Touraine, a leading French sociologist and leftist intellectual, suggests that the basis of power has changed as a result of these developments: "If property was the criterion of membership in the former dominant class, the new dominant class is defined by knowledge and a certain level of education."[9]

Neo-Marxists and technological determinists have stressed the extent to which theoretical and scientific knowledge has become the principal source of social and economic change, altering social structures, values, and mores in ways that have given considerable prestige and power to scientific and technological elites. The emerging strata of postindustrialism—whose roots are in the university, the scientific and technological worlds, the industries spawned by computers, the public sector, and the professions—have developed their own distinctive values.

Ronald Inglehart, the most important empirical analyst of postindustrialism, points out that "postmaterialist" value changes and the decline of class conflict are also functions of the growing climate of affluence in the last half-century. The generations that came of age during the second half of the twentieth century hold different values than their predecessors, who were reared in an atmosphere of economic scarcity and experienced severe economic depressions. Survey data gathered by Inglehart over the past quarter-century have shown clear generational effects and links to the massive growth in educational attainments that have made the expansion in high-tech and scientific pursuits possible.[10]

These developments have profoundly affected the political scene in industrially advanced societies. With the growth of market power in the economic arena, postindustrial politics has been marked by a decline in ideological conflict over the role of the state. The citizenry, now better-educated, has become increasingly concerned with noneconomic or social issues—the environment, health, the quality of education, the culture, greater equality for women and minorities, the extension of democratization and freedom at home and abroad, and (last, but far from least) questions of personal morality, particularly as they affect family matters and sexual behavior. In some polities, including France and Germany, environmental reformers have taken the lead in creating new Green parties, generally allied in coalition with the new social democrats.

Just as the United States has set a model for less statist, more market-oriented polities, more recently it has been in the forefront of the postmaterialist "new politics," which has traveled, so to speak, from Berkeley and Madison to Paris and Berlin. The French political analyst Jean-François Revel, writing in the early 1970s, noted that the newer forms of movement protest, whether in Europe or elsewhere, are "imitations of the American prototype."[11]

Many political analysts, while recognizing major reformulations by the left within their own countries, do not realize the extent to which these changes reflect developments that are common throughout the economically advanced democracies. To point out the magnitude and congruence of these events, I will summarize the ways in which left-wing politics in country after country has taken an "American" path. This, of course, does not mean that parties and ideologies are the same crossnationally. There are important variations reflecting diverse historical backgrounds, the varying nature of political cleavages, and the structural and demographic patterns underlying them. Yet the similarities among the polities are considerable. As Tony Blair has stressed, "it's a perfectly healthy thing if we realize there are common developments the whole world over."[12]

The New Social Democrats

Following a meeting of European social-democratic leaders with Bill Clinton in New York on 24 September 1998, Tony Blair proclaimed their new "third way" doctrine:

> In the economy, our approach is neither laissez-faire nor one of state interference. The government's role is to promote macroeconomic stability; develop tax and welfare policies that encourage independence, not dependence; to equip people for work by improving education and infrastructure; and to promote enterprise. We are proud to be supported by the business leaders as well as trade unions. . . . In welfare and employment policy, the Third Way means reforming welfare to make it a pathway into work where possible. It promotes fair standards at work while making work pay by reducing the taxes and penalties that discourage work and the creation of jobs.[13]

The 1997 British election, won overwhelmingly by the Labour Party after it had rejected its historic emphasis on public ownership, put an end to a century of socialist efforts to reduce the degree of private ownership or to eliminate it altogether. Tony Blair deliberately stressed his agreement with the free-market, smaller-government policies of Bill Clinton. Even before Clinton, Blair proclaimed that the era of big government was over and promised to govern from the center. Blair reformulated his party's image as "New Labour," a nonsocialist party that is not committed to working with the trade unions. He emphasized that he wants unions to cooperate "with management to make sure British industry is competitive." Peter Mendelson, then the ideologist of the Blairites, proudly asserted that Labour is now "a market capitalist party."[14]

Even more notable was Blair's advice to labor organizations in a 1994 article in the *New Statesman* that "it is in the unions' best interest not to be associated with one political party." Blair argued that unions "should be able to thrive with any change of government or no change in government"—this from the leader of a party largely founded by trade unions and subsidized by them for all of its history. During the 1997 campaign, the Labour Party released a special manifesto aimed at business promising that a Blair government would retain the "main elements" of Margaret Thatcher's restrictions on unions and would resist unreasonable economic demands. Blair noted in an interview that his administration would "leave British [labor] law the most restrictive on trade unionism in the Western world."[15]

The Labour Party's manifesto proclaimed: "Tax and spend is being replaced by save and invest." Its general election platform not only stated that "healthy profits are an essential motor of a dynamic market economy" but also emphasized that the goal of low inflation requires that wage gains be held down. It is not surprising that Baroness Thatcher, at the start of the 1997 campaign, said, "Britain will be safe in the hands of Mr. Blair." Speaking to a meeting of the Socialist International, Blair returned the compliment, saying, "There were certain things the 1980s got right—an emphasis on enterprise, more flexible labour markets." One of his first actions after taking office was to shift the power to control monetary policy and interest rates from the Treasury to the Bank of England. Another, taken after his first meeting with Bill Clinton on 31 May 1997, was to launch welfare reform designed to reduce the numbers on the dole by pressing single mothers to take paying jobs. At this meeting, Clinton and Blair asserted that the "progressive parties of today are the parties of fiscal responsibility and prudence."[16]

The same pattern is evident the world over. During the 1980s, the Labor governments of Australia and New Zealand cut income taxes, pursued economic deregulation, and privatized various industries. The Australian Labor party reached an "accord" with trade unions that resulted in reducing real wages by at least 1 percent in each of the eight years that Prime Minister Robert Hawke headed the government. The story is similar in New Zealand, where the Labour Party during 1984–90 ended "the tradition of taxation according to ability to pay," dismantled the welfare state, and privatized many state enterprises. According to a report in a social-democratic magazine, Prime Minister David Lange argued that "social democrats must accept the existence of economic inequality because it is the engine which drives the economy."[17]

The same pattern holds for the parties of the left outside the English-speaking world. The Swedish Social Democrats reversed their previous wage-growth, high–income-tax, and strong–welfare-state orientations and undertook several privatization measures as well. The late American socialist leader, Michael Harrington, reported critically that Prime Minister Olof Palme's government increased employment by reducing the real income of those with a job.[18]

In Spain, three-term Socialist prime minister Felipe González converted his party—Marxist in its initial post-Franco phase—into a supporter of privatization, the free market, and NATO. He once noted, in a near-Churchillian formulation, that a competitive free-market economy is marked by greed, corruption, and the exploitation of the weak by the strong, but "capitalism is the least-bad economic system in existence." *The Economist* described his economic policies as having made his government "look somewhat to the right of Mrs. Thatcher's."[19]

The oldest major Marxist party in the world, the Social Democrats of Germany (SPD), rejected Marxism at their Bad Godesberg conference in 1959. American political scientist Russell Dalton later commented on their program: "Karl Marx would have been surprised to . . . learn that free economic competition was one of the essential conditions of a social democratic economic policy." Speaking in 1976, Social Democratic Chancellor Helmut Schmidt argued that the interests of the workers required expanding profits, noting that "the profits of enterprises today are the investments of tomorrow, and the investments of tomorrow are the employment of the day after." The SPD's 1990 program noted in classical liberal fashion that within a "democratically established setting, the market and competition are indispensable." In 1995, Rudolph Scharping, then the SPD candidate for chancellor and currently minister of defense, emphasized that his party's historic assumptions had proven wrong, stating, "We Social Democrats created an overly regulated, overly bureaucratic, and overly professionalized welfare state."[20]

The chancellor elected in 1998, Gerhard Schröder, continues in this tradition. He sees the SPD not as part of the left but as occupying a "New Middle," a place where, as John Vinocur puts it, "words like 'risk,' 'entrepreneurial spirit,' and 'flexible labor markets' coincide with expressions of allegiance to social justice and fair income distribution." Schröder has promised to improve the German economy and reduce its high unemployment rate by lowering its "prohibitive labor costs" and "providing incentive for new capital investment." He notes that the SPD is "breaking with . . . statist social democratic attitudes. . . . [W]e've understood that the omnipotent and interventionist state doesn't have its place in the current circumstances."[21]

In his inaugural speech after being inducted as chancellor on 10 November 1998, Schröder stressed continuity with the outgoing Christian Democratic government of Helmut Kohl, saying, "We do not want to do everything differently, but many things better." To help reduce unemployment, he has cut corporate taxes from the maximum rate of 47 percent under Kohl to 35 percent, and has called for business and unions to cooperate in a formal "alliance for jobs." He also proposes to foster private pension schemes, to encourage personal responsibility, and to concentrate state subsidies and spending on the "truly needy," while, in the words of the *Financial Times,* linking "fiscal policy with supply side measures, including deregulation and the opening of markets."[22]

In the past, socialist parties created extensive welfare states that required a steadily increasing proportion of GDP (in some cases, more than half) to go to the government. Today, however, these same parties recognize that they simply cannot compete in the world market unless they reduce government expenditures. Their electoral situation forces them to try to appeal to middle-class and affluent skilled workers and high-tech employees. Hence, like Blair, Clinton, and Schröder, they seek to lower taxes, reduce welfare entitlements, and balance their budgets, but also to press for postmaterialist reforms aimed at cleaning up the natural, social, and economic environment. Even Sweden, the prototypical social-democratic polity, sped up its efforts to strengthen its economy by privatizing an additional 25 enterprises in 1999. Finland and Denmark have pursued similar policies under social-democratic leadership.

The only exceptions to the move away from state intervention among socialist parties have occurred in Norway and, to some extent, in France, both of which still favor extensive welfare policies (though not, it should be noted, nationalization of industry). Norway can retain a belief in "old-fashioned socialism" because of its abundant oil resources, which pay for its welfare state. The French left operates within a society in which *dirigisme,* the idea of a strong directing state, has been as much a part of the national culture as antistatism has been in America. Both the right and left in France have approved of a powerful state, an emphasis that goes back to the Empire, the Revolution, and the monarchy. Journalist Roger Cohen has noted that "the Gaullist attachment to the state and rejection of market reform encouraged the Socialists to keep further to the left, to distinguish themselves." As Ezra Suleiman, an academic authority on French politics, emphasizes, "The right can't let go of the state, so the left stays left."[23] Thus it is not surprising that the Socialists campaigned and won in 1997 promising a massive program of government-sponsored job creation and the protection of the welfare state from budget cuts.

Yet in an interview with *Le Nouvel Observateur,* socialist prime minister Lionel Jospin sounded like other European socialists in saying he favors a move away from "statism," with more decentralization and increased individual initiative.[24] He has praised the extensive privatization measures carried through by François Mitterrand during his 14 years as president. Jospin has also spoken of the need for France to emulate the American economy. In 1998, he criticized leftist disdain for the level of U.S. job growth, saying, "Contrary to what we have claimed and indeed believed, the jobs being created in the United States are not only, or even mainly, low-paid, dead-end jobs, but skilled ones in the service and high-tech industries." According to *The Economist,* Jospin has stressed that the French "could learn much about America's economic dynamism, the vitality of its research and innovation, its competitive spirit and capacity for renewal."[25]

Curiously, the model late-1990s country, frequently cited as such by European social democrats and others, is the Netherlands, with an unemployment rate of 6.5 percent in 1997 (far below the major Continental economies), and a growth rate higher than in Britain, France, or Germany. The Dutch, under a government headed by former union leader Wim Kok of the Labor Party, have kept down "wages, inflation and interest rates, and . . . [eased] the rules for hiring and firing and for opening new businesses." Unemployment benefits have been cut, while the rules for sick and disability pay have been tightened. Thomas Friedman of the *New York Times* described the policy as "U.S. style downsizing, privatizing, and loosening up of labor rules."[26]

In a "social pact" negotiated between the unions, then led by Kok, and the employers, labor agreed to limit wage increases to 2 percent a year. Whether due to these policies or not, the subsequent near-full-employment economy has led to an increase in income inequality, much as in the United States and other industrialized countries. In high-tech economies, the better-educated and highly skilled are much more in demand than industrial workers and the less skilled, and thus they are relatively much better paid.

Far from a politically "backward" United States following the lead of a more "progressive" Europe, the Old World left is now becoming more like the American left, as Lewis Corey had anticipated. Hence one may indeed say that, in political terms, the United States has shown Europe the image of its future. As European countries reached new heights of affluence and mass consumption, they began, as Antonio Gramsci had anticipated, to resemble the United States, with societies that are less stratified, less status-bound, and much better educated. Consequently, their less privileged strata are much less class-conscious than before. Today, Europe's now-nonsocialist "progressive" parties seek, as Adam Przeworski notes, to make capitalism more humane and more efficient. As François Mitterrand's former advisor Regis Debray put it, the objective of European socialist leaders is "to carry out the politics of the Right, but more intelligently and in a more rational manner."[27]

Old Terms, New Definitions

None of this is meant to suggest that the political divisions of modern democracy, conceptualized since the French Revolution on a spectrum between left and right, have disappeared. Democrats and Republicans, or social democrats and conservatives, still provide choices on the ballot, although their ideological bearings and internal factions are changing.[28]

Cleavages linked to social stratification are no longer the main correlates of a party's position on the left or right of the political spectrum. Issues revolving around morality, abortion, "family values," civil rights, gender equality, multiculturalism, immigration, crime and punishment, foreign policy, and supranational communities push individuals and groups in directions that are independent of their socioeconomic position. Yet most of these matters can be related to social ideology, which in turn correlates with religion and education.

The meanings of the terms "left" and "right" are changing. As we have seen, the parties of the left, although still identifying themselves as social democratic or socialist, have largely reconstituted themselves as liberals in the American sense of the word, emphasizing postmaterialist themes like environmentalism, equality for women and gays, minority rights, and cultural freedoms. The right has moved, in varying degrees, toward classical liberalism or libertarianism. The left stresses group equality and economic security; the right, equality of opportunity and the weakening of state power. Logically, the right should also support personal freedom, along the lines favored by nineteenth-century liberals, but the political alliances between economic conservatives and religious traditionalists have fostered cultural conservatism on issues relating to sex, the family, and style of life. Given the complex variations in the political cleavage structure, it is difficult today to specify a consistent pattern that differentiates left from right. For example, some advisers to new U.S. president George W. Bush have suggested that his outlook is "communitarian," a label previously associated with some advisers to Bill Clinton.

No major tendency, left or right, retains a belief in a utopia, a solution to all major problems through dramatically reconstructing society and polity. These post–Cold War conditions bode well for democratic stability and for international peace. It has become a truism that democracies do not wage war against each other, and most of the world is now democratic. While extremist movements and parties exist, all of them are relatively weak, at least in the West. The strongest are Jörg Haider's Freedom Party in Austria, with 27 percent of the vote, and Jean-Marie Le Pen's National Front in France, which is supported by 15 percent of the electorate. No other is close to these levels. There are no charismatic leaders, and little political enthusiasm. Youth, who Aristotle noted "have exalted notions . . . [and who] would rather do noble things than useful ones," are necessarily frustrated.[29]

Will this situation change? Of course it will; economies, and consequently societies, never remain in a steady state. The inner dynamics of market systems produce reverses in the business cycle that can threaten democratic stability. The Japanese collapse has replaced the Japanese miracle. France's move to the left in 1997 and Le Pen's support on the right were facilitated not only by the country's statist values but also by an unemployment rate of 12 percent. Demographic factors threaten to undermine the financial underpinnings of social security and health systems. The rise of new major players in the international arena, such as China, can and will result in new trade disequilibriums. But all these prospects and more are for the future.

For now, the end of the Cold War seemingly has given America and its ideology an almost total victory. The United States is now the *only* superpower. Its economy is the most productive. The major recent movements for egalitarian social change and for improving the quality of life—feminism, environmentalism, civil rights for minorities, gay rights—all diffused from America, much as the democratic revolutions of the nineteenth century had. The developed world has been more successful than ever in satisfying the consumption desires of its people, manual workers and intellectual strata alike.

All this should make for more conservative and smug societies. Yet the standards by which Western countries now judge themselves are derived from the French, American, and Marxist revolutionary creeds. These proclaim that "all men are created equal" and share the goal of "life, liberty and the pursuit of happiness." Yet all polities, even the classically liberal ones, must fail to live up fully to the inherently utopian objectives of libertarianism and egalitarianism. Americans still lean more to the libertarian side, Europeans to the egalitarian. Both tendencies favor freedom for all and strong juridical restraints on state power. Americans prefer a meritocratic, libertarian society with an effective but weak government. They will not attain these objectives in any absolute sense, but they will keep trying. It may be noted that socialists from Marx and Engels to Antonio Gramsci, Anthony Crosland, and Michael Harrington all have acknowledged that the United States came closer socially (though obviously not economically) to their ideological goal of a classless society with a weak state than any other system they knew in their lifetimes. Leon Samson, a left-wing American Marxist, concluded in the early 1930s that American radicals could not sell socialism to a people who believed they already lived in a society that operationally, though obviously not terminologically, was committed to socialist objectives.

America still has an ideological vision with which to motivate its young. Europeans are increasingly committed to a similar social vision, derived in large measure from the French Revolution and social democracy. Both accept the competitive market as the means to increase productivity, thereby diminishing differences in consumption styles linked to class. Both are enlarging the scope of higher education, with a consequent enhancement of access into elite ranks. Emphasis on status differences in Europe is declining. Economic inequality, of course, is still great, and even increasing during periods of technological innovation such as the present, because new skills are in much greater demand than old ones. But since patterns of deference and social class inferiority are declining, while access to information is widening with the spread of the Internet, power is becoming more dispersed. These profound social and economic changes will continue to reshape the nature of party cleavages in the coming decades, no doubt in ways that cannot now be fully anticipated. Yet just as the era of big government, according to Tony Blair and Bill Clinton, is now over, so the recent evolution of parties on the left heralds an end to class as the dominant cleavage structuring party politics. Parties in advanced industrial democracies will continue to sort themselves along a left-right spectrum, but "left" and "right" will never again be defined by the contest between socialism and capitalism. With the end of that grand ideological competition, the differences between parties have narrowed and become more fluid. Today, most parties lean toward the center on economic issues, while party systems float in search of a new grand line of cleavage. The social bases for that new defining cleavage may not emerge any time soon.

NOTES

1. Karl Marx and Friedrich Engels, "Unpublished Letters of Karl Marx and Friedrich Engels to Americans," in *Science and Society* 2 (1938): 368; H.G. Wells, *The Future in America* (New York: Harper and Brothers, 1906); Karl Marx, *Capital*, vol. 1 (Moscow: Foreign Languages Publishing House, 1958), 8–9. For Lenin's writings, see Harvey Klehr, "Leninist Theory in Search of America," *Polity* 9 (1976): 81–96.

2. Cited in R. Laurence Moore, *European Socialists and the American Promised Land* (New York: Oxford University Press, 1970), 70, 58, 102, and 77, respectively.

3. Max Beer, *Fifty Years of International Socialism* (London: George Allen and Unwin, 1935), 109–10.

4. Leon Trotsky, *The Living Thoughts of Karl Marx* (New York: Longmans, Green, 1939), 38–39.

5. Max Weber, *The Protestant Ethic and the Spirit of Capitalism* (New York: Charles Scribners and Sons, 1958), 64–65.

6. Harvey Klehr, "The Theory of American Exceptionalism," Ph.D. diss., Department of History, University of North Carolina–Chapel Hill, 130. The full discussion of Fraina-Corey is on pp. 126–30.

7. "ILO Highlights Global Challenges to Trade Unions," *ILO News*, 4 November 1997.

8. Daniel Bell, *The Coming of Post-Industrial Society* (New York: Basic Books, 1978); Radovon Richta, et al., *Civilizations at the Crossroads* (White Plains, N.Y.: International Arts and Sciences Press, 1969).

9. Alain Touraine, *The Post-Industrial Society: Tomorrow's Social History* (New York: Random House, 1971).

10. Ronald Inglehart, "The Silent Revolution in Europe: Intergenerational Change in Post-Industrial Societies," *American Political Science Review* 65 (December 1971): 991–1017. See also Ronald Inglehart, *Modernization and Postmodernization: Cultural, Economic, and Political Change in 43 Societies* (Princeton, N.J.: Princeton University Press, 1997).

11. Jean-François Revel, *Without Marx or Jesus* (Garden City, N.Y.: Doubleday, 1971), 6–7.

12. John F. Harris and Fred Barbash, "Blair Savors Colleague Clinton's Arm on His Shoulder," *Washington Post,* 30 May 1997, A27–28.

13. Tony Blair, "Third Way, Better Way," *Washington Post,* 27 September 1998, C7.

14. George Will, "Last Rite for Socialism," *Washington Post,* 21 December 1997, C7.

15. Tony Blair, "No Favours," *New Statesman and Society,* 28 November 1994, 33; Madaline Druhan, "Union Reforms Stay, Labour Leader Says," *Globe and Mail* (Toronto), 1 April 1997.

16. Tom Baldwin, "New Labour Manifesto Steals Old Tory Slogans," *Sunday Telegraph* (London), 30 March 1997, 1; John F. Harris and Fred Barbash, "Blair Savors Colleague Clinton's Arm on His Shoulder," A27–28; Alison Mitchell, "In London, 2 Young Guys Sit Talking About Democracy," *New York Times,* 30 May 1997, 1, 3.

17. Seymour Martin Lipset, "No Third Way: A Comparative Perspective on the Left," in Daniel Chirot, ed., *The Crisis in Leninism and the Decline of the Left* (Seattle: University of Washington Press, 1991), 184–85.

18. Michael Harrington, *The Next Left: The History of a Future* (New York: Holt, 1987), 130–31.

19. Tom Gallagher and Allan M. Williams, "Introduction," in Tom Gallagher and Allan M. Williams, eds., *Southern European Socialism* (Manchester: Manchester University Press, 1989), 3; "As González Glides Rightward," *The Economist,* 11 March 1989, Spain Survey.

20. Quoted in Seymour Martin Lipset, "No Third Way," 188–90; Rudolf Scharping, "Freedom, Solidarity, Individual Responsibility: Reflections on the Relationship Between Politics, Money and Morality," *The Responsive Community* 6 (Fall 1996): 53.

21. John Vinocur, "Downsizing German Politics," *Foreign Affairs* 77 (September–October 1998): 11–12.

22. Edmund L. Andrews, "Rivals Have Found Little to Fight Over in German Election," *New York Times,* 26 September 1998, A6; Ralph Atkins, "Schröder Pledges Strict Financial Control," *Financial Times,* 11 November 1998, 2.

23. Roger Cohen, "France's Old Soldier Fades Away," *New York Times,* 8 June 1997, E5.

24. Anne Swardson, "Jospin Takes a New Stand on Austerity," *Washington Post,* 22 January 1998, A24.

25. "Jospin Discovers America," *The Economist,* 27 June 1998, 50.

26. Thomas L. Friedman, "The Real G-7's," *New York Times,* 19 June 1997, A35.

27. Adam Przeworski, *Capitalism and Social Democracy* (Cambridge: Cambridge University Press, 1985), 206; Regis Debray, "What's Left of the Left?" *New Perspectives Quarterly* 7 (Spring 1990): 27.

28. François Furet, "Democracy and Utopia," *Journal of Democracy* 9 (January 1998): 79.

29. Aristotle, *Rhetoric,* in Richard McKeon, ed., *The Basic Works of Aristotle* (New York: Random House, 1941), 1404.

4

PARTIES ARE NOT WHAT THEY ONCE WERE

Philippe C. Schmitter

Philippe C. Schmitter is professor of political and social sciences at the European University Institute in Florence. He has previously taught at Stanford University and the University of Chicago and is the coeditor (with Guillermo O'Donnell and Laurence Whitehead) of Transitions from Authoritarian Rule *(1986). His most recent book is* How to Democratize the European Union . . . and Why Bother? *(2000).*

Although economists were no better prepared to understand and guide the course of the unexpected transitions from command to market economies than political scientists were ready to understand and guide the even more numerous transitions from autocracy to democracy, the economists did have one major advantage. They had a leitmotif which—if followed assiduously enough—seemed to guarantee success: *Get the prices right!*

Political scientists also had a slogan to peddle, but they were less assertive in using it (perhaps because they were less convinced than their economist brethren that it would work in all settings, times, and places): *Get the parties right!* For there is hardly a serious student of democracy who does not seem to believe that political parties provide by far the most important linkage between citizens and the political process *and* that party platforms provide the best possible means for aggregating diverse interests and passions into a coherent, system-wide mix of public policies *and* that competition between these parties provides the most reliable mechanism for ensuring the accountability of rulers *and* that cooperation within and between these parties provides the only feasible way of forming viable governments.[1] Unfortunately for the prestige of their discipline, political scientists are not so sure that they know what to do in order to "get the parties right." Economists, especially those of the hegemonic neoliberal persuasion, are very confident that they understand what it takes to "get the prices right"— and free trade in the international market conveniently tells them when they have reached their goal. Alas, there is no perfect market in political parties operating across national boundaries that can indicate when the right equilibrium has been attained!

In this essay, I shall explore critically this orthodoxy with respect to the leading role of political parties and ask whether or not other types of organized intermediaries might have significant roles to play in promoting the consolidation of democracy—at least in the contemporary period. But first, a brief *excursus* into the meaning of some of the key concepts.

Consolidation of democracy. Theoretically, the notion of consolidating democracy sounds puzzling and even oxymoronic. Intuitively, however, its meaning seems rather obvious. After a period of considerable uncertainty and of unknown duration, during which the previous autocracy "transits" to some other form of political domination, it becomes necessary to transform improvisations into stable rules and alliances under which actors can compete and cooperate on predictable terms. From a "war of movement" in which many have high expectations (and some have great fears) about the magnitude of change, the democratic struggle should settle into a "war of positions" along established lines of cleavage for mutually agreed-upon advantage.[2] *Consolidation could be defined as the process of transforming the accidental arrangements, prudential norms, and contingent solutions that have emerged during the transition into relations of cooperation and competition that are reliably known, regularly practiced, and voluntarily accepted by those persons or collectivities—that is, politicians and citizens—that participate in democratic governance.* If it sets in, the democratic regime will have institutionalized uncertainty in certain roles and policy areas, but it will also have reassured its citizens that the competition to occupy office and/or to exercise influence will be fair and circumscribed to a predictable range of outcomes. Modern, representative, political democracy rests on this "bounded uncertainty" and on the "contingent consent" of actors to respect the outcomes it produces.[3]

Nothing ensures that consolidation will be successful in all cases— unless one assumes (as very few analysts do these days) that democracy is either a functional requisite or an ethical imperative. Neither the level of economic development, the stage of capitalist accumulation, nor the hegemony of the bourgeoisie can automatically guarantee the advent, much less the persistence, of democracy. Nor is this regime outcome the inevitable product of some previously attained level of "civilization," literacy, educational attainment, or distinctive political culture. This is not to deny that affluence, a relatively equal distribution of wealth, an internationally competitive economy, a well schooled population, a large middle class, and a willingness to tolerate diversity, to trust adversaries, and to settle conflicts by compromise are not advantageous; it is just that democracy still has to be chosen, implemented, and perpetuated by "agents," real live political actors with their distinctive interests, passions, memories, and, why not, *fortuna* and *virtù*. No doubt, they will be constrained by the above developmental and cultural factors, but there is still plenty of room for making right or wrong choices. Even the most inauspicious setting can give rise to an attempt to democratize—such as Haiti, Mongolia, Benin, and Albania—and, who knows, some of them may succeed— see India, Costa Rica, Bolivia, Portugal, and Papua New Guinea, none of which seemed to stand much of a chance when they began changing regimes.

Let us not, however, be misled by all this emphasis on choice and voluntaristic action. *The core of the consolidation dilemma lies in coming up with a set of concrete institutions that politicians can agree upon and citizens are willing to support in a specific context.* Arriving at a stable solution, especially in the climate of exaggerated expectations that tends to characterize the transition, is no easy matter. Not only are the choices *intrinsically conflictual*—with different parties or politicians preferring rules that will ensure their own reelection or eventual access to power and different groups of citizens wanting rules that will ensure the accountability of their professional agents—but they are also *extrinsically consequential.* Once institutional choices are translated via electoral uncertainty into governments that begin to produce public policies, they will affect rates of economic growth, willingness to invest, competitiveness in foreign markets, distributions of income and wealth, access to education, perceptions of cultural deprivation, racial balance, and even national identity. To a certain extent, these substantive matters are anticipated by actors and incorporated in the compromises they make with regard to procedures, but there is much room for error and unintended consequence. In the short run, the consolidation of democracy depends on actors' and citizens' ability to come up with a solution to their intrinsic conflicts over rules; in the long run, it depends upon the extrinsic impact that policies made under these rules have upon social groups. Here is where the "objective structural realities" of levels of development, positions in the world economy, conflicts over sectoral product, and distributions of welfare and the "subjective preferences" of classes, generations, genders, *ethnies,* status groups, and situs reenter the picture with a vengeance. Given the likelihood that some time must elapse before the new rules of cooperation and competition produce observable results, it seems safe to assume that the process of consolidation will be a great deal lengthier than that of transition.

Representation and types of intermediaries. Whatever institutions are chosen and implemented during a change in regime, it is very likely that a central role will be assigned to mechanisms of representation.

Modern democracy—at least, in all polities above a certain scale—relies heavily on the indirect, if not vicarious, participation of its citizens. Rulers are held accountable—if at all—by competition and cooperation among intermediary agents who "re-present" the interests and passions of citizens, grouped in various categories and levels of aggregation, before public officials. Moreover, these intermediaries have become more organized, specialized, and professionalized over time in the roles they perform. And, as we shall see, they have recourse to a greater variety of channels of representation and levels of aggregation than in the past.

Which is one of the major reasons why it may not be so prudent to assume that most, if not all, of the work of representation will be performed by political parties—especially when it comes to accomplishing the very complicated task of consolidating a viable democratic regime. Just a moment's glance at any established liberal democracy reveals how many of these multiple channels between citizens/firms and authorities/agencies are filled with organizations other than parties. Even more disturbing is the observation that much of this activity by organized intermediaries has little or no relation to what parties supposedly do best: structure electoral choices and form governments.

Hence, consolidating contemporary democracy may be a more differentiated and variegated process than in the past. My suspicion is that many students of fledgling neodemocracies are committing one, or both, of two potential fallacies of anachronism: They tend to ignore the very substantial changes that have taken place in the nature and role of parties in established democracies, or they presume that parties in today's neodemocracies will have to go through all the stages and perform all the functions of their predecessors.

I believe that it is preferable to assume that citizens today—even in polities that have long suffered under authoritarian rule—have quite different organizational skills, are less likely to identify so closely with partisan symbols or programs, and are more likely to defend a much more variegated set of interests than in the past. Moreover, the new regimes are emerging in an international environment virtually saturated with different models of successful collective action. All this may not strictly preclude a hegemonic role for parties in the consolidation process, but it does suggest that they will be facing more competition from interest associations and social movements than their predecessors and that we should revise our thinking about democratization accordingly.

For simplicity's sake, let us delineate three generic types of intermediaries: *political parties, interest associations,* and *social movements.* All are organizations; all attempt to link the preferences of persons, families, and firms to various agents and agencies of government; all seek to aggregate the individual preferences of their members or categories into collective demands; all are protected by formal political rights of assembly and petition in democracies; all have some degree of autonomy in their internal processes; and all wish to influence the form and content of public policy. Within each type, needless to say, there are major variations in organizational structure, material resources, size of membership, degree of loyalty, extent of encompassment, strategies of influence, likelihood of success, and so forth—but what interests us most are the differences among these three types of intermediaries and how these differences might influence the consolidation of democracy.

The distinguishing characteristic of political parties is their role in the conduct of territorially based elections. They control the process of nominating candidates who, if they win, occupy specified positions of authority, form a government, and accept responsibility for the conduct of public policy. Interest associations seek to influence the direction of policy so that it will benefit particularly (and, if possible, exclusively) their own members, without competing in elections or being publicly accountable for these policies. Social movements are also in the business of trying to exert influence over policy without competing in elections or becoming accountable to the public as a whole, but the benefits that they typically seek would accrue, not specifically to their own members, but to a broad spectrum of the citizenry—even to foreigners, plants, animals, fishes, reptiles, and prospective beings from other planets. These different foci of activity tend to imply other modal differences in organizational structure, relations between followers and leaders, motives for participation, level and type of resource mobilization, dependence upon allies and external sources of support, and capacity to incite loyalty or hatred.

Needless to say, the three categories are not airtight; mutants and hybrids are being born all the time. Nor is it the case that every organization that calls itself a party, an association, or a movement really deserves the label. Lots of parties inscribed on the electoral lists never stand any realistic chance of winning and are therefore associations or movements "in disguise." Some interest associations can become so influential that they determine the occupants of specific government roles and are even "credited" by the public with direct responsibility for public policies. Some social movements pretend to speak for broad social categories but are really interested in promoting the welfare of their own members—in some cases only the welfare of their own staffs. The only claim that I am advancing for this trilogy, beyond its obvious utility in reducing a wide range of variance, is that there tends to exist greater variation in organizational characteristics across these categories than within them.

On the basis of this descriptive claim, I will advance the hypothesis that *these three types of intermediaries all play a significant role in the consolidation of neodemocracies* and, moreover, that *there is no longer any a priori reason to suppose that parties should be privileged or predominant in this regard.* Contemporary democratizers are the beneficiaries-cum-victims of a worldwide process of diffusion of organizational forms and techniques. Once their transitions from autocracy have begun and minimal rights of assembly and petition have been established, they are likely to be literally invaded by parties, associations, and movements of extraordinary variety—some of which had no previous experience or objective basis in the country. This is the exotic "flora and fauna" that neodemocracies must simultaneously deal with if they are to consolidate their regime changes, rather than the gradually shifting and usually sequenced emergence of intermediaries that populated the earlier cases of democratization. Political parties may have played that leading role in the past, but they will not necessarily do so in the present or future.

The Consolidating Functions of Parties

One way of exploring this rather unorthodox assertion is to take a (critical) look at the functions that political parties are supposed to perform, especially in light of what it is supposed to take to consolidate a democratic polity. The list of benevolent tasks ("eufunctions") that parties are capable of performing is very extensive. If one is to believe the literature, there seems to be almost nothing that political parties have not done, at one time or another. However, if one attempts to separate out those tasks that are only performed by some "super-party" (the German Social Democratic Party or the Swedish Social Democratic Labor Party have often been exploited to illustrate how many things democratic parties are capable of doing), the number of "functions of partisanship" shrinks considerably.

1) Political parties, first and foremost, should structure the electoral process by nominating candidates for office, by recruiting persons to participate actively in campaigns, and, thereby, by offering to citizens aggregated in territorial constituencies a choice between alternative sets of leaders. The successful performance of this function becomes considerably more difficult if one adds the caveat, proposed by Norberto Bobbio, that the alternative products offered to the "electoral consumer" should be real and significant in terms of citizen preferences. Let us call this the function of "electoral structuration."

2) Political parties should provide most citizens with a stable and distinctive set of ideas and goals (symbols) that anchor their expectations about democracy, orient them in a general way toward policy options, and make them feel part of the process of collective choice. Needless to say, this function of "symbolic integration" makes a significant contribution to success in performing the function of electoral structuration, although there is reason to believe that party identification can only be acquired gradually across several political generations.[4]

3) Political parties, once they have competed in the electoral process, should be capable of forming a government and of providing an internal structure to the legislative process—whether they do so alone or in alliance with other parties and whether the executive and legislative posts are independently or concurrently filled. Note that, in order to do this well, parties should be capable of maintaining a consistently high level of internal discipline during their terms in office, although to make this a strict functional requisite would surely disqualify many electoral groupings from acquiring the label of parties. We will call this the "governing function."

4) Underlying all of the above functions is a single assumption: *Political parties must be capable of aggregating the interests and passions of a significant proportion of the citizenry by channeling the expectations of these individuals, families, firms, associations, and movements through their internal processes and producing a program that mixes public policies in such a way as to satisfy the general demands of their constituents.* It should be noted that it is not required (or even expected) that the parties monopolize the "aggregative function" and, hence, force all individuals and collectivities to process their expectations through partisan channels. The process of representation is capacious enough that some persons and groups should find room to interact directly with authorities; it should be the system of political parties, however, that plays the most prominent role in packaging the more discrete and fragmentary demands into more manageable general objectives and proposals.

Not all individual parties perform all these functions.[5] Some engage in a much broader range of activities, including provision of entertainment, education in civic virtue, analysis of public policy, publication of newspapers, ownership or control of broadcasting facilities, provision of social services, staffing of public enterprises, management of cooperatives, recruitment and training of association and movement leaders, maintenance of public order, formation of shadow cabinets, creation of paramilitary forces, and distribution of prebends and the receipts from corruption. But when the system of political parties as an ensemble does not fulfill the above four "core" functions, or even when it finds itself competing heavily with other intermediaries to do so, one should question whether or not political parties are really so indispensable for the consolidation or even the simple perpetuation of democracy.

Note that I am *not* claiming that political parties do not make some contribution to the consolidation of democracy and I am certainly *not* predicting that they will somehow fade away in neodemocracies. As long as there are elections based on territorial constituencies, there will be organizations that call themselves political parties trying to control the nomination of candidates, to package them under a common label, and to win contested seats. What I *am* claiming is that those organizations are less and less capable of performing the functions that parties have performed historically and that our theorizing about the process of consolidation should be modified accordingly. For example, it may be the case that party systems can remain unconsolidated for some time— perhaps indefinitely—when all of the other partial regimes that make up a democracy are quite well consolidated. Just because voters remain volatile in their partisan preferences and the number and identity of parties fluctuates from one election to another, this does *not* necessarily mean that the regime as a whole has failed to consolidate itself.

Structuring Electoral Competition

"Electoral structuration" is the primary function for parties, in the sense that it is this activity that constitutes their strongest claim to a distinctive political role. And there is no question that organizing rival candidacies for office and campaigning for the vote of citizens in territorial constituencies were crucial for their initial prominence in most neodemocracies. Parties had relatively little to do with the timing and even the content of most transitions, but once credible elections had been convoked and their outcome was uncertain, parties took over center stage from the governing factions, interest associations, and social movements that (usually) had contributed more to bringing about a change in regime. Leaders, funds, energies, and expectations shifted toward those intermediary organizations that got their names onto the electoral lists. Depending on the party and electoral laws (which the initial parties often had a major role in drafting, hence, the consequent difficulty in deciding whether the electoral law "produced" the party system or vice versa), the number of parties that developed varied considerably. There were relatively few in Southern Europe, where the continuity with past labels was greater; more existed in Latin American parliamentary elections, and fewer in presidential elections, due to their polarizing effect; and many more sprang up in Eastern Europe where partisan continuity was lowest and the thresholds for registration of new parties unusually low.

The subsequent founding elections were usually held in an atmosphere of "civic orgy," with exceptionally high turnouts and the pageantry of a national revival. Only in Hungary did less than 65 percent go to the polls initially.[6] However, with almost monotonic regularity, the rate of abstention rose with each subsequent election. In Southern Europe, where regime consolidation has been greatest, the turnout rate has tended to stabilize within the relatively high range that is characteristic of well-established democracies in the rest of Europe. In Eastern Europe, where initial expectations were probably higher, the subsequent disenchantment *(desencanto)* with electoral contests has also been greater. In the Polish local elections of 1991, the turnout dropped to American levels: 34.1 percent.

It is in two important regards that parties do not seem to be capable of performing well their "historic" function of structuring electoral choices in a reliable and relevant fashion: the rise of nonparty or "antiparty" candidates and the higher rates of shifting party loyalties.

Not only have politicians without the support of major parties managed to get themselves nominated as candidates for high office and run on "antiparty" programs, but they have been rewarded for doing so by the electorate. Admittedly, this is predominantly a Latin American trait, with Alberto Fujimori of Peru as the prototype, followed by Fernando Collor and, subsequently, Fernando Henrique Cardoso in Brazil and Rafael Caldera in Venezuela. All were elected *despite* rather than *because* of the preexisting party system. In Argentina, Carlos Menem was duly nominated by "his" party, but he subsequently chose to follow policies diametrically opposed to those historically associated with it (and those under which he had campaigned). Nevertheless, the candidacies of Lech Wałęsa in Poland and Václav Havel in the Czech Republic have also been distinctly "supraparty," either in the sense that they were nominated without the manifest effort of a party or that their election did not depend on the support of a particular party or alliance of parties.[7] More and more, one gains the impression that there are independent political entrepreneurs buying an existing "party brand" or creating a new one exclusively for their own purposes, rather than the reverse that is presumed by the party literature. And even when an established party selects "its" candidate, the campaign and subsequent process of forming a government depend more upon that candidate's personality than on the party's organization, finance, or programs.[8] To North Americans, this may sound like a familiar story, but to Europeans (from whom most of the theorizing about the generic types and roles of parties has tended to come) this must seem like a perversion of the norm—if not a threat to democracy itself.

Citizens in the neodemocracies seem aware of these "loose couplings" between parties, their candidates, and their platforms and have responded opportunistically by switching their voting preferences between elections. According to data gathered by Maurizio Cotta on electoral volatility between successive elections, four of the new democracies after the Second World War had aggregate percentage shifts of 23 percent (Italy), 21 percent (Germany), 12 percent (Austria), and 6 percent (France)—roughly comparable to the length of their preceding autocracies.[9] In Southern Europe, the comparable figures between the first and second elections were 22 percent (Greece), 11 percent (Portugal), and 11 percent (Spain). But the biggest differences came between the second and third elections: 27 percent for Greece, 10 percent for Portugal, and a phenomenal 42 percent for Spain. Three of the post-1945 democracies, on the other hand, had markedly lower volatility in the second round (France is the exception). In Latin America, the volatility has been even greater,[10] and in Eastern Europe it has broken all records. For example, in Poland 70 percent of the electorate switched parties between the first and second elections—admittedly, the latter were held under different rules—and another 35 percent between the second and third. In Slovakia, the aggregate percentage shift was 41 percent, while it was a bit more stable in the Czech Republic at 28 percent. The only Eastern European country with an electorate that came even close to mimicking what Western European party systems had displayed almost 50 years previously was Bulgaria, which had only a 20 percent shift between the first and second elections and 36 percent between the second and third rounds.[11] Moreover, unlike the Southern European countries, where the volatility of voter preferences subsequently converged toward the European norm, it continues to remain high in Eastern Europe—with the notable exception of Hungary.

All this is not to deny that political parties are unbeatable as intermediaries when it comes to organizing territorial constituencies and simplifying voter choices—and all neodemocracies need a competitive system of parties if they are to fulfill the formal requisites for democratic status. What supraparty candidacies and electoral volatility do suggest, however, is that informal elite arrangements and independent citizen reactions are bypassing these channels and, presumably, decreasing the subsequent importance of party-structured legislatures and party-identified voters. Even the elections themselves seem less and less capable of providing citizens with a convincing link to the political process, as is witnessed by the falling rates of voter turnout.

Providing Symbolic Identity

The primary weapon that parties have in their effort to "fix" the electoral preferences of the citizenry is their capacity to manipulate symbols and memories in such a way that, over time, individuals come to identify exclusively with one party. Regardless of the candidate(s) a party chooses or the program(s) it espouses for a specific contest, its core identifiers will vote for it as the party that "naturally" represents them. Philip Converse has advanced a very elegant argument that this necessarily involves the intergenerational transmission of norms and, hence, is likely to take something on the order of 75 years or longer before the electorate as a whole has acquired this "anchor" for their political/electoral expectations.[12]

Except in the rare cases where the autocracy had been short-lived and parties from the former period could be easily revived—for example, Greece—most contemporary neodemocracies had to create a system of parties *ex novo*—often by borrowing names, symbols, slogans, and platforms from abroad or from the country's very remote past.[13] It quickly became apparent that these new parties were not going to be capable of replicating the heroic role that parties played in early democratizations.

For one thing, they have attracted very few card-carrying and dues-paying members—even when one compares them only with the post-1945 democracies. Italy probably represents the most "party-centric" case of consolidation during that period, and, appropriately, it has (or had) one of the highest rates of party membership among established democracies—about 14 percent. Greece with around 8 percent is the only neodemocracy in Southern Europe that comes even close. Only 4 to 5 percent of Portuguese and Spaniards admit to being members of a party.[14] South Korea, Estonia, Hungary, Lithuania, and Poland all report comparable or lower figures.[15] Only Bulgaria (22 percent), Ukraine (15 percent), Czechoslovakia (11 percent, before the separation), and Romania (9 percent) had higher proportions of the national sample in parties—and one suspects that this is to be explained mainly by the larger number of "hangers-over" from the previously dominant communist party.

In addition, the parties did not seem to be providing much of a diffuse political identity for citizens. When asked whether they felt close to any political party, national sample surveys reported as few agreeing as 19 percent in Poland, 36 percent in South Korea, and 37 percent in Ukraine, with most of the countries hovering around the 50 percent mark (Czechoslovakia, Estonia, Hungary, Lithuania, and Spain). Only in Bulgaria and Romania did it approach two-thirds of the adult population—and that presumably reflects greater continuity with the cadres of their respective communist parties. Part of the reason for this can be gleaned from responses to another question, which asked whether parties offered different policies. In all the above countries (except Poland and Ukraine) between 65 percent and 75 percent of those surveyed said that parties did not differ much from each other.[16]

These figures for membership and identification are so low that they call into question one of the central tenets of party advocates, namely, that only political parties are capable of "aggregating" the largest number of potential citizens and, therefore, of representing the broadest—that is, most public-regarding—range of interests. In many neodemocracies, sports clubs, neighborhood groups, religious associations, and trade unions have much larger actual memberships than do political parties—and one suspects they might even have a more socially heterogeneous and committed membership. This may not provide them with the capacity to aggregate member preferences into a "program for government," but factionalism, de-ideologization, and mediatization seem to have robbed most parties of that capacity as well.

More to the point, however, are the citizen perceptions of the "representativeness" of these different intermediaries. To my knowledge, no survey data on this issue exists for Southern Europe or Latin America, but there is apposite research on four Eastern European countries, thanks to the Central European University's data files on "The Development of Party Systems and Electoral Alignments in East-Central Europe." As reported by Gábor Tóka, the rankings show that political parties *as a category* do worse than most types of associations and movements, with environmental groups getting a particularly high rating. On the other hand, the respondents tended to give a higher ranking to their preferred party than to any specific association or movement. For example, those giving an equal or better rating to non-party representatives than to parties in general were 46 percent in Slovakia, 41 percent in the Czech Republic, 37 percent in Poland, and 30 percent in Hungary. In Slovakia, however, only 14 percent of the sample gave an absolutely better score to some association or movement than to any of the major parties. The proportion was 17 percent in the Czech Republic, 18 percent in Hungary, and 31 percent in Poland.[17] Admittedly, without comparable figures for other time periods or countries, it is hard to judge whether this represents a significant shift away from political parties as the "natural" representative intermediaries in the eyes of citizens.

There are, however, other less obtrusive indicators of the declining capacity of parties in neodemocracies to provide a stable and valued political identity: the absence or virtual disappearance of party newspapers; the substitution of paid for voluntary labor in campaigns; the decline in attendance at party congresses (if and when they are held at all); the failure of parties to penetrate, much less to control, associations and movements as they often did in the past (especially on the left); and, as the operational culmination of all these micro-level trends, the much higher levels of volatility in electoral outcomes and the much greater frequency with which governing parties are thrown out of office.

Forming Governments

Electoral structuration may be the most distinctive function of parties, but the most important when it comes to regime consolidation is their capacity to make (and unmake) governments. Regardless of how well parties present alternative candidates and provide attractive political identities, if they are incapable of playing a leading role in filling top political offices and supporting the policies of subsequent governments, they are in deep trouble as agents of democratization.

We have already hinted at one difficulty in performing this role:

relatively rapid turnover in power due to electoral volatility (or, in some parliamentary cases, factional defections that result in premature elections). Historically—that is, in the waves of democratization that accompanied World Wars I and II—one party tended to emerge as predominant because of its identification with the change in regime and usually remained in power for ten to twelve continuous years (for example, Ireland, Finland, West Germany, Italy, and Japan). In the post-1974 neodemocracies, the opposite has occurred. In all but two cases (Chile and the Czech Republic) the initially victorious party has been defeated in the first or second subsequent election—often by a large margin. Not only is this rapid turnover in power an unobtrusive indicator of malperformance of the first two generic party functions, but it is also a manifest sign that the new parties are having a difficult time forming and, especially, sustaining effective governments.

Part of the responsibility lies with the distinctive type of party that often emerged as the winner in the founding elections. They have been dubbed "forum parties" in that they provided a common platform for resistance against the previous autocracy by grouping together a wide range of disparate political formations. Initially, they were much closer to being social movements, and some were reluctant to transform themselves into parties. The Spanish Union of the Democratic Center of Adolfo Suárez was the prototype and, like its successors, collapsed into a multitude of factions once electoral competition really took hold—suffering the worst electoral defeat (a loss of 29.3 percent points between the elections of 1979 and 1982) in the history of modern democracy. Solidarity in Poland, Civic Forum and Public Against Violence in Czechoslovakia, Popular Front in Estonia, Democratic Russia in Russia, and the United Democratic Forces in Bulgaria had similar fates.

But this "birth defect" of some party systems is not enough to explain the pervasive pattern of unstable and (by inference) ineffectual party government. As we now approach the fifth and sixth postautocracy elections in some of these polities, we shall see whether this tendency will abate. Spain, Portugal, and Greece all passed through periods of relative stasis under the hegemony of a single party or alliance, but they seem more recently to have returned to the specter of frequent rotations in power. Granted that the winners in today's neodemocracies seem not to have enjoyed the same initial margins of victory as their predecessors after 1918 or 1945 (although I admit that this is just an impression, since I have not yet gathered the requisite data), and granted that the subsequent development of public opinion has made all elected governments more susceptible to being rejected for their association with poor economic performance (and I suspect, but cannot prove, that living standards, growth rates, and levels of employment declined more after democratization than previously—especially in Eastern Europe and the successor republics of the former Soviet Union). Still, something has changed in the way that winning parties or coalitions select leading government personnel and control their behavior in office. Ironically, this cannot be due to any reluctance on the part of the winners to assume the prerogatives of governing, occasional protestations to the contrary notwithstanding.

The "political class" that is forming in contemporary neodemocracies is much more likely to be composed of aspirant professional politicians, that is, persons who intend to live *from* and not just *for* politics. The "founding fathers" of most established democracies consisted of relative amateurs who had other professions and relatively little interest in perpetuating themselves in power. Neodemocratic politicos need continuous access to public authority (and more specifically to public money), since they often have no independent source of income to rely upon and since their parties alone are incapable of rewarding them materially or spiritually. Moreover, precisely because they have so few loyal dues-paying members, contemporary parties themselves have become much more reliant on public funding. There has also been a tendency for the new constitutions to refer more explicitly than in the past to the role of parties, even attempting to ensure them monopolistic access to specific funds and forums. The irony arises because, despite these efforts, parties in today's neodemocracies are less capable of exercising a monopoly over elite selection, of disciplining the sub-sequent behavior of those who are selected, or of ensuring that their program gets implemented when "they" are in power. Patronage, in the sense of favoritism in appointments to government jobs and awards of government contracts, continues to be a mainstay of political parties and may even have increased in importance under conditions of weak economic performance. Effective control over the macro aspects of public policy, however, has declined.

The most obvious development limiting the government-forming and policy-making role of parties in neodemocracies is "globalization/ regionalization." Greater and more complex forms of economic interdependence—reaching beyond the traditional spheres of foreign trade and overseas fixed investment into the productive structure of transnational enterprises and the instantaneous flows of speculative capital—have narrowed the range of "permissible" policies. Coupled with this has come the formation of so-called "intergovernmental organizations," such as the International Monetary Fund and the International Bank of Reconstruction and Development, at the global level or "supranational organizations," such as the European Union and its various policy agencies, at the regional level. Their leverage is all the greater since most neodemocracies inherited economies mis-developed, devastated, or deeply indebted by preceding autocracies and since the approval of an apposite international functional agency or membership in an appropriate regional organization has become a virtual *sine qua non* for attracting badly needed foreign investment. One of the most salient ways in which a neodemocracy can obtain such a certificate of good conduct is to place its macroeconomic management in the hands of technical experts whose competence is recognized by these very same international organizations. Needless to say, relatively few of these technocrats have any stable party affiliations, and their preferred solutions frequently clash head-on with the programs of parties, especially those on the left. Given the declining mobilizational capacity of these very same parties, it is increasingly unlikely that they will be able to contest the policies of their own technocrats.

My hunch, however, is that the decline in the viability of the government-forming function is not just the result of globalization or regionalization. Its deeper roots lie in the combination of greater professionalization of the role of politician and greater dependence upon the state for revenues and recognition. These obviously inter-related political factors are driving parties away from their earlier functions of structuration and identification, and that, in turn, makes it more difficult for them to control the behavior of governing elites on the grounds that they "re-present" the interests and passions of civil society and individual citizens. In the corporatist version, the shift is toward organizations—mostly recognized and monopolistic interest associations—that do not so much represent as intermediate between members and authorities and, in so doing, play a key role in forming the preferences of their members and in collaborating with authorities in the implementation of policies. In the more common pluralist version, the shift is toward weaker and less "identifiable" political parties and stronger and more "insistent" social movements—with less visible and highly specialized associations (and even individual firms) working unobtrusively in the background, exploiting direct contacts with public officials that circumvent partisan channels as much as possible. Not an encouraging picture for political parties no matter which direction one looks!

Aggregating Interests and Passions

Most of the normative case for the superiority of political parties as intermediaries seems to hinge on their ability to aggregate the interests and passions of citizens. *Because* parties are the only institutions capable of aggregating a broad spectrum of interests and passions, *therefore* they are the only ones legitimately entitled to rule in the name of society as a whole. Even though, by their etymological origin (if nothing else), they are bound to represent only a "part" of the citizenry, the competition between parties or the cooperation among parties when they form governments is supposed to compel them to offer general programs designed to appeal beyond their core militants and constituencies in ways that are denied to interest associations and social movements—no matter how hard the latter work at "catching" as many members as possible. Even if—as now seems often the case—parties have fewer members and—as sometimes seems the case—less reputable images than associations or movement, the process of competition in which they are engaged should force them to address larger issues and aspirations.

In earlier periods, the primary weapon of parties as interest aggregators was their articulation (one is tempted to say, their embodiment) of a distinctive ideology. By offering to citizens a comprehensive vision of how much better the society might look if they were given responsibility for governing, parties seemed to ensure that the political process would attend to "the will of the public as a whole" and not just the specialized interests of associations or momentary passions of movements.[18] With the decline in the credibility of most partisan ideologies and the convergence toward a relatively narrow range of general policy objectives, parties tended to shift toward a "catch-all" strategy after World War II that aimed at appealing to as many voters as possible, that is, to those closest to the median position on most issues.[19] Not only did this weaken their symbolic capacity, but it tended to encourage more opportunistic behavior on the part of the voters. Rather than aggregate "actively" by asserting a higher public purpose, parties aggregated "passively" by assembling a multitude of private purposes. This helped some of them, no doubt, to escape from their class or regional "ghettos" and to win general elections, but often at the expense of their functional performance.

Parties in the post-1974 neodemocracies (with a few marginal exceptions) are the beneficiaries-cum-victims of this prior decline in credible ideologies and constriction in feasible policy alternatives. Not only do they have less differentiated products to peddle, but most of them have virtually no accumulated "ideological capital" to draw upon.[20] Moreover, they have to cope with three additional difficulties in their contemporary efforts at aggregating interests and passions.

First, ideology was rarely the only aggregative device deployed by parties. They also tended to rely heavily on interorganizational linkages with other types of intermediaries. While this was particularly important for progressive parties in their allegedly "organic" connection with workers' movements, trade unions, and producer and consumer cooperatives, conservative parties also tended to have stable alliances with business and professional associations, lodges, and fraternal societies. Where they existed, farmers' parties were literally the electoral expression of agrarian associations. In neodemocracies, these linkages have proven much weaker—either because the entire realm of civil society was less developed prior to regime change or because, thanks to the belated timing of "free and fair" elections, newly emergent movements and associations are much more concerned with protecting their organizational autonomy. Moreover, in those cases where these units of civil society are being promoted by outside actors—that is, those famous nongovernmental organizations—they are being advised (even compelled) not to have any connection with political parties. In Southern Europe, strong and resilient ties existed among movements, associations, and parties at the beginning of the transition but weakened when the parties were forced by international constraints to resort to restrictive policies that conflicted with the specific interests of workers, retirees, and other "policy-takers."[21]

Second, the technology of electoral competition and, one is tempted to say, of politics in general has changed dramatically with developments in the mass media. Parties no longer own or control their own media. And they have only very limited channels of direct access to their members or potential voters (such as rallies, caucuses, and conventions). So, they must increasingly rely upon media owned and controlled by others to send out their message. And when that media is privately owned, competition among firms for audience shares and revenues tends to bias not only the access that different parties have to their respective publics but also the content of their messages. State ownership of the media—with a few honorable exceptions—virtually guarantees a bias in favor of the governing party. Effective aggregation of interests and passions, if it takes place at all, occurs not directly through channels internal to parties and their "sister" organizations but indirectly through the media before undifferentiated mass audiences. Especially when the message is transmitted via television, its form and content must be tailored to fit parameters imposed by this medium—which seems to have opened up the electoral process to telegenic candidates with little or no party experience or loyalty.

Third, closely coupled with the growing reliance on mass media another shift has come in the technology of contemporary electoral politics: the development and increased reliance upon opinion surveys and other polling devices to capture the expectations of mass publics. Candidates, even those who go through the ranks and are nominated by some regular party process, have tended to develop their own means of sounding out public opinion. They do not need to rely upon partisan channels for guidance; indeed, in their quest for vote maximization, they may become quite wary of such "biased" sources. Witness the enormous rise in the importance of political consultants—most of whom are proud of their ability to work across party lines. Not only has this already affected the electoral process in neodemocracies, but the consultants they employ (at least, initially) are often recruited from outside the country![22] My hunch is that this ready availability of public opinion data has undermined the aggregative role of parties per se. Not only does the information come to candidates independently of partisan channels, but they use it "passively" to position themselves as closely as possible to the median voter on each issue—irrespective of the compatibility of the positions they take. Parties abandon all pretense of "actively" intervening to form and direct the opinions of their members or followers toward some higher and more general set of goals. Once their candidate has won, he or she is saddled with a mishmash of incompatible (if popular) promises that cannot be satisfied simultaneously, thereby generating further disenchantment with the vacuousness of party platforms and the perfidy of party politicians.

Parties' Prospects

I would be the first to admit that what I have attempted above is what the French call a *réquisitoire*—a selective and, therefore, biased assemblage of observations intended to place the emerging political parties of neodemocracies in the worst possible light. No doubt, had I compiled more systematic data and evaluated them more objectively, I would have uncovered greater evidence that political parties in the countries that have democratized since 1974 have performed some critical functions during the subsequent attempts to consolidate their respective regimes.

Nevertheless, one of the major reasons that I am so convinced of the basic weakness of parties in these neodemocracies is that *virtually all the difficulties that they have been experiencing are also being experienced by contemporary parties in archaeodemocracies*. The crisis of representation and intermediation through partisan channels seems to be generic, not specific to those countries that have recently changed their mode of political domination.

This has been partially disguised by the fact that the older parties are still drawing on political capital accumulated during their "heroic age," when they did provide strong identities, offer dramatically different programs, produce major realignments in voter preferences, and form epochal governments that appealed to a broad range of citizen interests and resolved major social, economic, or military crises. At least since the mid-1970s, they have been spending this precious capital with each successive election. Only by substituting state funds for the decline in symbolic identifications and voluntary contributions and only by relying increasingly on the personal appeal of individual candidates (many of whom have little or no prior party experience), instead of on the compellingness of their programs, have parties managed to sustain their nominal prominence in the minds of most citizens.[23]

Students of political parties are fond of using the metaphor of the "gatekeeper" to describe their subject matter.[24] It seems to appeal to them to think of political parties as if they constituted a select and disciplined corps of actors, resplendent in their symbolic trappings, who effectively guard the Citadel of Government by keeping the special interests articulated by individuals, firms, localities, associations, and movements from disturbing the rulers, and by only letting through the gates those that have been aggregated into broader, and possibly more other-regarding, public interests. Moreover, for most of these students, the fewer the number of gatekeepers the better, since that should ensure a more encompassing process of aggregation.

But what if the gatekeepers were no longer guarding the real portals of access to political power? What if, inside the Citadel, there were an increasing number of specialized redoubts staffed by "guardians" recruited for their technical expertise and their nonpartisanship—each with its own secret passages?[25] And what if there were more and more political agents within the walls leaking information to the *hoi polloi* outside and letting them inside the Citadel discreetly? And what if the resplendent trappings of those gatekeepers were increasingly paid for from public funds rather than voluntary contributions, and their meager salaries were increasingly supplemented by money and status coming from the more affluent individuals and groups among the *hoi polloi?* Would students of democratic politics then spend so much of their time and effort studying political parties?

So, ironically and retrospectively, it may be fortunate that political scientists did not rely so heavily on that "Get the parties right!" slogan. For, under contemporary conditions, there may be no way to get them right—if by "right" one means that they should be capable of performing well all four functions and, thereby, playing a role comparable to that which they played in earlier processes of democratization.

Which is not to say that any of the other forms of organized intermediation between citizens and public authorities are likely to do much better! Interest associations and social movements are certainly more numerous and prominent than during previous waves of democratization, but that does not imply that either of them separately or both of them together can provide their members or followers with overarching collective identities, structure political competition in meaningful ways, govern (and accept responsibility for governing) the polity, and aggregate a diversity of social interests and passions into a coherent program of government. Contrary to the more organic versions of functionalism, there is no reason to expect that, simply because these tasks are not being adequately performed by parties in most neodemocracies, some other set of organizations will take them over. Nor do I see any a priori reason for assuming that all forms of intermediation are locked into a zero-sum struggle for attention, loyalty, funds, or whatever. Some democracies have strong parties, associations, and movements; others are weak in all of them; most have varied mixes of them.

What seems more probable is that neodemocracies, like many archaeodemocracies, are going to have to survive with a lot less aggregation and intermediation than in the past. Their political parties will produce a great deal less electoral structuration, symbolic identification, party governance, and interest aggregation than did their forerunners. What this implies for the quality of these neodemocracies is another issue!

NOTES

1. So instinctual is this faith in parties that it is sometimes inserted on top of what an author explicitly states. Samuel Huntington's status as a disciplinary guru is such that the following quote of his is frequently cited by contemporary students of democratization: "The vacuum of power and authority which exists in so many modernizing countries [and, allegedly, in so many democratizing polities—PCS] may be temporarily filled by charismatic leadership or by military force. But it can only be filled permanently by political organization. Either the established elites compete among themselves to organize the masses through the existing system, or dissident elites organize themselves to overthrow that system. In the modernizing world, he [*sic*] who controls the future is who organizes its politics." Samuel P. Huntington, *Political Order in Changing Societies* (New Haven: Yale University Press, 1968), 461. Cited in Geoffrey Pridham and Paul G. Lewis, eds., *Stabilizing Fragile Democracies: Comparing New Party Systems in Southern and Eastern Europe* (London: Routledge, 1996), 5. Although Huntington said "political organization," those who cite him presume (probably correctly) that he was exclusively referring to political parties—as if elites could not possibly organize and compete in other forms and forums.

2. The distinction between these two generic types of political struggle comes from Antonio Gramsci, *Selections from the Prison Notebooks,* Quentin Hoare and Geoffrey Nowell Smith, eds. and trans. (New York: International Publishers, 1971), 108–10, 229–39.

3. For this emphasis on uncertainty as *the* characteristic of democracy, see Adam Przeworski, "Some Problems in the Study of the Transition to Democracy," in Guillermo O'Donnell and Philippe C. Schmitter, eds., *Transitions from Authoritarian Rule: Prospects for Democracy* (Baltimore: Johns Hopkins University Press, 1986), 57–61. For the emphasis on the limited scope of uncertainty and its link to contingent consent, see Philippe C. Schmitter and Terry Lynn Karl, "What Democracy Is . . . and Is Not," *Journal of Democracy* 3 (Summer 1991): 75–88.

4. Philip Converse, "Of Time and Partisan Stability," *Comparative Political Studies* 2 (July 1969): 139–71.

5. For some reason, scholars working on the "generics" of political parties seem to keep coming up with four functions, even if they are almost never defined in exactly the same fashion. Two recent examples of "quadri-functionalism" are Klaus von Beyme, "Party Leadership and Change in Party Systems: Towards a Post-Modern Party State?" *Government and Opposition* 31 (Spring 1996), 135–59; and Wlodzimierz Wesolowski, "The Formation of Political Parties in Post-Communist Poland" in Geoffrey Pridham and Paul G. Lewis, eds., *Stabilising Fragile Democracies,* 229–53.

In their communication subsequent to the conference, Larry Diamond, Marc Plattner, and Richard Gunther suggest a more extensive list of six functions. My first function ("electoral structuration") seems to have collapsed their first two into one; otherwise, the correlation is close, even if the names are not. As for their sixth function ("political system integration and legitimation"), I treat it as a compound product of parties' having performed the other four or five—and I raise some doubts as to whether this function is still, in fact, unique to existing parties in neodemocracies. I am indebted to Manual Hidalgo for this clarification.

6. Poland is a confusing case in that turnout in the first round of its first contested election in 1989 was 62.7 percent, despite the negotiated and limited nature of the competition. In its first genuinely "free and fair" elections in October 1991, only 43 percent of the eligible voters turned out!

7. And, in the case of Poland's first presidential election (1990), a completely unknown candidate (resident in Canada!), Stanisław Tyminski, won 23.1 percent of the vote running for party "X"!

8. Consider the following unobtrusive indicator: the proportion of campaign literature (posters, pamphlets, flyers) that do not even mention the party affiliation of the candidate, just his or her picture or slogan. To the best of my knowledge, no one has ever gathered this information, but I suspect that it would show a steady tendency to increase over time—discounting, of course, for those countries where illiteracy or the law requires the use of party symbol or name.

9. Stefano Bartolini and Peter Mair have calculated the average electoral volatility among European established democracies as less than 8 percent. Stefano Bartolini and Peter Mair, *Identity, Competition and Electoral Availability: The Stabilisation of European Electorates 1885–1985* (Cambridge: Cambridge University Press), 27–34.

10. Michael Coppedge reports an average volatility score for the neodemocracies of Latin America of 30 percent. Michael Coppedge, "Freezing in the Tropics: Explaining Party Volatility in Latin America," paper presented at Midwest Political Science Association, Chicago (1995).

11. There is a third dimension to the performance of the electoral structuration function about which I have no data, only a suspicion. In the past, repeated elections under a stabilized party system usually had the effect of "nationalizing" the electoral process, that is, of reproducing more or less the same correlates of class, status, gender, religious affiliation, generational differentiation, and so forth with partisan preference across the national territory. My impression is that party systems in post-1974 neodemocracies have not tended to eliminate initial regional differences and may even have encouraged their expression. Of course, this could be due more to the fact that contemporary democratizations have often been accompanied by a decentralization of internal political and administrative *compétences* than to weaknesses in the emergent parties themselves.

12. Philip Converse, "Of Time and Partisan Stability."

13. Actually, the Greek case is a puzzling one in that the two major parties did change names, formal organizational structures, and many of their leading personnel, but nevertheless managed to reproduce most of the characteristics of the preauthoritarian party system. For a subtle account, see Michalis Spourdalakis, "Securing Democracy in Post-Authoritarian Greece: The Role of Political Parties," in Geoffrey Pridham and Paul G. Lewis, eds., *Stabilizing Fragile Democracies,* 167–85.

14. These data come from Leonardo Morlino, "Consolidation and Party Government in Southern Europe," *International Political Science Review* 16 (April 1995): 150.

15. Data contained in Doh Chull Shin, "Political Parties and Democratization in South Korea: The Mass Public and the Democratic Consolidation of Political Parties," *Democratization* 2 (Summer 1995): 35. The data on East European cases comes from a survey conducted by Laszlo Bruszt and Janos Simon.

16. See Doh Chull Shin, "Political Parties and Democratization in South Korea," 33. There is some controversy over the reasons for such low levels of party

identification in East Central Europe. Initially, several authors speculated that it stemmed from a general "cultural" antipathy generated by the previous meaning of party membership in a "Marxist/Leninist/Stalinist" system. Laszlo Bruszt and Janos Simon have stressed the importance of "amorphous" or "flattened" societies in which class differentiation does not offer a sufficient anchoring for collective identities and, hence, fails to produce reliable links to parties. Laszlo Bruzst and Janos Simon, "The Great Transformation in Hungary and Eastern Europe," in György Szoboszlai, ed., *Flying Blind: Emerging Democracy in East-Central Europe* (Budapest: Hungarian Political Science Association, 1992), 177–203. See also David Ost, "Labor, Class and Democracy: Shaping Political Antagonisms in Post-Communist Society," in Beverly Crawford, ed., *Markets, States and Democracy* (Boulder, Colo.: Westview Press, 1995), 177–203.

Bernhard Wessels and Hans-Dieter Klingemann confirm the absence of class-related voting but document that other social differentia are correlated with partisan preferences: age, education, union membership, religiosity. Nevertheless, Wessels and Klingemann conclude that "there is not yet an entirely clear relationship between social structure and the vote, especially not with respect to class. And if a relationship exists, it does not always fulfill the expectations derived from the Western experience." See Bernhard Wessels and Hans-Dieter Klingemann, "Democratic Transformation and the Prerequisites of Democratic Opposition in East and Central Europe," Veröffentlichung der Abteilung, "Institutionen und sozialer Wandel," Wissenschafts-zentrum Berlin für Sozialforschung, FS III 94–201, pp. 12–15.

17. Gábor Tóka, "Parties and Electoral Choices in East-Central Europe," in Geoffrey Pridham and Paul G. Lewis, eds., *Stabilizing Fragile Democracies,* 103. After noting that the ratings for political parties in general tend to be unfavorable, Tóka concludes that "the overwhelming majority of citizens tend to find their best political representative in a political party rather than other organizations" (p. 104).

18. Juan Linz and Alfred Stepan offer a typical (and recent) example of such an assumption: "A consolidated democracy requires that a range of political parties not only *represent* interests but seek by coherent programs and organizational activity to *aggregate* interests." See Juan Linz and Alfred Stepan, *Problems of Democratic Transition and Consolidation* (Baltimore: Johns Hopkins University Press, 1996), 274.

19. The *locus classicus* for the identification and (critical) observation of this trend is Otto Kirchheimer, "The Transformation of the Western European Party System," in Joseph LaPalombara and Myron Weiner, eds., *Political Parties and Political Development* (Princeton, N.J.: Princeton University Press, 1966), 177–200.

20. The one obvious exception to this, the communist parties of Southern Europe and Latin America—some of which played a sustained role in the resistance against autocracy—saw their electoral strength (and party membership) dwindle with each successive election after the change in regime. It should be noted that in Spain and Portugal this was the case before the collapse of the Soviet Union served to discredit even further their ideological appeal.

21. While, admittedly, I have not examined this systematically, I have not detected in neodemocracies (nor in most established democracies) the inverse trend, which seems to be affecting the party system in the United States, where a dramatic increase—not decrease—in interorganizational linkages has been taking place. One party (the Republican) has been virtually taken over by a social movement (the Christian Coalition); the other party (the Democratic) has benefited from an extraordinary revival in its links to the trade union movement.

22. The one item of new political technology that does not (yet) seem to have affected neodemocracies (or most established European democracies) is the

computerized mailing list of potential contributors. Whether it is because of higher mail costs, less reliable delivery, the absence of relevant data files, or the presence of laws protecting data confidentiality, they have been spared this innovation— which, if I am to judge by the daily volume of appeals in my mail, has become a major source of funding for candidates (and, occasionally, for parties) in the United States.

23. One of the most extreme manifestations of this decline is *partitocrazia,* that is, an extreme inflation of the role of parties, both with regard to the staffing of public positions and the profiting from public policies. The term was invented in Italy but has been applied to other polities, such as Belgium. See Kris Deschouwer, Lieven De Winter, and Donatella Della Porta, eds., *Partitocracies Between Crisis and Reform: The Cases of Italy and Belgium,* special issue of *Res Publica* 28 (1996): 215–35; and Lieven De Winter, "The Italo-Belgian Partitocratic Type Compared to Fourteen West-European Countries," paper presented at the 1996 Annual Meeting of the American Political Science Association, San Francisco, September 1996.

According to my interpretation, "party-ocracy" is a product of weakness, not strength. The more that a given party loses its traditional stock of voluntarily supplied symbolic resources and fails to control major areas of policy making due to transnational and technocratic forces, the more dependent it becomes upon resources provided directly or indirectly by the state. As a result, the advantages of partisanship become more concentrated in the higher echelons of the party organization and the temptation to profit personally increases correspondingly— hence, the strong odor of corruption that accompanies the term.

24. David Easton seems to have originated it: David Easton, *The Political System: An Inquiry into the State of Political Science* (New York: Knopf, 1971).

25. On the role of guardians in modern democracies, see Robert Dahl, *Democracy and Its Critics* (New Haven: Yale University Press, 1989), 52–64.

5

THE PARTY EFFECTS OF ELECTORAL SYSTEMS

Giovanni Sartori

Giovanni Sartori *is Albert Schweitzer Professor Emeritus in the Humanities at Columbia University. He was previously professor of political science at the University of Florence and at Stanford University.* His books include Parties and Party Systems *(1974),* The Theory of Democracy Revisited *(1987),* Comparative Constitutional Engineering *(1994), and, most recently,* Homo Videns *(1998) and* La Sociedad Multietnica *(2001).*

To debate whether electoral systems are an independent or dependent variable is pointless. For we are not dealing with an intrinsic independence; we are simply asking different questions. Electoral systems are assumed to be an independent variable when the question is "What do they do?" If the question is, instead, how electoral systems come about and why are they chosen, then the electoral system is treated as a dependent variable. And that is all there is to it.

Taken as an independent variable and, indeed, as a causal factor, electoral systems are assumed to affect the party *system,* not parties *per se.* Yet it stands to reason that a modification of the system of parties must also be of consequence for the component elements of the system, namely, for its parts. Note, however, that this argument goes from system to party, not from party to system. As hypothesized, the causal chain is that electoral systems cause the party system, which in turn causes parties per se to be as they are.

The argument must begin, then, with the influence of the electoral system on the party system. I must also challenge from the start the view that "any theory making electoral systems a fundamental causative factor in the development of party systems cannot be sustained."[1] For this is still the prevailing view.[2]

As is well known, the first author to state in law-like form how electoral systems influence the party system was Maurice Duverger. His first law reads: "The plurality single-ballot system tends to party dualism." His second law reads: "The double-ballot [plurality] system and proportional representation tend to multipartism."[3] These laws have been deluged with criticisms and certainly display major weaknesses. The Duverger laws posit that electoral systems affect (that is, reduce or multiply) the number of parties, and yet Duverger never indicates how parties are to be counted. The related point is that a causal relationship is verifiable only if the effect is clearly specified, whereas the effect of the first law (party dualism) is accordion-like, and the effect of the second law equally suffers from excessive imprecision. Another major and almost fatal weakness of Duverger's treatment is that he never states the conditions under which his laws apply or, conversely, do not apply.[4]

These drawbacks have led, unfortunately, to an outright dismissal of the nomothetic approach. When Douglas Rae took up the matter in his influential *The Political Consequences of Electoral Laws,* he did not build cumulatively on Duverger but switched instead to a different track. Rae posits a general "fractionalization effect" of electoral systems (whether or not they lead to fragmentation) and provides a statistical measure for it—his well-known "index of fractionalization." Whatever the merits and shortcomings of Rae's index,[5] the point is that, with Rae, the political-science profession enters a path of measurements whose gains in precision are outweighed by major losses of understanding.

While Duverger looked at concrete party systems (even though he did not identify them correctly), the quantitative literature that goes from Rae to Rein Taagepera and Matthew Shugart simply leaves us with arbitrary cutting points along a continuum. For example, Rae defines "two-party competition" (note, not two-partism as a system) as a state of affairs in which "the first party holds less than 70 percent of the legislative seats and the first two parties together hold at least 90 percent of the seats."[6] Why not less than 60 percent and, cumulatively, 80 percent? And what do these ratios or proportions entail in terms of systemic properties? This is what we are not told. Likewise, Taagepera and Shugart come up with what they call a "generalized Duverger's rule" which reads as follows: "The effective number of electoral parties is usually within + 1 unit from N = 1.25 (2 + *log* M)."[7] Now, and quite aside from the fact that the empirical fit of the rule is poor, as they admit, what is the explanatory value of their "effective parties" measure? Not only are we left with a pure and simple counting of parties (of dubious empirical validity) but what is it that we have? The authors themselves ask: "Is the new rule on the number of parties a law, a hypothesis, or an empirical data fit?"[8] And their candid reply simply is: "For practical matters, it really does not matter." Well, no: It matters.

The issue is whether electoral systems "cause" something, and if their effects can be rendered in terms of law-like generalizations. And laws can hardly be formulated unless we are clear-headed as to how they relate to causal analysis, to condition analysis, to probability and determinism, and, conclusively, to how they are confirmed or disconfirmed.[9]

So, if nothing of this nor the difference between law and hypothesis matters "in practice," then the business of knowing has been put out of business. Because there can be no real knowing without logic, whereas what is currently considered and called "methodology" is method without *logos,* techniques that have largely lost their logical backbone and component element.

Restating the "Laws"

Reverting, as it were, to "logical knowing," the question is: Can the impact of electoral systems be stated in terms of law-like rules that are both predictive of single events (not only of classes of events) and verifiable? But first, what do we mean by "law"? We mean, I assume, a generalization endowed with explanatory power that detects a regularity that allows predictions. So a law is required to assert more than a regularity and cannot consist of a mere generalization. And the point to bear in mind is that the explanatory power of a law is just as crucial as its predictive power.

Another preliminary point bears on the conditions under which a law applies or does not apply. Hundreds of critics point to hundreds of occasions in which the electoral system fails to produce the predicted effects. But a law, any law, can hold only when it applies and cannot be disconfirmed by cases to which it does not apply. Water boils at 100° C at the sea level, not at the top of Everest; bodies fall at the same acceleration, regardless of shape and size, in a void. Likewise, the laws that specify the effects of electoral systems apply only to party *systems,* that is to say, to the stage at which a loose collection of notables gives way to a structured ensemble of parties. Unstructured systems made of shapeless and volatile units escape electoral engineering and are "lawless."[10]

Let us come to some specifics. First of all, what do electoral systems affect? At first blush, the direct effect of an electoral system appears to be on the voter. However, the electoral system also has a direct effect on the number of parties (the format of the party system) since it establishes how votes are translated into parliamentary seats. Other effects are instead derivative. We shall come to them in due course.

The effect of an electoral system *on the voter* can be constraining (manipulative) or unconstraining. If it is unconstraining, then an electoral system has no effect—and that is that. The effect of an electoral system *on the party system* can either be reductive (it reduces or compresses the number of parties) or not—and in the latter case we have again a non-effect. A pure system of proportional representation (PR) is ineffective in both respects: It does not have a manipulative impact either on the voter or on the format of the party system.[11] Pure proportionality, however, is rare. Regardless of the mathematics of proportionality, a small district (for example, a district that elects two to five members) brings about impure proportionality. The rule of thumb here is that the smaller the district, the lesser the proportionality. Conversely, the larger the district, the greater the proportionality. Israel and the Netherlands thus rank among the pure PR systems in that they elect, respectively, 120 and 150 MPs in a single, nationwide constituency.

The bottom line then is that when electoral systems are effective, they reduce the number of parties. This brings us back to the question of how parties are to be counted. Duverger, I have already noted, had no answer for this question, and his assessment was not only impressionistic but also utterly erratic. Yet if we assume that electoral systems "cause" the number of parties, then we must know how this number is to be determined. Clearly, parties cannot be counted at their face value. In my work, I have used the notion of *relevant party,* where relevance is a systemic assessment based on two criteria, namely, the coalition potential or blackmail potential of any given party.[12] Most authors instead abide by measures of fragmentation (Rae's index of fractionalization and the like) and currently speak of "effective party." The quantitative determinations are, to be sure, easy to obtain since they are machine-made. Unfortunately, they miss *relevance* (as I define it) since they tell us just about nothing about whether and in what manner a party affects the party system as a whole.

I now submit the rules ("laws") that govern the effects of electoral systems on the number of parties.[13]

Rule 1: A plurality system cannot produce by itself a nationwide two-party format, but under all circumstances it will help *maintain* an existing one. Hence, whenever a two-party format is established, a plurality system exerts a brakelike influence.

Rule 2: A plurality system will *produce,* in the long run, a two-party format (not the eternalization of the same parties, however) under two conditions: first, a party system structured by nationwide parties and, second, if the electorate which is refractory to whatever pressure of the electoral system happens to be dispersed in below-plurality proportions throughout the constituencies.[14]

Rule 3: Conversely, a two-party format is *impossible*—under whatever electoral system—if racial, linguistic, ideologically alienated, single-issue, or otherwise incoercible minorities (which cannot be represented by two major parties) are concentrated in above-plurality proportions in particular constituencies or geographical pockets. If so, the effect of a plurality system will only be reductive vis-à-vis the third parties that do not represent incoercible minorities.

Rule 4: Finally, PR systems also obtain *reductive effects*—though to a lesser extent—in proportion to their nonproportionality; and particularly whenever they are applied in small-sized constituencies, establish a threshold of representation, or attribute a premium. Under these conditions, PR too will eliminate the smaller parties whose electorate is dispersed throughout the constituencies; but even a highly impure PR will not eliminate small parties that thrive in concentrated above-quota strongholds.[15]

Let it be underscored that with single-member districts, the electoral system exerts its influence discretely, district by district. Hence a two-party system requires "nationwide parties" (as stated in Rule 2), that is, comes about only if the same two parties are the major contestants in all (or almost all) constituencies. Let me also explain why my rules largely hinge upon the distribution of electorates, and specifically upon knowing whether or not incoercible *above-plurality* or, as the case may be, *above-quota* minorities happen to be geographically concentrated or dispersed. This is so because my rules apply only when the stage of local fragmentation of politics is over. At this point we are simply left, therefore, with the allegiances that remain unaffected by the advent of a structured party system.

One may ask why the number of relevant parties (the format of party systems) is so important? This is because the format explains and predicts the mechanics, that is, the *systemic characteristics* of distinctive types of party systems. In my analysis, I sort out three major systemic patterns: 1) *two-party mechanics,* that is, bipolar single-party alternation in government; 2) *moderate multipartism,* that is, bipolar shifts between coalition governments; 3) *polarized multipartism,* that is, systems characterized by multipolar competition, center-located coalitions with peripheral turnover, and antisystem parties.[16]

I cannot explicate the above in any detail, aside from pointing out that as the analysis moves from the classification to a typology of party systems, the decisive variable turns out to be systemic *polarization,* defined as the distance (ideological or other) between the most distant relevant parties. So the question now is: Will the format be followed by the expected, corresponding mechanics (functional properties)? Given structural consolidation as a necessary condition and polarization as the intervening and, to some extent, dependent variable, I hypothesize as follows:

Hypothesis 1: When the single-member plurality formula produces a two-party format (Rule 1 and 2), the format will, in turn, produce a two-party mechanics if and only if the polarization of the polity is low. With high polarization, the two-party mechanics breaks down. However, since a two-party mechanics implies centripetal competition, it tends to lessen systemic polarization.[17]

Hypothesis 2: Assuming a below-quota dispersion of the incoercible minorities (if any), impure PR formulas are likely to allow for one or two parties above the two-party format, that is, three-four parties. This format will, in turn, engender the mechanics of moderate multipartism if and only if the polity does not display high polarization.[18] However, since

moderate multipartism still is bipolar-converging (centripetal competition), it will not tend to increase systemic polarization.

Hypothesis 3: Relatively pure or pure PR systems easily allow for a
five-to-seven-party format. Even so, under conditions of medium-low
polarization, the coalitional mechanics of moderate multipartism are
not impeded. Under conditions of high polarization, however, the format
will display the mechanical characteristics of polarized multipartism,
thereby including a multipolar competition that eventually heightens
systemic polarization.

Thus far I account for just one causal factor, the electoral system.
Another causal factor at play may be the party system itself. That is to
say, a strongly structured and well-entrenched party system performs as
a *channelling force* of its own. Thus the party system as a system of
channelment may, by itself, "cause" the staying power of a party
configuration *as is.* Vide Austria, whose two-party format has resisted
for some 40 years (until the rise of Haider's Freedom Movement) the
fragmenting lures of PR. But the substitution of an independent variable
with another does not pose any problem to my laws, which can easily
incorporate an alternative causal factor.[19] Still, I detect an incompleteness
in my analysis that has long escaped me, and that I must now confront.

The New Case: From PR back to Plurality

My argument and my laws implicitly assume a movement from
majoritarian to proportional systems. For this has been, historically, the
unfailing direction of change. PR was first introduced in 1889, and no
democracy switched back from proportional to plurality elections for
the next 70 years. (France did exactly that in 1959.) In France's transition
from the Fourth to the Fifth Republic, there was no apparent *resistance
power* of PR, in the sense that the return to majoritarianism went
smoothly and achieved its purpose (albeit slowly). Thus the eventfulness
of this unprecedented event went unnoticed. But when Italy attempted
a similar comeback from PR to plurality in 1994 and in 1996, the attempt
failed miserably and indeed backfired. So here we have a problem that
has yet to be tackled.

Why has France succeeded and Italy failed? The first reason is that
the two countries have followed different paths. France astutely adopted
a double-ballot plurality system reinforced by increasingly heightened
thresholds of exclusion (today of 12.5 percent); and the aggregate impact
of this electoral arrangement was reinforced, as of 1962, by direct-
majoritarian presidential elections. Italy has done nothing of the sort. It
adopted a single-shot plurality system[20] with an insufficient threshold
of exclusion, and has thus far not had a directly elected president. Clearly,
the Italians' major mistake was to assume that single-ballot plurality
elections would, per force, perform "reductively." Thus the major reason

why Italians have failed to curtail the number of parties lies in their failure to adopt a double-ballot system. Yet the success of the French comeback has obscured the intrinsic difficulties that confront the dismantling of an entrenched pattern of party fragmentation.

Note that in Italy a single-ballot plurality system has not only failed to reduce the number of parties; it has actually backfired in producing more parties, a still higher level of fragmentation. Until the early nineties, the "relevant" parties in Italy numbered six (plus or minus one) with PR; with plurality they have currently grown to 12 (plus or minus two). Why did they multiply? This is the question that goes to the heart of the problem.

The answers lies, I suggest, in the (originally Downsian) notion of blackmail party. Remember that "blackmail potential" is one of my two criteria for establishing party relevance. And the point now is that a switch from PR to plurality extends "relevance," that is, *provides relevance to hitherto irrelevant parties.* The reason for this is simple. With a winner-take-all system, victory or defeat may be decided by one or two percentage points. Thus even very small parties—as long as they have a core of strongly identified voters—may display crucial blackmail leverage. True, with plurality elections a small party cannot win, but it can easily endanger the winning chances of the major parties. Under this circumstance, and given a state of entrenched fragmentation, the Italian electoral game has, in fact, been played by "paying out" the minor parties (of each family), that is, by granting them on the drawing board a given number of seats in exchange for their staying out of the race. Paradoxically, in the case at hand, it is not PR but the winner-take-all system that multiplies parties (by extending and facilitating their relevance).

Clearly, then, returns from PR to plurality require a new engineering not covered by current know-how. The new problem is how to cope with a new kind of blackmail potential. Note that this new problem is entirely created—since all other circumstances remain equal—by the electoral system. It will have to be remedied, therefore, by electoral counter-measures. Here the firm point is that substituting PR with a single-ballot plurality system will not, in all likelihood, reduce the number of parties. Indeed, this remedy is likely to boomerang. Even a double-ballot system, however, will not cure party fragmentation if it is "closed" (that is, if it admits to the run-off only the first two frontrunners), because in this case blackmail maneuverings can still be quite effective. A third warning is that electoral alliances —the French *apparentement*—should be prohibited whenever an electoral system has thresholds or premiums. For, clearly, alliances circumvent thresholds of exclusion and defy the aggregative intent of majority premiums.

Bearing these provisos in mind, in the case of Italy, I have proposed at the parliamentary hearings an "open" double ballot system that admits to the run-off the first four runners.[21] One can, however, think of other ways of disposing of extreme fragmentation. In the case of Israel, for example, I would recommend a PR system that provides majority premiums for the first two parties in this proportion: 20 percent to the first, 15 percent to the second.[22] We then have the solution adopted in Chile as of 1989: a two-member PR system. While this system is especially intended to reinforce the second-place finishers, the minimal size of the constituencies does crush the smaller parties (even though Chile permits electoral coalitions).

Misunderstood Electoral Systems

Up to this point I have dealt with the effects of electoral systems. But what about the causal factor itself? Is everything clear at this end of the argument? Not really. Moreover, the understanding of electoral systems leaves much to be desired. For a number of voting methods are both misclassified and misunderstood. Electoral systems are fundamentally divided into majoritarian and proportional and thus defined by reciprocal exclusion: All majoritarian systems are not proportional and, conversely, all proportional systems are not majoritarian. So far, so good. But PR systems have been devised by mathematicians and a respectable mathematician must seek perfect proportionality. Thus mathematicians have ignored ordinal proportionality and have confined PR to *equal quotas* (or quotients), that is, to systems that allocate seats to equal shares of the voting returns. Assume, however, that we encounter—as was the case in Japan until 1993—four-member constituencies (average) that elect the first four most voted candidates. What kind of system is that?

For Lijphart and others, it is a variety of the limited vote (the voter has fewer votes than there are seats) in which each voter has only one vote. Therefore, they argue, it is a single nontransferable vote system (SNTV) which is best considered "a semiproportional system rather than a plurality system."[23] But the above makes little, if any, sense. First of all, it makes no sense at all to wonder whether the Japanese system may be considered a plurality system, for it is certainly not. Secondly, in all standard PR systems voters have fewer votes than there are seats, and with PR, it is normal for voters to have just one nontransferable vote. Therefore, it is an untelling redundancy to consider Japan an SNTV case. Thirdly, under what criterion is Japan best considered semiproportional? This is a purely impressionistic assessment. PR systems have always been considered more-or-less pure (or impure). Along this continuum, is there a cut-off point for the notion of "semiproportional"? The answer is no, and therefore this notion has no classificatory value.[24]

But why on earth have most scholars, in attempting to classify the Japanese case, trapped themselves in these tortuosities? In my opinion, the Japanese system was quite simply an *ordinal proportional system* characterized by personalized voting (in lieu of list voting) and by small constituencies (and thus of the impure, least proportional variety). So why does this straightforward understanding of the case escape us? The reason is the mathematical bias that establishes that proportionality can be achieved only via equal quotas, whereas proportionality can also be achieved, I submit, by having candidates elected in multimember constituencies on the basis of the highest portion (proportion) of the returns. Nor is it a foregone conclusion that ordinal proportionality is necessarily more imperfect (impure) than quota-based proportionality. For this matter (the degree of correspondence of votes to seats) is decided far more by the constituency size than by algorithms.

Moving on, double-ballot systems (also called two-round systems) represent both a neglected and highly misunderstood area of electoral systems. An expert of the stature of Richard Rose assimilates and indeed subordinates the double ballot to the alternative vote.[25] His argument is as follows:

> The two-ballot plurality systems used in France's Fifth Republic is a *variant* of the alternative vote. . . . The difference between the Australian and French forms of alternative vote is limited, but of practical importance. Both systems . . . heavily penalize parties which have a large vote, but more enemies than supporters. Both ask voters to state more than one preference. But the Australian system leaves it to the voter to decide his preference, ordering candidates *all at once* in a single ballot. By contrast the French system also gives an initiative to the candidates and parties after the results of the first ballot are in.[26]

With due respect, the above is a misreading. Firstly, it is the double ballot that has many variants, not the alternative vote. If anything, then, the double ballot should be the genus of which the alternative vote is a species. Anyway, the double ballot is not necessarily a single-member majoritarian-plurality system; it can also be an ordinal proportional method of electing candidates in multimember (if small) constituencies. Furthermore, the similarities perceived by Rose are, if anything, dissimilarities. The alternative vote requires an absolute majority. The French parliamentary double ballot requires only a plurality; the former "orders" the candidates, the latter does not; the former does not allow voters to change their vote, the latter does. These are hardly "limited" differences.

So why assimilate the double ballot to something else? In this manner one misses that the system's unique characteristic—that the voter *revotes*—is also its central characteristic. All other electoral systems are one-shot; the double ballot, and the double ballot only, is a two-shot system. With one shot the voter shoots very much in the dark; with two shots he or she shoots, the second time, in full daylight. This entails, among other things, that in the first round the voter is free to express his first preference, that is, to engage in "sincere voting." It is only in the second round that he is subjected to the constraints of the electoral system. Note, moreover, that when the voter is pressured in the run-off to vote for less preferred candidates, this constraint largely becomes the constraint of actual voting distributions (not, as in the single-ballot plurality system, of the electoral system).[27]

Misinterpretations and ambiguities also plague the notion of "mixed system," the formula that has currently charmed Italy, Russia, Japan, New Zealand, and other countries. The notion originates with the German electoral system, and its popularity is largely due to a misunderstanding. For the German system is mixed, in the sense that half of the members of the Bundestag obtain a personalized vote (in single member constituencies), but is proportional in the far more important respect that the seats are *all* allocated proportionally on the basis of the PR list voting.

Alleged electoral experts are equally misguided in attributing importance to the German additional member system (AMS), that is, to its variable Bundestag membership. For instance, Pippa Norris writes that the most striking phenomenon in recent years has been the shift in New Zealand, Italy, and Japan "away from the extremes of proportional *and* majoritarian systems toward the middle ground of the 'additional member system' used in Germany."[28] But Italy and Japan do not have additional members and AMS is not a middle ground of anything, for it only ensures proportionality. Let it be added that the German system is not mixed in outcome (since it produces a fully proportional parliament). It is equally wrong to assume that Germany displays a three-party format because it mixes PR with plurality. German parties have been reduced by the Constitutional Court—which has outlawed communists and neo-Nazis—not by the electoral system.

Germany and its false witnessing aside, when is a mixed system veritably mixed? And what are the merits of plurality-PR mixes? A frequently held opinion is that mixed systems are "the most attractive forms of solution to meet otherwise contradictory imperatives."[29] I agree that we are faced with contrary (though not contradictory) imperatives, namely, the function of mirroring (exact representation), and the function of functioning (efficient government). But are mixed systems a solution that combines, as the claim goes, the best of both worlds?

Let me first provide this definition: A veritable mixed system is such if and only if *both* the voting method and the allocation of seats are in part majoritarian and in part proportional. Thus a veritable mixed system must combine a proportional with a majoritarian translation of votes into seats. The current Italian, Japanese, and Russian electoral systems qualify as mixed under the aforesaid criterion. In Italy since 1994, 75 percent of the seats are filled via plurality districts, while the remaining 25 percent of the seats are filled according to proportional criteria. In

Japan the mix is 60 percent (plurality) to 40 percent (proportional), whereas in Russia the mix is an even 50:50. As I have already noted, the result of Italy's mixed system across two elections has been counter-productive.[30] In Russia, under existing conditions no electoral system can be expected to do much, yet the choice was a poor one.[31] And in Japan three years of disappointing coalition-maneuverings have helped the LDP to restore its own single-party government.[32]

So far with the veritable mixed systems. Other countries are equally called mixed, albeit misleadingly, for here we fail to distinguish between two different kinds of mixtures. In the first kind (the one that is correctly called *mixed*) we have plurality-proportional mixes both in input and in output, as we know to be the case of Italy, Japan, and Russia.[33] In the second one (that can be called *mixed-proportional*), the mixture is incomplete: it is only in input, for the output is fully proportional. Indeed, in Germany as well as in New Zealand, a proportional compensation is provided (in parliamentary seats) for any disproportionality arising from the plurality elections. Hence the systems in question unequivocally perform as proportional systems based, in part, on personalized voting. The interesting case in this category is New Zealand, in that here we have a switch from plurality to PR. And while the German "proportional mix" has been of almost no consequence, New Zealand's switch has already brought about the novel experience of coalition uncertainty.[34]

Overall, the record of both the veritable and incomplete mixes has been erratic.[35] But this record still is, for most countries, a very short one. And since one or two elections cannot tell with any assurance how electoral "mixes" might work when routinized, my objection is, in terms of principle, that electoral systems should have *one logic* that conforms to their purpose. Hence all the mixed systems, including the incomplete ones, are objectionable in that they confuse voters and, secondly, require parties to become Janus-faced. PR permits, as Fahrquharson puts it, "sincere voting," that is, it encourages voters to express their first preferences freely, while majoritarian electoral systems require voters to engage in "strategic voting," that is, to express second best, calculated preferences (attuned to the likely winners). To require an ordinary voter to engage simultaneously in sincere (proportional) and in strategic (majoritarian) choices is a sure way of blurring them. By the same token, parties too are prompted to engage in schizophrenic behavior. For parties that coalesce in the plurality contests fight against each other in the PR setting. So are we looking at the best of two worlds or, instead, at the best way of producing a bastard, a parliament that serves no purpose? For the ultimate question always is: Electoral systems to what end?

The ultimate end of PR is *representative justice*. The ultimate end of majoritarian elections is *governing capacity*. Clearly these are contrary goals. To be sure, these goals are amenable to trade-offs: more governability in exchange for less proportionality, or, more proportional justice for less governability. But these trade-offs should not lead to solutions that are neither fish nor meat, that is to say, to non-solutions. One of the two ends—representativeness or governability—must have clear priority and prevail over the other.

Note that I do not hold that one goal is intrinsically superior to the other. I hold that we are confronted with a choice that should not be eluded by "mixes." Thus while Arend Lijphart believes that PR is inherently superior to plurality and that a consociational model of governance is inherently superior to the Westminster model, my view is, instead, that when a proportional parliament produces paralyzed coalition governments, we should seek majoritarian electoral remedies. Unfortunately we hardly know how to do that.

The Influence on Parties

Let me turn to the last item on my agenda. Thus far I have dealt with the impact of the electoral system on the voter and with its effects on the party system. As I have indicated at the outset, this is the causal path that we are logically required to follow. Yet it is clearly the case that the electoral system also shapes parties per se. When the whole is affected, its parts are affected; and, conversely, the parts affect the whole to which they belong.

Note, firstly, that with a majoritarian system, one either wins or loses in each constituency, whereas in a proportional system, winning and losing are only a matter of greater or smaller shares. And if the very notion of winning is different, at the very least the tactics of party competition must be different. In one case the loser loses all; in the other it just loses something (perhaps just one or two percentage points). So different electoral systems bring about different ways of competing, and this affects how parties are, that is, their competitive nature.

A similar point can be made with regard to the notion of responsibility. When an electoral system maintains or brings about two-partyism, by the same token it brings about single-party government, and thus an identifiable responsibility: who is responsible, in governing, for what. When, instead, electoral systems cause multipartyism, by the same token, they generally bring about coalition governments. If so, the more numerous the coalition partners (for example, in Italy with PR they have generally been five), and the more frequent the coalition changes, the less the voter can attribute responsibility to any specific party. With coalition governments, responsibility becomes fuzzy. One may thus say that different electoral systems engender "differently responsible" and/ or "differently irresponsible" parties (in the sense that I have just indicated), in that few parties facilitate, and many parties obfuscate, the perception of responsibility in party governance.

However, the single most important direct effect of the electoral system on parties per se bears on whether party splitting is penalized and party aggregation rewarded. As we have seen, when a nation-wide two-party system is in place, a plurality system is a powerful factor in maintaining two-partyism. And we have also seen that double-ballot systems can be rendered strongly aggregative. Conversely, unless they are extremely impure, PR systems hardly penalize party fragmentation and party splits, thus allowing for small-to-minute parties. Therefore, whether we have few large parties or a host of small-sized parties is a direct consequence of the electoral system. In short, electoral systems control party numbers (in the manner indicated by my laws).

It is also assumed that a single-member-district system enhances "personalized" politics, whereas list systems of proportional representation reinforce "party-based" or party-centered politics. On the same grounds, majoritarian systems are assumed to lead to constituency-based (local) politics and thus to decentralized parties, whereas PR is assumed to uphold centralized and stronger parties. Yet these seemingly obvious expectations turn out to be fraught with exceptions. This is so because we are now dealing with *indirect* or derivative effects and thus, with distal causality. And the more a causal trajectory or a causal linkage is lengthened, the more it allows for intervening variables. Yes, on its own accord, a single-member-district system does enhance person-based and locality-centered politics. But this tendency can be effectively counteracted by party strength (as in England). And another decisive intervening variable here is who controls the financing of politics: the party as a centralized entity or the candidates themselves. The general point is, then, that the more we move into the area of indirect effects, the more we enter into multicausality and thus the more the electoral system turns out to be one of many causal factors. And I cannot unravel multicausal complexities here.

Are parties in decline? If they are, electoral systems have little say on that. The enfeeblement of parties cannot be ascribed to voting methods. But the effects of electoral systems remain unchanged, as stated, regardless of whether the nature and centrality of parties change.

NOTES

1. Vernon Bogdanor, "Conclusions," in Vernon Bogdanor and David Butler, eds., *Democracy and Elections: Electoral Systems and their Political Consequences* (Cambridge: Cambridge University Press, 1983), 254, 261.

2. Somewhat amazingly, even in the recent *Handbook of Electoral System Design* (Stockholm: International Institute for Democracy and Electoral Assistance, 1997), there is no reference whatsoever to "laws" that may monitor the designing of electoral systems.

3. I quote from Maurice Duverger, *Les Partis Politiques*, 2nd ed. (Paris: Armand Colin, 1954), 247, 269 (my translation).

4. These and further critiques are spelled out in Giovanni Sartori, "The Influence of Electoral Systems: Faulty Laws or Faulty Method?" in Bernard Grofman and Arend Lijphart, eds., *Electoral Laws and Their Political Consequences* (New York; Agathon Press, 1986), 43–45.

5. I discuss them in Giovanni Sartori, *Parties and Party Systems: A Framework for Analysis* (New York: Cambridge University Press, 1976), 307–15; and in Giovanni Sartori, "The Influence of Electoral Systems," in Bernard Grofman and Arend Lijphart, eds., *Electoral Laws and Their Political Consequences,* 45–46, 51, 65–66.

6. Douglas Rae, *The Political Consequences of Electoral Laws* (New Haven: Yale University Press, 1971), 93.

7. Rein Taagepera and Matthew Soberg Shugart, *Seats and Votes: The Effects and Determinants of Electoral Systems* (New Haven: Yale University Press, 1989), 145.

8. Ibid., 145.

9. On all these points, see Giovanni Sartori, "The Influence of Electoral Systems," 49–52.

10. See Giovanni Sartori, "The Influence of Electoral Systems," 55–56; and Giovanni Sartori, *Comparative Constitutional Engineering: An Inquiry into Structures, Incentives, and Outcomes,* 2nd ed. (New York: New York University Press, 1997), 37–38.

11. We generally speak of a "multiplying effect" of PR. This is, however, a manner of speech, for the multiplication is not "caused" by PR but results from the "removal of obstacles" brought about by PR.

12. See Giovanni Sartori, *Comparative Constitutional Engineering,* 33–34, and, for the full argument, Giovanni Sartori, *Parties and Party Systems,* 119–25, 300–19. It is apparent that my relevance criteria apply to parliamentary systems. The number of parties is of lesser importance in presidential systems.

13. I draw them and repeat from Giovanni Sartori, *Comparative Constitutional Engineering,* 40–45.

14. For reasons explained later, I deliberately avoid specifying whether the plurality system in question is of the single-ballot or double-ballot variety. Here the assumption is that one of the two will perform as predicted.

15. To illustrate sketchily, Rule 3 applies nicely to the Canadian case. That is, the rule accounts for the fact that, despite plurality, Canada has a three-four-party format, whereas Rule 4 applies nicely to Ireland and Japan (with small three-to-five member constituencies), to Greece, Spain, and Austria (which also have relatively small constituencies of, respectively, five, six, and seven members), and also helps explain (on account of the exclusion clause) the format of the German Federal Republic.

16. This typology is developed at length in Giovanni Sartori, *Parties and Party Systems,* 125–211 and 273–93. For easier consultation, see Peter Mair, ed., *The West European Party System* (Oxford: Oxford University Press, 1990), a reader that carries the gist of my party theory (316–49).

17. The underlying assumption of the hypothesis is that low polarization corresponds to a unimodal, bell-shaped distribution of opinions and that when most voters cluster around the central, middle area of the political spectrum, party competition is (must rationally be) center-converging. Conversely, high polarization corresponds to a bimodal, two-peaked distribution with a hollow center. This

entails that competition is center-fleeing, and that two-camp entrenchments block the swinging of the pendulum. A recent work bearing on these issues is Reuven Y. Hazan, *Centre Parties: Polarization and Competition in European Parliamentary Democracies* (London: Pinter, 1997).

18. High polarization generally results from ideological distance. However, it can also reflect ethnic and/or religious conflict. Let it be added that polarization can equally be party-triggered, in the sense that in a given system, parties may find divisive and conflictual politics rewarding.

19. See Giovanni Sartori, *Comparative Constitutional Engineering,* 44–45.

20. More precisely, the new Italian electoral system is "mixed" in this proportion: 75 percent of the seats are allocated by plurality and 25 percent on a proportional basis. This majoritarian incompleteness, however, does not affect my argument.

21. This formula is implemented by a proportional compensation (on national lists) for the parties admitted to the run-off that drop out. My expectation is that this arrangement would lead to two-cornered final races and that it would eliminate blackmail at both electoral stages.

22. The percentages are purely illustrative. The advantage of this "premium method" is that it strongly encourages party aggregations (especially if electoral alliances are not permitted). Its standard alternative—a majority premium for the winning electoral coalition—simply fabricates a heterogeneous majority that maintains all its pre-coalition conflicts.

23. Bernard Grofman and Arend Lijphart, eds., *Electoral Laws and Their Political Consequences,* 154–55.

24. Note, incidentally, that the Japanese system was devised to favor medium-sized parties and that its proportionality would have been "normal" had that intent been achieved.

25. To wit, the alternative vote is a "preferential" majority system, used in single-member districts, in which voters use numbers to mark their preferences on the ballot paper. If no candidate achieves an absolute majority of first preferences, votes are reallocated until one candidate attains the required 50 percent majority. The alternative vote is used in Australia.

26. Richard Rose, "Elections and Electoral Systems," in Vernon Bogdanor and David Butler eds., *Democracy and Elections,* 32–33 (my emphasis).

27. For further considerations, see Giovanni Sartori, *Comparative Constitutional Engineering,* 10–12, 61–69.

28. In "The Politics of Electoral Reform" issue of the *International Political Science Review* 16 (January 1995), Introduction.

29. Patrick Dunleavy and Helen Margetts, "Understanding the Dynamics of Electoral Reform," *International Political Science Review* 16 (January 1995): 24.

30. For a detailed account, see Leonardo Morlino, "Is There an Impact? And Where Is It? Electoral Reform and the Party System in Italy," *South European Society & Politics* 2 (Winter 1997): 103–30.

31. In the 1995 Duma election, of the 18 parties running with PR party lists, only four crossed the 5 percent threshold of exclusion. Thus nearly 50 percent of the votes were wasted, producing an enormous overrepresentation of the first four parties. On the other hand, 43 parties competed in the single-member constituencies,

and excessively multicornered races produced winners with 20 percent of the constituency vote. It is apparent that some double-ballot system would have performed better.

32. To be sure, this is not a prediction. Remember, however, that the downfall of the LDP (Liberal Democratic Party) resulted from a split, not from any major defeat. Thus if and to the extent that the LDP holds together as the major single party, as its self-interest recommends, it is well positioned to do very well in the plurality contests and to bring home its proportion (a major one) in the PR arena. Somewhat paradoxically, the new mixed system is easier for the LDP to handle than the earlier one.

33. The IDEA *Handbook of Electoral Design* calls this a "parallel system," thus correctly distinguishing it from the "mixed member proportional" (MMP) system, which is New Zealand's name for the German "personalized proportional system" *(Personalisierte Verhältniswahl)*. I object, however, to the "parallel system" denomination, for labels are required to be descriptive. Since in this case we exactly have a mixed system, why not say so?

34. The 1996 election has produced a two-party coalition government (National Party and New Zealand First) that controls a bare majority (61 seats out of 120) of Parliament. To be sure, very thin majorities also occur in England; but with coalition government, "minimal winning coalitions" generally perform with great difficulty and represent the worse possible solution.

35. The full list of electoral mixes adds up to some 15 countries. In Latin America, the important cases are Venezuela (semi-mixed) and Mexico (mixed-mixed). In Eastern Europe, the peculiar case is Hungary, with a double ballot variety of mixed system. The point, however, is that mixed systems are indeed a mixed bag that must be sorted out.

II

Parties and Party Systems After Reform

6

THE THREE PHASES OF ITALIAN PARTIES

Leonardo Morlino

Leonardo Morlino is professor of political science at the University of Florence and served as president of the Italian Association of Political Science in 1998–2001. He is the author of a hundred essays and books, published in several languages, including Italian, English, Spanish, French, and German. His most recent books include Democracy Between Consolidation and Crisis: Parties, Groups, and Citizens in Southern Europe *(1998) and* Democrazie e democratizzazioni *(forthcoming).*

In the early 1990s, Italian democracy entered a period of upheaval that seems to be over at the beginning of the subsequent decade. Since the 1950s, a highly developed party system has been a key aspect of Italian democracy and a basic condition for its consolidation.[1] This system lingered even when those large, well-developed parties were no longer necessary. Therefore, the major political upheavals of the 1990s had their greatest effects on the parties and the party system. In this chapter, the crisis and transformation of Italian parties will be considered by examining three topics: the state of the parties at the beginning of the postwar democracy; the pre-1990s changes to the parties and the party system; and the political developments of the past decade. A concluding section will seek to explain the changes and relate them to the general experience of West European democracies.

Since the postwar Italian republic was founded in 1948, its party system has been characterized by high organizational complexity. Thanks to many societal and political cleavages[2] and a proportional electoral law with a very low threshold for representation, a large number of parties became established. They included not only the two major parties—the Christian Democratic Party (DC) and the Italian Communist Party (PCI)—but also a number of midsize and small parties spread throughout the ideological spectrum. The half-century duration of this party system juxtaposed the traditional postwar parties with new parties that came out of the movements of the 1960s and early 1970s—Radicals, Greens,

Proletarian Democracy—and localist or "anti-politics" parties of the 1980s, such as the Northern League.

Since there were three groups of parties created in different periods, different models of party organization also coexisted. Even among the traditional, early postwar parties, organizational models varied from mass parties (such as the DC, the PCI, or the Socialists [PSI]) to elite or opinion parties (Republicans, Liberals, and Social Democrats). For the parties formed during the 1970s or after, the problem of organizational change was minor—they never attempted to organize themselves according to the traditional models or never developed a central nonparliamentary organization. Since the problems of political change and organizational decline are paramount only for the traditional parties, their condition in the early 1960s needs to be described.

The Three Mass Parties

At the end of the main consolidation phase in the early 1960s, the party system was clearly institutionalized. By some indicators, the electorate and the number of parties also stabilized. Total electoral volatility was very low: 4.5 percent in 1958 and 7.9 in 1963 (see Table 3 on p. 134).[3] The partisan stability of the electorate was very high: The correlation coefficients (r) between the elections of 1963 and those previous are .95 for PCI, .80 for the PSI, and .90 for the DC.[4] There was very little change in the high degree of fragmentation of the party system: .74 in 1958 and .76 in 1963 (see Table 3).

The party organizations were also well established. The three main parties exhibited at least two different models of a mass party. The DC was a denominational party, already very close to being a catch-all party,[5] and the Communist Party was the classic party of mass integration. The Socialists attempted to imitate the Communist model, although with limited success. A similar mass-party model also shaped the neofascist Italian Social Movement (MSI), which had abandoned the traditionally fascist model of a hierarchically organized mass party with militias, as well.[6] The smaller Republican and Liberal parties were opinion parties, that is, elite moderate parties able to win votes and support by convincing the electors and public about their positions on several specific issues. Despite their recurring references to the socialist mass-party model, the Social Democrats (PSDI) were actually somewhere between a mass party and party of notables.[7] In fact, the organization and character of these small traditional parties were mostly shaped by their participation in government as junior partners to the DC.

There was, however, considerable distance between a party's organizational model and its actual organization. Most of the DC's formal organization existed only on paper.[8] The attempt by party secretary Amintore Fanfani (1954–59) to create a modern mass party with a large

TABLE 1—MEMBERSHIP RATES[1] AND LEVELS[2] IN THE MAIN MASS PARTIES

PARTY	1946	1953	1958	1963	1968	1972	1976	1979	1983	1987	1992	1994	1996
DC/PPI	7.5	10.5	11.3	13.7	13.7	14.1	9.6	9.9	11.4	13.7	7.4	5.4	6.7
	603	1,141	1,410	1,622	1,696	1,823	1,365	1,384	1,384	1,812	n/a	233	173
PSI	8.1	22.7	11.5	11.5	n/a	17.5	14.4	13.2	13.4	11.3	1.0	n/a	n/a
	860	780	487	492	n/a	560	509	473	567	621	51	43	38
PCI/PDS	47.5	34.9	27.1	20.8	17.6	17.4	14.4	15.8	14.8	14.7	12.2	8.9	8.5
	2,068	2,134	1,819	1,616	1,503	1,585	1,814	1,761	1,635	1,508	770	698	675
PRC											5.4	4.9	3.9
											119	113	127
MSI/AN	n/a	n/a	n/a	n/a	n/a	8.3	9.6	9.0	6.6	7.2	8.6	6.2	8.2
			240	200	239	217	174	165	165	181	324	487	
N. LEAGUE											4.1	3.0	1.1
											140	n/a	100
FI												0.1	1.5
												5	n/a

[1] The membership rate is the number of party members as a percentage of the total number of votes cast for the party.
[2] Membership levels are listed in thousands.
Sources: Membership rates for the Communists: Celso Ghini, "Gli inscritti al partito e alla FGCI, 1943/1979," in Massimo Ilardi and Aris Accornero, eds., *Il Partito Comunista Italiano: Struttura e storia dell'organizzazione 1921–1979* (Milan: Annali della Fondazione Feltrinelli, 1982); for the Christian Democrats: Maurizio Rossi "Un partito di 'anime morte'? Il tesseramento democristiano tra mito e realtà," in Arturo Parisi, ed., *Democristiani* (Bologna: Il Mulino, 1979), 27; for the Socialists: Valdo Spini and Sergio Mattana, eds., *I quadri del PSI* (Nuova Guaraldi, Quaderni del Circolo Rosselli, 1981), 56; and from official party sources for membership data in the 1980s and 1990s. Membership levels until 1992, see Luciano Bardi and Leonardo Morlino, "Italy," in Richard S. Katz and Peter Mair, eds., *Party Organizations: A Data Handbook on Party Organizations in Western Democracies, 1960–90* (London: Sage Publications, 1992); after 1992, see official party data.

membership, a central organization, and, above all, a diffuse peripheral structure was largely a failure. In this early period, there was steady growth in DC membership, both in total and as a proportion of its votes (see Table 1 above), but the electoral strength of the party largely lay in the support of Catholic organizations. The DC's heavy dependence on external organizations signaled its weak institutionalization. Membership grew more rapidly in the South than in the North,[9] reflecting the growing importance of clientelistic relationships during this period. Also important was the internal organization of factions. There were at least six during those years, and they had their own de facto structures, including press agencies or media support.[10] Relatedly, a network of notables was very important in recruitment at the local level.

The organization and membership of the Italian Communist Party (PCI) was completely different.[11] In the new statute of 1957 (following the 1956 Hungarian uprising), the rights of members were stressed, but the key Leninist-Gramscian features of the organization were basically unchanged. The concept of "democratic centralism" remained fundamental. Decisions were made by the leaders, from above, but the members had to be convinced. The mechanism of appointment of party officials from above also remained the same. In addition, any activity aimed at the formation of autonomous factions within the party continued to be strictly forbidden.

Although the PCI's leadership was as dominant as that of the DC, in the PCI the "activists"—the most ideologically driven and active militants—were the party's greatest asset. These activists did much of the work of the party for free, including running campaigns locally and creating and distributing propaganda.[12] Organizationally, the Communists had a capillary network at the local level, grounded in cells and sections arranged along functional and territorial lines. Yet the cells that should have been flourishing—those in the workplace—never fully developed.[13] Additionally, instead of carrying out its originally intended activities, such as strikes, protests, riots, and even revolution, the PCI took up peaceful democratic actions, including electoral campaigns and the parliamentary representation of worker and peasant interests. Thus what began as a Leninist party was transformed into a classic integration party.

This organizational transformation was compounded by a steady decline in Communist Party membership (see Table 1 on the previous page). The ratio of party members to party voters, though still higher than those of the other mass parties, was also clearly dropping. By the 1960s, the passionate large-scale mobilization of the late 1940s had disappeared. In addition, in this period there was a clear perception that the moment of a possible radical social revolution was over.

Another difference between the DC and the PCI was the role played by ancillary organizations. Catholic organizations supported the DC electorally and politically but retained their autonomy. The PCI, on the other hand, was able to create partisan, peasant, women's, and cultural organizations that were highly dependent on the party. The strength of these groups helped both to generate the PCI's strong electoral showing in the 1950s and to prevent the party from becoming socially isolated.[14]

The third major mass party of the period, the Italian Socialist Party (PSI), had some organizational features of its own. Although PSI leader Rodolfo Morandi attempted to give the party Leninist characteristics in the late 1940s and early 1950s, these did not last when the decision was made to enter a governing coalition with the DC in the early 1960s. While formally similar to the PCI, the organization of the PSI had local units structured territorially, without any success in building communist-style cells. The reduced grassroots participation increased the importance of the provincial federations, which became the bases for the power of local notables. These notables developed a number of important factions that after 1957 became more and more autonomously organized.

By 1960, the PSI's membership was fairly stable (see Table 1 on the previous page) after a sharp decline between 1955 and 1957. However, the PSI was organizationally weaker, with a much lower ratio of militants to members: 1:50 compared to 1:23 in the DC and 1:18 in the PCI. The

PSI also lacked the PCI's strong ancillary organizations. The presence of the Socialists as minority partners in many of the Communist organizations was merely a remnant of the links between the two parties that existed until the mid-1950s.[15]

Party Staffing, Financing, and Parliamentary Components

Party staffing. Among the mass parties, a more developed organization and greater membership correlate with a larger party staff, more party financing, and a weaker and more dependent parliamentary component. While no precise figures on party staff and finance exist from the early 1960s, Galli puts the whole staffs of PCI and DC officially at a few thousand, as compared to about one thousand working for all other parties.[16] Unofficially, however, a large number of civil servants had been working for their respective parties for years in "red areas," in Catholic regions, and in the South. All three parties benefited from this and thus, in a clientelistic fashion, filled government positions in the communes and provinces.

Party finance. In the absence of any state subvention or law on campaign financing (issues that would be first addressed in 1974 and 1985, respectively), there are no official figures from this period on the amount of money expended for party activities. Nevertheless, some funding sources were well known at the time and have been recently confirmed by documents and witnesses. For the DC, most party financing came from the so-called black funds of public economic agencies, which went to party branches and internal factions. Another source was the private contributions of industrial entrepreneurs, mainly from the oil sector and construction firms. For the Communists, massive financial support came directly and indirectly (mainly through import-export firms) from the Soviet Union, enabling an enormous party apparatus and the Communist hegemony in ancillary organizations where the Socialists were also present. From the end of the 1940s until 1956–57, the Communists generously financed the PSI, thereby maintaining close relations between the two parties. When the Autonomist faction gained control of the PSI in the late 1950s and broke with the Communists, the PSI had a serious financial crisis, [17] only resolved when the party entered the center-left cabinets in the 1960s and gained sources of financial support similar to those of the DC.

The parliamentary party. In the early 1960s, the three major parties varied on how much autonomy they granted to their parliamentary components. The 1957 PCI statute, in fact, mentions neither members of parliament (MPs) nor parliamentary groups. In the PSI, parliamentary group presidents were allowed to participate in the meetings of the

Socialist Central Committee, but without the right to vote. For the Christian Democrats, however, MPs were ex-officio participants in national party conferences, a number of them were members of the DC National Council, and the presidents of parliamentary groups were members of the national executive. By statute, however, the DC's parliamentary party was dependent on the central party.

During this period, all three parties required a period of activity in the party before being elected to the Parliament. The longest period of socialization was in the PCI; a shorter period was common in the DC, where some MPs (about 15 percent) were elected without having held any party office; and an intermediate period was common among the Socialists.[18] The party with the greatest overlap between party leadership and parliamentary membership was still the DC, while the PCI had the lowest.[19]

The same pattern holds for the role of parliamentary leadership. The leaders of the PCI's parliamentary groups had their bases in the party, they were appointed by central party bodies without any open competition or participation of the parliamentary groups, and parliamentary leadership positions were not relevant to party leadership struggles. The DC was similar in the first aspect, but there was competition for parliamentary leadership positions and the parliamentary groups had a say in the process. Moreover, in the DC (and to a large extent the PSI), the party had several leaders, and parliamentary leadership positions became an additional resource in internal competition for party offices.[20]

Smaller Parties

An important difference between the neofascist Italian Social Movement (MSI) and the other small parties must be stressed. Despite its relatively small electoral support (averaging 5.3 percent in the 1950s), the party statutes described a mass party, not a militia party of the fascist type. The MSI's relationship with the fascist experience was reflected in ideology and leadership rather than in organization. In fact, its organization was similar to that of the Socialists, with local sections, provincial federations, a Central Committee, and a strong central secretary and national leadership. The MSI also had ancillary organizations, such as youth, student, and veterans' groups. In all of these features the MSI simply paralleled the three larger Italian mass parties, although the provincial secretary had greater power on his federation and at the same time more dependence from the center. In the mid-1950s the secretary claimed to have half a million members in 3,700 sections (although reliable data are lacking). Later figures were much lower, above all during the crisis of the early 1960s. Also as in the PSI, the dependence of parliamentary groups on the party leadership was well established during the 1950s.[21]

During the 1950s, the combined mean electoral strength of the Liberals, the Republicans, and the Social Democrats—recurring cabinet partners of the DC—was slightly under 10 percent.[22] In spite of their statutes, redrafted during this decade, all three were opinion parties with very influential parliamentary groups. Moreover, all of them had youth, women's, and university organizations (which sometimes conflicted with the central party); all had a mass tradition in a few areas; and all published newspapers. At the same time, however, they had a very limited number of members (under 200,000 for the Liberals and the Social Democrats in 1956–58, and fewer than 50,000 for the Republicans in 1963).

Parties and Society

One common measure of the relationship between parties and civil society is party identification.[23] Many factors may explain identification with or membership in a party, including ideology, party polarization, party propaganda, and clientelism. Each of these factors is important to understanding the strength of Italian party identification at the end of the 1950s. In a 1956 Doxa survey, 76 percent of Italians declared their identification with a party. Generally speaking, however, the data on party identification in Italy are poor. Thus it is more effective to analyze the actual network of relationships between the parties and various sectors of civil society.

It is well known that the 1950s were a "decade of political society,"[24] when parties dominated Italian civil society. The main elements of this pattern of domination were the relationship between parties and religious organizations, particularly between the DC and Catholic organizations; the particularistic relationship between parties and unorganized social groups or individuals; and the relationship between parties and interest groups, particularly business organizations and trade unions.

During the first decades of Italian democracy, the DC was defined by its closeness to various religious organizations and the Vatican. The Catholic subculture and strong religious attitudes in the North were the core of Christian Democratic electoral strength;[25] in fact, several authors labeled it a confessional party. For the leftist parties, Marxist ideology performed the same function as religion: linking a number of civil-society sectors—during this period the lower classes—to the parties.

Clientelism was at the core of the particularistic ties between some parties (such as the DC, the Liberals, and the Social Democrats) and civil society in parts of the South. This system was basically set up in the 1950s with the establishment and enlargement of the public economic sector, the creation of the Cassa per il Mezzogiorno (a public fund for development in the South), and the passage of various bills.[26]

In the agricultural sector, the association of large and middle-sized landowners, Confagricoltura, needed to defend the interests of its members in the new democratic context and ended up approaching the government party.[27] At the same time, however, it sought to develop a privileged relationship with other rightist parties[28] and thereby to apply pressure on the DC both internally and externally. The association of small landowners, Coldiretti, was also closely connected with the DC, having been created by the party with the help of the Church. Although the DC's de facto delegation of agricultural policy to Coldiretti may indicate otherwise, the association was in fact dominated by the party. Indeed, the presence of Coldiretti members in the Ministry of Agriculture and in parliamentary committees was paralleled by the presence of DC party members in the executive bodies of the association.

In the industrial sector the DC also dominated, through its penetration of public economic agencies and the marginalization of organized left groups. During the 1950s, the DC dominance of the industrialists became clear when the business association, Confindustria, suffered organizational splits and a decline in both membership and political initiative. At this point, the DC was weaker in terms of parliamentary seats but considerably stronger on other levels, due to the expansion of the public sector and the management of credit facilities by the public banks, as well as the demobilization and fragmentation of entrepreneurs.

With the trade union sector, although the DC dominated the Catholic union (the Italian Confederation of Labor Unions, or CISL), there was also some degree of union penetration of the DC at the parliamentary level through the creation of an intraparty faction. Nevertheless, the autonomy of the DC meant that it did not passively submit to the union's policy positions. A confirmation of the party's domination of the trade union is the fact that during this period, the latter never took up a clearly autonomous position in the area of industrial relations. Only in the early 1960s did one see a clearer differentiation of their respective roles.

The influence of the parties of the left in their union (the Italian General Confederation of Labor, or CGIL) or that of the Republicans in the Italian Union of Labor (UIL) hardly needs explanation. There was a common belief in a certain role for the union in the party that ensured party dominance in the formulation of policy. Thus both the UIL and the CGIL were subjected to the marginality of the parties to which they were linked. The unions did not even consider trying to avoid party domination because it allowed them access to the party electoral lists and to the parliamentary arena in general. Moreover, one of the main channels of leftist party activism was precisely participation in trade-union activity.

Expansion of the public sector was crucial to party–interest group relations. In the agricultural sector, the Federconsorzi, a network of public agencies to help people active in the entire sector in their various activities (purchasing of seeds, agricultural appliances and machines, selling of products, and so on), as well as agrarian reform agencies, public pension agencies, and the Cassa per il Mezzogiorno conditioned all relations between the incumbent DC and the interest associations. The same applied to the industrial sector. The relationship between government parties and entrepreneurs or trade unions was defined by the role of such public-sector agencies as the Institute for Industrial Reconstruction, the Ministry for State Investments, and the Cassa per il Mezzogiorno in the industrial sector, as well as the public banks.[29] For ideological reasons, the left supported the expansion of the public sector, not understanding until too late the major political side effects.[30]

By the end of the 1950s there was a well-defined network of relationships between parties and interest groups, and more generally between parties and civil society. This was the Italian style of party government, characterized not only by party colonization of the public sector and penetration and control of civil society but also by party "occupation" of the bureaucracy and (with the continual replication of similar coalition governments as a result of a highly proportional electoral system) the absence of any possibility of alternation in government.[31]

Changes to the Major Parties Before the 1990s[32]

In the early 1960s, the DC created a new center-left coalition government, with the PSI in a pivotal role. Consequently, competition in the governmental party system grew, creating a greater need for material and political resources. In order to maintain and strengthen their organizations, party leaders (and parties) began drawing on resources in the public sector, which was booming as a result of strong economic growth and the importance of public-sector development in the center-left program. This, in turn, reinforced the dependence of civil society on the parties. Another important change was the implementation of regionalization in the early 1970s, which contributed to the emergence of more autonomous, regionally based intraparty groups.

Party memberships. During the 1960s, 1970s, and 1980s, total party membership declined by only about 3 percent, to about 4,150,000. Even allowing for the considerable expansion of Italy's electorate (by about 28 percent between 1963 and 1992), this reflected a remarkable resilience of Italian parties. By the 1990s, however, membership in the three most important parties collapsed. This sudden drop can be explained by the gradual reduction of party alignment with the Catholic and communist subcultures—a development that unfolded gradually but became evident in the 1990s. The strong grip of the parties on the political system and on some key elements of civil society may have been the main reason for the delay.

The evolution of DC membership illustrates the sudden nature of the Italian party crisis. Membership figures seesawed throughout the period, reflecting the party's uneven organizational fortunes, with highs of over 1.8 million in 1973 and 1988 and a low of just under 1.1 million in 1977. In December 1992, Secretary Mino Martinazzoli announced his decision to "re-found" the party by erasing membership records and asking all prospective members (old and new) to file new applications. The projected reform also attempted to implement a regionalization of the party's organization. Efforts to improve the party's machinery during the 1970s and the 1980s had disappointing results, but they confirm that organizational defects predated the crisis of the 1990s by at least two decades.

This period also saw the progressive erosion of the DC's privileged relationship with the Catholic subculture and a parallel process of secularization. Nonterritorial branches, called *sezioni ambiente,* were created to replace Catholic organizations as party contacts with civil society. In 1991, however, these accounted for little more than 5 percent of the DC's 13,700 branches. In fact, by the mid-1980s, many DC branches were little more than empty shells, with no permanent quarters let alone telephones or other equipment, while others were inactive save at election time.[33]

Party organization. The strength of the DC's formal organization also appears to have been inflated. While delegates to the party's National Congress were allocated on a regional basis according to the party's share of the electorate, they were nominated and elected in regional congresses on the basis of registered membership: hence the powerful incentive to inflate such figures. Indeed, the notion of membership in the DC was very weak. Ordinary members had very little contact with the party's organization or participation in any of its activities. The burden rested mostly on the party activists, with five or six in each branch. Many of them held salaried public offices, allowing them to work almost full-time for the party and thus greatly reducing the party's need for permanent staff.

As for the official staff of the party, it decreased from about 800 to 500 in the late 1980s under pressure from the economic crisis. At the same time, diminishing electoral support and growing judicial and public scrutiny of civil-service appointments decreased the traditional parties' opportunities to use public office holders (especially at the local level) and civil servants as party activists. The result for the DC—as well as for the other traditional parties—was unavoidable organizational streamlining.

For the Communists, perhaps the most important postwar organizational change was the disappearance of the cell as the basic organizational unit. At the 1979 party congress, only about 2,000 factory cells were represented, the *sezione* having become the basic territorial unit. This change marked the transition to a much more pragmatic posture, from a mass-integration to a catch-all party. The notion of membership underwent a parallel evolution. In the 1940s, every member was a militant, and in the mid-1950s at least 350,000 communists still had leadership functions.[34] By the late 1960s, however, most party activities were carried out by only a handful of members in each of the 12,000–13,000 branches,[35] and a decade later the PCI's membership was described simply as *iscritti* (literally "enrolled"), a status that could easily be further downgraded to "sympathizers" or just "voters."[36] The rising red tide of the mid-1970s probably attracted "exchange" voters who sought personal advantages through membership, only to give it up once it was clear the party had lost its bid for power.[37] Yet there are deeper reasons for the PCI's organizational and electoral decline. Italy's industrial and agricultural populations—historically the PCI's largest constituencies—have been shrinking steadily, and the party's insistence on preserving its privileged relationship with these groups could only harm it in the long term. The party's rate of attracting new members was almost halved, and its membership composition changed drastically; as students disappeared, industrial and agricultural workers decreased, while pensioners and housewives became more prominent.

The PSI's structure changed little in the 1960s through the mid-1970s, despite its move from opposition to government and its consequent organizational troubles (including the separation of a left-wing faction and the merger, and subsequent split, with the Social Democrats). Power remained concentrated in the hands of faction leaders. PSI factions, unlike those of the DC, never represented a channel for the party to establish links with selected sectors of civil society, and the competition among them hampered the party's ability to attract members.[38] The relative importance of the party's geographic (the industrial North) and functional (the working class) constituencies continued to decline.

In the PSI, the apparently considerable changes implemented during Bettino Craxi's secretariat (1976–93) were mostly meant to consolidate his leadership rather than to give the party a more efficient and flexible organization, and they proved insufficient to prevent the PSI's downfall in the 1990s. The grassroots remained very weak and were active only at election time.[39] Weak participation and personalism strengthened the provincial federations and favored the consolidation of local factions. If not for the strong leadership of Craxi, the party might have become a quasi-federal organization. Ironically, Craxi's success was partially rooted in his political capabilities, but it was even more the result of the general expectation of PSI electoral success in light of the Communist decline and DC weakness.

Party finance. Only by exploring the complex and often illegal funding relationships that existed between political parties and organized (or even individual) interests can one understand Italian party organizations during the 1960s–80s. Although official data are inadequate and unofficial information is still very difficult to obtain, we can surmise that Italian party organizations were enormously expensive. In 1974, a new party financing law standardized and made public party budgets. The law prohibited party financing by public (wholly or partially state-owned) companies. By establishing strict and cumbersome regulations and procedures, the law actually made *legal* contributions very difficult as well. Moreover, the law never achieved its major goals. Political corruption and the involvement of public companies in illegal party financing have not disappeared and may have increased enormously. The law also created a party financing fund that could only be increased by legislation—a major problem when the costs of campaigning rose dramatically after the mid-1970s, due to both the "media revolution" (allowing previously banned private broadcasting) and the "office revolution" (with expensive communication technologies like computers and fax machines). Finally, although officially Italian parties were sparsely staffed and salaries low, staff expenses were the only expenditure item to reveal real increases in all three major parties' official budgets. During the 1980s, the rising expense of campaigning coincided with increasing competition inside the governing coalition between the DC and the PSI, since by then the Communists were completely legitimized.

In this competitive context, parties could hardly afford to give up funding from public companies; hence the explosion since the 1970s of the *tangenti* (kickback) system. A study of political corruption cases states that, between 1979 and 1987, Italian parties received on average at least 60 billion lire per year (in 1986 lire, that is, roughly US$45 million) in illegal funding, equal to about 75 percent of the total public funds for parliamentary parties.[40] After the unprecedented crackdown following the *mani pulite* (clean hands) inquiry started in January 1992, revised estimates revealed the total amount illegally obtained by Italian political parties to be 3.4 trillion lire per year, at least ten times the total official income of all Italian political parties (about 280 billion in 1989).[41]

Organizational changes. Despite the continuing centralized control of parliamentary personnel recruitment, a number of changes occurred. After the mid-1970s, the composition of parliamentary parties became less reflective of parties' links with particular social classes. More than half of all MPs were now professionals; even among Communist MPs, farmers and workers had all but disappeared by the end of the 1980s. Intra-elite relationships and formal power structures also changed dramatically.

The most radical transformation occurred in the PCI. However, its monolithic structure remained unchanged at the top elite level long after the Leninist model had been largely abandoned at the grassroots. The absolute dominance of the PCI's top executive bodies persisted. Although the PCI often declared the Parliament to be the Italian political system's central institution,[42] the parliamentary party constantly remained in a subordinate position. This subordination was visible in many respects: First, while there was relatively low parliamentary participation in the party's executive bodies, top party executives monopolized the party's parliamentary leadership positions. Second, national executive bodies remained solely responsible for parliamentary candidate selection. Third, there always were sharp differences in seniority between backbenchers and frontbenchers (the only ones normally allowed to spend more than two terms in parliament).[43] Fourth, at any given time, no less than 70 percent of PCI members of parliament were professional politicians and therefore dependent on the party apparatus for their very livelihood. Finally, even when one of the two parliamentary groups sought greater autonomy, it was nullified by Italy's perfect bicameralism, because of the total absence of coordination between the groups in the Senate and the Chamber of Deputies.[44]

Although the PCI remained formally committed to democratic centralism until 1990, alterations in its organization appeared at least six years earlier.[45] After its unprecedented victory in the 1975 local and regional elections, the party had to recruit a huge number of new local and regional executives, and their diverse socializations created tensions.[46] Democratic centralism, however, managed to survive until the mid-1980s, when new procedures allowed groups comprising at least 20 percent of the regional congress delegates to nominate national congress delegations; this paved the way for the transformation of internal "tendencies" into factions.[47] In order to give each new faction adequate representation, the Central Committee kept expanding (from 128 members in 1960 to 357 in 1990), losing its executive connotations. The Committee's new representative character was also evident in the deliberate emphasis on gender representation—the share of women grew from 8 percent in 1960 to one-third in 1990.[48]

In the Socialist Party, on the other hand, stratarchic elements and factionalism were always present and were formalized in 1959 with the adoption of proportional representation in all internal party elections. Between 1976 and the early 1990s, however, the party's power structure was profoundly modified by Bettino Craxi's personal leadership.[49] During this period, the PSI changed from a mass party into what has been described as a quasi-monocratic party—the qualifier made necessary by the clear division of labor between the top and intermediate levels of the party leadership.[50] The consolidation of Craxi's leadership was evident in a number of institutional changes containing the disruptive factional fights that characterized the party prior to 1976. The modifications included direct election of the party secretary by the national congress; the creation of a new six-member inner cabinet making all important decisions; the transformation of the 141-member Central Committee into a 473-member National Assembly; and a gradual tripling in size of the National Executive (to 110 members in 1993), coupled with a progressive decrease in its powers.[51]

The growing concentration of power at the top of the PSI was paralleled by the growing autonomy of provincial federations. Under Craxi, the party became increasingly oriented to the electorate. Elected positions grew in importance, especially at the local level, due to the party's pivotal position between the DC and the PCI on most local and regional councils. The consolidation of local leadership by PSI administrators was the price the national leadership had to pay for the social pact at the national level and for electoral support. The success of Craxi's national strategy— to develop an inner circle of leaders whose fortunes were clearly connected to his own—was not matched by a parallel success at the regional level. The Italian political system's two-tiered power structure was mirrored by a two-tiered resource flow, which gave the PSI's periphery almost complete political and financial autonomy. Although the national leadership had a free hand in making the major strategic decisions and even in drawing up parliamentary candidate lists, they seldom exercised any influence on local government alliances or even decisions. Between 1974 and 1987, official financial transfers from the party center to the periphery declined from 38.1 percent to 15.6 percent of the total budget, but the local groups were unfazed.[52] The ever-expanding "alternative" party-financing system funneled sufficient resources to meet regional demands and provided enough rewarding private-sector positions to accommodate the personal ambitions of regional PSI leaders.

The Although the DC still maintained some mass-party characteristics, it was the Italian party that most closely approached the catch-all party model.[53] The growing importance of the parliamentary component and the unquestionable importance of internal factions (as linkages between the party and selected sectors of society) reflected the party's electorate-centered orientation. These characteristics were reinforced after 1960, especially in 1964 with the adoption of proportional representation in the National Committee elections, thereby institutionalizing factions.[54] Further changes that year increased the importance of provincial federations in determining parliamentary candidacies and consequently strengthening the autonomy of the parliamentary component. Moreover, DC leaders always had difficulty getting the full support of elected party officials, including at the national level. After the 1976 parliamentary elections, which saw a unique 37 percent turnover in parliament, DC parliamentary groups became more autonomous, as demonstrated in early 1978 by their strong opposition to the Secretariat's strategy of alliance with the PCI.

The DC's lack of internal discipline appears to explain why its leaders recurrently attempted to strengthen the party's organization, but reform attempts could alternatively be seen as responses to the demands of disgruntled factions or even frustrated younger cohorts. The demand of young groups explains a radical faction reshuffling in 1975–76, yet this did not bring about significant turnover in the party's representative and executive bodies. Moreover, the party's formal leadership structure was never significantly altered. Again, factional dynamics were crucial in the DC elite's internal power relations. In the mid- to late-1970s, Benigno Zaccagnini tried to build up the party organization's intermediate and local levels, hoping to replace the factions and to better reflect the new, increasingly secular image the party intended to project. The party's organization, however, remained dominated by the personal networks and electoral machines of local notables.

Parties and Society Before the 1990s

The nature of the relationship between parties and social groups has changed, especially since the late 1960s. This was the consequence of the growth of civil society, which caused or simply coincided with a decline of ideology and a growth of independent opinion in the Italian electorate.[55] It could be argued that Italy's multiparty system delayed the development of catch-all orientations toward the electorate, but reliable time series data on party identification are sorely lacking. In one of the few studies on this topic, Renato Mannheimer stresses that, on his five-point scale, less than one-quarter of his respondents fell into the two highest identification categories while another quarter qualified as weak identifiers.[56] Since the 1950s, there seem to have been *qualitative* changes in Italian electoral behavior loosely comparable to changes in party identification. Renato Mannheimer and Giacomo Sani affirm that opinion voters (those who vote on the basis of their opinions on specific issues and not on some party identification), practically nonexistent during the 1950s, had become much more numerous than other kind of voters.[57] Based on other data, however, Roberto Cartocci concludes that identified voters (that is, those who maintain a strong party identification[58]) still prevail in the Center-North and exchange voters, who receive clientelistic rewards for their votes, are dominant in the Center-South, whereas opinion voters are only of marginal importance.[59]

Following the upheavals of 1968 and the often spontaneous factory actions, industrial relations became the most important field for labor action.[60] This gave the unions greater autonomy and strength, with several important consequences: more independence from political parties; the near-unification of the three major confederations (CGIL, CISL, and UIL); and the development of an autonomous role in relationships with the government and the state. These developments actually laid the bases for a possible, but always problematic, separation between unions and political parties.

On the whole, however, during the 1980s the PCI's hegemony over the unified workers movement was undoubtedly broken. Prime Minister Craxi's unprecedented decision to modify by decree the *scala mobile* (the cost-of-living adjustment) split the union movement and, within the CGIL, split the Communist component from the Catholic and Socialist ones. Subsequently, the failure of the national referendum, strongly favored by PCI, to overturn the decree confirmed the end of Communist hegemony in the labor movement. The late 1980s also saw the emergence of powerful autonomous unions and COBAS (*comitati di base,* or grass-roots committees), which organized mainly teachers in public schools, civil servants, and railroad workers.

In the mid-1970s, DC attempts to interfere in the nomination of Confindustria's president caused a split within that organization that was hidden only by the successful candidacy of the prestigious CEO of Fiat, Gianni Agnelli.[61] This marked a turning point, as Agnelli and his successor, Guido Carli, often bypassed the government and the parties to negotiate directly with the labor unions. The most important product of this approach was the 1975 creation of the *scala mobile.* Confindustria also established a privileged link with the Republican Party, believing it to be an independent defender of "efficiency and competition against the centralization and bureaucratization of the economy."[62] In practice, Republican ministers took up the role, previously held by Liberals, of presenting Confindustria point of view to the government.

Yet the DC's dominant economic position was not endangered. The agricultural association, Coldiretti, remained supportive, though its importance gradually declined as Italy's agricultural sector shrank.[63] The DC's power over the economy, however, was mainly the sum of its numerous links with individual firms or entrepreneurs' associations; these made up for the agricultural decline and the more distant relationship with Confindustria.

The secularization and decline of ideology during the 1960s strongly conditioned the parties' relations with their various ancillary organizations. When the importance and membership of traditional organizations declined with the gradual erosion of subcultures, parties tried to develop new structures and strategies to "open up" to new social actors and movements. The DC all but lost its most important link with civil society, Catholic Action, whose membership dropped from 3.3 million in the mid-1960s to 550,000 two decades later and whose positions on crucial issues—such as the 1974 divorce and 1981 abortion referenda—were not as supportive as the party had expected. The party's relationship with the Catholic Association of Italian Workers (ACLI) followed a different pattern, but the results were similar. The ACLI also suffered a serious membership drop, due to splits in the 1970s precisely over the movement's ties with the DC. While the relative positions of the PSI and the PCI within the various leftist organizations remained basically unchanged, the PCI's hegemonic influence declined considerably during the 1980s. Moreover, membership in many of these organizations, rather than an expression of political sympathy for the sponsoring party, was very often instrumental, bringing, for example, discounts on cinema and theater tickets.

All in all, the traditional parties' links with civil society were declining, in qualitative if not always quantitative terms. Young people in particular resisted regimentation in the traditional parties' organizational structures. Once again, the PCI suffered the most, with membership in the Federation of Communist Italian Youth plunging in the 20 years following the 1968 protests. A similar decline was registered among MSI youth affiliates. The DC and PSI fared better, but the more secular DC youth movement was vigorously challenged by Comunione e Liberazione, a 60,000-strong, extremely militant Catholic youth organization.[64]

Until the 1970s, the Italian parties both published official party newspapers and controlled some important "independent" newspapers. In fact, the moderate or even conservative line of many of these newspapers was guaranteed by party-sponsored appointments of editors and journalists. A 1976 Constitutional Court ruling ended the state monopoly of radio and television broadcasts, but it did not substantially change the relationship between parties and the media.[65] The ruling permitted an overnight explosion of private local TV stations, which by the mid-1980s were concentrated into three national networks owned by media tycoon Silvio Berlusconi. His successful attempt to go beyond the limits posed by the Constitutional Court was made possible by Bettino Craxi's personal support. With this move, Craxi redressed the TV media balance, which was at the time heavily pro-DC.[66]

Thus, on the whole, the consolidated *partitocrazia* persisted throughout the 1960s and 1970s. In fact, party control of huge sectors of the Italian economy expanded considerably during this period and had deep historical roots. The complex network of party-controlled holding companies and their subsidiaries (banks, social security, and welfare agencies) was created during the Fascist era. Through this control, the DC created an autonomous power base, whose continuing expansion permitted the party to share it with other governing parties. In the mid-1980s, public companies accounted for about 30 percent of sales and 50 percent of investment, and state-controlled banks accounted for at least three-quarters of Italian banking.

Old and New Parties Since the Early 1990s

Since the early 1990s, Italian political parties have radically transformed, though some had begun to change earlier. Several have undergone a major facelift; others have virtually disappeared; and brand new parties have emerged. The key changes occurred in 1991, 1994, and 1998–99 (see Table 2 on the following page), but they can be traced back to the growth of local lists and environmentalist groups in the mid-1980s.[67]

The PCI was the first party to undergo a crisis (especially in electoral performance) and a profound transformation. This gradual process came to a head with the fall of the Berlin Wall in November 1989. However,

TABLE 2—ELECTORAL CHANGES (1987–99)[1]

PARTY	1987	1992	1994	1996	1999
PROLETARIAN DEMOCRACY	1.7	-	-	-	-
COMMUNIST REFOUNDATION	-	5.6	6.0	8.6	4.3
ITALIAN COMMUNISTS	-	-	-	-	2.0
DEMOCRATS OF THE LEFT	26.6	16.1	20.4	21.1	17.4
THE NET	-	1.9	1.9	-	-
GREENS	2.5	2.8	2.7	2.5	1.8
CHRISTIAN DEMOCRACY (DC)/PPI	34.3	29.7	11.1	6.8	4.3
LISTA PRODI-DEMOCRATS	-	-	-	-	7.7
SOUTH TYROLEAN PEOPLE'S PARTY (SVP)	0.5	0.5	-	-	0.5
REPUBLICAN PARTY (PRI)	3.7	4.4	-	-	0.5
ITALIAN RENEWAL (DINI)	-	-	-	4.3	1.1
DEMOCRATIC ALLIANCE (AD)	-	-	1.2	-	-
RADICAL PARTY/LISTA BONINO	2.6	1.2	3.5	1.9	8.5
SOCIALIST PARTY (PSI)	14.3	13.6	2.2	-	2.0
SOCIAL DEMOCRATS (PSDI)	2.9	2.7	-	-	-
SEGNI PACT	-	-	4.7	-	-
CHRISTIAN DEMOCRATIC UNION (CDU)	-	-	-	5.8	2.1
CHRISTIAN DEMOCRATIC CENTER (CCD)	-	-	-	-	2.6
FORZA ITALIA (GO ITALY)	-	-	21.0	20.6	25.2
LOMBARD/NORTHERN LEAGUE	1.3	8.7	19.4	10.1	4.5
LIBERALS (PLI)	2.1	2.8	-	-	-
SOCIAL MOVEMENT/NATIONAL ALLIANCE	5.9	5.4	13.5	15.7	10.3
SOCIAL MOVEMENT-FIAMMA TRICOLORE	-	-	-	0.9	1.6
OTHER PARTIES	1.6	4.6	3.6	1.7	3.6

[1] Percentages are Lower Chamber proportional results.
Source: Official returns by Italian Ministry of Interior.

the integration of the PCI into Italian democracy began with two previous events: the "historic compromise" of 1973, which aimed to form an alliance with Catholic forces and even with the DC; and the PCI's support for Prime Minister Giulio Andreotti during a difficult period of terrorist attacks in 1978–79. In spite of these openings, the PCI's links to the Soviet Union were always viewed by some as a sign of the party's antidemocratic nature. The disintegration of the Soviet Union in 1991 eclipsed these fears but at the same time confirmed the bankruptcy of the communist alternative.

In February 1991, the PCI adopted a new name, the Democratic Party of the Left (PDS), and new logos.[68] A more orthodox communist segment created a splinter party, the Communist Refoundation, with roughly one-third the electoral size of the PDS. PDS membership continued to decline in the early 1990s. Organizational inadequacy and strategic ambiguity, however, may be responsible for at least some of the declining electoral fortunes and for the party's inability to redirect its links with civil society. The result was an entrenchment of local interests, and consequently, the progressive pulverization of a party structure that had seemed monolithic.[69]

The other important change was the formation, growth, and success of the Northern League, whose first party conference was held in February 1991. A product of various Leagues and other local lists from Veneto, Lombardy, and Piedmont, this new party occupied the space left vacant by Catholic culture following secularization in those regions. It is rooted in precise territorial identities and has successfully exploited the tax-payers' protest and other localist, anticentralist, antiparty, and anti-South positions. The ability of the Northern middle classes to express these various discontents electorally was facilitated by the disappearance of the communist-anticommunist cleavage after 1989.[70] Always higher than the European average, popular dissatisfaction in Italy grew significantly at the end of the 1980s, mainly due to the economic crisis.[71]

These considerations also help to explain the crisis of the DC, which came to a head in 1992–94 as the result of two other factors: the new electoral laws and the *mani pulite* anticorruption investigation led by Milanese prosecutors. The most interesting effect of the new electoral law (which introduced a much more majoritarian system) was the "anticipated reaction." Even before March 1994—when the first elections under the new law were to take place—internal divisions split the DC into different groups, as the members anticipated the anticenter, bi-polarizing impact of the reform.[72] The powerful delegitimizing impact of the *mani pulite* followed from the spectacular media coverage and the 1992–94 follow-up to the investigation, which showed how pervasive corruption and illegal party financing were. The DC leadership was closely identified with corruption and, even more dramatically, accused of colluding with organized crime in the South. The complex network of illicit relationships was integral to the DC's power base and could not be spontaneously eliminated. In the early 1990s, the secession of part of the Sicilian DC created the Network, an anti-Mafia Catholic group, but had little effect on the rest of the party. In 1992, Mario Segni's formation of the Populars for Reform showed more promise, but its greater appeal was probably due to the new climate in the country. A constituent assembly was called in July 1993 to reform the party and renew its leadership (by denying the right to participate in party activities to anyone involved in the investigations), but all decisions were postponed until a party congress to be held in late 1993. Following the replacement of the party secretary in 1993 and a long intraparty struggle, a new Italian Popular Party (PPI) was born in January 1994, an event that was preceded and accompanied by schisms on both the left and right.

A similar story may be told about the fortunes of the Socialist Party. Its crisis and breakdown resulted directly from the *mani pulite* inves-tigations, which had three major effects: First, they decapitated the party's leadership. In addition to Craxi (who was charged with corruption and other criminal violations for laws on party finance), the investigations forced out Claudio Martelli and many other party leaders among the 66 indicted PSI parliamentarians. Second, they dried up the party's main sources of revenue, forcing many local headquarters, especially in the North, to close or downsize. Third, the investigations utterly shocked PSI voters and caused their unprecedented flight of support, once again predominantly in the North. The PSI vote plummeted from 13.6 percent in 1992 to 2.2 percent in 1994 (see Table 2 on p. 126). As a result of the investigations, the post-Craxi PSI immediately lost its monocratic character. Following Craxi's resignation in early 1993, the party witnessed a major struggle for a new secretary and the departure of some leaders to join new parties before breaking up completely following the 1994 elections. After 1992–93, the Craxian model of party was just a historical remembrance and the final lost opportunity for the Socialists.

Partly as a result of its strong performance in the local by-elections in 1993, the right-wing MSI seized the political initiative and created the National Alliance (AN) with the support of some defections from the DC. The AN, led by MSI secretary Gianfranco Fini, softened some of its right-wing positions, and the secretary has been very careful to convey a democratic image. A further decisive step toward democratic integration was the inclusion of the AN in the 1994 cabinet of Silvio Berlusconi. In spite of this, the continuing presence of neofascist midlevel elites and some unfortunate declarations in favor of the previous fascist experience have roused the suspicions of the foreign press and most of Italy's centrist and leftist leaders. Paralleling the secession of the hard-line Communist Refoundation from the PDS, a small group of nostalgic neofascists withdrew from the AN to form another party (MSI-FT), an event that was taken as proof of the democratic integration of the AN.

The second phase of change (1992–94) saw the continuing *mani pulite* investigations and the adoption of the new electoral laws in 1993.[73] In hindsight, however, the most important element in this phase was the foundation of a new party, Forza Italia (FI). As the 1994 elections approached, it became evident that the delegitimation and crisis of the DC, the PSI, and the other small centrist parties had created a vacuum in the middle of the electoral spectrum.[74] In founding FI in January 1994, television magnate Silvio Berlusconi sought to fill this vacuum. Within only a few weeks of its birth, and following a massive barrage of television advertising, opinion polls indicated that FI would become the largest party in the new parliament. The ownership and control of three national television channels and virtual control of several other local networks gave Berlusconi's party an enormous advantage during the electoral campaign. By carefully monitoring opinion polls, Berlusconi, one of Italy's richest entrepreneurs, with vast experience in advertising, determined the issues that could capture the floating center/center-right voters and later addressed those issues in his electoral propaganda.

After the 1994 elections, the political landscape continued to shift dramatically. During the second half of the decade, electoral and governmental coalitions continually reshuffled. A bipolar electoral tendency was established within a system that remained multiparty, with a wide-spread perception of the pivotal role of centrist parties and the resulting competition for that space. There were a few failed attempts at constitutional reform and a number of external inputs that shook the self-referentiality of parties (a process of internal decision making in which the concerns of internal leaders and groups dominate over the external attention to voters and their opinions). Those external factors have included the social and economic problem of unemployment, the necessity of cutting the budget deficit, and all the political, economic, and military obligations of participation in the European Union. The late 1990s were also characterized by more fluid relationships between parties and civil society as well as low or even nonexistent political participation. These moments expressed apathy, alienation, and dissatisfaction, but at the same time opened space for movements based on specific issues or particular leaders,[75] as evidenced in the successes of the radical Emma Bonino as well as Antonio Di Pietro and Romano Prodi in the 1999 elections.

Party Organizations and Civil Society in the 1990s

The many changes of party names and symbols or even splits and mergers might actually have little significance. They might be little more than a facelift, behind which leaders, structures, and even policies remain the same. To assess the depth of change in parties, one must examine the organizational adjustments—a task made more difficult by the reluctance of party leaders to reveal their liabilities. The changes in Italian party organization also evince long-term trends that are emerging gradually in other European countries as well.[76]

One major change has been the sustained deterioration of the parties' presence and diffusion in civil society, implying the end of the traditional mass parties. The membership of the new and successor parties is both smaller and of lesser importance. During the 1970s and 1980s, party elites continued to be the main actors in Italian politics, which was still characterized by patronage in the allocation of resources. The old reasons for a large party membership declined mainly because of the deradicalization of the DC and the PCI, a related decline of ideology, and the development of the political role of television after 1983. New middle-to-large parties like Forza Italia and the Northern League have relatively low memberships, and their leaders have no plans to create mass parties. In the League, members are militants coopted from above, resulting in something rather close to a cadre party; in Forza Italia, members are components of local electoral committees or promoters of a "product," centered around the leader and founder of the party, with no role to play outside election campaigns.

As in the past, among the new parties there continue to be different organizational models, although elements of both the professional-electoral party[77] and the cartel party[78] are hard to detect in the new parties. The successors to the PCI—the PDS, then DS, and the Communist Refoundation—managed to preserve some of the PCI's grassroots structures. Although by 1991 the PDS had decided, as had the other traditional parties, to rely on a leaner organization, the PCI's tradition of offices and militants did not disappear completely. The PDS maintained a few elements of the old mass-integration party, including vertical ties and some importance of members and membership. Thus the feeling of belonging to a community was still widespread, but the community had become a place more for leisure than for discussing politics. This means that very little of the traditional party is left, and then mainly in the old "red" regions. When the increasingly important role of the parliamentary party is considered, the PDS seems closer to the model of the "modern cadre party" than that of a professional-electoral party.[79]

The National Alliance is the other contemporary party that sees membership as relevant.[80] After its reshaping and renaming in 1995, the party seems to be in transition from a traditional mass-integration party to a party-movement, all in an effort to acquire moderate votes, particularly in the South. Although the old structures are becoming obsolete, the party militants remain an important organizational resource for improving electoral results. Organizational change is also necessary for a party whose "old guard" generation is slowly but unavoidably declining and whose extreme neofascist youth support is difficult to socialize.[81] The transition will certainly be very difficult and will probably be more evident in the words of the ambitious leader than in any actual transformation of the party. Additionally, the central role of the leader will probably continue to be emphasized and will even be strengthened by the media's personalization of contemporary politics.

The Northern League formally has a more traditional view of membership, characterized by low admission requirements and generic membership obligations. In practice, however, members are stratified into four categories: *supporters,* who have no voting rights or obligations but who give financial support; *militants,* who have local voting rights, low political autonomy, and "active militancy" obligations, emphasizing manual rather than intellectual activities;[82] *full members,* who are appointed by the National Assembly after demonstrating "excellent militant commitment" and who have national voting rights; and *founding members,* with lifetime voting rights at the national level.[83] The League has also developed a strong organization manned by voluntary workers (many of them young). It is a markedly hierarchical party with a strong leader and central office controlling finances, electoral campaigns, and party policy, and managed like a private business.

Since 1990, the League has metamorphosed from a protest party into a governmental party, back into a protest, antisystem party, later into a protest movement-party, and then again into a governmental party with a radical but no longer antisystem program. It has abandoned its most radical goal—secession—but still has a strong leader, which may define it as a charismatic party. Moreover, the impact of governmental experience in 1994 and the increasingly autonomous role of its parliamentary component had very important consequences. Being solidly rooted locally but not nationally, the League was unable to bear the strains and pressures of internal dissent. The leadership of Umberto Bossi was challenged, especially on the issue of participating in the Berlusconi cabinet. The crucial moment came in early 1995 when Bossi regained full control of the organization and turned it back into a protest and movement party, expressing the dissatisfaction of the North. The regional and local elections of April 1995 strengthened his leadership, as did the national elections of 1996, even though the party declined electorally (see Table 2 on p. 126).

With its dominant role for the leader, direct mobilizational appeal, low membership rate, strong vertical organizational, ancillary organizations,[84] and intolerance of dissent, the League may appear to be an updated version of the traditional mass party, with integrative features. Yet it could also be defined as a "modern cadre party," only without a professional leadership group or internal democracy. Organizing along these lines is made possible by the marginal identity of League supporters and the hostility directed toward it by people with different political leanings. Thus the recent electoral decline of the League could be due to the waning of both the marginal identity and the hostility in the North, making it more difficult to keep active militants. Moreover, it may also be the ultimate consequence of the lack of space for dissent and of all the unavoidable conflicts between Bossi and local League leaders, once they became the incumbent authorities in the communes or provinces.

The organizational structure of Forza Italia went through two distinctive phases—genesis and consolidation. The creation of the party was carefully planned during the second half of 1993, and it was launched and organizationally developed in the three months before and during the March elections. The key organizational role was performed by the staff of Publitalia, an advertising company that is part of Berlusconi's Fininvest conglomerate. In a few days, they set up 13,000–14,000 clubs with about 80 people per club. The clubs were vertically connected to a national association of clubs (ANFI), which guided their politics. FI may thus be considered a new kind of *business-firm/party,* given the key roles performed by Publitalia and Berlusconi. However, the experience of being in office in 1994 and the conflicts with its coalition partners created internal dissent and clearly distinguishable groups, though no factions. In this genetic phase the party had two organizational structures, the clubs and the tiny (5,000-member) party organization, which

conflicted with one other. The clubs had the potential to become independent electoral bases for candidates. Nevertheless, the party was defined
by three features: its overriding orientation was to winning votes (the
electoral component); Berlusconi's leadership was undisputed and connected to the very life of the party (the charismatic component); and the
electoral structure had been set up by an advertising firm (the professional
component).

Forza Italia's second phase—organizational consolidation—began
when the party entered the opposition at the end of 1994. When it had to
cope with the regional and local elections, the tension between local
club autonomy and strong central leadership was overcome. After the
organizational changes of 1995 and 1997,[85] the party was ruled even
more by cooptation from above. Appointments were always made by the
next level up in the hierarchy, and the possible conflicts and autonomy
of clubs were resolved *a priori* by the affiliation of the few remaining
clubs with the party. (In 1999, there were only about 1,500 clubs.)
Moreover, the parliamentary component was controlled by Berlusconi,
who remained as strong a leader as during the party's founding. The
most important developments, however, concern the locally elected
representatives of the party: This new political class neither is cohesive
nor strongly identifies with the party,[86] but it is well connected with
small and mid-size entrepreneurial interests.[87] In parliament, a third of
the FI-elected representatives in 1994 were industrial entrepreneurs,
landowners, or tradesmen. It is likely that such an electorally oriented
party will enlarge its appeal to encompass other sectors of the moderate
middle class and, in doing so, become the true heir to the DC, at least in
terms of social representation, while being a completely new party in
terms of organization. The FI's very low membership rate is indicative of
the image that the party tries to convey—an image very distant from that
of a traditional mass party. For a new party without tradition or real
activists, this is the best tactic to get electoral support in a passive society
if complemented by a continuous presence on TV and by incumbency.
In this vein, winning the 2001 parliamentary election, after the success
in the 2000 regional ones, was a vital achievement for the party and its
leader, who led a prolonged electoral campaign. The FI's huge success
in the 2001 election will stabilize the party even more with its three new
components vis-à-vis the origin (see above): the leader who created a
personalistic party,[88] the professional group who also made the victory
possible, and the mid-level, parliamentary, regional and local elites,
who are the most solid supporters of such a party. The departure of the
entire FI elite from their party positions to fill the numerous governmental
positions of ministers, undersecretaries, presidents of regions and
provinces, mayors, and parliamentarians or councillors in the different
representative assemblies will not undermine the party, as it would have
undermined a traditional mass party a few years ago. The light

organization can be set up, frozen, and revitalized again in a short span of time, above all after a period of continuous incumbency. The new Italian Popular Party, although formed by former Christian Democrat elites, is by no means heir to the DC. The PPI cannot depend on the political unity of the Catholic vote, which is now largely spread among various parties, Forza Italia included. Despite this diffusion and the secularization of the past three decades, the PPI tries to maintain the old Christian Democratic connections, particularly with some sectors of the Church hierarchy, the Catholic associations, and the Catholic workers' groups.[89] The electoral results of the 1999 European elections, where the party lost more than 30 percent of its previous electorate, illustrate the decline of this political force (see Table 2 on p. 126), which in 2001 tried to revitalize itself through an alliance with the other centrist, moderate groups related to the old DC within the center-left, and particularly with the Democrats, until 1999 led by Romano Prodi. In principle, the strategy of Catholic appeal makes some sense, in that the Catholic network (though less political than in the past) is probably the only one that is still present in contemporary Italian civil society. The success of this approach, however, has been undermined by the existence of other centrist political groups with former DC leaders and by the appeal to Catholics of Forza Italia and the AN, which are powerful competitors of the Popolari.

The picture would not be complete without discussing the presence of new political movements. At least since the end of the 1960s, student, worker, civil rights, and later ecological movements (among others) have been prominent politically. After a few years, when the influence of such actors waned, in the early 1990s, a single-issue movement was born around electoral reforms. Two referenda were passed on these issues: the first changed the way of voting by giving the voter the possibility of expressing only one preference vote within the chosen party list (1991); the second one set the bases for a much more majoritarian formula for parliamentary elections (1993). A third electoral reform referendum, which would have increased the majoritarian aspect, failed in April 1999 because of low turnout. Although this failure may suggest that single-issue movements no longer appeal to citizens, other movement-parties emerged in 1999 and successfully competed in the European elections. The Democrats, led by Romano Prodi, Antonio di Pietro and many popular city mayors, won 7.7 percent, and the list led by Emma Bonino, a well-known radical member of the European Commission, won 8.5 percent. These movements can be successful in a period of low participation and antiparty attitudes through their use of political marketing and heavy coverage by the media.

The weakening of the once-powerful links between parties and civil society was a major characteristic of the crisis of the late 1980s and early 1990s.[90] The unions became autonomous actors that can oppose the governing party, even if that party is their traditional partner. The

TABLE 3–MAIN MEASURES OF PARTY SYSTEM CHANGE (1946–99)

YEAR	TEV	IBV	PF	ENP
1946	-	-	.79	4.3
1948	22.8	12.9	.66	2.6
1953	13.3	4.6	.76	3.6
1958	4.5	1.0	.74	3.4
1963	7.9	1.3	.76	3.7
1968	3.4	1.4	.75	3.6
1972	4.9	1.1	.76	3.6
1976	8.2	5.4	.72	3.1
1979	5.3	0.7	.74	3.4
1983	8.5	0.3	.78	4.0
1987	8.4	1.1	.78	4.1
1992	16.2	5.2	.85	5.8
1994	41.9	5.8	.87	7.3
1996	17.7	6.6	.86	6.3
1999[1]	23.4	1.0	.91	7.2

TEV = Total electoral volatility, the sum of the absolute value of all changes in the percentages of votes cast for each party since the previous election divided by two.
IBV = Inter-bloc volatility, the following are the blocs. Left: Proletarian Democracy, Communist Refoundation, Italian Communists, Democrats of the Left (former PCI), The Net, Greens, PPI-Prodi-SVP-UD-PRI, Democrats (Prodi), Italian Renewal (Dini), Socialist Party (PSI), Republican Party (PRI), Social Democrats (PSDI), Democratic Alliance (AD); Right: Radical Party (Lista Pannella), CDU, CCD, FI, Lombard/Northern League, Segni Pact, Liberals (PLI), Social Movement/National Alliance, Social Movement–Fiamma Tricolore. Christian Democracy (DC-PPI) considered right for1946–92, then PPI considered Left.
PF = Rae's index of fractionalization; see Douglas W. Rae, The Political Consequences of Electoral Laws (New Haven: Yale University Press,1967), 56.
ENP = effective number of parties; based on Markku Laakso and Rein Taagepera's formula which is as follows: $P_e = \dfrac{1}{\sum_{i=1}^{n} P_i^2}$ Markku Laakso and Rein Taagepera, "Effective Number of Parties: A Measure with Application to West Europe," Comparative Political Studies 12 (April 1979): 3–27.

[1] 1999 results from European election, all others from general legislative elections. For the computations of volatility between 1996 and 1999, votes for the two communist parties (Communist Refoundation and Italian Communists) were considered disaggregated in 1999; similarly, votes for Democrats (Prodi) and PPI, South Tyrolean People's Party, and Republican Party were considered disaggregated in 1999; as were the votes for the CDU and the CCD.
Source: Computation on official returns by Italian Ministry of Interior.

Confindustria plays a political role closer to that of a party than an interest group. The entire clientelistic system fell into deep crisis with the breakdown of the DC and then the privatizations of the late 1990s. Finally, most ancillary organizations have become independent, with some exceptions in the "red areas." In addition to all this, the 1980s saw the end of the strong "blackmailing" role of the parties, thanks to a complex decision-making process that takes place in different national and European arenas. The fading of linkages is also evident in the sharp decline in party identification, which dropped from about 40 percent in the early 1980s to about 27 percent in 1993–94, with a high proportion of no answers (28 percent in 1994, an election year, compared to an average of 2.5 between 1977 and 1981).

A Diachronic Comparison

There are five summary points in this analysis of the three major phases of political parties in Italy. First, the 1950s and early 1960s were characterized by a coexistence of different organizational models, which disproved the hypothesis of organizational homogenization[91] and showed how strong traditions, ideologies, and consequent party identities may endure. In the late 1990s, different organizational models once again coexist—an outcome of residual traditions and identities as well as the sheer number of parties. In fact, as shown by Table 3 above, party fragmentation was higher.

Second, in all three phases, the maintenance of organizational structures has been easier for parties with stronger identities, such as extreme or radical parties. This means that the DS and even more the Communist Refoundation, on one side of the spectrum, and the AN and the MSI-FT, on the other, may try to maintain their old identities and related organizations with loyal militants. The same may hold true for the Northern League, which has a strong militant identity. When those parties compete for moderate votes, however, they tone down their extreme identities and thereby make organizational maintenance more difficult. This may eventually lead to a destructuring of midsize parties with hegemonic ambitions in their area, such as DS and AN, once the old militants of both parties fade from the scene. In a sense, these two parties have the most serious organizational problems with the disintegration of their old solid bases and their difficulties in changing into a light party structure such as Forza Italia.

Third, at present, four or even five models of party organization coexist: the elite party, the "modern cadre party," the electoral party or, more precisely, the personalistic party, and the movement-party. About the first there is nothing new to add. They are tiny parties that sometimes have a leader with his own electoral and parliamentary base, and they have low institutionalization and no organization. Parties such as the Christian Democratic Center (CCD) and the United Christian Democrats (CDU) on the center-right, and the Italian Renewal (RI) and the Democratic Union for Europe (UDEUR), which in 2001 merged in an alliance with others within the center-left coalition, are good examples. The ironic aspect is that all of them are the small phoenixes born out of the ashes of the old Christian Democracy. In fact, all of them are the development of DC factions, able to change into autonomous small parties and persist.

The "modern cadre party" is much more interesting and new. It is the outcome of a transformation of the mass party that has not followed Otto Kirchheimer's predictions.[92] These parties have a strong leader, a small group of professionals, militants tied to the party vertically, a reduced number of members, a low or very low membership rate, and an electoral strategy aimed at creating and maintaining identities. The AN and the DS are close to this model, while the Northern League is rather closer to an anachronistic mass party with deferential militants/members.

The electoral party has no links or relationships with the old mass parties. As conceptualized by Panebianco,[93] it is characterized by a stress on personal leadership and specific issues, and by a small organization composed of professionals with marketing and communication expertise. Forza Italia is very close to this kind of a party. But a few additional characteristics make FI even closer to the model of the "personalistic party" (as discussed by Richard Gunther and Larry Diamond in chapter 1 of this volume). In fact, the prominent role of Berlusconi in every aspect and activity of the party well justifies this label. Of course, this is a personalistic party, but not an unconsolidated structure. As mentioned above, after three elections and almost a decade, the vested interests of a large elite around Berlusconi are very strong and are bound to be additionally strengthened because of the party's incumbency at both the central and local levels, and because the centrist and moderate space where the party rooted itself will be still there in the coming years. This organizational model has permanently entered Italian politics, as often happens just by chance, but it will last, and if not with Berlusconi then with another leader in a similar organizational formula within the larger electoral model.

Lastly, the movement-party is an actor in between a party and a movement and places a particular stress on mobilization and participation with regard to a single issue or set of issues. The radicals of Bonino's list are close to this model while the Democrats of Prodi and Di Pietro took some characteristics of the movement-party but also some features of the old elite party. They may be the expression of a transitional phase that is almost over in Italy. If so, they are bound to either disappear or transform into more institutionalized actors.

It would be illusory to think that the coexistence of different party models is due to destructuration and changes in party organization, since such coexistence was already present in the 1950s. Today, however, it is no longer due to different traditions and identities. Rather, the explanation seems primarily to lie in the high levels of party fragmentation: A large number of parties makes the homogenizing impact of stable competition difficult, if not impossible. In spite of its wider empirical importance, the cartel party is not present in the Italian picture, for several reasons.[94] The Italian system lacks the stability that is at the root of the cartelization of parties. Some features of the cartel party, such as public financing of parties and access to the television, apply by law to all parties in Italy, and so no distinction among parties is possible in this respect. Moreover, the distinction between members and non-members is still relevant in Forza Italia, the PDS, and the Northern League. Parties in Italy are still seen as distinct, public but nonstate agencies. Finally, the competition among parties remains vigorous, contradicting the collusion implied by cartelization.

Fourth, does the evidence from the three phases of Italian political parties suggest that parties are in decline in Italy? Yes and no at the same time. No doubt, party organizations and functions have changed. After the crisis and breakdown of the DC, there are no Italian denominational parties. The mass party and the catch-all party are no longer present in Italy, or in the rest of Europe, but their heritage and their remnants remain in the League, the AN, and the DS. In addition, new models, such as the personalistic party and the "modern cadre party," have appeared.

Moreover, although parties continue to perform the same functions as

they did thirty years ago, for many activities—such as societal representation or interest articulation and aggregation—they no longer do so exclusively. Those functions are now also performed by unions and other
interest associations, as well as by the media. At the same time, the gate-
keeping role of parties, which was an important characteristic of the consolidating period,[95] slowly faded away, and by the 1980s was no longer
a key aspect of Italian politics.

Finally, the explanations of these changes again coincide with general
European trends, including secularization, the decline of ideology,
technological development in the media, and the articulation and growth
of civil society. In the Italian case, however, other reasons can be recalled,
particularly for the changes of the 1980s and the 1990s. Prominent among
these causes were the gradual integration of the communist left, political
dissatisfaction, the disappearance of Fascist collective memories, and
the demand for higher efficacy in solving all the problems with which
Italian politics must cope.[96]

NOTES

1. See Leonardo Morlino, *Democracy Between Consolidation and Crisis: Parties, Groups and Citizens in Southern Europe* (Oxford: Oxford University Press,
1998).

2. Class conflict, religion, center/periphery, and system support have been the
main cleavages in Italian politics since 1946, although the first one was most salient
for decades. According to Paolo Farneti, there are five salient cleavages in Italian
politics: the reform/revolution cleavage, the religious one, the institutional division
(fascism/antifascism), that regarding the government of economy (market versus
state), and the international cleavage. See Paolo Farneti, *Il sistema dei partiti in
Italia 1946–1979* (Bologna: Il Mulino, 1983), 46–50.

3. Leonardo Morlino, *Democracy Between Consolidation and Crisis.*

4. See Giorgio Galli, ed., *Il comportamento elettorale in Italia* (Bologna: Il
Mulino, 1968), 217.

5. Otto Kirchheimer, "The Transformation of the Western European Party Systems," in Joseph LaPalombara and Myron Weiner, eds., *Political Parties and Political
Development* (Princeton, N.J.: Princeton University Press, 1966).

6. Marco Tarchi, *Dal MSI ad AN: Organizzazione e strategie* (Bologna: Il Mulino,
1997).

7. See Carlo Vallauri, ed., *L'arcipelago democratico: Organizzazione e struttura
dei partiti italani negli anni del centrismo (1949–1958)* (Rome: Bulzoni, 1981).

8. For a detailed analysis of the organization during those years, see Gianfranco
Poggi, ed., *L'organizzazione partitica del PCI e della DC* (Bologna: Il Mulino,
1968).

9. See Gianfranco Poggi, ed., *L'organizzazione partitica del PCI e della DC;* and
Maurizio Rossi, "Un partito di 'anime morte'? Il tesseramento democristiano tra
mito e realtà," in Arturo Parisi, ed., *Democristiani* (Bologna: Il Mulino, 1979).

10. See Alan Zuckerman, *The Politics of Faction: Christian Democratic Rule in Italy* (New Haven: Yale University Press, 1979); Giovanni Sartori, *Correnti, frazioni e fazioni nei partiti politici italiani* (Bologna: Il Mulino, 1973); Giovanna Zincone, "Accesso autonomo alle risorse: le determinanti del frazionismo," *Rivista Italiana di Scienza Politica* 2 (1972): 139–60.

11. See Gianfranco Poggi, *L'organizzazione partitica del PCI e della DC;* Massimo Ilardi and Aris Accornero, eds., *Il Partito Comunista Italiano: Struttura e storia dell'organizzazione 1921–1979* (Milan: Annali della Fondazione Feltrinelli, 1982); Sidney Tarrow, *Peasant Communism in Southern Italy* (New Haven: Yale University Press, 1967).

12. See, for example, Giorgio Galli, *Il bipartitismo imperfetto: Comunisti e Democristiani in Italia* (Bologna: Il Mulino, 1966), 166. In these years there is also more detailed research on a sample of militants of DC and PCI; see Francesco Alberoni, ed., *L'attivista di partito* (Bologna: Il Mulino, 1967).

13. See Gianfranco Poggi, ed., *L'organizzazione partitica del PCI e della DC,* 132.

14. See Agopik Manoukian, ed., *La presenza sociale del PCI e della DC* (Bologna: Il Mulino, 1968).

15. The following authors give a good picture of Socialist organization in the early 1960s: Wolfgang Merkel, *Prima e dopo Craxi: le transformazioni del PSI* (Padua: Liviana, 1987); Valdo Spini and Sergio Mattana, eds., *I quadri del PSI* (Quaderni del Circolo Rosselli, Nuova Guaraldi, 1981); Antonio Landolfi, *Il socialismo italiano: Strutture comportamenti valori* (Roma: Lerici, 1968); Franco Cazzola, *Il partito come organizzazione*; Liliano Faenza, *La crisi del socialismo in Italia 1946-66* (Bologna: Edizioni Alfa, 1967); and Samuel Barnes, *Party Democracy: Politics in an Italian Socialist Federation* (New Haven: Yale University Press, 1967).

16. Giorgio Galli, *Il bipartitismo imperfetto,* 167–68.

17. See Antonio Landolfi, *Il socialismo italiano,* esp. 119.

18. Maurizio Cotta, *Classe politica e parlamento in Italia* (Bologna: Il Mulino, 1979), 176–78. With regards to a more comprehensive analysis of Italian patterns of recruitment for the three major parties, see pages 196 and following.

19. Maurizio Cotta, *Classe politica e parlamento in Italia,* 102–3.

20. Ibid., 352–54.

21. For all the data concerning the MSI see Piero Ignazi, *Il polo escluso: profilo del Movimento Sociale Italiano* (Bologna: Il Mulino, 1989, 253–310) and the official documents of the party in Carlo Vallauri, *L'arcipelago democratico.*

22. More precisely it was 9.2 percent, with Liberals at 3.2 percent, Social Democrats at 4.5 percent, and Republicans at 1.5 percent.

23. On this topic with special reference also to Italy see Renato Mannheimer, *Capire il voto: Contributi per l'analisi del comportamento elettorale in Italia* (Milan: Angeli, 1989).

24. Paolo Farneti, "Introduzione" to Paolo Farneti, ed., *Il sistema politico italiano* (Bologna: Il Mulino, 1973), 31–40.

25. See esp. Paolo Farneti, ed., *Il sistema politico italiano.*

26. See Gianfranco Pasquino, "Italian Christian Democracy: A Party for All

Seasons?" in Sidney Tarrow and Peter Lange, eds., *Italy in Transition: Conflict and Consensus* (London: Frank Cass, 1980), 95; and Luigi Graziano, *Clientelismo e sistema politico: Il caso dell'Italia* (Milan: Angeli, 1980).

27. See Leonardo Morlino, ed., *Costruire la democrazia: Gruppi e partiti in Italia* (Bologna: Il Mulino, 1991).

28. Mainly the Liberals, but in some areas of the South also the two small monarchical parties and the MSI.

29. For a reconstruction of this course see Marco Maraffi, *Politica ed economia in Italia: La vicenda dell'impresa pubblica dagli anni trenta agli anni cinquanta* (Bologna: Il Mulino, 1991), especially chs. 7–8. This author stresses the role of Fanfani in the construction of the public sector.

30. See ibid., 222–23.

31. See Gianfranco Pasquino, "Party Government in Italy: Achievements and Prospects," in Richard Katz, ed., *Party Governments: European and American Experiences* (Berlin: Walter de Gruyter, 1987).

32. This section is based on research directed by Leonardo Morlino on the Italian party organizations (1945–89), within an international research project led by Richard Katz and Peter Mair. A partial result of the research is now in Luciano Bardi and Leonardo Morlino, "Italy: Tracing the Roots of the Great Transformation," in Richard Katz and Peter Mair, eds., *How Parties Organize: Change and Adaptation in Party Organizations in Western Democracies* (London: Sage Publications, 1994, 242–77).

33. Maurizio Rossi, "Sezioni di partito e partecipazione politica," *Polis* 1 (1987): 67–102.

34. Celso Ghini, "Gli iscritti al partito e alla FGCI, 1943/1979," in Massimo Ilardi and Aris Accornero, eds., *Il Partito Comunista Italiano*, 241.

35. Giorgio Galli, *Storia del PCI* (Milan: Bompiani, 1976).

36. Enrico Casciani, "Dieci anni di reclutamento nel PCI," Il Mulino 30 (1981): 310–26.

37. See Arturo Parisi and Gianfranco Pasquino, "Changes in Italian Electoral Behavior: The Relationships Between Parties and Voters," in Peter Lange and Sidney Tarrow, *Italy in Transition: Conflict and Consensus*, 6–30.

38. Gianfranco Pasquino and Maurizio Rossi, "Quali compagni, quale partito, quale formula politica? Un'indagine sul PSI," *Il Mulino* 29 (1980): 78; Sergio Mattana, "La struttura e la base sociale del PSI," *Quaderni del Circolo Rosselli* 1 (1981), 59; Wolfgang Merkel, *Prima e dopo Craxi*, 60.

39. Wolfgang Merkel, *Prima e dopo Craxi*; see also Maurizio Rossi, "Sezioni di partito e partecipazione politica."

40. Franco Cazzola, *Della corruzione: Fisiologia e anatomia di un sistema politico* (Bologna: Il Mulino, 1988) 138–39.

41. See interview in *La Repubblica* (20 February 1993): 7. More recent research on corruption confirms how widespread it was and how it made it possible to maintain complex organizations. See Donatella Della Porta and Alberto Vannucci, *Un paese anormale: Come la classe politica ha perso l'occasione di Mani Pulite* (Rome-Bari: Laterza, 1999).

42. Antonio Baldassarre, "I gruppi parlamentari comunisti," in Massimo Ilardi and Aris Accornero, eds., *Il Partito Comunista Italiano,* 446.

43. Ibid., 461 et passim.

44. Ibid., 471–72.

45. Gianfranco Pasquino, "Programmatic Renewal and Much More: From the PCI to the PDS," 4.

46. Piero Ignazi, *Dal PCI al PDS* (Bologna: Il Mulino, 1992), 93; Chiara Sebastiani, "I funzionari," in Aris Accornero, Renato Mannheimer, and Chiara Sebastiani, eds., *L'identità comunista: I militanti, le strutture, la cultura del PCI* (Rome: Editori Riuniti, 1983) 99–105.

47. Piero Ignazi, *Dal PCI al PDS,* 95.

48. See Luciano Bardi and Leonardo Morlino, "Italy," in Richard Katz and Peter Mair, eds., *Party Organizations: A Data Handbook on Party Organizations in Western Democracies, 1960–90* (London: Sage Publications, 1992) and Piero Ignazi, *Dal PCI al PDS,* 113.

49. Oreste Massari, "Le trasformazioni nella direzione del PSI: la direzione e i suoi membri (1976–1984)," *Rivista Italiana di Scienza Politica* 17 (1987): 403.

50. Aldo Di Virgilio, *La crisi del PSI,* forthcoming.

51. Wolgang Merkel, *Prima e dopo Craxi,* 67.

52. Aldo Di Virgilio, *La crisi del PSI.*

53. Paolo Farneti, *Il sistema dei partiti in Italia 1946–1979* (Bologna: Il Mulino, 1983), 202.

54. Robert Leonardi and Douglas Wertman, *Italian Christian Democracy: The Politics of Dominance* (London: MacMillan, 1989), 109.

55. Paolo Farneti, *Il sistema dei partiti in Italia 1946–1979,* 156.

56. Renato Mannheimer, *Capire il voto.* This is consistent with a previous survey, which found that "in the mid-80s a portion of the electorate oscillating between 40 and 50 percent could be considered at least to some extent identified with a party."

57. Ibid., 58.

58. See Arturo Parisi and Gianfranco Pasquino "Changes in Italian Electoral Behavior: The Relationships Between Parties and Voters."

59. Roberto Cartocci, *Elettori in Italia: Riflessioni sulle vicende elettorali degli anni ottanta* (Bologna: Il Mulino, 1990).

60. Marino Regini, "Labour Unions, Industrial Action, and Politics," in Sidney Tarrow and Peter Lange, eds., *Italy in Transition: Conflict and Consensus,* 49–50.

61. Liborio Mattina, "I gruppi imprenditoriali, i sindacati e lo stato nella crisi e riaggiustamento del sistema industriale italiano," mimeo (Firenze: DISPO, 1989) 12–13; Alberto Martinelli, "Organised Business and Italian Politics: Confindustria and the Christian Democrats in the Postwar Period," in Sidney Tarrow and Peter Lange, eds., *Italy in Transition: Conflict and Consensus,* 83.

62. Alberto Martinelli, "Organised Business and Italian Politics: Confindustria and the Christian Democrats in the Postwar Period," 83.

63. Robert Leonardi and Douglas Wertman, *Italian Christian Democracy: The Politics of Dominance,* 217.

64. Luigi Accattoli, "Il Movimento Popolare: forza e limiti di un messianismo politico" in Piergiorgio Corbetta and Robert Leonardi, eds., *Politica in Italia: Edizione 1988* (Bologna: Il Mulino, 1988), 293–313.

65. Pier Paolo Giglioli and Gianpietro Mazzoleni, "Processi di concentrazione editoriale e sistema dei media," in Raimondo Catanzaro and Filippo Sabetti, eds., *Politica in Italia: Edizione 1990* (Bologna: Il Mulino, 1990), 205.

66. Carlo Marletti, "Partiti e informazione televisiva: la nomina di Enrico Manca a presidente della Rai," in Piergiorgio Corbetta and Robert Leonardi, eds., *Politica in Italia: Edizione 1987* (Bologna: Il Mulino, 1987).

67. See Leonardo Morlino and Marco Tarchi, "The Dissatisfied Society: Protest and Support in Italy," *European Journal of Political Research* 30 (1996): 41–63; and Leonardo Morlino, *Democracy Between Consolidation and Crisis.*

68. See Leonard Weinberg, *The Transformation of Italian Communism* (New Brunswick: Transaction Publishers, 1995); and Carlo Baccetti, *Il PDS: Verso un nuovo modello di partito?* (Bologna: Il Mulino, 1997).

69. Steven Hellmann, "The Italian Communist Party Between Berlinguer and the Seventeenth Congress," in Robert Leonardi and Raffaella Nanetti, eds., *Italian Politics: A Review* (London: Frances Pinter, 1985), 59–60.

70. See Ilvo Diamanti, *La Lega: Geografia, storia e sociologia di un nuovo soggetto politico* (Rome: Donzelli, 1995).

71. The relationship between economic dissatisfaction and political dissatisfaction is shown for 1983–84 in Brad Lockerbie, "Economic Dissatisfaction and Political Alienation in Western Europe," *European Journal of Political Research* 23 (1993): 281–93. During 1984–1994, the average percentage of people who declared themselves "not very satisfied" or "not at all satisfied" "with the way democracy works" was 73.2 percent in Italy compared to 44.7 percent in all other EC countries combined. See Leonardo Morlino and Marco Tarchi, "The Dissatisfied Society."

72. The idea of "anticipated reactions" was introduced by Carl Friedrich. On the impact of the new electoral laws see Leonardo Morlino, "Is There an Impact? And Where is it? Electoral Reform and Party System in Italy," *Southern European Society & Politics* 2 (1997): 103–30.

73. For details on the electoral laws, see Roberto D'Alimonte and Alessandro Chiaramonte, "Il nuovo sistema elettorale italiano: quali opportunità," *Rivista Italiana di Scienza Politica* 23 (1993): 513–48.

74. The local by-elections in important towns in June and November–December 1993, held under the new majoritarian law approved in March 1993, had an immediate polarizing impact, and their results, on the whole favorable to the leftist coalition, also contributed to Berlusconi's decision to enter politics.

75. See Leonardo Morlino and Marco Tarchi, "The Dissatisfied Society."

76. The following discussion is based on the preliminary results of a research project directed by Leonardo Morlino.

77. Angelo Panebianco, *Modelli di partito* (Bologna: Il Mulino, 1982).

78. Richard Katz and Peter Mair, "Changing Models of Party Organization and Party Democracy: The Emergence of the Cartel Party," *Party Politics* 1 (1995): 5–29.

79. Ruud A. Koole, "The Vulnerability of the Modern Cadre Party in the Netherlands," in Richard Katz and Peter Mair, eds., *How Parties Organize.*

80. Marco Tarchi, *Dal MSI ad AN,* 399–415.

81. See Leonardo Morlino and Marco Mattei, "Vecchio e nuovo autoritarismo nell'Europa Mediterranea," *Rivista Italiana di Scienza Politica* 22 (1992): 137–60.

82. See Roberto Biorcio, "La Lega Nord e la transizione italiana," *Rivista Italiana di Scienza Politica* 29 (1999): 80.

83. Marco Tarchi, *La Lega* (Bologna: Il Mulino, forthcoming).

84. See Roberto Biorcio, "La Lega Nord e la transizione italiana"; see also Roberto Biorcio, *La Padania promessa* (Milan: Il Saggiatore, 1997).

85. For 1995, see Marco Maraffi, "Forza Italia dal governo all'opposizione," in Mario Caciagli and David I. Kertzer, eds., *Politica in Italia: Edizione 1996* (Bologna: Il Mulino, 1996), 139–57; for 1997, see Emanuela Poli and Marco Tarchi, "I partiti del polo: uniti per che cosa," in David Hine and Salvatore Vassallo, *Politica in Italia: Edizione 1999* (Bologna: Il Mulino, 1999), 79–100.

86. Caterina Paolucci, "Forza Italia: un marchio in franchising?" *Rivista Italiana di Scienza Politica* 29 (1999): 481–516.

87. Alessandro Tonarelli, "Gli amministratori locali di Forza Italia," *Rivista Italiana di Scienza Politica* 29 (1999): 89–120.

88. Mauro Calise presents Forza Italia as a personalistic party. See Mauro Calise, *Il partito personale* (Bari: Laterza, 2000), chs. 5 and 7.

89. See also Roberto Cartocci, *Tra Lega e Chiesa* (Bologna: Il Mulino, 1994).

90. See Leonardo Morlino, *Democracy Between Consolidation and Crisis,* chs. 1 and 7.

91. See Otto Kirchheimer, "The Transformation of the Western European Party Systems."

92. Ibid.

93. Angelo Panebianco, *Modelli di partito,* 481.

94. See Richard Katz and Peter Mair, "Changing Models of Party Organization and Party Democracy."

95. See Leonardo Morlino, *Costruire la democrazia.*

96. See Leonardo Morlino and Marco Tarchi, "The Dissatisfied Society."

7

JAPAN'S "1955 SYSTEM" AND BEYOND

Bradley Richardson

Bradley Richardson is professor of political science and University Distinguished Scholar Emeritus at Ohio State University. Currently he is director of that university's East Asian Studies Center and Center for Japanese Studies. His many publications include The Political Culture of Japan *(1974) and* Japanese Democracy: Power, Coordination, and Performance *(1997).*

Japan has the oldest competitive party system in the non-Western world. Although, as in Europe, Japan's first electorate was restricted to a small portion of the population—principally rural landowners—political parties began contesting elections in 1890. By 1925 the suffrage was extended to all males, forcing parties and their candidates to mobilize voters at all levels of society. In 1946 this imperative was further extended when women were given the vote and more offices were contested in public elections. Before World War II, only the lower house of Japan's parliament and some local officials were elected. Since 1946, however, members of both houses of parliament have been selected through competitive elections, along with political executives and assemblies in cities, towns, villages, and prefectures (roughly equivalent to American or German states, even though the Japanese system is unitary in design). Extending the scope of electoral competition obviously provided more challenges to party organizations and candidates.

Relatively stable electoral alignments and the dominance of the conservative movement were the hallmarks of the Japanese party system in most of the prewar era. Similar patterns generally prevailed after World War II, with certain exceptions (see the Table on the following page). One was the late 1940s, a time when purges by the Allied occupiers of quite a few prewar politicians encouraged many inexperienced people to seek election under self-designated party banners. The result was an unusual number of small parties alongside a few larger organizations. There were also divisions in both the dominant conservative and opposition camps. Over time, however, the number of parties declined,

TABLE—RESULTS OF JAPAN'S POSTWAR ELECTIONS

HOUSE OF REPRESENTATIVES ELECTIONS: PERCENTAGE SHARES OF NATIONWIDE VOTE

	1946[1]	1949[1]	1953	1958	1963	1967	1972	1976	1979	1980	1983	1986	1990	1993	1996[2]	2000[2]
LIBERAL DEMOCRATS	43[1]	52[1]	66[1]	58	55	49	47	42	45	48	46	49	46	37	39/33	41/28
LIBERAL PARTY																3/11
CLEAN GOVERNMENT PARTY						5	8	11	10	9	10	9	8	8	2/13	
RENEWAL PARTY														10		
JAPAN NEW PARTY														3	1/1	
HARBINGER PARTY														3		
NEW FRONTIER PARTY															28/28	28/25
DEMOCRATIC PARTY															11/16	
DEMOCRATIC SOCIALISTS					7	7	7	6	7	7	7	6	5	4		
SOCIAL DEMOCRATS	18	14	27*	33	29	28	22	21	20	20	20	17	24	15	2/6	4/9
JAPAN COMMUNISTS	4	4	2	3	4	5	10	10	10	9	9	9	8	8	13/13	12/11

HOUSE OF REPRESENTATIVES ELECTIONS: PARLIAMENTARY SEATS

	1946	1949	1953	1958	1963	1967	1972	1976	1979	1980	1983	1986	1990	1993	1996[2]	2000[2]
LIBERAL DEMOCRATS	234	233	310	287	283	277	271	249	252	298	258	306	275	223	239	233
LIBERAL PARTY																22
CLEAN GOVERNMENT PARTY						25	29	55	57	33	58	56	45	51		31
RENEWAL PARTY														55		
JAPAN NEW PARTY														35		
HARBINGER PARTY														13	2	
NEW FRONTIER PARTY															156	
DEMOCRATIC PARTY															52	127
DEMOCRATIC SOCIALISTS					23	30	19	29	35	32	38	26	14	15		
SOCIAL DEMOCRATS	92	48	138	166	169	170	118	123	109	110	115	85	136	70	15	19
JAPAN COMMUNISTS	5	35	1	1	0	0	38	17	39	29	26	26	16	15	26	20
TOTAL SEATS	464	466	466	467	467	486	491	511	511	511	511	512	512	511	500	480

[1] Total for conservative or socialist movement.

[2] There are two figures for total vote shares for the 1996 and 2000 elections. The first figure pertains to shares of single-member–district votes aggregated on a nationwide basis, the second to shares of aggregated regional PR district votes. Vote and seat aggregates are divided roughly into conservative, middle-of-the-road, and left blocs. Generally parties that mobilize more via candidate support groups (for example, Liberal Democrats and Liberals) do better in single-member districts while parties that solicit more support as parties do better in PR districts.

Sources: Jichisho, Senkyobu, *Shugiin Giin Sosenkyo, Saiko Saibansho Saibankan Kokumin Chosa Kekka Shirabe* (Tokyo: 1990); Seiji Koho Senta, *Seiji Handobukku* (Tokyo, 2001); and Ministry of Home Affairs website for the 2000 election.

and some movements themselves consolidated by 1955. From that point until 1989–93, one conservative party—the Liberal Democratic Party (LDP)—dominated elections at all levels and in most settings. Because of the relative stability of party alignments and a deep ideological and Cold War foreign-policy rift between the conservative LDP and Japan's opposition parties, the period after 1955 came to be called the "1955 system."

The second postwar exception to stable electoral alignments and clearcut conservative dominance came after the mid-1970s, in Japan's largest cities. Electoral changes in Japan's growing urban areas resulted in the reduction of the LDP's parliamentary representation to less than a majority, down from nearly two-thirds of the Diet seats in 1955–67.[1] Despite losses in large urban districts and a later issue-driven setback in the 1989 House of Councillors election, the LDP's domination continued with only relatively minor adjustments until mid-1993, when more than 50 members of parliament (MPs) left the LDP to form two new conservative parties. After that event—the beginning of a third era of instability and conservative shrinkage—Japan was ruled for a while by non-LDP governments and later controlled by an LDP-Socialist coalition. But, starting in 1996, the LDP has once again had a near majority in the lower house of parliament (the House of Representatives). The LDP is again Japan's dominant party, although cooperation with other parties is necessary to pass legislation, especially in the upper house (the House of Councillors).[2]

We can conceptualize the postwar evolution of the Japanese party system in terms of five distinct periods:

1) 1946–55: Conservative dominance accompanied by frequent changes in party composition and names within the conservative movement and a split in the Socialist movement, culminating in 1955 with the formation of the LDP and the joining of the left and right wings of the Socialist movement to form the Japan Socialist Party, or JSP (multiparty becoming essentially a three-party system in 1955).

2) 1955–93: The 1955 system characterized by conservative hegemony under the LDP, including, however, a secular decline in conservative strength; accompanying suburban development around large cities, and the appearance of two new significant minor parties, the Democratic Socialists and the Clean Government Party (Komeito); for a while growing success on the part of the Socialists (now Social Democratic Party of Japan, or SDPJ) also contributed to conservative decline (five-party system).

3) 1993–94: Defections of LDP parliamentarians to form the Harbinger Party (Sakigake) and Renewal Party (Shinseito) or to join the Japan New Party (Nihon Shinto), led by Morihiro Hosokawa, Conservative prefectural governor and later prime minister (seven-party system).

4) 1994–96: Merger in December 1994 of the Japan New Party,

Democratic Socialists, Clean Government (national element only), and Renewal parties to form the New Frontier Party (Shinshinto), following formation by the same parties of a Reform coalition in May 1994 and a second coalition of the same name in September of that year (four-party system).

5) 1996–present: Formation of the Democratic Party of Japan (Nihon Minshuto) in September 1996 from elements of the SDPJ and Harbinger Party; establishment of the Liberal Party (identified in some sources as the New Liberal Party) in January 1998 with strong Renewal Party representation; and the reemergence of the Clean Government Party as a national party (seven-party system).

The Table on p.144 indicates the vote shares of the main parties in selected elections during the postwar era. From this it can clearly be seen that only three political movements have been participants in all postwar elections—the conservatives (LDP after 1955), the Communists, and the Socialists (Social Democrats after 1994). The LDP's dominance of Japanese politics, despite fluctuations in its vote, is also visible. The JSP/SDPJ's fortunes have also varied, first growing apace with urbanization in the 1960s but later declining as other urban-based opposition parties presented themselves. The Communist Party has been present throughout the postwar era as a minor party and has gained some strength over time.

I have chosen to emphasize the LDP's organizational characteristics as the basis for identifying a Japanese party type because of the long dominance of Japanese politics by the LDP—and the even longer dominance by conservative movements in general. The LDP's long-time role as the largest party also influenced some of its organizational characteristics, and for this reason I will pay some attention to the organization of the JSP/SDPJ where it is different from that of the LDP.

How Parties Are Studied

Historically, research on political parties has been dominated by comparative political sociology.[3] American parties research and historical institutionalism also offer concepts relevant to the development of party typologies. Quite a bit of early research on political parties focused on their structural properties, especially relationships between party elites and lower echelons or followers,[4] or the nature of formal party organs and mass elements.[5] The status of party structures inside parliamentary parties was also considered.[6] Allocations of power and authority in particular parties were often inferred from these structural interpretations. Sometimes the emphasis on structure was extended to address the degree of internal organization or interlevel articulation.[7] Often parties were treated as unitary political actors, an assumption that carries over even into today's party literature. Parties' internal policy making and recruitment processes were not examined in detail, and party change was frequently seen as the result of external environmental forces. Basic party format was also said to reflect party goals, ranging from simply winning elections to broader concerns of "cultural integration," without reference to how those goals were chosen.

Applying a structural model like those just described would leave out much of what is important about Japanese parties. Japan's largest parties have always been heavily factionalized, even though factions have no role in formal party organization charts. Personal networks are also pervasively important, while a variety of other informal groups populated party organs or linked different party levels and units. Once the informal nature of Japanese parties is appreciated, it is clear that party structure is more complicated than previously thought: Formal party organization is pretty much centralized on paper, but informal relationships make the party stratarchical or decentralized at many points.[8] Japanese parties, and especially the LDP, are largely bottom-up organizations, based on candidate constituency organizations and upward interest articulation via a variety of social and organizational networks.

Political sociology's emphasis on structure and organization can also lead to the neglect of internal party processes and their implications for the distribution of intraparty power. Japan's party politics are often believed to be consensual, clandestine, and manipulated by elites from the top. This view is far from reality. Looking at political processes inside parties shows that the LDP and other parties are actually conflict systems as well as organizational frameworks. Affairs within the dominant LDP and other parties were (and are) conflictual and in most instances transparent, whether decision making concerns leader recruitment, candidate selection, policy choices, or parliamentary strategy. Herbert Kitschelt's argument that contests between plural elites set basic party strategies in some kinds of Western European parties is a good starting point for portraying this important characteristic of Japanese parties, but I find that Japanese parties display much more conflict involving many more kinds of groups than even his pioneering work suggested.[9]

In addition to the prevalence of intraparty conflict, Japan's large parties also provide examples of institutionalized groups, norms, procedures, and patterned expectations, which serve at most times to dampen or help resolve conflict or to promote party integrity in some way. Indeed, quite a bit of Japan's alleged political consensualism reflects the prevalence of multiple channels and processes dedicated to conflict management.

The message of this chapter is four-fold: First, Japanese parties are more than unitary formal organizations; they also include many important informal groups and personal networks that display different characteristics than the formal organs. Following Maurice Duverger's emphasis on mass-level party organization as the defining characteristic of party types, the importance of informal groups and social networks that operate inside or parallel to formal party organs leads me to call the LDP a "mass personalized-network party." Second, there are multiple party hierarchies, and influence is multidirectional. The party's structure is more stratarchical than hierarchical. Third, parties are political systems with enormous amounts of internal conflict, and the scope and nature of this conflict affects parties' structural characteristics and power distribution in important ways. Finally, parties develop many traits as institutions, but institutions in this instance are more contingent upon other forces than the new institutionalist literature would assume. The Liberal Democrats are an example of "conditional institutionalization"— intraparty affairs demonstrated many institutionalized characteristics until the party's underlying coalitional arrangements began to fray in the late 1980s and 1990s as the result of accusations of leader corruption. From this experience we learn the importance of Angelo Panebianco's observation that parties are ultimately coalitions, not solely organizations or institutions.[10] When coalitions fail, institutions also collapse. Party institutions in quiet times shape behavior, but they are contingent upon coalition health—they are not inevitable determinants of behavior under all conditions. Japanese parties are a hybrid of formal and informal structural characteristics, combined with power distributions reflective of internal political processes, and the parties' very organizational integrity is conditional.

Formal and Informal Organization

The Liberal Democratic Party was created in 1955 by the merger of the then-existing Liberal and Democratic Parties. Its formation followed a decade in which the Japanese conservative movement fragmented and recombined, and party names frequently changed. The LDP self-consciously modeled itself after the British Conservative Party and other European parties that had strong central institutions and permanent national and local organizations.

The formal organization of the LDP provides for five clusters of formal organization: leadership positions, strategy councils, parliamentary and intraparty representative bodies, and several other organizational units. These clusters made the overall party arrangements not dissimilar to the organizational characteristics of West European parties of "cultural integration."[11] Leadership is vested in a party executive composed of a president, a vice-president (not always appointed), and an executive council. There is also a secretary-general, who assists the party president in the administration of party affairs and who traditionally has been the party president's spokesman and a major figure in the formation of legislative and electoral strategies. There are also party caucuses and legislative strategy committees in both houses of the national parliament, which act as liaisons and sounding boards in the often complex relationship between party leaders and rank-and-file parliamentarians. In addition, the LDP holds an annual representative conference that brings together top officials and members of parliament, plus persons selected by the party's prefectural organizations. The LDP has several other national organs dedicated to functions such as internal finance and election management. Reflecting the LDP's long domination of national government, there is also a major intraparty forum for policy formulation, the Policy Affairs Research Council (PARC). The PARC in turn has its own highly developed internal organization, including a deliberative council, divisions (which are parallel to government ministries and Diet committees), investigative councils, and various other internal policy bodies concerned with ongoing issues of political importance either to LDP clientele or to the parliamentary give-and-take between parties. The PARC has been likened many times to an intraparty legislature, especially since some of its organizational components function much like American congressional committees by holding hearings or by lobbying other PARC sections on behalf of favored policies.[12]

In spite of an elaborate formal organization, the LDP has displayed more clearly than perhaps any other party in the industrialized world the importance of informal organization to the operation of formal institutions. Factions were the most important of the informal groups in the LDP. During the LDP's long period in power, factions collectively chose party and government leaders and supported candidates in elections. Local party factions and politicians' groupings also existed and periodically challenged central party influence over gubernatorial and parliamentary candidate selection. In addition, informal policy groups and clusters of politicians with similar interests played important roles in party policy making, while informal consultational processes at times replaced and often complemented formal procedures. Finally, most candidates in elections at all levels had informal political machines.

Until 1993, LDP factions were the most visible of the party's several kinds of internal informal groups.[13] For a while after the 1993 debacle, the factions retreated to the status of "study groups," only to reemerge again after 1994 to regain at least some of their earlier prominence.[14] Although varying in size in the 1980s from 14 members to as many as 136, the LDP factions were generally similar in character. Factions within the LDP have always been groups of followers of a particular politician. Before the formation of the Liberal Democratic Party in 1955, the most prominent conservative leaders, Shigeru Yoshida and Ichiro Hatoyama, each had personal followings. There were also some other leader-centered groups in the pre-1955 parties. Soon after the formation of the LDP, factions appeared among followers and proteges of Yoshida and

Hatoyama. This was the beginning of several faction lineages that have dominated LDP internal politics to the present. There were typically five to eight identifiable factions within the party, and sometimes other minor groups as well.

In the 1950s, factions reflected personal loyalties between party heavyweights and their followers. Because factions were identified by the name of their leader, the belief persisted that internal relationships followed a traditional patron-client model.[15] But the pure patron-client relationship—to the degree it had existed—was replaced over time by an organizational framework in which the faction leader was more a manager than a patron. It is necessary therefore to look beyond personal loyalties to determine the reason for factions' existence and cohesiveness.

In spite of some apparent changes over time in internal relationships, factions were always held together by the self-interest of members and leaders. Factions provided services for their members, and the members in turn were supporters of the factions. Faction leaders used their factions' memberships to launch coalition-building efforts to win top positions in the party and the government. The size of a faction, measured in number of members, was a bargaining resource to gain positions. Factions were the voting blocs from which party leadership coalitions were assembled.[16]

Thus, as with other kinds of political structures (including coalitions of all kinds), factions were based on an exchange of political resources between ordinary faction members and a faction's leader.[17] For LDP factions, the basic quid pro quo was the provision of access to party and government positions and funding support for members in exchange for members' support for faction leaders in contests for party leadership. Factions reduced the uncertainty of members' political lives by making careers more predictable. Over time, this intrafaction exchange of resources became at least as important to faction solidarity and continuity as personal loyalties and feelings, or even various specific inducements by leaders to promote solidarity—although these also contributed to faction maintenance.

Furthermore, factions provided a variety of services and resources to their members above and beyond stable career expectations. Faction leaders and their lieutenants made campaign speeches in members' home constituencies and provided funds to help members with campaign expenses. Factions also represented incumbent members and newly sponsored candidates in the intraparty negotiations over which candidates would receive a party's official endorsement. Even after the establishment of a proportional representation system in upper-house elections in 1982—which theoretically might have enhanced the role of the party's formal organization—candidate positions on the party lists were said to be determined by factional interests. Finally, faction leaders provided members with regular money allowances, which helped them maintain a constituency organization between elections and host constituents when they visited Tokyo. Faction leaders also provided their followers with New Year's gifts of money, known as *o-mochi dai*, and gifts at the summer *chugen* season (a Buddhist time of remembrance). They also helped their members represent the interests of their electoral constituencies through personal introductions to ministry officials and help with influencing PARC committees and party leaders. Indeed, even after the factions suffered a decline in status after the LDP's 1993 implosion, Japanese newspapers reported that some junior Diet members still thought that factions were important to their ability to effectively process petitions from constituents.[18]

Nelson Polsby has described the American Congress as "institutionalized" because of its durability, autonomy (that is, boundaries), and internal complexity.[19] Clearly the LDP factions have met the test of institutional durability in several ways. Most of the LDP factions formed in the 1950s were subsequently passed on to new leaders when a faction leader retired from politics or died. The stability of factions—until the LDP's loss of power in July 1993—and their more recent reemergence have also reflected the importance of their functions, such as the role of factions in personnel assignments described earlier. The continuity of factions also reflects the strong personal commitment of members to their factions. Like the lifetime employees of major firms, faction members seldom switched allegiance to a different intraparty group—demonstrating that boundaries have clearly existed as well.

Factions also meet the criterion of internal complexity. Over time, each faction has developed many of the organizational characteristics of a Japanese-style political party, including a hierarchy of formal offices (chair, vice-chair, secretary-general) and policy and election committees. Some factions even had a secretariat. Often there were also intrafactional groups of junior, middle-ranking, and senior members (seniority being based on number of times elected to the Diet), plus an informal intrafaction group of retired (or very senior) members. This last kind of group resembled the party's Supreme Consultative Council, which was made up of former prime ministers and House of Councillors presidents. Most factions also had informal power structures, for example, the "seven magistrates" of the Takeshita faction and the "court nobles" of the Miyazawa faction.

The LDP factions also engaged in many activities and rituals that further contributed to both their durability and their organizational complexity. Meetings of officers and members were held often, in some instances every week. "Study" meetings and dinners for members of different internal groups were also held regularly. Summer retreats in mountain resorts provided another opportunity for faction members to get together. In some factions new members were reportedly given special training much like new company employees under the lifetime employment system. Each faction also had newsletters and other forms of internal communication.

Procedural norms that developed over time also contributed to the institutionalized character of LDP factions and to the resolution of intrafaction disputes. A rigidly defined rule of seniority was used to select faction members for cabinet and party positions. By establishing exactly what kind of position a person would get after being elected a certain number of times, it helped prevent conflict among intensely ambitious people. Faction members could be sure that they would receive certain kinds of appointments as they advanced in seniority, and faction leaders parceled out appointments in a predictable way. If a faction's seniority rule was sometimes violated—when a junior member was promoted ahead of turn or when a senior politician entered a faction laterally—the ensuing uproar served to underline the importance of this norm.

Candidate Election Organizations

Electoral machines are the second of the LDP's most important informal party groups. These machines, or support associations *(koenkai)* in their most recent manifestation, typically have been found in older, small-business–dominated urban districts, in small cities and towns, and in the countryside during much of the time since the end of World War II.[20] A typical candidate's machine is a coalition of local social and political elites.[21] In rural areas, the usual coalition has included town-assembly members, heads of farm or fishery cooperatives, and officers of other local groups, like voluntary firefighters. Hamlet (now district) heads might also be included. Sometimes the electoral organizations of prefectural and local assembly members have been used by parliamentary candidates to augment their own organizational strength. In some cases, a Diet member's machine might even piggyback on a prefectural assembly member's electoral coalition. Urban secondary organizations, especially local small retailers' associations, have also been part of candidate electoral networks, much as secondary groups have been linked with party organizations in other countries.

Under the multimember-district election system prevailing until 1994, a candidate's electoral machine normally focused on one geographical part of a constituency and consisted at the most of a couple hundred local leaders, though larger groups were sometimes seen. In one exceptional case, former prime minister Kakuei Tanaka's famous Etsuzankai organization in Niigata prefecture comprised 315 affiliated municipal assemblymen, 26 mayors, and 11 prefectural assemblymen.

Candidates' local machines support a variety of activities to maintain voter loyalty. National politicians appear regularly at local school athletic days, shrine festivals, and meetings of local interest groups to cultivate support. Local and national politicians also respond to solicitations from communities and local groups to help support local events financially. Even after major corruption scandals in the late 1980s threatened many politicians' normal funding sources, incumbent Diet members were still making donations to support local festivals and other special events, according to newspaper accounts.

The extent to which national politicians give money or some kind of token presents at election time in exchange for voting support, another allegedly typical practice, has never been known precisely, although it is believed to be widespread. My own interviews with local assemblymen indicate that politicians give more gifts at the time of their first candidacy than later, when they are better known and have established a record of representing their constituency. According to recent newspaper accounts, however, most incumbents still send presents of money to newly married couples and make donations at funerals when these events involve their supporters. Many Diet members also hold formal dinner parties for their most loyal supporters, and some pay most of the costs of vacation trips for members of their supporters' associations. Some Diet members are renowned for their largesse: The last event held by Tanaka's organization was reportedly a weekend trip for 11,000 people to a hotsprings resort at an alleged cost of $1.4 million.

Frequent gifts and heavily subsidized trips are a Diet member's way of demonstrating personal consideration and concern for supporters. Another way to demonstrate personal attention is by sending greeting cards. Greetings are sent at New Year's and also in midsummer during the *chugen* season. Even Diet members who travel abroad are expected to send greeting cards to their followers. Sometimes these number in the thousands. As one Diet member confided to me in an interview, "Personality is judged by how one observes the ordinary ways of the world." The ways of the world are costly for many Japanese politicians.

Whatever the motivations of politicians and followers, the activities and expenditures for constituents help to preserve the integrity of the electoral base of incumbent Diet members as well as to provide a ticket to election for some new candidates. Ordinary voters also gain the satisfaction of being recognized by an important person. In this view, displays of concern and money convince voters that the donor is a responsible person who observes the norms of Japanese culture regarding obligation and downward loyalty. Another important part of securing a local base of support is the representation of local interests, both those tied to a specific place and those tied to the occupations of the people who live there. Tanaka's organization was an excellent example: The provision of public works in every corner of his Niigata district was one of the reasons for his enormous electoral success. Some of the more costly and unusual projects captured national attention and became legendary. Construction of expressways and high-speed train lines with

connections or station stops at rural towns and the provision of hot-
water systems in village streets to facilitate automatic snow removal
were among the better known of Tanaka's constituency projects.[22]

Pluralism and Conflict in Political Recruitment

The structural approach to party organization always stressed the
character of vertical aspects of formal party formats, such as the
relationship between party executives and parliamentary, national, and
local party elements. A similar emphasis on interlevel relationships has
been adopted by most observers of Japanese politics, who have
characterized the formal organization of the Liberal Democratic Party
between 1955 and 1993 as an inverted pyramid.[23] According to this
view, policy making, recruitment, and strategy were concentrated at the
national level. Decisions on electoral and parliamentary strategy were
also centralized, at least in theory. In contrast, local party branches
often were (and are) inactive, and membership was often nominal or
even reflected loyalty to a particular Diet member more than to the
party. Despite efforts to develop mass-level party organizations, the
party's national organs were widely believed to be better developed and
more visible than grassroots organization.

Some of the ideas about the LDP's formal organization are clearly
valid. However, informal organizational patterns, which are often
neglected by the structuralist school, can present a different picture of
party structure than those suggested by formal party arrangements. For
example, in the case of the LDP, decisions about which candidate will
be assigned the party's approval are more stratarchical or even
decentralized than centralized, given the need to negotiate with local
factions and interests. There is usually a strong upward flow of pressure
on behalf of local interests, which affect national party decisions via the
policy-making influence of *zoku* members. (*Zoku,* meaning families or
tribes, are informal, sometimes even secretive, clusters of Diet members
interested in a common policy area.) In many senses, the party is
organizationally more like two pyramids, one inverted and one standing
on its base. The first describes the formal organization and activities
that are centralized; the second recognizes that Diet members' political
machines have provided the party with extensive and intimate contacts
among constituents that have resulted in the upward communication of
local and regional interests to national party councils. Other aspects of
informal organization presented in this chapter complete the picture of
a frequently downwardly responsible party apparatus, in which the formal
shape is the only sign of centralized party power.

There is also more to party organization than just vertical
relationships. Parties can be horizontally fragmented or integrated as
well. As in Kitschelt's portrayal of European ecological and socialist

parties, conflict occurs *within* every level of Japanese parties, including the LDP, as well as *between* national, prefectural, and local domains.[24] The allocation of executive positions was one such source of intraparty conflict within the LDP. Between 1955 and 1993, the recruitment of Japan's most important political elites took place inside the Liberal Democratic Party. Both party and government leaders were chosen by coalitions of intra-LDP factions, since, in the case of government leadership, the LDP's domination of the Diet ensured that intra-LDP decisions were normally promptly ratified in the parliament. The intraparty coalitions were founded on agreements to support a particular leadership team in exchange for the allocation of positions to each participating faction.

The LDP leadership coalitions were short-lived and occasionally quite fragile. New LDP presidents were typically selected every two years, though there were major exceptions to this rule in some instances. A turnover in cabinet appointments took place even more frequently, as governing coalitions sought to give more supporters top positions.[25] In the first seven years of the 1980s, Japan changed cabinets (but not prime ministers) an average of once every 12 months. Coalition agreements supporting a particular prime minister could also be renegotiated, as potential leaders were always waiting in the wings. Conflict between factions over who would become party leaders was intermittently intense throughout the era of the LDP's domination, at times even threatening the party's ability to function effectively in designing party policies and strategies.

When making leadership choices, the LDP functioned much like a multiparty system. If a cabinet reshuffle or change in party leadership seemed to be in the offing, each LDP faction developed a coalition strategy consisting of both efforts to form an alliance with other factions and a slate of cabinet or party positions to be allocated to the faction in exchange for their support of a new interfactional leadership coalition. Faction leaders also cultivated relationships with other factions as part of their coalition strategy. Their goal was to acquire a sufficient number of allies among the large factions to end up in the winning coalition. Sometimes precoalition alignments already existed, based on personal ties between faction leaders. In other cases, enmities between certain leaders precluded faction alliances. Similar friendships and enmities between top politicians continue to exist in the LDP and other parties today.

The informal factions in the LDP made careers predictable through the application of promotion norms. At the same time, even the factions themselves were often centers of intense internal conflict. Intrafaction conflict reflected in part the inevitable clash of faction members' personal ambitions and personalities, especially senior politicians near the pinnacle of a faction's hierarchy of influence. Indeed, feuds between established or rising politicians were nearly constant in intrafaction as well as intraparty politics. On various occasions, those who supported certain senior politicians within a faction grouped together, and the formation of such a group signaled someone's ambition to become faction leader and eventually prime minister. When the death or retirement of a faction leader dictated a change, subfaction heads mounted aggressive campaigns for the faction leadership. Conflicts among these subfactions or their leaders at times led to splits in factions. Although most factions have been stable over time, occasional faction splits are a reminder of the fragility of faction coalitions and the intensity of interpersonal and intergroup conflicts.

Sometimes factions were divided between their junior and senior members. These intergenerational cleavages usually reflected younger faction members' feelings of distance from faction leaders. Junior members of the Miyazawa faction reportedly felt isolated from the group of mainly exbureaucrats who led the faction. In other cases, junior faction members were upset when they felt that the credibility of their faction was declining, as happened when leading members were associated with some kind of scandal. The juniors were fearful that corruption accusations would weaken the faction's ability to get party and government positions for its members, always a dominant concern.

Policy-Making Pluralism

LDP factions were mainly concerned with personnel matters, but other important intraparty groups were concerned with policy, and policy cleavages in the LDP have at times been profound. Pluralism in internal policy (and sometimes even ideology) was the rule during most of the LDP's time in power. Considerable intra-LDP conflict reflected the presence of organized policy groups and policy tribes within the party. Policy groups like the Asian Problems Research Association, the Afro-Asian Problems Research Association—both of which were concerned with China policy—and various other groups contributed to intra-LDP policy pluralism at different times. For example, even though many LDP members were nominally anticommunist in the early postwar era, differences of opinion among the two China policy groups repeatedly stalled intraparty debate on Japanese relations with mainland China and Taiwan in the 1960s and were stumbling blocks to achieving rapprochement between Japan and mainland China for many years.

In the 1980s, the LDP moved even further away from a politics of ideology, and nonideological issues like administrative reform, proposals for a new tax regime, and farmers' concerns dominated party agendas. Groupings of LDP Diet members (*zoku*) interested in specific policy areas, such as agriculture, construction, small business, or education, were a source of intra-LDP pluralism.

The *zoku* phenomenon points out the importance of the LDP's role in transmitting sectoral, regional, and local interests. After its formation in 1955, the LDP was aligned with many of Japan's most important interest groups and population sectors. The party subsequently expanded its interest coalition by building ties with an increasingly broader constellation of interests.[26] So inclusive was the scope of the LDP's interest coalition that the party was clearly a "catch-all" party, according to the Otto Kirchheimer view of parties' relationships with social sectors and private interests. Although facilitating success at the polls, the diversity of interests served by the LDP sometimes made intraparty policy agreement difficult. Policy making had its own dynamic, with groups vying for influence over policy positions. At times, there were even sharp divisions within the leadership that weakened their influence over party decisions. On some occasions, internal party conflict was so great that party leaders were called on mainly to mediate between intraparty groups.

Party leaders sometimes had to give in to rank-and-file pressure and ratify policies initiated by informal groups within the party. The repeated accommodation of farm-group demands provides one such example. In other cases, party leaders held the line against intraparty pressure. The party center prevailed in 1988, for example, when Prime Minister Takeshita and other party leaders pushed tax reforms through the Diet in the face of intense opposition from fellow party members representing regional and small retailers' interests—even though the previous year a similar move by a Nakasone-led government had been thwarted.

Interestingly, although individual leaders of some LDP factions had reputations as hawks or doves on security issues, the factions themselves generally did not have strong ideological or policy coloring. Lacking cohesive opinions on most issues, members and leaders of factions could be expected to refrain from involvement in policy matters. Nevertheless, competition for party leadership positions sometimes became entangled with policy processes. When that happened, particularly when the extension of a party president's term was at stake or when a new LDP president was to be selected, factional politics became a part of policy making and party strategy.

Resolving Internal Conflict

I have shown that the LDP was a political system with attendant conflict between intraparty groups and factions, and even inside the all-important factions. Analysis of intraparty decision making also demonstrates that there were a variety of institutionalized intraparty mechanisms for dampening or resolving conflict. The most visible of these mechanisms governed recruitment of top party and government leadership, including arrangements within party factions that dictated how positions were allocated.

Party recruitment of leaders and cabinet members via interfactional coalitions was governed by a mixture of formal rules and informal norms specifying in general terms when, how, and how often leaders would be selected. The expectations involved in forming (and removing) LDP leadership coalitions provide evidence of the regularized nature of intraparty processes. Often there were tentative understandings within the LDP regarding the probable order of succession to the party presidency. Most of the time a particular "generational" window of opportunity existed for a small number of senior party figures. The window was determined by several expectations: how long an incumbent leader would survive as party president, how many credible aspirants there were, and whether and when a new generation of aspirants for office would make a challenge to replace the existing generation. The concept of leadership generations, or clusters of possible leaders classified by age, was used widely in journalistic accounts of intra-LDP personnel decisions. Usually only the leaders of some of the large factions were expected to become party president and therefore were included in this group. The current LDP has reportedly returned to calculate leadership coalition possibilities based on these same expectations.[27]

When and how a party president had to step down was also a matter of intraparty understandings. Generally it was assumed that a party president would serve for two two-year terms, at the most. Most leaders in the 1970s and 1980s lasted only one term. Exactly when a president had to step down was based on political credibility, as judged by the factions and their leadership. Failure of the party to do well in parliamentary elections, extremely poor performance in monthly opinion polls, or failure to move the LDP legislative agenda through parliament were all used to discredit incumbents. Weak leadership performance prompted other factions to try to terminate the incumbent leadership coalition and select a new leader.

Another norm at work from the 1980s on was the concept of "fair shares," or the distribution of party and government seats to nominees from all factions on the basis of faction size. The resulting LDP interfaction leadership coalitions were of an "all-party" variety, rather than a few allied "mainstream" factions taking all of the seats, which had been the case earlier. The choice of all-party coalitions reflected an increased need for party unity after electoral losses in the 1970s, as well as an application of a fair-shares norm observable in various other aspects of Japanese politics, including budget formulation and Diet committee management. The interpersonal rivalries and differences in leader ideologies that had produced mainstream versus anti-mainstream divisions earlier in the postwar era had also moderated.

To recapitulate: Factions simultaneously enhanced and reduced conflict within the LDP. Because factions were institutionalized and had strong jurisdictional interests in regard to party leadership recruitment, competition between them was at times very intense. At the same time, like seniority norms in the U.S. Congress, the intrafaction and interfaction seniority norms in the LDP made political life more certain and conflict less inevitable. The presence of institutionalized intraparty factions also stabilized party life in other ways. The same intraparty factions contested choices of top LDP personnel year in and year out, with usually only minor, slow changes in leading personnel. Stable factions and an institutionalized factional system lent an overall regularity to the behavior and expected behavior of important actors in intraparty political processes. Competition for top positions and expectations about this competition were firmly structured, and this stability, combined with party procedures and norms, made orderly transfers of power possible—despite occasionally enormous intraparty conflicts and centrifugal pressures.

The LDP: Coalition or Institution?

The Liberal Democratic Party was stable and institutionalized between 1955 and 1993. In spite of frequently intense internal competition and conflict, it retained its organizational integrity for nearly 40 years. Then, in 1993, two groups of LDP Diet members defected to form new parties, followed by several individual MPs acting on their own. The defections and associated events threw the LDP and Japanese politics into disarray in 1993–94. At least two dozen new intraparty and interparty reform groups, several splinter groups, and one new multiparty movement were formed (and in some cases disappeared) within only 15 months. How can the contradiction between the LDP's long rule and elaborate organizational arrangements and its sudden partial collapse and recent organizational chaos be explained?

To answer this conundrum requires an appreciation that political parties are inevitably coalitions built on an exchange of resources.[28] They may develop institutionalized patterns as organizations, but all parties are still inherently coalitional in nature. Coalitions can last a long time, but under some conditions they are also very fragile and may collapse. Even though a party organization appears to be firmly established, continuation depends on whether enough party politicians continue to believe that the party should exist. If coalitional agreements fall apart, existing organizational arrangements become less meaningful, or even irrelevant. The LDP is a coalition that has existed to serve the interests of its members, its leaders, and its local interest-group constituency by winning elections, formulating policy proposals, and providing a system for recruiting party and government leaders. By working together, party politicians were able to gain political offices, represent constituencies, and formulate policies that advanced the principles of the dominant intraparty and clientele groups. The existence of the party served both the substantive concerns of its multiple constituencies and those of its leaders and rank-and-file members.

Historically, LDP politicians gained government positions and intraparty policy influence in exchange for accepting party policies, procedures, and norms. As long as the coalition met politicians' needs, the party continued to exist. When the party and its leadership lost credibility in 1992–93 in the face of corruption scandals, the party's *raison d'être* was weakened. For the LDP members who defected (nearly 20 percent of its MPs did), it had failed entirely, and exit was the preferred choice.

In reality, the coalitional nature of the LDP was intermittently and repeatedly visible in the periodic crises that had threatened the party's very existence since its formation in the 1950s. Loss of confidence in party leadership, coupled with internal factionalism and group conflict, brought the LDP near collapse several times. Intraparty conflict and reactions to that conflict contributed to opposing "dynamics" in the LDP. One dynamic was the persistence of party institutions and procedures, including those we described earlier, that promote integration and solidarity. The other was an intermittent tendency toward fragmentation and crisis. LDP internal conflict in earlier periods nearly led to party collapse in 1958–60, 1974, 1976, and 1979–80. In each instance, the party and its leadership were perceived by the rank-and-file and the mass media as lacking credibility. In every instance, the internal disagreements reflected doubts, within and outside the party, that the party could continue to win elections—a matter of special importance to rank-and-file members who had not been elected enough times to feel confident of reelection in the face of declining party credibility. Usually a party crisis was associated with the formation of new groups that sought to remedy the party's problems, either within the party's existing format or through reform. Protests by local and prefectural party units were also typical.

LDP reactions following the major corruption scandals of 1988–93 were similar to those in earlier crises. Leading politicians lost credibility after accusations that they had profited from purchases of Recruit Company stock on the basis of insider information or that they had accepted bribes from Sagawa Kyubin, an express trucking company. Junior LDP Diet members formed several intraparty reform groups out of frustration with the party leadership. These groups, and other groups formed as a reaction to them, included a 48-member cross-faction Free Renovationist league, a "liberal" reform-oriented policy group called Heiseinokai, and the allegedly right-wing Association of Persons Concerned over Basic State Problems. A number of other intraparty groups were also active at this time, including the Hirakawa Society, the Liberal Society Forum, the Utopia Study Group, and the Liberal Reform League. The creation of these and other reform and antireform groups was symptomatic of the anxiety of LDP Diet members. As the party began to lose credibility and formerly secure careers seemed in doubt, different groups sought solutions to party problems. As in past crises, starting a new political party was one consideration.

Specific events and the loss of LDP leadership credibility contributed to each LDP crisis. Factional competition was also a factor in some, but not all, cases. But the LDP crisis dynamic went beyond interfactional competition. Factions attempted to take advantage of events that were causing alarm among party politicians and therefore added to the general anxiety. In each case, severe intraparty conflict, perceptions of failed leadership, and election losses all contributed to a growing feeling that the party's very survival was threatened.

The intermittent fragility of the party coalition was further demonstrated by the outbreak of hostilities between the national party and its local components. In the most recent crisis (1988–93), several local LDP federations took up the protest against the central party leadership and passed resolutions demanding party reform and accountability. One prefectural organization threatened to secede from the party. Later in 1989, prefectural delegations at the annual summer meeting of representatives of local party chapters reiterated demands for party reform. Nine LDP members of the Fukuoka prefectural assembly asked for "*en masse* resignation of all LDP officers suspected of Recruit scandal involvement." Similar demands came from LDP members of the Nagoya city assembly and the Kagawa prefectural assembly.[29]

Local disagreements with the national party's leadership at times of crisis reflected the stratarchical and sometimes highly fragmented nature of local-national party relations, even in normal times. Local-national squabbles over parliamentary and gubernatorial nominations during the era of LDP hegemony were routine and sometimes involved national and prefectural factions along with the formal party organs. In 1991, for example, the LDP secretary-general and some members of the Tokyo metropolitan prefecture party disagreed over the choice of a nominee for the governorship of Tokyo. Incidents like that occurred with every major postwar election. Cleavages within local party groups were fairly common as well.

The 1988–93 crises forced several top party officials to resign and eventually culminated in defections from the party by groups intent on forming new conservative parties. LDP prime minister Noboru Takeshita had to resign in 1989 because of his involvement in the Recruit scandal. LDP prime minister Kiichi Miyazawa, whose leadership was characterized as very weak from the beginning of his term in 1991, was forced to step down in 1993. A total of 56 LDP Diet members left the party.[30] These events culminated in the LDP's loss of its majority in the Diet, ending its longtime, sometimes singlehanded domination of Japanese politics. When a group of centrist and moderate left parties came together in August 1993, the previously unthinkable event of a non-LDP coalition government became a reality. Although the LDP survived multiple crises and internal conflicts and maintained its institutional integrity in a "Perils of Pauline" fashion, it existed by virtue of its coalitional nature. Until 1993, the payoffs of positions, power, and, for some, ideological opposition to communism— along with the party procedures that constrained conflict—held together an otherwise fragmentation-prone political movement. The LDP regained power in an alliance with the SDPJ in mid-1994 and later returned to hold a near-majority in the lower and most important house of the Japanese parliament, even while participating in a three-party coalition to increase its parliamentary clout in both houses.

Since 1993, intraparty politics in the LDP have remained highly pluralistic, while decision-making procedures have been generally less predictable than before 1993. For a variety of reasons, the Liberal Democratic Party's overall organizational structure appears to be weaker and less institutionalized than in the past. Initially, the factions were discredited both because of alleged corruption by various faction leaders and by the strong condemnation of the faction system from MPs who had not been elected enough times to feel secure in the face of the corruption issue. When the LDP once again came into power, however, the factions and other informal institutions reappeared, although without the confidence they had shown previously. Once again it is obvious that the institutionalization of structures and procedures depends at least partially on what the institutions provide for their participants.

Japan's Other Parties

The LDP model of a semi-institutionalized but highly fragmented and even fragile coalitional structure can be seen elsewhere in Japanese politics. Fragmentation not unlike that in the LDP was often evident in the second largest party, the Socialist (now Social Democratic) Party. Indeed, despite the attention given by the SDPJ to building a strong central and local organization like its European counterparts,[31] and even though the party has always been smaller than the LDP, the number of factions and intraparty ideological groups has often been greater than in the conservative party. In normal times, then, the SDPJ could be described as more fragmented than even the LDP. Social Democratic factions and policy groups also split and regrouped fairly often. For example, the Socialist Association, the largest left-wing group in the party, split in 1986 over the party executive's efforts to move toward allegedly greater realism on fundamental domestic and foreign policy issues. Forty of the 50 members of the Socialist Association on the 134-person party secretariat resigned. An internal fragmentation pattern like that of the LDP was again apparent in the SDPJ in 1989–90 and later when junior

Diet members formed reform groups and local party organizations rebuked the party center. Although the SDPJ did not lose overall credibility as a party to the same degree as the LDP, by the early 1990s more than ten new groups had been established by party members struggling to redefine themselves in light of the rapidly changing conditions of Japanese politics.

The SDPJ has at times mirrored LDP organization in several other ways. A generational divide like that in the LDP was a prominent feature of the recent divisions in the SDPJ. For example, 60 SDPJ members of parliament elected for the first time in 1990 subsequently established two important new groups, New Wave and New Power. Not long thereafter, New Wave members requested that the party leadership resign, blaming them for the past failure of the SDPJ to gain power. New Power members also criticized the party leadership for election losses in 1991. Several other intraparty policy or reform groups—Social Democracy Forum, Action New Democracy, Sirius, New Generation Political Forum, Leadership 21, and Society 91— were also formed in the early 1990s. In 1992, one of Japan's major dailies reported: "With the successive establishment of new policy groups centering on young Diet members, the SDPJ is showing signs that its composition will become fluid. . . . Responding to the distrust in politics . . . and arguments for political reorganization in labor circles, this may be the spark that ignites an explosion on the opposition party side."[32] Meetings were also held at several points in late 1992 to discuss possibly setting up a new middle-of-the-road party to include parts of the LDP, the right wing of the SDPJ, and centrist parties—a potentiality which later became reality with the formation of the Democratic Party in autumn 1996. Internal fissures, generational challenges, and centrifugal dynamism were not properties of the LDP alone.

A Mass Personalized-Network Party

This chapter has described the main structural characteristics of Japan's long-dominant party—the Liberal Democratic Party—and the multiparty political system in which it has operated. I have indicated that the LDP is a mixture of formal organs and informal groups, with tendencies to centralization, stratarchy, or decentralization varying with specific functions—electoral mobilization, special-interest issues, parliamentary strategy, or national policy. National issues and foreign policy are resolved within central party leadership groups, including the Policy Affairs Research Council. Party policy and related parliamentary strategies are authored in PARC debates and hearings, as well as in the party's senior executive groups. But *zoku,* interest-group, and policy-group pressures make these processes highly pluralistic. There are also inputs and pressures from rank-and-file MPs bent on expressing their own and their constituencies' policy preferences, with the result that otherwise centralized party processes have a strong element of stratarchy.

The recruitment of candidates for election and the award of party labels thereto are often governed by local-national factional coalitions and at some times face insoluble conflicts leading to excess candidacies and local party splits. Recruitment decisions concerning party leadership are decided within the party's top organs and relationships but are also highly competitive as the result of intraparty factionalism.

It is difficult to encapsulate all of the organizational and structural dimensions displayed within the LDP in a single term. The same would be true, but less so, for other Japanese parties, especially smaller groups with fewer than 50 members in the Diet. In order to capture the importance in the LDP of both formal and informal mass-party characteristics (lots of organizations at all levels of the party and society), the party structure can be summed up as a "mass personalized-network party" or even "post-clientelistic personalized-network party." The use of these terms would conform to Duverger's predilection for using base qualities, such as cadre, branch, or militia, to symbolize some overall traits of inevitably complex organizations. Personal networks are important in all LDP activities (and those of other Japanese parties), and the parties' internal relationships are based to no small degree on an exchange of resources between persons in different parts or levels of the party. Factions are based on personalized networks and exchanges. So are the relationships employed in the representation of group interests and local concerns or, for that matter, the networks involved in accommodating the desires of different factions for top positions.

Turning to the important issue of party durability suggests still another party type. In this chapter, I have abandoned the frequent political-sociological preference to see parties as unitary organizations that change as the result of environmental adaptation. Instead, I have examined intraparty political processes and their responses to both internal and external political forces. This in turn led me to characterize the LDP as an example of "conditional institutionalization." The account of LDP processes showed that payoffs satisfying all persons in the party coalition were important to party survival and the maintenance of apparently well-institutionalized procedures and factional allegiances. Although the LDP was a conflict-ridden party from the very beginning, over time mechanisms like well-defined career advancement norms, a fair-shares concept, and regularized expectations about top executive turnover helped the party work its way out of its internal problems, and sometimes external troubles as well. When the LDP's problems became so great that party members could not be sure that their careers would survive, however, even institutionalized mechanisms and relationships embedded in the party's culture were themselves vulnerable.

External crises of party leadership credibility were the sources of internal breakdown in even seemingly institutionalized aspects of party procedures. Perhaps the enormous scope of societal interests encompassed within the party made the LDP organizationally unwieldy by generating conflict overload. Perhaps the numbers of important informal groups vying for influence had a similar effect. Perhaps the very importance of informal personal networks and the myriad small intraparty groups and candidate machines relative to the more limited scope of the party's formal organization contributed to the fragility of the party's institutionalized components. Whatever the choice of typology, two prominent features of the LDP's organization need to be kept in mind: There has been and still is enormous internal vertical and horizontal pluralism, reflecting the LDP's dominant status in Japanese politics and the broad scope of its interest relationships. There are also procedures, norms, and other systemic regularities that helped to hold the party together, but only as long as the party coalition served its purposes.

The LDP was—and continues to be—an important and integral part of Japanese political processes. The LDP and other parties run candidates in elections, mobilize voters, influence MP careers, select party and government leadership teams, develop parliamentary and governance strategies, seek policy goals, and generally occupy the most visible space in the Japanese political system. Both the scope of the LDP's policy concerns and the size and complexity of its mass constituency resulted in a proliferation of interests and party units covering perhaps as much as 75 percent of the affairs of governance between 1955 and 1993. The scope of the LDP's domination has declined somewhat, but political parties in general still collectively dominate policy making where legislation is involved. Despite the widespread and accurate belief that the bureaucracy does a lot, Japan's party-based ministry relationships and party-system–based parliamentary processes are central to political life. A slight weakening of internal party structures since 1993—factions for a while described themselves as "study groups," and a number of groups and individuals deserted the LDP for other parties—can give the impression of some party decline. But Japanese parties, viewed as combinations of formal and informal elements, still play the central role in most aspects of politics. Parties nominate candidates, and party factions allocate funds to support campaigns; party factions play a giant role in elite recruitment, while both formal and informal intraparty groups manage policy processes, develop and implement parliamentary strategies, and coordinate policy proposals with the bureaucracy.

It should be evident by now that my interpretation of Japanese political parties' organizational and structural characteristics eludes simple causal characterizations of intraparty relationships. This would include interpretations in principal-agent theory that assume the primacy of election-system effects on politicians' motivations and behavior and, therefore, on intraparty organization.[33] Rather than seeing the electoral system as the dominant driving force underlying politicians' behavior in Japan, however, I agree with Richard Gunther, who has shown that electoral institutions alone do not shape behavior but rather influence both parties and electorates *in combination with other factors.*[34] In Japan such "other factors" include the Japanese preference for deep constituency mobilization, which creates candidates who are very hard to dissuade from running. I would suggest that party organization, structure, and all internal relationships and processes are influenced by several variable clusters. These include, without any specific priority: the opportunities afforded by local community society for electoral mobilization; the influence of supra-community secondary organization affiliations of particular parties; the scope of societal interests addressed by a particular party, party goal, or ideology; and, relatedly, the distribution of intraparty elite preferences on goals and ideology at particular times in parties' development.

The LDP and other large Japanese parties have represented a mixture of two party types from the alternatives presented in chapter 1 of this volume. Viewed in terms of formal structure, Japanese parties are quite similar to European mass parties with elaborate national organizations and attempts to form active local party chapters. There are also large residual elements of exchanges between ordinary voters and party candidates reminiscent of clientelistic parties. Nevertheless, nowadays the exchanges are more personalistic than purely clientelistic. The patrons can be relatively low-level elites, and Japanese society is no longer stratified on the basis of wealth and status to the extent implied in the clientelistic model. I believe the term "mass personalized-network party" best fits the Japanese case in the present epoch.

NOTES

1. Relatedly, in 1983–86 the LDP formed a coalition with a small conservative breakaway group—the New Liberal Club—in order to strengthen its influence over the parliamentary process.

2. LDP success has varied in inverse proportion to the size of election districts, according to what might be called a mobilizational theory of Japanese elections. The party has done worse in House of Councillors elections where election districts are based on prefecture boundaries (as U.S. senators are in states) and are therefore larger and harder to organize than in the case of the much smaller House of Representatives districts. A 1994 electoral law reform created even smaller House of Representatives districts than the ones in effect throughout most of the postwar era. All Japanese parliamentary candidates have support organizations of some kind, but their constituency efforts are more effective in smaller than in larger districts.

3. The terms used in this chapter—process, structure, and organization—need to be defined. Process refers to the events and behaviors of everyday politics or what parties and politicians do in a particular time period to win elections, pass laws, and so on. Structure implies longer-term patterns in behavior and relationships. Organization implies the provision for a specific arrangement of internal units and a prescribed hierarchy of authority.

4. Robert Michels, *Political Parties: A Sociological Study of the Oligarchical Tendencies of Modern Democracy* (New York: The Free Press, 1962).

5. Maurice Duverger, *Political Parties: Their Organization and Activity in the Modern State* (New York: Wiley and Sons, 1963); Sigmund Neumann, ed., *Modern Political Parties: Approaches to Comparative Politics* (Chicago: University of Chicago Press, 1956), 395–421.

6. Kurt Shell, "The Socialist Party of Austria: A Party of Integration," in Kurt Shell, ed., *The Democratic Political Process: A Cross-National Reader* (Waltham, Mass.: Blaisdell, 1969).

7. Maurice Duverger, *Political Parties*.

8. Samuel Eldersveld, *Political Parties: A Behavioral Analysis* (Chicago: Rand McNally, 1969). According to Eldersveld, stratarchy describes a condition where national, state, and local party units are independent of each other rather than being subordinated to central organizational units or elites. In Japan, we use the term to indicate that parties have bottom-up as well as top-down structures, with the result that an average pattern might be considered to be stratarchical.

9. Herbert Kitschelt, *The Logics of Party Formation: Ecological Politics in Belgium and West Germany* (Ithaca, N.Y.: Cornell University Press, 1989); Herbert Kitschelt, *The Transformation of European Social Democracy* (New York: Cambridge University Press, 1994).

10. Angelo Panebianco, *Political Parties: Organization and Power* (Cambridge: Cambridge University Press, 1988).

11. Sigmund Neumann, *Modern Political Parties*.

12. Nihon Keizai Shimbunsha, *Jiminto Seichokai [The Liberal Democratic Party Policy Affairs Research Council]* (Tokyo: Nihon Keizai Shimbunsha, 1983).

13. Robert A. Scalapino and Junnosuke Masumi, *Parties and Politics in Contemporary Japan* (Berkeley: University of California Press, 1962); Nathaniel Thayer, *How the Conservatives Rule Japan* (Princeton, N.J.: Princeton University Press, 1969); Haruhiro Fukui, *Party in Power: The Japanese Liberal Democrats and Policymaking* (Berkeley: University of California Press, 1970); Hans Baerwald, *Party Politics in Japan* (Winchester, Mass.: Allen and Unwin, 1986); Ronald J. Hrebenar, ed., *The Japanese Party System: From One Party Rule to Coalition Government* (Boulder, Colo.: Westview, 1986).

14. Gerald Curtis, *The Logic of Japanese Politics: Leaders, Institutions and the Limits of Change* (New York: Columbia University Press, 1999); Bradley M. Richardson, *Japanese Democracy: Power, Conflict and Performance* (New Haven: Yale University Press, 1997).

15. Tsuneo Watanabe, *Habatsu: Nihon Hoshuto no Bunseki* [Factions: An Analysis of the Japanese Conservative Party] (Tokyo: Kobundo, 1964).

16. Japanese political-science folklore—as well as recent essays on Japanese political rationality—stresses the help that factions provide their members at election time as the main reason that factions exist in the LDP. In reality, politicians generally have three dominant concerns: getting reelected, obtaining top positions in the party and government, and influencing policy. The informal factions in the LDP satisfied the second of these goals and played a role in the first. Their contribution to the third was less central, although at times interfactional competition did affect policy making. See J. Mark Ramsayer and Francis McCall Rosenbluth, *Japan's Political Marketplace* (Cambridge, Mass.: Harvard University Press, 1993).

Japanese-studies folklore has also attributed the existence of internal party factions to Japan's pre-1994 multimember-constituency House of Representatives electoral system. Intraparty competition between candidates in large parties was said to underwrite the very existence of the faction system. In my own view, this is an unacceptably simple explanation.

17. Harumi Befu argues that exchange relationships are the dominant form of social relationship in Japan. Harumi Befu, *The Group Model of Japanese Society and an Alternative* (Houston: Rice University Studies, No. 66, 1980).

18. Aversion to the LDP's factionalism has a long history among Japanese scholars and political journalists. Factions have been seen over and over as the root of high-level corruption scandals, insomuch as the costs of supporting a faction are inevitably very high. The resulting popular bias against factions has led to frequent intraparty commitments to end factionalism, but this has not happened.

19. Nelson Polsby, "The Institutionalization of the U.S. House of Representatives," *American Political Science Review* 62 (March 1968): 144–68.

20. In the 1960s, these supporters' associations were found more in cities than in rural areas, reflecting, among other things, the lower density in urban areas of "natural" social relationships available to politicians for use at election time. Nowadays, supporter associations have penetrated the countryside as well. One national newspaper reported in 1989 that 40 million Japanese voters were enrolled in such associations—over half the electorate and roughly ten times the number of members claimed by the LDP.

21. Gerald Curtis, *Election Campaigning Japanese Style* (New York: Columbia University Press, 1971).

22. Jacob M. Schlesinger, *Shadow Shoguns: The Rise and Fall of Japan's Postwar Political Machine* (New York: Simon and Schuster, 1997). Such efforts by Tanaka did more than just address local people's desire for improved public services and transportation. They also provided business for construction companies and jobs for construction workers—a frequent off-season source of employment for farmers. Nationally, substantial portions of the annual general account budget have been spent on local public works to shore up Diet members' reputations and develop the public infrastructure. In 1955, the portion spent on public works was 14 percent, in 1965 it ballooned to 22 percent, and in the mid-1980s the amount was still a hefty 13 percent.

23. Chalmers Johnson, *Who Governs? The Rise of the Developmental State* (New York: W.W. Norton, 1995).

24. Herbert Kitschelt, *The Logics of Party Formation;* and Herbert Kitschelt, *The Transformation of European Social Democracy.*

25. Cabinet tenure has been very short in Japan; in other countries this is often a sign of government instability. In Britain, cabinets lasted for an average 50 months in the postwar period. Cabinets were reshuffled annually in Japan between 1945 and 1993. Indeed, Italian and Japanese cabinets in the 1980s were of roughly equal durability, and Italy is usually said to be a country of unusual leadership volatility. Given especially that the period of LDP rule was mainly a time of government stability, the frequency of cabinet replacement is striking. The answer to this conundrum lies in the motivation for cabinet change. In Italy, cabinets fell because of intense internal disagreements. In Japan, they were replaced to reallocate positions to new teams of aspiring politicians and indicate the importance of senior personnel appointments to politicians, both as personal goals and as a currency in election campaigns.

26. Muramatsu Michio and Ellis Krauss, "The Conservative Policy Line and the

Development of Patterned Pluralism," in Kozo Yamamura and Yasukichi Yasuba, eds., *The Political Economy of Japan: Vol. I—The Domestic Transformation* (Stanford, Calif.: Stanford University Press, 1987), 516–54; Yutaka Tsujinaka, *Rieki Shudan* [Interest Groups] (Tokyo: Tokyo Daigaku Shuppankai, 1988).

27. Contending faction leaders within an eligible generational cohort reportedly agreed on an even more refined order of succession to the party presidency. When Prime Minister Nakasone resigned in 1987, one of a "new" generation of three large-faction leaders was expected to succeed as party president and prime minister after Nakasone. When the smoke cleared after intra-elite negotiations, Noboru Takeshita was the choice of the outgoing party president, but it was said that Shintaro Abe would succeed Takeshita by agreeing not to contest Takeshita's preceding him. Whether or not all the published rumors about private succession agreements are true, an intraparty seniority rule of this kind could help keep conflict under control through its effect on faction leaders' expectations.

28. Angelo Panebianco, *Political Parties.*

29. These actions by local party organs, including several in largely rural areas, occurred at the same time as anti-LDP sentiment among farmers and small-business people in spring 1989. Farmers were worried about an anticipated opening of Japanese markets to foreign agricultural imports while the small businesses opposed increased taxes on retail sales and expansion of competition from lower-priced products from the growing numbers of superstores.

30. Defections from the LDP and the formation of new parties in 1993 had several motivations. Some who left the LDP were frustrated by the failure of Prime Minister Miyazawa to carry out political reform in the face of the party's loss of credibility in the corruption scandals (some saw reform as merely a political necessity; others believed that it was worthwhile in and of itself). There was also an element of opportunism. Ichiro Ozawa, a former rising star inside the LDP and a follower of Shin Kanemaru, left the LDP to expand his personal influence, as well as to ostensibly promote reform. Ozawa said that politics must be "modernized" by eliminating the LDP. In a sense, the actions of the former Takeshita faction Diet members (including Ozawa) who established the Renewal Party represented the spread of LDP factionalism beyond the party's boundaries.

31. Maurice Duverger, *Political Parties;* and Herbert Kitschelt, *The Transformation of European Social Democracy.*

32. Bradley M. Richardson, *Japanese Democracy.*

33. Thomas R. Rochon, "Electoral Systems and the Basis for the Vote: The Case of Japan," in John C. Campbell, ed., *Parties, Candidates and Voters in Japan: Six Quantitative Studies* (Ann Arbor: Center for Japanese Studies, Michigan Quantitative Studies in Japanese Studies, No. 2, 1981), 1–28; Rein Taagepera and Matthew S. Shugart, *Seats and Votes: The Effects and Determinants of Electoral Systems* (New Haven: Yale University Press, 1989); Gerald W. Cox, *Making Votes Count: Strategic Coordination in the World's Electoral Systems* (New York: Cambridge University Press, 1997); J. Mark Ramsayer and Francis McCall Rosenbluth, *Japan's Political Marketplace.*

34. Richard Gunther, "Electoral Laws, Party Systems and Elites: The Case of Spain," *American Political Science Review* 83 (September 1989): 835–58.

III

Developing and
Postcommunist Systems

8

POLITICAL DARWINISM IN LATIN AMERICA'S LOST DECADE

Michael Coppedge

Michael Coppedge is associate professor of government at the University of Notre Dame and director of the Quality of Democracy working group at the Helen Kellogg Institute for International Studies. He is the author of Strong Parties and Lame Ducks: Presidential Partyarchy and Factionalism in Venezuela *(1994) and numerous other publications, including "Venezuela's Vulnerable Democracy," which appeared in the July 1992 issue of the* Journal of Democracy.

Are parties in decline? In many ways, this is like asking whether musicians' performances have declined. Even in classical music, or the relatively stable and legitimate party systems of Western Europe, it is a difficult question to answer simply because styles and tastes change. For this reason, the editors of this volume rightly ask whether the perception of party decline might be the result of judging contemporary parties by old-fashioned models. They therefore suggest that we propose new models for describing parties and that we evaluate parties according to their ability to perform certain basic functions.

The question becomes even harder to answer when the focus shifts to Latin American parties. To continue the musical analogy, we are no longer talking about Mozart and Beethoven; parties in Latin America are more like pop musicians in several respects. First, there has been tremendous turnover. While there have been a handful of perennial favorites and a modest number that last a decade or so, there have also been quite a few "one-hit wonders," or *fenómenos*. Second, most parties, like most bands, have never succeeded in winning much of a following. Third, there has always been a wide range of quality. Just as there are great bands and awful ones, there have been parties that perform their basic functions well and others that are dysfunctional in various ways and to varying degrees. This is true across the countries of the region and within most of the countries as well. Finally, we must ask whether a classical model rooted in Western Europe was ever a useful standard. For all these reasons, the question must be reformulated before it can be answered in the case of Latin American parties.

I reformulate the question in several ways. First, given the accelerated pace of change in Latin America, what is the nature of change over the past ten to 15 years rather than over many decades? Second, are there any systematic differences between the parties that were important 30 years ago and those that were important at the end of the 1990s? Third, because high turnover makes it impractical to compare the same parties over time, have party *systems* become more functional or less so in recent years? And finally, do the forces that drive the process of turnover favor the survival of parties with certain characteristics?

There are only a few general tendencies across these cases. In the long run, population growth, urbanization, and the spread of the mass media have modified some of the ways in which the best organized parties operate. Although they continue to mobilize supporters during election campaigns, they rely less on routine mobilization and socialization through party-affiliated social organizations. Those that once hoped to finance themselves through dues collection have become dependent on outside campaign financing instead. And all parties that can afford it rely extensively on polling and the mass media to tap public opinion and get out their message.

In all other respects, individual parties have experienced very little organizational change. However, many parties have been, in effect, replaced by other parties with different organizational characteristics. This process of replacement can be understood as "political Darwinism": the survival of the parties best adapted to the political environment of austerity and economic stagnation during the "lost decade" (from 1982 until the early 1990s). This environment tended to select in favor of right or center-right governing parties, and personalistic or center-left opposition parties. Differences in initial conditions, economic perfor-mance, and skill at adaptation meant that different party systems evolved in different directions. Surprisingly, however, these changes rendered party systems in the major countries less functional only in Brazil, Ecuador, and Peru. This article illustrates these tendencies with brief case histories of Acción Democrática (AD) in Venezuela, Alianza Popular Revolucionaria Americana (APRA) in Peru, and the Partido Justicialista (PJ, or the Peronist party), in Argentina.

Change in the Major Parties

In some Latin American countries it is normal for parties to shrink or disappear. In 166 twentieth-century legislative elections in 11 Latin American countries, approximately 1,200 parties competed.[1] Of these, only 15 participated in all the elections held in their country, and only three contested as many as 20 elections. More than 80 percent ran in just

TABLE 1—CUMULATIVE ELEC-
TORAL VOLATILITY, 1982–95

COUNTRY	FROM	TO	CUMULATIVE VOLATILITY
Peru	1980	1995	86.0
Brazil	1982	1994	64.3
Ecuador	1979	1994	61.4
Bolivia	1980	1993	53.4
Venezuela	1978	1993	42.8
Argentina	1983	1995	37.0
Mexico	1979	1994	36.4
Colombia	1982	1994	27.0
Chile	1973	1993	24.8
Costa Rica	1982	1994	23.9
Uruguay	1971	1993	17.7

Source: author's data.

one election before becoming defunct.

Another way to measure the degree of change after 1982 is to calculate volatility rates using the election closest to 1982 as a baseline and the most recent election as an endpoint.[2] Table 1 reports these rates of change for the 11 Latin American countries with the most electoral experience. Table 1 shows that the initial party systems of Peru, Brazil, Ecuador, and Bolivia sustained severe damage, with less than half of their party systems remaining in the same form. The Peruvian party system of 1980 was nearly wiped out. Major parties in Venezuela, Argentina, and Mexico also lost a great deal of support. Only in Chile, Colombia, Costa Rica, and Uruguay did the pre-1982 party systems remain more or less intact. In these countries much of the change consisted of some splintering and name changes, in addition to some healthy vote fluctuation.

The generally high rate of turnover makes it impossible to trace long-term changes in the characteristics of all parties. However, some generalizations are possible with respect to the small number of parties that managed to survive several decades. Among these there have been parties that match, in some respects, several of the types defined by Richard Gunther and Larry Diamond in chapter 1 of this volume. As in Europe, the parties that predominated in the few countries that had competitive (though rarely fair) elections despite restricted suffrage during the late nineteenth and early twentieth centuries were parties of local notables. Among them were the early incarnations of the Chilean Conservative and Liberal parties, the larger Costa Rican parties before the 1948–49 Revolution, the Civilista party of Peru's "Aristocratic Republic" (1895–1919), and in some respects the state- and family-based oligarchic parties that distributed patronage during Brazil's Old Republic (1888–1930).[3] Many of these parties were more identified with a single national notable—in some cases, the party even took a leader's name, for example, Montt-Varistas and Calderonistas—than was typically the case in Europe, and more Latin American leaders may have become notable on the battlefield than in peaceful pursuits, but in other respects, this type fits.

As suffrage expanded, some parties prospered by being, or becoming, clientelistic. Indeed, Colombia's Liberals and Conservatives, which dominated electoral politics for a century, are very well described by Gunther and Diamond's definition of this type.[4] Although no other large party in the region fits the definition quite as well, most Brazilian parties since 1945 and some small regional parties in Argentina could qualify if they are allowed to have some identifiable programmatic stance. Uruguay's Blancos and Colorados could be called clientelistic, but only if a hierarchical structure and lower-class or poorly educated clients are not essential to the definition.[5] It must also be said that virtually all electorally successful parties in Latin America, even the more ideological ones, have learned to cultivate clientelistic ties at the grassroots. This tendency is a natural consequence of competing for the votes of poor citizens with little formal education.

An expanded suffrage also made it possible for socialist and Leninist parties to build a base of electoral support. Most Latin American countries have had several parties that attempted to mobilize the working class in support of some kind of socialist agenda. However, none of these has enjoyed success comparable to that of the major socialist, social democratic, or labor parties of Europe. One of the most successful was the Chilean Socialist Party, but the fate of Allende's government is well known. These parties' success was limited because industrialization came later to Latin America and never transformed society to the same degree that it did in Europe. Also, the suffrage tended to be extended relatively quickly in Latin America, creating incentives to organize broader cross-class coalitions.[6] So a different type of party often occupied the political space that included the emerging working class: the "national revolutionary" parties, which sought to unite the middle class, workers, and peasants behind a diffuse nationalistic and anti-oligarchical platform.[7] Although they initially fit the category of "nationalist" parties, their base of support was so broad that they tended to evolve into catch-all parties, though with two qualifications. First, they were all heavy practitioners of clientelism. Second, several of them built extremely strong party machines for recruitment, mobilization, and patronage distribution, unlike the catch-all type described by Gunther and Diamond. These parties were structured around sectoral organizations designed to mobilize unions, peasants, students, and some middle-class occupational groups. This family included the Alianza Popular Revolucionaria Americana (APRA) in Peru, Acción Democrática (AD) in Venezuela, Liberación Nacional (PLN) in Costa Rica, the Partido Revolucionario Dominicano (PRD) in the Dominican Republic, and for some scholars, Mexico's Partido Revolucionario Institucional (PRI) and Bolivia's Movimiento Nacional Revolucionario (MNR).

In a region with a population that was for centuries more than 90 percent Catholic (at least nominally), religious parties have been defenders of Christianity against secularization rather than defenders of one religion against another. This religious versus secular divide was the most salient cleavage in nineteenth-century Latin America, often resolved through violent means. Notable- or *caudillo*-led conservative parties inherited the proclerical side of this struggle at the turn of the century, but outside of Colombia it was already losing importance. However, in the 1930s and 1940s, progressive Catholic social teaching inspired some younger politicians to found Christian Democratic parties, which eventually enjoyed great electoral success in Chile, Venezuela (COPEI), and El Salvador, and some success in Peru (Partido Popular Cristiano) and Ecuador (Democracia Popular). They fit Gunther and Diamond's category of "denominational" parties only approximately, however, because they were not denominational in the strict sense of admitting only Catholics or Christians as members; they were only loosely inspired by the Church, and therefore depended very little on the local bishop's backing for their legitimacy; and they have also depended on clientelism and, in some cases, personal charisma, much like clientelistic and personalistic parties. As Protestant churches have grown in membership since the 1980s, a few parties have emerged as their vehicles, but none is yet a major force in politics. Neither can it be said that Latin America has any true religious fundamentalist parties.

Most Latin American countries have some ethnic diversity, but centuries of racial intermarriage blurred ethnic lines and strong pressures for assimilation kept the proportion of self-identified ethnic minorities small. These tendencies discouraged the formation of ethnicity-based parties, and they were complemented by active repression or cooptation of occasional attempts to build indigenous parties in some countries.[8] Nevertheless, in Bolivia, where perhaps 60 percent of the population identifies with Aymara- or Quechua-speaking indigenous groups, various "Katarista" parties sprang up after 1980. And in Ecuador, movements of the indigenous peoples of the Sierra, the Amazon, and the coast united in the 1990s. At first they preferred direct action over party politics, but toward the end of the decade they began to contest elections in alliance with unions, students, and small leftist parties, gaining a secure foothold in the party system. The "congress party" type, however, is absent in Latin America, probably because the ethnic cleavage lacks salience. National unity movements formed around class issues instead.

This discussion so far omits some important and fascinating political forces—Peronism and the Unión Cívica Radical in Argentina; Acción Popular and Alberto Fujimori's vehicles in Peru; the Concentración de Fuerzas Populares and the Partido Social Cristiano in Ecuador; Aliança Renovadora Nacional/Partido Democrático Social (ARENA/PDS), Partido de Movimiento Democrático Brasiliero (PMDB), and Partido dos Trabalhadores (PT) in Brazil; Partido Acción Nacional (PAN) and Partido de la Revolución Democrática (PRD) in Mexico; and others. It is tempting to slap one of the remaining labels—catch-all, programmatic, or personalistic—on these parties and be done with them, but this solution would mischaracterize them. Most of them, as well as most of those described already, are to some degree clientelistic, to some degree programmatic, and to some degree personalistic. These parties would rest uneasily in ideal-type categories that are not really mutually exclusive to begin with. Gunther and Diamond's expanded typology is a commendable effort, as previous typologies were indeed overly simplistic, but at some point it becomes counterproductive to shoehorn additional parties into even this improved classificatory scheme.

The fact is that partisan reality is still more complex. In reality, each party is unique and any strategy for simplifying this complexity encounters tradeoffs. One strategy is to define qualitative labels for various party characteristics—"working-class," "hierarchical," "clientelistic," "institutionalized," etc. When such labels fit well, they are revealing and useful. But in many cases, parties vary in the *degree* to which they represent a class or practice clientelism or are hierarchically structured, and so on, so assigning such labels without qualification or quantification can introduce distortions. A second strategy is to aggregate characteristics into types: parties that have a socialist ideology *and* a Leninist organization *and* a national base; or parties that have a charismatic leader *and* no clear program *and* practice clientelism; etc. Again, these types can be extremely useful when they fit, but given the unique combinations that all parties represent, one must either define myriad combinations to include every party or settle on a few combinations that fit some parties well, others partially or vaguely, and still others not at all. Gunther and Diamond deserve just credit for *not* aggregating some characteristics that others lumped together, but the many exceptions and qualifications mentioned above demonstrate that problems of aggregation remain for the Latin American cases. Some extra combinations would be required to flesh out the typology: catch-all parties with strong, hierarchical organization; personalist parties with definite programmatic commitments; and parties led by highly ideological elites who depend heavily on clientelistic practices at the base, among others. We need either more types or further disaggregation to do justice to the rich variety of parties in the world.

A third strategy is to narrow the focus to certain characteristics: just programmatic goals, or just organizational structure, or just the social base of support. The most valuable service Gunther and Diamond have performed is to unify disparate typologies that were focused on selected characteristics. This is a valuable service because it is unlikely that any narrow typology will tell us everything we could possibly need to know about a party. Different characteristics matter for different ends. A hierarchical organization, for example, may tell us something useful about a party's internal democracy and recruitment patterns but nothing about its coalition strategies, campaign styles, or impact on public policy.

Given the inherent limitations of typologies for describing cases faithfully and generating appropriate hypotheses, my own preference would be to abandon the search for an adequate typology. We would progress more rapidly by narrowing attention to whatever party characteristics theory holds to be relevant for the phenomenon of interest and measuring these characteristics as precisely as possible. This is what is attempted in the comparative analysis below, which leads to some generalizations about the kinds of parties that have electorally prospered or declined in Latin America, and why. Electoral success may not be one of the party characteristics highlighted as important by this volume's guiding typology, but perhaps that is because it is so essential that it is taken for granted. Yet in Latin America, electoral success cannot be taken for granted over the long term. For that reason, even though a one-chapter survey of parties in 20 countries must be selective, electoral success is the one characteristic that can least be ignored.

Has the nature of these important parties changed over the decades? In four respects, yes. First, most of these parties, if they existed before the 1950s, used to mobilize and socialize their membership through party-affiliated sports clubs, dining clubs, literacy workshops, and discussion groups, much as mass-based parties in Europe did in the 1930s. All of these activities have greatly declined as a consequence of population growth, urbanization, rising standards of living, greater personal autonomy, and higher levels of education. Most have fallen into disuse if they exist at all. Second, many of these parties initially attempted to be self-financing through dues collection; this effort was never all that successful, so now all of them have become dependent on outside public and private donations. Third, technological change has led all important parties in Latin America to make extensive use of polling, mass-media campaign advertising, and increasingly sophisticated U.S.-style campaign techniques. Fourth, more and more parties are experimenting with primaries for the selection of their candidates for president, congress, and governorships.

These secular changes might suggest that major Latin American parties have turned away from personal contact and face-to-face patron-client relationships as socialization and mobilization techniques. There is some change in this direction, but it should not be exaggerated because the new techniques often supplement the old ones rather than replacing them. For example, almost all of these parties continue their mass mobilization efforts during campaigns, partly because bringing supporters to rallies is one of the few ways local brokers can demonstrate that they can get out the vote and thus are valuable to the party leadership. As long as clientelism is rampant in Latin American politics, the mass mobilization will continue. And as long as poverty and deep inequalities plague Latin American societies, clientelism will remain a favorite political tool.

Change in Party Systems

Because the parties mentioned so far are only a small fraction of all the parties and are not representative of the others, it is necessary to examine changes in a country's whole *system* of parties. This can be done by identifying certain basic functions that party systems should perform and certain structural characteristics of party systems that are functional according to these criteria, as well as analyzing indicators of these characteristics. Party systems matter for democracy in two principal ways. First, they are the chief vehicles for representation, and therefore affect the quality of democracy. Second, they affect governability, especially in the legislative arena, and therefore indirectly affect the stability of a democratic regime in the long run. Both good representation and governability require legitimacy and are enhanced when there is strong party identification. In the long run, good representation promotes governability.[9] In a more immediate sense, however, what is good for democracy is not always good for governability, or vice versa, and for this reason we have conflicting notions about what sort of party system would be "best" for stable democracy. Because many people focus exclusively on the long-term compatibility between representation and governability, it is instructive to compare party systems at the extremes of fragmentation and polarization in order to highlight the tradeoffs that present themselves in the short term.

If our goal were perfect representation, we would want a large number of parties, to illustrate all possible combinations of positions on all relevant issues, as well as rigid parties that resist compromising on the mandate received from the voters and have sharp issue differences with other parties. Such a party system would be highly representative in the most pure sense of the term. But it would also tend to be divisive, polarized, and indecisive, and therefore dangerously inclined toward ungovernability in the legislative arena in the short term. If our goal were perfect governability, we would want just one highly pragmatic party that strives for consensus and whose activists are always willing to compromise to achieve it, in order to guarantee and mobilize full support for whatever the government decides to do. Such a party would be wonderful for governability (unless it alienated a substantial body of citizens and allowed them to organize an antisystem force), but it would also be the very antithesis of democracy.

In the real world, we are willing to sacrifice some democracy and some governability in order to achieve as much as possible of both. Thinking about these tradeoffs is a useful way to identify a standard for evaluating how functional a party system is for stable democracy. With respect to fragmentation, there should be enough parties for meaningful competition but not so many that it becomes difficult to form governments and make decisions. A minimum of two parties is a reasonable lower limit. If there are, in effect, fewer than two parties (in the sense that there is one party that is much larger than any other), then the system is insufficiently competitive because the largest party is expected to win control of the national executive all the time. The

Laakso-Taagepera index of the Effective Number of Parties, which ranges from 1.00 to infinity, counts parties after weighting them by their shares of the votes or seats, producing an "effective" number of parties that can be expressed in fractional terms, such as "2.63 parties."[10] This index has become the standard indicator of party-system fragmentation in political science.

Meaningful competition can also occur between more than two parties, but at some point further fragmentation undermines governability by making it harder to form a working majority in the legislature. Many cutoffs for this perilously large number of parties are conceivable, but one conservative standard is the number at which it becomes impossible for just two parties to form a majority. This number depends on the size of the largest (and presumably governing) party. If the largest party controls more than half the seats, a coalition is unnecessary; if it controls less than a quarter, any majority coalition must include at least three parties. When the largest party controls between one-quarter and one-half of the seats, it becomes impossible to form a two-party majority when there are 4.0 to 4.5 parties in the system (the maximum is 4.57 parties, when the largest party controls 37.5 percent of the seats).

With respect to polarization, the parties should take positions that are distinctive enough to provide the voters with a meaningful choice, but these positions should not be so far apart that they interfere with the construction of majorities for legislation and governing. One indicator of polarization (Index of Polarization, or IP) is the dispersion of the vote away from the relative center of the party system, which takes on values between zero (all of the vote in one ideological bloc) and 100 (half of the vote at each of the ideological extremes).[11] A minimum functional level of polarization would be 25, which is the lowest level that guarantees that no bloc wins more than half the vote and therefore ensures some competition between blocs. The maximum functional level of polarization can be set at 60, which corresponds to a perfectly even distribution of voters among all blocs. (This "flat" distribution marks the threshold between the "unimodal" or "single-peaked" distributions that are more concentrated than dispersed and the "bimodal" distributions that are more dispersed than concentrated.)

The Figure on the following page depicts changes in the levels of party-system fragmentation and left-right polarization in the 11 countries surveyed here using these two indicators. Lines in the figure define the functional ranges of fragmentation and polarization. As shown here, functional party systems have between 2 and 4.57 effective parties (calculated on the basis of seats) and are from 25 to 60 percent polarized. The figure also displays a line for each country that begins at the fragmentation and polarization levels at the "initial" elections as defined in Table 1 on p. 175 and ends at the corresponding values for the "final" election in the period of analysis. Overall, during this period there was an increase

FIGURE—CHANGES IN FRAGMENTATION AND POLARIZATION, 1982–95

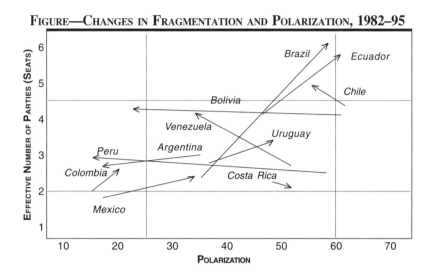

in fragmentation and polarization (as well as an association between these two tendencies). But in order to evaluate these changes it is essential to consider each party system's starting point and the magnitude of the change, for these facts determine whether fragmentation and polarization made these party systems more functional or less so.

Brazil and Ecuador suffered severe fragmentation and polarization that moved their party systems into a zone of great dysfunctionality. Mexico and Colombia also experienced growing fragmentation and polarization, but because they began with too little of each, these changes were in the direction of more meaningful and competitive elections. Venezuela, Uruguay, and Costa Rica experienced some changes, but not of sufficient magnitude to move them out of the functional zone.

Partial changes occurred in other countries. During this period in Bolivia, the party system remained fragmented (though not excessively so as two-party coalitions could still be formed), but the level of polarization declined dramatically by 1993 (after a surge in 1985) to a borderline low level. Similarly, Peru maintained a manageable number of parties, but leaped from excessively high polarization in 1980 to excessively low polarization in 1995, due to the dominance of Fujimori's depoliticizing Cambio 90/Nueva Mayoría. In Chile, left-right polari-zation was lower in the 1990s, although some intense conflict remained over constitutional issues. Fragmentation increased to a potentially dysfunctional level, but the decline in polarization more than compensated for it, as solid multiparty coalitions sustained the first two democratic governments after Pinochet. The Argentine party system was not too fragmented in the 1980s, but in the base year (1973) it was dysfunctionally polarized. The polarization index IP does not reflect polarization well in Argentina because the principal dimension of

TABLE 2—PUBLIC OPINION ABOUT PARTIES AND DEMOCRACY

	ARGENTINA	BRAZIL	CHILE	MEXICO	PERU	URUGUAY	VENEZUELA
CONFIDENCE IN PARTIES[1]							
MUCH/SOME	27	17	33	40	21	41	16
LITTLE/NONE	73	83	67	60	79	59	84
FEELINGS TOWARD PARTIES[2]							
CLOSE	9	13	10	17	6	26	11
SYMPATHIZER	30	22	28	37	42	46	26
NOT CLOSE	61	67	64	48	52	30	65
REGIME PREFERENCE[3]							
DEMOCRACY	82	48	54	57	58	86	64
AUTHORITARIAN	12	25	19	17	26	8	23
MAKES NO DIFFERENCE	7	27	27	26	16	6	14
SATISFACTION WITH DEMO-CRATIC PERFORMANCE[4]							
SATISFIED	53	31	34	24	47	59	38
UNSATISFIED	47	69	66	76	53	41	62

[1] "Por favor dígame para cada una de las instituciones que le voy a leer, cuánta confianza tiene usted en ellas: mucha, poca o ninguna? Los partidos políticos."
[2] "Respecto de los partidos políticos, cómo se siente ud.: muy cercano, algo cercano, sólo simpatizante o no cercano a ninguno?"
[3] "¿Con cuál de las siguientes frases está ud. más de acuerdo? 1. La democracia es preferible a cualquier otra forma de gobierno; 2. En algunas circunstancias, un gobierno autoritario puede ser preferible a uno democrático; 3. A la gente como uno, nos da lo mismo un régimen democrático que uno no democrático."
[4] ¿En general, diría Ud. que está muy satisfecho, algo satisfecho, algo insatisfecho o insatisfecho o muy insatisfecho con el funcionamiento de la democracia en el país?
Source: Miguel Basáñez, Marta Lagos, and Tatiana Beltrán, *Reporte 1995: Encuesta Latino Barómetro: Opiniones y actitudes en Latinoamérica; Economía, sociedad, política y asuntos internacionales* (May 1996), 91, 103, 50, and 51.

competition was historically between Peronists and everyone else rather than between left and right.[12] By 1995, competition was perhaps insufficiently meaningful in left-right terms, but still quite meaningful in Peronist–anti-Peronist terms.

In summary, there were significant improvements in levels of fragmentation and polarization in Mexico; a partial improvement in Argentina, Chile, and Colombia; no net change in Bolivia, Costa Rica, Uruguay, and Venezuela; a partial decline in Peru; and disaster in Ecuador and probably Brazil. Eight of the 11 systems functioned as well as before or better, and only three deteriorated overall. The number of improvements is rather surprising, in view of the difficult economic times the region was going through. However, the claim that some Latin American party systems became *more* functional does not mean that they were functioning *well,* and still less that Latin American democracy in general was thriving. Many of these party systems started from great dysfunctionality; delegative democracy was on the rise in Argentina, Peru, and Venezuela at least; the drug trade was spreading corruption in the Andean region and Mexico; indigenous peoples were underrepresented in the same countries; the military was incompletely subordinated to civilian leadership in Bolivia, Chile, and Peru; the courts and the rule of law were weak everywhere except Costa Rica and Chile; and human rights were violated far too often.

These conditions make it easier to understand why Latin Americans held their parties and other institutions in such low esteem in the mid-1990s. As Table 2 on the previous page shows for seven countries, most Latin American respondents in the Latinobarómetro survey of 1995 claimed to have little or no confidence in parties and, except for Uruguayans and perhaps Mexicans, claimed not to be close to any party. These subjective evaluations of parties correspond closely with the objective classifications of parties in the Figure on p. 182. Two of the countries (excluding Costa Rica, which was not included in the 1995 Latinobarómetro survey) that ended up on the zone of functionality—Uruguay and Mexico—had fewer negative evaluations of parties than all the rest, and the country with the most dysfunctional party system, Brazil, also had the most negative evaluations. (Chile is the only outlier here, probably due to the unusual degree of cooperation among the parties in the governing coalition, which has moderated the problems associated with fragmentation and polarization.) These poor evaluations did not affect Latin Americans' majority preference for democracy in principle (see Table 2), and they had only a light relation to the predominant dissatisfaction with actual democratic performance. These data suggest that political parties do *not* help legitimate the political system in these countries. If anything, the legitimacy of democracy may engender a reluctant toleration of parties in the population.

Political Darwinism

It should be clear by now that party politics in Latin America is a harsh struggle for survival with few survivors. It could be aptly called "political Darwinism" because there are several parallels between the evolution of party systems and the evolution of natural species. Both natural selection and the more artificial selection of political parties by voters involve competition for limited resources, whether votes or food; the winners of this competition grow (in popular support or numbers) while the losers decline and eventually become extinct; the survivors tend to reproduce themselves more or less faithfully for the next round of competition, although with some capacity for innovation; and the best adaptations to the environment are favored for growth and survival in future rounds.[13]

This view of the process suggests that four basic conditions shape the evolution of parties and party systems: 1) the amount of stress to which the party system is subjected; 2) the nature of the stress, which determines which party characteristics are rewarded and which are punished; 3) the vulnerability of the parties to this kind of stress; and 4) the parties'

TABLE 3—BIGGEST WINNERS AND LOSERS IN LATIN AMERICAN ELECTIONS, 1982–95

	COUNTRY	PERIOD	% CHANGE	GOVERNED?	POSITION
BIGGEST LOSERS					
Unión Democrática y Popular	Bolivia	1980–93	-38.7	Y	center-left
Democrático Social (PDS)	Brazil	1982–94	-37.2	Y	right
Acción Popular	Peru	1980–95	-36.3	Y	center
Conc. Fuerzas Populares	Ecuador	1979–94	-28.8	Y	personalist
Unión Cívica Radical	Argentina	1983–95	-25.9	Y	center
Revolucionario Institucional (PRI)	Mexico	1979–94	-23.9	Y	center(-right)
PMDB	Brazil	1982–94	-23.4	Y	center
AND-MIR alliance	Bolivia	1985–93	-22.0	Y	center-right + center-left
APRA	Peru	1980–95	-20.5	Y	center-left
Conservador	Colombia	1982–94	-18.8	Y	center-right
COPEI	Venezuela	1978–93	-17.2	Y	center-right
Acción Democrática	Venezuela	1978–93	-16.4	Y	center-right
Liberación Nacional (PLN)	Costa Rica	1982–94	-10.5	Y	center-left
Nacional (Blancos)	Uruguay	1971–93	-8.8	Y	center-right
Izquierda Democrática	Ecuador	1979–94	-8.5	Y	center-left
Renovador Nacional (PRN)	Brazil	1990–94	-8.5	Y	personalist
Colorado	Uruguay	1971–93	-8.4	Y	center(-left)
BIGGEST WINNERS					
PRE-EXISTING PARTIES					
Social Cristiano (PSC)	Ecuador	1979–94	+17.8	Y	right
MNR	Bolivia	1980–93	+15.4	Y	center-right
Acción Nacional (PAN)	Mexico	1979–94	+14.3	N	center-right
Frente Amplio	Uruguay	1971–93	+12.5	N	left
Unidad Social Cristiana	Costa Rica	1982–94	+11.3	Y	center-right
Justicialista (Peronist)	Argentina	1983–95	+5.5	Y	center(-left)
EMERGING PARTIES					
Cambio 90/Nueva Mayoría	Peru	1985–95	+52.1	Y	personalist
Frente Grande/FREPASO	Argentina	1991–95	+20.9	N	center-left
La Causa R	Venezuela	1978–93	+20.4	N	center-left
Social Democrático Brasileiro	Brazil	1986–94	+17.1	N	center-left
Roldosista Ecuatoriano (PRE)	Ecuador	1979–94	+16.8	Y	personalist
P. Revolución Democrática (PRD)	Mexico	1988–94	+16.7	N	center-left
Nacional Velasquista (PNV)	Ecuador	1979–94	+14.2	N	personalist
Conciencia de Patria	Bolivia	1985–93	+14.3	N	personalist
Unión Cívica Solidaridad	Bolivia	1989–93	+13.8	N	personalist
Convergencia Nacional	Venezuela	1988–93	+13.8	N	personalist
Por la Democracia (PPD)	Chile	1973–93	+11.8	Y	center-left
Democracia Popular	Ecuador	1979–94	+8.2	N	center-left

capacity to adapt appropriately. How did each of these conditions apply to Latin America after 1982? Did they combine to select in favor of parties with certain characteristics?

Table 3 on the previous page ranks the biggest winners and losers in elections during the "lost decade" and provides some clues about the selection criteria of the Darwinian struggle for survival. First, all of the biggest losers were governing parties at some time during this period. Apparently incumbency was frequently very costly. However, this was not always the case, as some of the biggest winners in the region were also governing parties, such as the Partido Social Cristiano (PSC) in Ecuador, the MNR in Bolivia, and Alberto Fujimori's Cambio 90/Nueva Mayoría. This suggests that the real impact of incumbency was to raise the stakes, because governing parties were held most directly responsible for government performance. A second tendency was that among the parties that predated the initial election, the biggest winners were usually on the right or center-right.[14] Only one of the six was on the left, and the one that is sometimes considered center-left—Peronism's Justicialista party—shifted decisively to the center or even center-right by the late 1980s under the leadership of Carlos Menem. Third, among the new parties, the biggest winners were all either personalist or center-left parties. The implications of these last two tendencies are cloudy until the parties' governing status is also taken into account; then it seems likely that there were three types of parties that tended to do especially well after 1982: personalist parties, governing parties to the right of center, and left-of-center parties in the opposition.[15]

All of these observations can be tested more rigorously with a larger sample of cases and data that are less aggregated. Such a test is reported below, and it confirms these ideas and adds some others. But first the theory must be fleshed out further.

The amount and type of stress. Parties are pressed to adapt whenever their environment changes in ways that affect the voters' beliefs and priorities. Many aspects of the politically relevant environment have changed rapidly in Latin America, creating (to a different degree in each country) regime change, rapid urbanization, economic boom-and-bust cycles, rising drug trafficking and related crime, high and wildly varying inflation, deepening social inequalities, terrorism, guerrilla war, and economic liberalization. Any party would be sorely challenged to adapt well to any of these conditions, so it should not come as a surprise that the stressful environments in Latin America coincide with volatile party systems. The average party-system volatility in Latin America is 29.3 percent in the 11 countries examined here, compared to an average of 8.6 percent in Western Europe from 1885 to 1985.[16] The figures reported are both average, not cumulative, volatility, using the same counting rules. Any one of the kinds of change listed above could be cited to account for the large volatility gap between these two regions.

One type of stress was particularly common and particularly severe in Latin America in the period after 1982: economic stress. The 1980s were such rough times for Latin America that they are referred to as the "lost decade." Only Colombia and Chile registered significant improvements in per capita GDP in this period; it fell 5 percent in Venezuela, 8 percent in Argentina, 20 percent in Bolivia, and 27 percent in Peru.[17] As a result, between 1980 and 1992, inequality increased in Argentina, Bolivia, Brazil, Chile, Costa Rica, Mexico, and Venezuela; it decreased only in Colombia and Uruguay.[18] Inflation was generally higher than levels that would be tolerated in Western Europe and the United States, and it reached the nightmarish rates of 2,938 percent in Brazil (1990), 3,087 percent in Argentina (1989), 7,482 percent in Peru (1990), and 11,749 percent in Bolivia (1985).[19] A plausible working hypothesis, therefore, is that voters tended to reward parties that could claim credit for taming inflation, restoring economic growth, and improving the standard of living. Similarly, one may suppose that they tended to punish parties that made the economic situation worse in these respects.

Parties' vulnerability to stress and capacity to adapt. Voters do not treat all parties the same, however: In some countries voters are reluctant to question their party identification even if their party wrecks the economy or someone else's party produces a boom. In other countries, voters are far more generous in their rewards and more harsh in their punishments. The former type of party has a "solid" base of support; the latter, a "fluid" base. The strength of party identification therefore mediates the impact of economic performance on the vote. Identification with major parties is considered to be fairly strong in Argentina, Chile, Colombia, Costa Rica, Uruguay, and Venezuela, but fairly or extremely weak in Ecuador, Brazil, and Bolivia.[20] However, the strength of identification can vary among parties within the same country and can also change over time.[21]

Beyond whether a party's base of support is solid or fluid, the impact of economic performance also depends on whether the party is in the government or in the opposition. While incumbents may be held responsible for economic performance, the opposition is not in a position to take the credit or the blame, whatever the case may be. Therefore, we would expect governing parties that reduce inflation to grow, and those that make it worse, to decline. These effects should be greater for parties with a fluid base than for parties with a solid one, and the tendencies should be more clearly defined for governing parties than for opposition parties.[22]

Table 4 on the following page shows how the fates of selected governing and opposition parties varied, depending on the strength of identification, incumbency or opposition, and government success in fighting inflation. These estimates are based on regression analysis of 132 cases—the 23 most extreme cases reported in the table, plus 109 cases in which inflation rates were much lower. (For details, see the

TABLE 4—SELECTED EXAMPLES OF ELECTORAL SUCCESS AND FAILURE
UNDER EXTREME INFLATION

	COUNTRY	YEAR	CHANGE IN INFLATION	% CHANGE IN VOTE ACTUAL	% CHANGE IN VOTE PREDICTED
OPPOSITION PARTIES WITH A SOLID BASE					
FALLING INFLATION					
Unión Cívica Radical	Argentina	1991	-2,916	-0.2	+1.5
Unión Cívica Radical	Argentina	1993	-161	+1.3	+1.6
P. Unidad Social Cristiana	Costa Rica	1986	-78	+12.4	+1.6
MEAN				**+4.5**	**+1.6**
RISING INFLATION					
Justicialista	Argentina	1989	+2,964	+3.5	-2.3
P. dos Trabalhadores	Brazil	1990	+2,812	+1.3	+9.2
MEAN				**+2.4**	**+3.4**
GOVERNING PARTIES WITH A SOLID BASE					
FALLING INFLATION					
Justicialista	Argentina	1991	-2,916	-4.6	-3.4
Justicialista	Argentina	1993	-161	+3.0	-2.0
P. Liberación Nacional	Costa Rica	1986	-78	-7.3	-6.8
MEAN				**-3.0**	**-4.1**
RISING INFLATION					
Unión Cívica Radical	Argentina	1989	+2,915	-7.9	-1.0
OPPOSITION PARTIES WITH A FLUID BASE					
FALLING INFLATION					
Acción Democrática Nacionalista	Bolivia	1989	-11,734	-7.6	-6.9
Mov. de la Izquierda Revolucionaria	Bolivia	1989	-11,734	+11.7	+0.4
Coordinadora Democrática (CODE) +PPC	Peru	1992	-7,408	-24.6	-19.6
Frente Grande	Argentina	1993	-161	+3.7	+3.7
MEAN				**-4.1**	**-5.3**
RISING INFLATION					
Acción Democrática Nacionalista	Bolivia	1985	+11,702	+16.0	+10.1
Mov. Nacionalista Revolucionario	Bolivia	1985	+11,702	+10.2	+9.0
P. Democrático Social	Brazil	1990	+2,812	+1.5	+8.4
P. da Frente Liberal	Brazil	1990	+2,812	-8.7	+3.2
FREDEMO	Peru	1990	+7,318	+11.0	+5.8
MEAN				**+6.0**	**+7.3**
GOVERNING PARTIES WITH A FLUID BASE					
FALLING INFLATION					
Mov. Nacionalista Revolucionario	Bolivia	1989	-11,734	-4.7	+16.0
Cambio 90/Nueva Mayoría	Peru	1992	-7,408	+32.3	+13.6
MEAN				**+13.8**	**+14.8**
RISING INFLATION					
Unión Democrática Popular	Bolivia	1985	+11,702	-32.5	-27.1
PMDB	Brazil	1990	+2,812	-30.7	-27.5
APRA	Peru	1990	+7,318	-25.6	-25.3
MEAN				**-29.6**	**-26.6**

Appendix to this chapter.) All of the expected relationships hold true, but only at the extremes experienced by the cases included in the table.

The tendencies observed are as follows: 1) Parties with a solid base of support found it electorally costly to govern and electorally beneficial to be in the opposition. 2) Economic performance had no significant impact on this tendency among parties with a solid base: Governing

TABLE 5—IMPACT OF ECONOMIC PERFORMANCE ON VOTE FOR FOUR TYPES OF PARTIES

RELATION TO PRESIDENT	STRENGTH OF PARTY ID	INFLATION FALLING	INFLATION RISING
opposition	solid	+	+
opposition	fluid	–	+
governing	solid	–	–
governing	fluid	+ +	– –

parties were not more harshly punished if they raised inflation than if they lowered it, and opposition parties did not profit from worsening inflation more than they profited from price stabilization.[23] For parties with a fluid base of support, however, the changes were much larger, and both governing and economic performance mattered. 3) Opposition parties with a fluid base were hurt a little by falling inflation and helped a little by rising inflation. 4) On the other hand, governing parties with a fluid base were helped a lot by falling inflation and hurt a lot by rising inflation. These relationships are summarized in Table 5 above. As Table 3 on p. 185 indicates, there are some notable exceptions, because elections are not simply referendums on economic performance. The explanation offered here merely traces some general tendencies that account for 38 percent of the variance; 62 percent must be explained by other factors. These factors could be characteristics of the competitive environment such as noneconomic issues or economic issues besides inflation; or other forms of adaptation, such as leadership, campaign styles and tactics, and alliances and boycotts.

A note on emerging parties. As noted above, parties change by replacement as well as adaptation. If there are any commonalities among the emerging parties in Latin America it would be good to identify them. It cannot be said, however, that the new parties that emerged to completely or partially replace old major parties were necessarily to the right or to the left, or even that they tended to be personalistic; there were examples of all three. However, two generalizations can be made.

First, emerging parties tended to be reactions against some major party that failed to adapt, and therefore they tended to be its opposite in some respects. Some characteristics of emerging parties differed greatly from country to country, depending on what sort of party they were replacing. In reaction to the iron discipline of AD and COPEI, La Causa R in Venezuela was opposed, on principle, to requiring its activists to toe any party line. But in Brazil, where most parties—and especially the PMDB—were notoriously uncohesive, one of the most successful emerging parties was the PT, which achieved the tightest discipline of any party in the system. In Mexico, both the PAN and the PRD were committed to political democracy and voluntary participation, in contrast to the authoritarian mobilization techniques of the dominant PRI. Peru presents perhaps the most extreme case, in which Fujimori's Cambio 90/Nueva Mayoría reacted against the legacies of the previous AP and APRA governments by trying not to be a party at all.

Second, the new parties favored by voters are those that had a credible chance of winning, which in turn was a function of two qualities. One was experience in governing at the regional or local level. In Mexico, PAN was the opposition party that had won the largest number of local elections before 1988 and the largest number of governorships before 1994. In Venezuela, La Causa R first became nationally prominent through the governorship of its leader, Andrés Velásquez, in the eastern state of Bolívar. And in Brazil, the PT won quite a few municipal elections in major cities before its presidential candidate, Luis Inácio "Lula" da Silva, made it to the presidential runoff in 1989. The other token of credibility was earned if the new party had splintered away from one of the old major parties. This probably gave an advantage to the PRD in Mexico, led by Porfirio Muñoz Ledo and Cuauhtémoc Cárdenas, both formerly of the PRI; to Chile's Partido por la Democracia (PPD), led by Ricardo Lagos of the Socialist Party; to Convergencia Nacional in Venezuela, led by Rafael Caldera, the founder of COPEI; to the Frente Grande and Frente del Pais Solidario (FREPASO) in Argentina, led by the Group of Eight and José Octavio Bordón, all ex-Peronists; and to the Partido Roldosista Ecuatoriano in Ecuador, which split away from the Concentración de Fuerzas Populares (CFP) in the early 1980s.

Adaptation: Three Case Studies

The rewards for economic stabilization in the post-debt-crisis environment explain why most of the biggest winners among established parties were on the right or center-right: Fighting inflation was a natural part of their agenda, for which little adaptation was required. For the governing parties to the left of center, survival required a wrenching adaptation. For them, implementing stabilization and structural adjustment meant reversing many of the policies they had championed for years—expansion of the state sector, aggressive regulation of the private sector, extensive state intervention setting wages and prices— and postponing attempts to reduce poverty and inequality. Often it also meant recruiting economic advisers from pro-market institutes and turning a deaf ear to demands coming from unionized workers who traditionally had been a source of strong support.[24] For these parties, the 1982–95 period was a Mephistophelian environment that presented them with a Faustian bargain: Surrender your soul and you can live forever; otherwise, you will die. Most left-of-center parties either would not or could not keep such a bargain. Of the ten elections held with center-left parties as incumbents, only three took place while inflation was falling. By contrast, inflation was falling during 53 percent of the elections with center incumbents, 73 percent with center-right incumbents, and 63 percent with incumbents on the right.

Among the qualitative changes in parties with which this volume is concerned—changes in recruitment, electoral mobilization, issue structuration, and societal representation—the most interesting examples were adaptations by center-left parties to the conservative environment. Case studies of three historically center-left parties will illustrate the dimensions of change and their consequences. Each was well-established, began with strong identifiers in the electorate, mobilized trade unions, and governed during part of this period. But these three parties responded to the challenges of the time differently. APRA in Peru *mis*adapted— zigging to the left when it should have zagged right—and brought about its own destruction.[25] Acción Democrática in Venezuela resisted adaptation, by withdrawing support from its own leaders who turned toward the market, and lost 40 percent of its voters.[26] The Justicialista party in Argentina, however, followed Carlos Menem to the right and won more votes, but underwent profound internal reorganization in the process.[27]

Before beginning, it should be noted that many characteristics of these three parties did not change significantly during this period. All three had long suffered from a poverty of practical policy ideas, which forced them to depend heavily on outside advisers for policy guidance in government. All three parties practiced very tight discipline in congress, and in Peru and Venezuela this discipline extended beyond the legislature. Other practices varied across the parties, but nevertheless remained constant over time. All of them mobilized voters with a mix of clientelism, mass meetings, and mass media, but better access to campaign funding enabled Acción Democrática (AD) to do all of these more intensively. Leadership was more personalized in APRA and the Partido Justicialista (PJ) than it was in AD, and procedures for recruitment and promotion were less institutionalized in the PJ. There are probably two reasons for the lack of change in these respects. The first is that every large party creates its own organizational subculture early in its existence, and this subculture tends to reproduce itself faithfully.[28] The second is that these parties had few incentives to adapt these aspects of their organizational life. Rather, the kind of adaptation required by the political environment after 1982 concerned the parties' ideological positioning and relations with labor and business. Therefore, whatever changes occurred in the ways parties recruited leaders, mobilized voters, and formed or sustained governments were not the result of adaptation, but instead the replacement of old parties by new ones that performed these functions differently.

APRA: Misadaptation and replacement. The Alianza Popular Revolucionaria Americana (APRA) was founded by Víctor Raúl Haya de la Torre as an alternative to communism that would unite workers, peasants, and the middle class behind an anti-oligarchical program. From the 1930s to the mid-1960s it enjoyed a cult-like adherence among a substantial proportion of the urban middle class and workers in industry and export agriculture.[29] By the mid-1960s it exercised paternalistic control over 75 percent of the trade unions in Peru. It also informally sponsored paramilitary squads called *búfalos* that took violent action against rivals. At its peak, the party had an extensive grassroots organization that involved activists in a wide range of activities, including rallies, lectures, cooperatives, and soccer clubs. In 1945–48 and 1956–58, however, APRA briefly backed two relatively conservative governments; and during the 1963–68 presidency of Fernando Belaunde, Haya joined the conservative former dictator Manuel Odría to block attempts at land reform. In the increasingly pro-reform context of the time, such actions eroded APRA's support base, especially among organized labor.

The transition to democracy after 1978 coincided with three challenges to APRA in addition to the debt crisis, which hit Peru early. One was the radicalization of many voters by the leftist military government of General Juan Velasco Alvarado (1968–75), which had nationalized major industries, set up agricultural cooperatives, established close ties to Cuba, and placed former Socialist and Communist politicians in charge of some urban social programs.[30] During the 1970s and afterwards, most unions affiliated themselves with the leftist Confederación General de Trabajadores Peruanos (CGTP) rather than APRA's Confederación de Trabajadores Peruanos (CTP). The youth wing, Juventud Aprista Peruana (JAP), was even more radicalized, to the point of being openly and explicitly Marxist. A second challenge was the need to renovate the leadership, as most of the well-known leaders were quite old and discredited by Haya's past compromises. Finally, the most serious challenge of all was the death of Haya himself in 1979. Although he had taken on several leaders in their twenties and thirties as proteges, he left neither a clear successor nor a means for choosing one, so the party languished in a leadership vacuum for the next four years.[31]

The leader who eventually emerged as the winner of the presidential candidacy nomination in late 1983 was 34-year-old Alan García. Before long, activists treated him as the unquestioned leader, much as they had treated Haya, and it fell to him to guide APRA's adaptation to the post-1982 political environment. At first he planted the party firmly in the center, where it was abundantly rewarded. Then he unexpectedly swerved to the left, which cost the party dearly.

García's 1983–85 presidential campaign was designed to reshape APRA in order to attract votes outside its traditional base. One promise was targeted at radicalized workers and students: an announcement that Peru would use no more than 20 percent of its export earnings for servicing the foreign debt. (He lowered this figure to 10 percent on inauguration day.) This promise was also appealing to many voters who were not otherwise very radical, however, and most of his other appeals were directed toward less radical groups. He encouraged the formation of middle-class "Civic Communities" to endorse his candidacy; he initiated consensus-building talks with the armed forces and the Church; he publicized the most technical policy studies Apristas had to offer (which were still not as detailed or rigorous as those of their rivals); he criticized unionized workers for being a labor elite less deserving of state support than the unemployed and underemployed; he repudiated some of Haya's anticapitalist utterings; he distanced himself from the party's violent past; and he advocated a "social pact" with business.[32] The overall effect was to cast APRA in the role of a pragmatic, reasonable, moderate reformist alternative to the growing left. This strategy led to the party's greatest electoral success ever: García won 47.8 percent of the vote in 1985, compared to less than 36 percent in all previous elections in which the party had run its own candidate.

At first, García was an extremely popular president, with approval ratings over 80 percent in his first year and over 60 percent in his second.[33] But in July 1987 he suddenly shifted to the left by nationalizing all remaining private domestic banks, insurance companies, and finance corporations. This move instantly alienated the international financial community (which already distrusted García's heterodox policies), Peruvian business leaders, opposition leaders on the right, and even most leaders of APRA—none of whom had been consulted before the decision was made—without winning the support of the parties on the left.[34] The economy shuddered, then collapsed, and from this point on APRA suffered an unbroken series of disasters: García's approval rating immediately plummeted to 30 percent; within months, a rival wrested control of the APRA congressional delegation from him; some CTP unions joined general strikes in 1988 and 1989; JAP youth began defecting to the Movimiento Revolucionario Tupac Amaru (MRTA, the same terrorist group that held hostages in the Japanese embassy for four months in 1997); and the party's share of the vote shrank to 25 percent in 1990. In 1995, further discredited by Alberto Fujimori's economic success and his virulently antiparty rhetoric, APRA's share shrank to 6.5 percent—yielding just 6.7 percent of the seats in congress and 4 percent of the presidential vote—not enough to maintain its registration as a national political party. García himself went into exile in Colombia to escape corruption charges.[35]

Peru is a clear-cut case of a change in the nature of parties due to replacement rather than adaptation. The major party in Peru after 1990 was Cambio 90/Nueva Mayoría, the personalist vehicle of Alberto Fujimori, which controlled 67 of the 120 seats in congress as a result of the 1995 election. Its only ideology was to back whatever Fujimori wanted to do, without question. It had no grassroots presence. It screened candidates in focus groups and took polls to set priorities. It went farther in the direction of the unmediated electronic executive than any other party in the region, and perhaps the world. Conaghan has argued that "Peru's party system has ceased to exist in any meaningful sense."[36]

Acción Democrática: Resistance and decline. Acción Democrática (AD), like APRA, was founded to bring together the middle class, workers, and peasants into a nationalistic anti-oligarchical alliance. Unlike APRA, it was very successful at winning power. After seizing power jointly with military conspirators in 1945, it won Venezuela's first fair presidential election in 1948 with more than 70 percent of the vote, and won five of the eight presidential elections after the restoration of democracy in 1958. Although AD was fairly radical for its time in the beginning, by 1958 it had become a slightly center-left catch-all party. It won the votes of Venezuelans from all classes, occupations, and regions, and in this respect was indistinguishable from its principal rival, the Social Christian party COPEI. Unlike many catch-all parties, however, AD had a Leninist organizational structure explicitly based on democratic centralism, and it actively enforced party discipline among its legislators, leaders, and militants at the national, state, and local levels. As late as 1995 it was still expelling hundreds of members for ignoring the party line in local elections.

In addition to being tightly disciplined, AD aggressively penetrated most organizations in civil society aside from the Church and private businesses.[37] Through infiltration, cooptation, and the creation of parallel organizations, AD and the other major parties succeeded in placing party members as leaders of student governments, professional associations, and unions. These leaders then mobilized their organizations in support of their party during and between elections. AD was much more successful than other parties at gaining control over labor unions and federations, and in winning the most important offices at the head of the peak labor confederation, the Confederación de Trabajadores de Venezuela (CTV). The labor wing of AD was therefore a large and valuable component of the party. However, AD's labor leaders habitually deferred to the party line in exchange for party support for labor demands in the long run. And to the extent that the labor wing had influence over party affairs, it was counterbalanced by the influence of the state party bosses, who used their regional patronage machines to deliver large blocs of votes at national party meetings. In general elections, both state bosses and labor leaders turned out large numbers of activists for open-air rallies, caravans, and processions, all festooned with party posters, banners, T-shirts, hats, and other paraphernalia. Since about 1973, parties have also made heavy use of high-tech polling, campaign consultants, and slick television ads, but not at the expense of this old-fashioned type of electoral mobilization.

During the long intervals between major national party meetings, however, a much smaller group of leaders made party decisions. Formally, that body was the National Executive Committee (CEN); informally, it was a group of five to seven leaders known as the *cogollo*. And when the president came from AD, the *cogollo* normally did its best to reach agreement with the president privately so that president and party could appear united in public. When the national leadership was united, the *cogollo* had the power to dictate the party line to the Parliamentary Fraction and state and local party leaders. But when the national leadership was divided, as often occurred during the selection of the presidential candidate, de facto leadership reverted to state party bosses and labor leaders.

When the debt crisis hit Venezuela, AD resisted adaptation every step of the way. One president temporized with heterodoxy with the full support of the party; the next veered toward neoliberalism, but the party blocked his way; and when the next presidential candidate also endorsed the turn to the market, he and his supporters were marginalized, leaving the organization in the hands of an extremely pragmatic general secretary who supported minimal liberalizations only reluctantly and semipublicly. Jaime Lusinchi (1984–89) followed heterodox policies throughout his term, so there was not much of an attempt at adaptation for the party to resist. Lusinchi's policies were supported by a majority of the CEN, the Parliamentary Fraction, and the labor wing.[38] Lusinchi's successor was Carlos Andrés Pérez, also from AD, who surprised everyone by announcing a shock economic liberalization package at his inauguration. Due to the concentration of policy-making authority in the executive branch in Venezuela, he managed to implement the easier parts of his program, but he was a very unpopular president throughout his term. As time passed, AD became less willing to support further reform, and after the two unsuccessful coup attempts in 1992, the party left its president without support and Pérez's economic liberalization stalled. A minister in the Pérez cabinet wrote: "Pérez's own party, Acción Democrática, having spent most of the 1980s profiting from the many opportunities to serve as broker between society and the state, adamantly opposed any changes resulting in reduced government intervention."[39] AD leaders were not happy when Pérez was impeached in 1993, but they expelled him from the party anyway while he awaited sentencing on corruption charges.

It could be argued that AD adapted in other ways. In 1988 and 1989, for example, the party voted for two electoral reforms that provided for the direct election of governors and mayors, as well as the election of half of the national deputies in single-member districts. These reforms were designed to make public officials more responsible to their own constituents and less responsible to national party leaders. It may appear that AD was adapting to the environment either by lessening *partidocracia* (the distortion of democracy by excessively strong parties) or by creating a diversion away from the economic situation. In reality, the party per se was not enthusiastic about political reform, either. The electoral reform was pushed by Pérez during the campaign itself, which was the time of his greatest influence over the party; as soon as the law went into effect, other party leaders took steps to minimize its decentralizing effects by, for example, exerting tight control over nominations for governor, mayor, and national deputy. When grassroots demands arose for further constitutional reform in 1992, AD took the lead in delaying, watering down, and ultimately shelving the major reform bill. In spite of these efforts to resist adaptation, several governors or mayors with a regional base of support began to challenge the national leadership. One of these, Claudio Fermín, won the presidential nomination in a primary. He was very much the candidate of renovation, with calls for thorough economic liberalization and more openness and participation within the parties. But in the 1993 election, Fermín won only 23.6 percent of the vote, the worst performance ever for an AD candidate. After the election, hundreds of his supporters were purged from the party and Fermín himself was treated so coldly by other party leaders that he took refuge in the United States for several years.

Although AD was not hurt as badly as Peru's APRA, both it and COPEI lost considerable support. From 1973 to 1988 they never won less than a combined 74 percent of the legislative vote; in 1993, they won only 46 percent, and in 1998, 36 percent. In presidential races, they customarily shared 90 percent of the vote until 1988; but in 1993 their combined share was 54 percent. In 1998, COPEI backed an independent candidate rather than attempt to win on its own, and then at the last minute both parties threw their support to a different independent, together contributing only 11 percent to his vote total.

The largest new parties that have filled the vacuum left by AD and COPEI are all either personalist or center-left, and all are in some ways reactions against the traditional parties. In 1993, one was Convergencia Nacional, the personalist vehicle of Rafael Caldera, who abandoned COPEI and won the presidential contest. The other that year was La Causa R, a center-left party that explicitly campaigned against the AD-COPEI "establishment." It was committed to being the opposite of AD in several ways: it was responsive to the union rank-and-file rather than cooptative and controlling; pluralistic rather than disciplined; and respectful of the autonomy of new social movements.[40] In 1998, independents dominated the field. For much of the long campaign, the frontrunner was Irene Sáez Conde, a former Miss Universe who earned a reputation as an efficient and honest mayor. Her star fell, however, when she accepted COPEI's endorsement, which voters interpreted as "the kiss of death." Much of her support then went to Henrique Salas Römer, a state governor who also had a reputation for efficiency and honesty. But the big winner in 1998 was the candidate who combined all of these characteristics. Hugo Chávez Frías was the charismatic leader of a personalistic movement, the Movimiento V República (Fifth Republic Movement); he employed populist rhetoric, even if he was not certifiably on the center-left, and was allied with the center-left Movement Toward Socialism (MAS) and the Causa R splinter Patria Para Todos; and he vowed to wipe out corruption, which he associated with the traditional parties. Furthermore, it was clear that he stood for radical change, as he was the leader of a nearly successful coup attempt in February 1992. No one else could have better personified the tendency of new parties to be reactions against the old ones.

The Peronists: Adaptation and growth. Even more than APRA or AD, the Partido Justicialista (PJ) in Argentina depended organizationally on the support of trade unions, monopolized union support, and gave the unions a prominent leadership role in the party. Before the late 1980s, the unions were customarily allocated one-third of the positions on the National Council; 1983 presidential candidate Italo Luder was backed strongly, if customarily, by the unions; 35 of the 115 PJ deputies were associated with the unions; and the head of the metalworkers union, Lorenzo Miguel, served as party president in 1983–84.[41] The PJ was not exclusively a socialist or labor party, however, for three reasons. First, there was a strong element of personalism toward Perón before his death in 1974, and toward Carlos Menem after 1987. (In the intervening years the party struggled to produce a new unifying leader.) Second, because of its apparently all-encompassing diversity, the PJ for decades claimed to not even be a party, which would represent only a part of society, but instead a movement of the entire Argentine *pueblo*.[42] And third, the party enjoyed vibrant grassroots organization structured around neighborhoods and provinces, not just sectoral organizations such as unions. Because identification with Peronism was so strong, there were self-mobilizing, unofficial *unidades de base* (base units) in practically every neighborhood, often more in working-class neighborhoods; these were grouped together into local clientelistic factions called *agrupaciones* by brokers called *punteros*. The *agrupaciones* fed informally into the provincial factions that constituted the provincial parties, and the national party encompassed most of the provincial Peronist parties. Nevertheless, while not strictly a labor party, the PJ was more of a working-class party than AD or APRA, as there was a very significant differentiation of Peronist and anti-Peronist vote by class.

In spite of the strong working-class base of support, it is less clear that the PJ possessed a center-left ideology. Its prominent leaders spanned the entire left-right spectrum, from the Montoneros on the extreme left and the Peronist Youth of the 1970s on the left, to Herminio Iglesias, López Rega, and the *Guardia de Hierro* ("Iron Guard") on the right or far right.[43] Moreover, the corporatist labor interests that were dominant in the party before 1985 were often labeled "conservative." However, this conservatism consisted of nationalism, clericalism, and sympathy for authoritarianism rather than support for economic liberalization. Before 1989, most of the party's prominent leaders and fractions shared an opposition to many of the pro-market reforms that were being prescribed for Argentina and other Latin American countries emerging from the debt crisis. Privatization was up against especially vehement opposition due to its perceived negative impact on the Peronist unions. Even the anti-union "Renewalist" faction that won control of the party in 1985 was on the center-left in economic terms; its attack on the unions was directed only at the unions' power within the party organization and parliamentary caucus.

Menem himself adapted to the 1982–95 environment by shifting to the right. In 1985–87, as governor of La Rioja province, he had backed the "Renewalist" faction led by Antonio Cafiero that called for internal democratization of the party, institutionalization of the party organization, and a return to what it viewed as the party's ideological heritage on the center-left. Once the corporatist union leadership was defeated by the Renewalists, however, Menem broke with Cafiero to launch his own candidacy for the presidential nomination. During the campaign, his economic program was vague, and many feared (or hoped) that he would turn out to be a populist. Once in office, however, his shift to the right became clear. With the pro-business Unión del Centro Democrático as a coalition partner, and with the help of ministers recruited from prominent business groups and think tanks, Menem aggressively decontrolled prices, liberalized trade, sold off state enterprises, and cut the budget. By 1993 inflation was down to 10.6 percent and still falling, while investment poured in and growth returned.[44]

What is amazing is that Menem managed to keep the support of most of his party while carrying out this shift to the right. It helped considerably that the marginalization of the old "orthodox" labor wing had already been accomplished by the Renewalists. Led by Antonio Cafiero, this faction amended the party charter to reduce labor representation in the National Council from one-third to only 17 positions out of 110 (15 percent). It also promoted primaries for the selection of legislative candidates, which reduced the number of labor legislators from 35 to six. Even more importantly, the Renewalists sidelined all of the old labor representatives. Ever since the 1960s, an informal labor confederation known as the "62 organizations" had been the de facto representative of labor within Peronism. Cafiero simply refused to recognize this body, choosing to deal instead with a more cooperative set of labor leaders, though he did not grant them a formal role in the party. Menem encountered union opposition, especially from public employees opposed to privatization, but managed to hold onto most union and non-union support within the party. For example, the peak labor confederation CGT organized only one general strike during Menem's first term, compared to 13 during the 1983–89 government of Raúl Alfonsín. Some union leaders were brutally repressed; others were coopted; a few made their peace with market capitalism; and still others grumbled but stayed within the party.[45] But almost all union leaders backed Menem for reelection in 1995.

Non-union opposition within the party was also skillfully marginalized. Due to the weak institutionalization of the party organization, Menem had little trouble in arranging for the lateral entry of nonpoliticians into party leadership positions, displacing politicians whose entire careers had been spent in Peronism.[46] His one setback was the departure of the "Group of Eight" deputies, who defected in protest against Menem's shift to the right and his authoritarian style. Overall, however, this defection was not very costly because Menem maintained the PJ's share of the vote despite the defection of the Group of Eight and Governor José Octavio Bordón, who ran as the presidential candidate of FREPASO and won a startling 29 percent of the vote. Such was the success of Menem's adaptation that even though Bordón had been a Peronist, his party drew votes away from other parties, principally the Radicals.[47]

Patterns of Change

Latin America's parties and party systems are too diverse and dynamic to provide a simple answer to broad questions about the decline of parties.[48] They have changed in the past two decades, but then, they have always been changing; some parties lost mobilizational capacity and hierarchy, though they were not that common in the region to begin with, and some (Costa Rica and Uruguay) have not changed very much at all.

However, we *can* identify certain tendencies in the nature of this change. First, the nature of individual party organizations—centralization, discipline, cohesion, recruitment, mobilization, socialization, financing—seems to change very slowly, if at all. In the meantime, it is more likely that the party will be sidelined in the volatile electoral environment. Therefore the primary mechanism of change in parties is replacement by other parties rather than internal reform. Second, this evolutionary process, akin to Darwin's principle of natural selection, tends to favor the survival of parties that are well adapted to the political environment. Parties are not the passive objects of the process, as they possess some capacity to adapt. Those that adapt well survive; those that stubbornly refuse to adapt, or misadapt, lose votes and move toward extinction. Third, in the "lost decade" of approximately 1982 to 1995, the environment selected in favor of governing parties of the center-right or right and opposition parties that were either personalist or left of center. But the environment has probably changed already, so we can expect to see different sorts of parties favored in future elections. In particular, the environment seems to favor the center-left over the center-right. By September 2000, Fujimori's approval ratings had declined enough to make his reelection either extremely close and at least partially fraudulent, Hugo Chávez remained popular with a populist platform, and the Peronists had been turned out of office by a center-left alliance.

Evaluating the consequences of these changes is a separate question, and its answers are not simple either. Changes that improve the quality of representation sometimes weaken governability, and vice versa. Whether or not a change takes a party system into or away from a zone of functionality (defined by a happy medium of fragmentation, polarization, and other characteristics) depends on the starting point and the nature, magnitude, and direction of the change. In Latin America, the party system became less functional for representation and governability in Brazil and Ecuador but more functional in both respects in Colombia and Mexico. It became less functional for representation in Peru and possibly Argentina, and less governable in Venezuela (see the Figure on p. 182). In the other four major countries, there was either no significant change or a gain in one respect that was offset by a loss in another. This summary assessment is not a cause for celebration, but it should temper the much more negative impression left by a handful of dramatic electoral upsets (by Collor in Brazil, Fujimori in Peru, ADM-19 in Colombia, Caldera and Chávez in Venezuela) that were the focus of disproportionate media coverage and scholarly discussion. In view of the grim economic environment, we should have expected party-system change to be much worse. Perhaps a quiet, sober celebration would be in order after all.

Appendix: A Model of the Impact of Inflation Changes on Changes in Legislative Vote Shares

The dependent variable for this model is the change in the percentage of the vote won by a party from one legislative election to the next. The sample consists of 132 such changes for parties that had been, were, or would become major parties in 11 Latin American countries from 1978 to 1995. The sample therefore includes all the presidential parties and all major opposition parties in this period in Argentina, Bolivia, Brazil, Chile, Colombia, Costa Rica, Ecuador, Mexico, Peru, Uruguay, and Venezuela.

Two of the independent variables are control variables. The first is simply the percentage of the vote won by the party in the previous election. This is included because the percentage of the vote that is potentially available to add to a party's share is 100 minus its previous share. Parties that are already large may shrink easily, but they find it difficult to grow beyond a certain point. Small parties have a greater potential for growth, but they can lose only so many votes before they are eliminated. The negative coefficient of the lagged vote correctly specifies these different constraints on large and small parties. The second control variable is the percentage of the vote won previously by parties that merged with the party of interest (a positive number) and the percentage of the vote currently won by parties that split away from it (a negative number). When these splits and mergers occur (only 10 instances are included in this sample), they have an obvious direct impact on vote shares. Controlling for them makes it possible to estimate the impact of economic performance with less bias.

The only indicator of economic performance used here is the change in ln(inflation) from the last year of the previous government to the last year of the current government. Lower inflation is represented by positive numbers and higher inflation by negative numbers. The model reported below contains interactions between economic performance as measured in this way, on the one hand, and incumbency and the strength of party identification, on the other (see note 20 on party ID).

- $\Delta\ln(\text{inflation})_{\text{incumbents with fluid base}}$ represents the change in logged inflation for all incumbent parties with a fluid base of support.
- $\Delta\ln(\text{rising inflation})_{\text{opposition with fluid base}}$ applies to all opposition parties with a fluid base, but only if inflation was rising.
- The model also includes a dummy variable for all parties classified as having a fluid base of support. The OLS regression estimates are:

$\Delta\text{vote} = 11.03$ $-0.32*\text{lagged vote}$ $-7.30*\text{weak ID}$ $+0.46*\text{splits and mergers}$
     $(2.00)**$ $(0.05)**$ $(1.74)**$ $(0.19)*$

$+3.32*\Delta\ln(\text{inflation})_{\text{incumbent with fluid base}}$ $-2.14*\Delta\ln(\text{rising inflation})_{\text{opposition with fluid base}}$
     $(0.76)**$ $(0.90)*$

$N = 132$, Adjusted $R^2 = .381$
Standard errors are in parentheses. * = significant at the .02 level; ** = significant at the .0001 level

NOTES

The author is grateful to the editors, Charles Kenney, Marcelo Leiras, Scott Mainwaring, Pierre Ostiguy, and Gábor Tóka for their many valuable contributions to this analysis, and to Miguel Basáñez for permission to use the 1995 Latinobarómetro data.

1. I define parties simply as organizations that compete in legislative elections. This definition necessarily includes many ephemeral organizations that managed to get on the ballot, and it excludes some political organizations that were never willing or able to compete in elections.

2. The volatility index is the sum of the absolute values of the differences of the shares won by all parties from one election to the next, halved to adjust for double-counting. This index was first defined in Mogens Pedersen, "The Dynamics of European Party Systems: Changing Patterns of Electoral Volatility," *European Journal of Political Research* 7 (1979): 1–26. Although volatility is normally calculated for pairs of consecutive elections, it may apply to any pair of elections. The index reported in Table 1 applies to the first and last elections in the periods listed. This method better reflects cumulative change over a long span of time because it measures all the changes that last, and only changes that last. The more commonly reported average volatility in consecutive elections counts changes that are subsequently undone. For example, if two parties' shares in four elections were 65–35, 45–55, 55–45, and 60–40, the average volatility would be $(20 + 10 + 5) / 3 = 11.7$, while cumulative volatility would be only 5.0, better reflecting a system that is very similar at the beginning and the end of the period.

3. Karen L. Remmer, *Party Competition in Argentina and Chile: Political Recruitment and Public Policy, 1890–1930* (Lincoln: University of Nebraska Press, 1984); Scott Mainwaring, *Rethinking Party Systems in the Third Wave of Democratization: The Case of Brazil* (Stanford, Calif.: Stanford University Press, 1999), 64–70; Ciro F. Cardoso, "Central America: The Liberal Era, c. 1870–1930," in Leslie Bethell, ed., *The Cambridge History of Latin America* (Cambridge: Cambridge University Press, 1986), 197–227; and David Scott Palmer, *Peru: The Authoritarian Tradition* (New York: Praeger, 1980), 18–67.

4. Ronald P. Archer, "Party Strength and Weakness in Colombia's Beseiged Democracy," in Scott Mainwaring and Timothy R. Scully, eds., *Building Democratic Institutions: Party Systems in Latin America* (Stanford, Calif.: Stanford University Press, 1995), 164–99.

5. Luis Eduardo González, "Los partidos políticos y la redemocratización en Uruguay," *Cuadernos del CLAEH* 36 (1986): 25–56.

6. Michael Coppedge, "The Evolution of Latin American Party Systems," in Scott Mainwaring and Arturo Valenzuela, eds., *Politics, Society, and Democracy: Latin America* (Boulder, Colo.: Westview Press, 1998), 171–206.

7. Robert J. Alexander, "The Emergence of Modern Political Parties in Latin America," in Joseph Maier and Richard W. Weatherhead, eds., *Politics of Change in Latin America* (New York: Praeger, 1964), 119; John Martz, *Acción Democrática: Evolution of a Modern Political Party* (Princeton, N.J.: Princeton University Press, 1966); Grant Hilliker, *The Politics of Reform in Peru: The Aprista and Other Mass Parties of Latin America* (Baltimore: The Johns Hopkins University Press, 1971), 1–15.

8. Donna Lee Van Cott, "Party System Development and Indigenous Populations: Theoretical Reflections on the Bolivian Case," *Party Politics* (2000).

9. Arend Lijphart, *Democracies: Patterns of Majoritarian and Consensus Government in Twenty-One Countries* (New Haven: Yale University Press, 1984) 106–14.

10. The effective number of parties is the reciprocal of the sum of squared party shares. Its value is 2.0 for a 50–50 party system and 4.0 for the 25–25–25–25 party system. When parties are unequal in size, it usually takes on fractional values. This indicator was originally described in Markku Laakso and Rein Taagepera, "Effective Number of Parties: A Measure with application to Western Europe," *Comparative Political Studies* 12 (1979): 3–27.

11. The relative center can be farther to the right or the left than the absolute center as defined in the classification criteria and is operationalized here as the Mean Left-Right Position of all parties in the system (MLRP). MLRP measures how far to the left or the right the average party was in each election, based on the left-right positions of all the parties and their shares of the vote. This indicator assumes that all parties classified left (whether Christian or secular) are approximately twice as far from the center as parties classified center-left, and right parties are twice as far to the right as the parties of the center-right. This assumption permits the calculation of MLRP as: right % + .5 center-right % − .5 center-left % − left %. The formula for left-right polarization is therefore: |1−mlrp|*right % + |.5−mlrp|*center-right % + |−.5−mlrp|*center-left % + |−1−mlrp|*left %, where mlrp = MLRP/100. The index can reach its maximum only when half of the vote goes to the right and half to the left; if all of the vote went to just one extreme, polarization would be zero because the relative center would be at the extreme as well and there would be no dispersion. It is important to remember that this is an indicator of *left-right* polarization only and does not reflect the intense personal, ethnic, ins-outs, or other rivalries that sometimes exist between parties that are relatively close in left-right terms.

12. See note 43 for elaboration.

13. This conception of party-system evolution as the product of both the environment and choices by leaders was first developed at length in Seymour Martin Lipset and Stein Rokkan, "Cleavage Structures, Party Systems, and Voter Alignments," in Seymour Martin Lipset and Stein Rokkan, eds., *Party Systems and Voter Alignments: Cross-National Perspectives* (New York: The Free Press, 1967), 1–64. It has been further developed more recently in Angelo Panebianco, *Political Parties: Organisation and Power* (Cambridge: Cambridge University Press, 1988); and Herbert Kitschelt, *The Transformation of European Social Democracy* (Cambridge: Cambridge University Press, 1994).

14. All left-right ideological labels applied to parties in this chapter come from a comprehensive classification of 97 percent of the parties in the major countries of

Latin America. I drafted a classification myself, obtained feedback from 53 country specialists, then did my best to reconcile their suggested corrections consistently over time and across countries. This project is fully documented in Michael Coppedge, "A Classification of Latin American Political Parties," Kellogg Institute Working Paper No. 244 (November 1997).

15. Methodological sophisticates will object that I have selected on the dependent variable for all the arguments in this paragraph. They are correct, but I have done so only to generate hypotheses that are tested with a larger and far more appropriate sample below.

16. Michael Coppedge, "Freezing in the Tropics: Explaining Party-System Volatility in Latin America," paper presented at the 1995 Meeting of the Midwest Political Science Association, Chicago, 6–8 April 1995; and Stefano Bartolini and Peter Mair, *Identity, Competition, and Electoral Availability: The Stabilization of European Electorates, 1885–1985* (Cambridge: Cambridge University Press, 1990).

17. For Peru and Ecuador, IMF, *International Financial Statistics 1992;* for other countries, United Nations Economic Commission for Latin America and the Caribbean, *Social Panorama of Latin America 1994* (Santiago, Chile: ECLAC, 1994), Tables 1 and 19. Dates are 1980–92 in Argentina, Bolivia, Chile, and Colombia; 1981–92 in Costa Rica, Uruguay, and Venezuela; 1979–82 in Brazil; 1980–90 in Peru; 1979–90 in Ecuador; and 1984–92 in Mexico.

18. United Nations Economic Commission for Latin America and the Caribbean, *Social Panorama of Latin America 1994* (Santiago, Chile: ECLAC, 1994), 35–45. Comparable data were unavailable for Ecuador and Peru.

19. Peak inflation 1980–85: *Anuario estadístico de América Latina y el Caribe 1988* (Santiago, Chile: CEPAL, 1988), 94–95; peak inflation 1986–95: Inter-American Development Bank, "Average Annual Growth of Consumer Prices," available at *http://iadb6000.iadb.org/int_data/pri2.html.*

20. No cross-nationally comparable data on the strength of party identification in Latin America yet exist. One study tracks the stability of self-reported party preferences in Argentina, Chile, Mexico, and Venezuela, but the survey questions are not strictly comparable and cover only four cases. Lauro Mercado Gasca, "Visiting Party Loyalties in Latin America," paper prepared for the 20th International Congress of the Latin American Studies Association, Guadalajara, Mexico, 17–19 April 1997. Comparable instruments were used in the 1995 and 1996 Latinobarómetro surveys in eight countries, but a one-year span is not long enough to justify inferences about the stability of party loyalties, and the data have not been shared with the scholarly community. An independent assessment based on the best data available is Scott Mainwaring and Timothy Scully, "Introduction: Party Systems in Latin America," in Scott Mainwaring and Timothy Scully, eds., *Building Democratic Institutions: Party Systems in Latin America* (Stanford, Calif.: Stanford University Press, 1995), 17–21. The coding of my data coincides with Mainwaring and Scully's conclusions.

21. Here, PRI and PAN in Mexico, PT in Brazil, and the UCR and PJ in Argentina are treated as having a solid base of support, while PRD in Mexico, PMDB and PFL in Brazil, and Frente Grande and FREPASO in Argentina are treated as having a fluid base. In Peru, identification with APRA was strong before 1968 but weak afterwards.

22. Robert Dix, "Incumbency and Electoral Turnover in Latin America," *Journal of Interamerican Studies and World Affairs* 26 (1984): 435–48; George A. Quattrone and Amos Tversky, "Contrasting Rational and Psychological Analyses of Political Choice," *American Political Science Review* 82 (1988): 719–36; Martin Paldam, "How Robust Is the Vote Function? A Study of Seventeen Nations over Four Decades," in Helmut Norputh, Michael Lewis-Beck, and Jean Dominique Lafay, eds., *Economics and Politics: The Calculus of Support* (London: Sage Publications, 1991).

23. There is no way to know whether the insignificance of economic performance for solid parties is due to their strong ID or to the fact that none of them happened to experience inflation changes of 3,000 percent or greater. Also, it is possible that the association between strong ID and inflation is no accident, as solid governing parties may be less likely to allow inflation to surge to such extraordinarily high levels.

24. Catherine Conaghan, James Malloy, and Luis Abugattas, "Business and the 'Boys': The Politics of Neoliberalism in the Central Andes," *Latin American Research Review* 25 (1990): 3–30.

25. Other cases include Izquierda Democrática, the CFP in Ecuador, and PMDB in Brazil.

26. Similar cases of resistance and decline are the Radicals in Argentina, Acción Popular in Peru, and the Blancos and Colorados in Uruguay.

27. Other parties that adapted and grew were the Christian Democrats and the Socialists in Chile. More conservative parties prospered electorally without having to adapt as drastically. Examples are the PUSC in Costa Rica, the Social Christian Party in Ecuador, and MNR in Bolivia which, despite having led the 1952 Revolution, was already right of center by 1985.

28. Angelo Panebianco, *Political Parties,* ch. 4.

29. Grant Hilliker, *The Politics of Reform in Peru: The Aprista and Other Mass Parties of Latin America* (Baltimore: Johns Hopkins University Press, 1971), 74–82.

30. The best study of the impact of this government on voters is Susan C. Stokes, *Cultures in Conflict: Social Movements and the State in Peru* (Berkeley: University of California Press, 1995).

31. Carol Graham, *Peru's APRA: Parties, Politics, and the Elusive Quest for Democracy* (Boulder, Colo.: Lynne Rienner, 1992).

32. All of this evidence comes from Carol Graham, *Peru's APRA,* 84–91.

33. Martín Tanaka, "Los espejos y espejismos de la democracia y el colapso de un sistema de partidos: Perú, 1980–1995, en perspectiva comparada," paper prepared for delivery at the 1997 meeting of the Latin American Studies Association, Guadalajara, Mexico, 17–19 April 1997, 26.

34. Carol Graham, *Peru's APRA,* 111–21.

35. In 1995, Fujimori raised the signature requirements for registering a national party from 100,000 to about 490,000 signatures, which the remnant of APRA failed to meet. It nevertheless ran many candidates as independents in the November 1995 mayoral races, and privately claimed to have elected about 1,000. Private communication from Charles Kenney, 29 May 1997.

36. Catherine Conaghan, "The Irrelevant Right: Alberto Fujimori and the New Politics of Pragmatic Peru," paper prepared for the conference on "Conservative Parties, Democratization, and Neoliberalism in Latin America: Mexico in Comparative Perspective," Center for U.S.-Mexican Studies, University of California–San Diego, 31 May–1 June 1996.

37. Michael Coppedge, *Strong Parties and Lame Ducks: Presidential Partyarchy and Factionalism in Venezuela* (Stanford, Calif.: Stanford University Press, 1994), ch. 2.

38. Lusinchi was not able to impose his choice for the presidential nomination, but this was because most state bosses and national leaders considered the alternative more electable, not because of any disapproval of Lusinchi's policies. Michael Coppedge, *Strong Parties and Lame Ducks*, chs. 4 and 6.

39. Moisés Naím, *Paper Tigers and Minotaurs: The Politics of Venezuela's Economic Reforms* (Washington, D.C.: Carnegie Endowment for International Peace, 1993), 47.

40. Margarita López Maya, "El ascenso en Venezuela de la Causa R," paper presented at the 18th International Congress of the Latin American Studies Association, Atlanta, Georgia, 9–13 March 1994.

41. I am deeply indebted to Steven Levitsky for his detailed descriptions and insights into Justicialist party organization, as analyzed in Steven Levitsky, "Crisis, Party Adaptation, and Regime Stability in Argentina: The Case of Peronism, 1989–1995," paper prepared for delivery at the 1997 meeting of the Latin American Studies Association, Guadalajara, Mexico, 17–19 April 1997.

42. James McGuire, "Political Parties and Democracy in Argentina," in Scott Mainwaring and Timothy Scully, *Building Democratic Institutions,* 200–46.

43. I am also deeply indebted to Pierre Ostiguy for his "Peronism and Anti-Peronism: Social-Cultural Bases of Political Identity in Argentina," paper prepared for delivery at the 1997 meeting of the Latin American Studies Association, Guadalajara, Mexico, 17–19 April 1997. Ostiguy argues that the diversity within the Peronist and anti-Peronist blocs obscures the fact that they are consistently divided by what he calls the "high-low" cleavage. Those at the high end of this divide are "refined," cosmopolitan, and inclined to favor formal procedures; those at the low end are "crude," localist, and personalist or *caudillista*. It is a class cleavage defined in sociocultural rather than economic terms. In this scheme the Peronists, Montoneros, and Carapintadas are "low" and the Radicals, Socialists, UCeDé, and FREPASO are "high."

44. I am again heavily indebted to Steven Levitsky, "Crisis, Party Adaptation, and Regime Stability in Argentina," for these arguments.

45. Steven Levitsky, "Populism is Dead! Long Live the Populist Party! Party Adaptation Through Coalitional Realignment in Peronist Argentina," paper prepared for delivery at the 1995 meeting of the Latin American Studies Association, Washington, D.C., 28–30 September 1995, 20–24.

46. Steven Levitsky, "Crisis, Party Adaptation, and Regime Stability in Argentina."

47. Ibid., 4–5.

48. Michael Coppedge, "The Dynamic Diversity of Latin American Party Systems," *Party Politics* 4 (1998): 547–68.

9

TOWARD MODERATE PLURALISM: POLITICAL PARTIES IN INDIA

E. Sridharan and Ashutosh Varshney

E. Sridharan is academic director of the Institute for the Advanced Study of India at the University of Pennsylvania and an editor of forthcoming volumes on coalition politics in India, the constitution of India, and political parties in India. Ashutosh Varshney is associate professor of political science at the University of Michigan, Ann Arbor and author of Ethnic Conflict and Civic Life: Hindus and Muslims in India *(forthcoming, 2001).*

Since its independence in 1947, India has maintained its democratic institutions, except for a brief period of 19 months between 1975–77. Elections have become deeply institutionalized and are now the widely accepted way for parties to come to power and form governments. Since the first universal-franchise elections were held in 1952, 12 more elections for the central parliament have been held, as have many more elections for the various state assemblies. Between 1947 and 1999, power has been transferred peacefully to competing political parties seven times at the central (federal) level. Since 1967, the state and central governments have often been formed by different parties. Since 1977, incumbent governments at both levels have repeatedly been thrown out of power. Newspapers have always been free of government control, and television has been free since 1991. Subjecting the government of the day to unsparing scrutiny is viewed as a matter of right by journalists. The judiciary has on the whole maintained institutional autonomy, though it has periodically been pressured to follow the wishes of the executive. The election turnout has continued to climb, at times exceeding turnouts in several advanced Western countries, including the United States. Starting with 45.7 percent in the first general elections in 1952, the turnout grew to more than 60 percent in the 1990s.[1]

India's political parties are viewed as both the heroes and villains of the country's democratic experiment. Without their ingenuity, citizen mobilization, and vigorous participation, the democratic system obviously would not have worked. But they are often also accused of weakening the democratic vigor of the country by practicing "immoral politics," raising funds illegally for campaigns, rarely caring for the poor except in rhetoric, and embracing only instrumental short-term benefits and shunning long-term perspectives on national welfare. On the whole, however, there has been no serious argument against the principle that elections in which political parties freely contest one another should decide who the country's rulers ought to be.

A meaningful discussion of India's political parties and party politics requires that we view both against the backdrop of the nation's salient social cleavages. It is difficult to cram Indian materials into the conventional concepts of parties and party systems developed with West European parliamentary systems in mind. India's extraordinary social diversity and complexity—regional, linguistic, ethnic, religious, economic, and, most distinctively, caste—create multiple and cross-cutting cleavages. Even though India's political institutions are the same as those of many Western democracies (a parliamentary system, a first-past-the-post, or FPTP, electoral system, single-member electoral districts, and federalism), the country's social diversity powerfully influences the evolution of the party system and the political and organizational behavior and electoral strategies of political parties, generating results that are quite different from other parliamentary federal systems.

India's social diversity thus forms the organizing theme of our chapter. How do India's multiple, cross-cutting lines of diversity, in light of the country's federalism and first-past-the-post elections, shape its party politics? Together, the diversity and institutional features of the polity have created an increasingly *plural*—but not sharply *polarized*—party system at the national level. They have also led to a wide and often confusing array of political parties. The system, however, is marked by what Susanne and Lloyd Rudolph have called a persistent centrism.[2] India's pluralism is of a moderate variety, not one of unmanageable extremes that might take the polity toward disintegration. It tends to moderate extreme centrifugal tendencies, forcing parties and groups to compromise.

In this chapter, we discuss three aspects of India's party politics: the impact of a first-past-the-post electoral system and federalism on political parties; changes in the nature of the party system from a one-party–dominant system to moderate pluralism in the presence of multiple, cross-cutting cleavages; and changes and continuity in the nature of major political parties since 1947. For focus and brevity, we will concentrate on four of the most important national parties: the Congress party, which has ruled India for much of its independence since 1947; the Hindu nationalist Bharatiya Janata Party (BJP), which has become the biggest party in India in the second half of the 1990s; the Janata family of parties, which has been the third most important political force since 1977, but has also shown signs of disunity and disintegration; and finally, the communist left. Although it is small, the communist left has persisted

TABLE 1—INDIA'S RELIGIOUS PROFILE

RELIGIOUS GROUP	% OF POPULATION
Hindus	82.0
Muslims	12.1
Christians	2.3
Sikhs	2.0
Buddhists & Jains	1.2

Source: Census of India, 1991.

and become politically more important, as no one party can any longer dominate the political landscape and form a government on its own. In the more competitive political marketplace of India today, even small players can carry some weight.

In order to set our political discussion in context, we begin with a description of India's social diversity and its main cleavages. In the next section, we will ask why India does not develop a two-party system, which one would theoretically expect from Duverger's law. In the third section, we will describe the changes that have occurred within the party system. In the fourth section, we will discuss the historical evolution, character, ideology, social base, and organizational features of the major political parties—the Congress party, the BJP, the Janata family of parties, and the communist left. Finally, we will pull the various threads together in the conclusion.

Social Pluralism

India has been called the most socially diverse country in the world, with four cleavages—religious, linguistic, caste, and tribal—often noted. These cleavages give a good sense of the larger diversity.

India's religious tapestry is composed of Hinduism, Islam, Buddhism, Christianity, Sikhism, Jainism, and (pre-Islamic Persian) Zoroastrianism, of which Hinduism and Islam have the largest followings (see Table 1 above). Numbering more than 110 million in 1991 and spread virtually all over the country, Muslims constitute India's biggest minority, though their absolute numbers, in relative terms, amount to only 12.1 percent of the population. Though a smaller minority overall, Sikhs are a majority in one state, and Christians a majority in some smaller states. There is also a Muslim-majority state, Jammu and Kashmir.

The linguistic mosaic is even more varied: Twelve languages are spoken by more than 5 million people each (see Table 2 on the facing page), and another four languages by more than a million each. Since Indian federalism is linguistic, most languages, though not all, have a state of their own, which essentially means that the official language of each state is spoken by a majority of its inhabitants. Each state in the federation thus not only is a linguistic homeland but also contains a linguistic diaspora.

Racial diversity is present, though it has virtually no importance in politics. The tribal-nontribal distinction primarily calls attention to the approximately 8 percent of India's population, excluding Jammu and Kashmir, that lives in central and northeastern India, is itself racially

TABLE 2—LANGUAGES SPOKEN BY MORE
THAN 5 MILLION PEOPLE EACH (1991)

LANGUAGE	PERSONS SPEAKING AS MOTHER TONGUE	PERCENTAGE OF POPULATION
Hindi	337,272,114	39.85
Bengali	69,595,738	8.22
Telugu	66,017,615	7.80
Marathi	62,481,681	7.38
Tamil	53,006,368	6.26
Urdu	43,406,932	5.13
Gujarati	40,673,814	4.81
Kannada	32,753,676	3.87
Malayalam	30,377,176	3.59
Oriya	28,061,313	3.32
Punjabi	23,378,744	2.76
Assamese	13,079,696	1.55

Source: Census of India, 1991.

diverse, and is heavily dependent on forest-lands for livelihood. The tribals have a new name in independent India, the Scheduled Tribes (STs), which essentially means that they are listed in a separate schedule of the constitution for affirmative action.

Of all the social cleavages in India, caste distinctions are the most varied and confusing. Caste is a defining feature of the Hindu social order. In its pristine purity, which goes back centuries, this social order consisted of a three-fold hierarchy based on birth, amounting to an ascriptive division of labor. At the top were the priests and scholars (the *Brahmins*), the warriors (the *Kshatriyas*), and the businessmen (the *Vaishyas*). Peasants, artisans, and servicemen were the lower castes of the second category (the *Sudras*). A third category, the "untouchables," existed at the bottom of the hierarchy, effectively outside the caste system. Each caste had different rights and privileges; the lower the caste, the fewer the privileges. After independence, the first category (the *Brahmins, Kshatriyas,* and *Vaishyas*) came to be known as the upper castes, and the third category (the "ex-untouchables") as Scheduled Castes (SCs). The second and middle category (the *Sudras*) was given a new name—the "other backward castes" (OBCs). Numerically, upper castes today constitute roughly 17.6 percent of the population, the SCs about 16.5 percent, and the OBCs 43.7 percent (see Table 3 on the following page).

How did independent India seek to attack this vertical hierarchy? Reserved quotas in political representation (both in federal and state legislatures), public employment, and institutions of higher education constituted the first track. Only those placed at the bottom of the hierarchy, however—the ex-untouchables (now SCs) and the STs—were given the benefits of affirmative action. These two groups made up 22.5 percent of the total population. As a result, 22.5 percent of the openings in public sector jobs, educational institutions, and legislatures were reserved for the SCs and STs.

The OBCs were originally excluded from the list of beneficiaries. There were two arguments: that the untouchables and tribesmen, not the OBCs, had historically suffered the worst indignities; and that the OBCs, constituting more than 40 percent of the population, had numbers on

TABLE 3—INDIA'S CASTE COMPOSITION

GROUP	% OF POPULATION
Upper Castes	16.1
Lower Castes	43.7
Scheduled Castes (SCs)	16.5
Scheduled Tribes (STs)	8.1
Non-Hindu Minorities	17.6

Note: Since no caste census has been taken since 1931, these figures should be seen as best guesses, not exact estimates. They are sufficient to show the overall magnitudes, however. Also, the upper castes in this calculation include the "dominant castes" that are no longer considered deprived, even though they were ritually not placed in the upper category. Sources: Government of India, Report of the Backward Classes Commission, vol. 1, 1ˢᵗ part (Mandal Commission Report, 1980), 56; and Census of India, 1991.

their side, and could use their numbers to influence the distribution of political power in a democracy. In southern India, for example, the OBCs used their numbers democratically to challenge, and later overthrow, the political hegemony of the *Brahmins*. In the 1970s, faced with pressures from below, the government constituted the Mandal Commission to investigate afresh whether affirmative action should cover the OBCs as well. In 1980, the Commission gave its report, recommending the extension of affirmative action to the OBCs. An OBC quota of 27 percent, the Commission said, should be added to the 22.5 percent already reserved for ex-untouchables and tribesmen. Half of public employment and half of the seats in higher-education institutions would thus be reserved, and nearly 67 percent of India would be eligible for such reservations. It is this group—the OBCs, the SCs, and the STs—that today's "lower caste" parties have mobilized as a new political constituency. They are not fully united for reasons outlined below, but they are on the whole no longer under the control of upper castes.[3]

How Political Institutions Have Shaped Parties

Against the background of social diversity summarized above, what are the effects of a first-past-the-post system and federalism on the evolution of party politics nationally and in the states?[4] Duverger's law— that the FPTP system would inevitably lead to a two-party system[5]—is gradually working itself out at the state level in India, creating two-party or two-alliance systems in an increasing number of states, but it is not leading to a similar outcome at the national or central level.

Table 4 on the facing page summarizes the vote shares of the various leading parties since 1952. In the first five national elections (from 1952 to 1971), India had a one-party–dominated multiparty system in which the Congress party received a plurality of more than 40 percent of the vote, while the second-largest party could win only about 10 percent. This gap enabled the Congress party consistently to win a majority of parliamentary seats. In 1977, however, the party lost for the first time to an alliance of almost the entire opposition. In 1980 and 1984, the Congress recovered its position, but the opposition consolidated into larger chunks. In the 1989, 1991, 1996, 1998, and 1999 elections, the Congress plurality

TABLE 4—VOTE SHARES OF SIGNIFICANT PARTIES, 1952–98 (PERCENTAGES)

	Party	1952	1957	1962	1967	1971	1977	1980	1984	1989	1991	1996	1998	1999
	Congress	45.0	47.8	44.7	40.8	43.7	34.5	42.7	48.1	39.5	36.5	28.8	25.8	28.3
CONGRESS SPLINTERS	Congress (O)					10.4								
	Trinamul Congress												2.4	2.6
	TMC											2.2	1.4	0.6
HINDU NATIONALIST	BJP	3.1	5.9	6.4	9.4	7.4			7.4	11.5	20.1	20.3	25.6	23.8
	Shiv Sena											1.4	1.8	1.6
LEFT PARTIES	CPI	3.3	8.9	9.9	5.0	4.7	2.8	2.6	2.7	2.6	2.5	2.0	1.8	1.5
	CPI(M)				4.4	5.1	4.3	6.1	5.7	6.5	6.2	6.1	5.2	5.4
ANCESTORS OF JANATA FAMILY OF PARTIES	PSP	5.8	10.4	6.8	3.1	1.0								
	SSP	10.6		2.7	4.9	2.4								
	Swatantra			7.9	8.7	3.1								
	Janata Party						41.3							
	Janata Party (Secular)							19.0						
	Lok Dal (1984)							9.4	5.6					
JANATA FAMILY, POST 1989, MAIN FACTIONS	Janata Dal									17.7	11.8	8.1	3.2	0.9
	Samajwadi										3.4	2.9	5.0	3.8
	RJD												2.7	2.8
	Biju Janata Dal												1.0	1.2
	Samata Party											2.2	1.8	3.1
	BSP											3.6	4.7	4.2
MAIN REGIONAL PARTIES (last two are Tamil Nadu parties)	Akali Dal									3.3	3.0	0.8	0.8	0.7
	TDP									1.5	2.0	3.0	2.8	3.7
	AIADMK									2.3	1.6	0.6	1.8	1.9
	DMK											2.2	1.5	1.7

Party Acronyms: CPI: Communist Party of India; CPI(M): Communist Party of India (Marxist); PSP: Praja Socialist Party; SSP: Samyukta Socialist Party; BSP: Bahujan Samaj Party; TDP: Telugu Desam Party; AIADMK: All India Anna Dravida Munnetra Kazhagam; DMK: Dravida Munnetra Kazhagam; TMC: Tamil Maanila Congress; WBTC: West Bengal Trinamul Congress; Congress (O): Congress (Organization); RJD: Rashtriya Janata Dal.

Notes: 1) The Congress (O), TMC, and WBTC are all sometimes Congress splinter groups; WBTC is currently allied to the BJP. 2) The PSP, SSP, Swatantra, Congress (O), Janata Party and its 1980 splinter, Janata Party (Secular), and Lok Dal are all ancestors of the Janata family of parties of the post-1989 period, which encompasses the Janata Dal, Samajwadi Party, RJD, and Biju Janata Dal. The Samata Party is also a Janata Dal offshoot, but is presently allied to the BJP. 3) The TDP (Andhra Pradesh regional party). AIADMK, DMK (Tamil subnationalist), Akali Dal (Sikh subnationalist, Punjab-based), and Shiv Sena (Hindu nationalist, Maharashtra-based) are significant regional parties. 4) Janata Dal in 1999 denotes the Janata Dal (Secular), while Samata Party in 1999 denotes Janata Dal (United). 5) In general, vote shares for smaller parties are given only for those years in which they are significant or in which the parties are significant for the formation and survival of governments. 6) Earlier names of the same parties, for example, of the BJP, are omitted in the interest of brevity.

Sources: David Butler, Ashok Lahiri, and Prannoy Roy, *India Decides: 1952–1991* (New Delhi: Living Media India Limited, 1995) for 1952–91 data. See also Election Commission of India, *Statistical Report on General Elections, 1996, to the Eleventh Lok Sabha, Vol. 1 (National and State Abstracts), Statistical Report on General Elections, 1998, to the Twelfth Lok Sabha, Vol. 1 (National and State Abstracts),* and *Statistical Report on General Elections, 1999, to the Thirteenth Lok Sabha, Vol. 1 (National and State Abstracts),* for 1996, 1998, and 1999 data; V.B. Singh, ed., *Elections in India,* vol. 2 (New Delhi: Sage Publications, 1994) for data on TDP, AIADMK, and DMK only for 1989 and 1991.

fell to 39.5 percent, 36.6 percent, 28.7 percent, 25.9 percent, and 28.3 percent, respectively—short of the figure needed for a seat majority—resulting in hung parliaments. Simultaneously, the vote shares of the second party or alliance and the third party or alliance rose, thereby narrowing the gap and making the system more competitive. The trend in vote shares has inevitably led to the decline of the hegemony of the Congress party: In terms of vote shares, the party retained its first-place standing even in the 1998 and 1999 elections (its two worst ever), but by less than a 1 percent and 4.6 percent margin, respectively. As Table 5 on the following page shows, in terms of parliamentary seats (a total of 545), it came second in 1996 (with 140 seats to the BJP's 161), in 1998 (with 141 to the BJP's 182), and in 1999 (with 114 to the BJP's 182).

The state-level party system has evolved into a two-party system in most cases, or at least a two-alliance system. In all states except three (Uttar Pradesh, Bihar, and Karnataka), the party systems have become bipolar.[6] It is, however, a situation of "multiple bipolarities"—with different pairs of parties/alliances dominating in different states. The pattern is as follows: Congress versus the Left Front (West Bengal until 1996, Kerala, and Tripura); Congress versus the BJP (Madhya Pradesh, Rajasthan, Himachal Pradesh, Gujarat, and Delhi); Congress versus Janata Dal (Orissa and Karnataka, until 1996); Congress versus the regional party (Andhra Pradesh, Punjab, Jammu and Kashmir, Assam until 1996, and the northeastern rim states except Tripura); Congress versus the regional party/BJP alliance (Maharashtra in the 1990s, Punjab since 1997, Haryana since 1996, and Orissa since 1998); and one regional party versus another (Tamil Nadu). Electoral victories nationally depend on state-level swings, which can go in opposite directions even in adjacent states.

These results only partially confirm Duverger's law, supporting it at the state level but not at the national level. Why is that so? Let us begin with why Maurice Duverger thought first-past-the-post would lead to a two-party system, and then discuss why India differs from that law-like expectation. According to Duverger, the "mechanical effect" and the "psychological effect" are the two mechanisms responsible for the decimation of third parties and the emergence of two-party systems under FPTP. The mechanical effect is simply that under FPTP, those parties getting above a certain percentage of the vote tend to get overrepresented in terms of seats, while those falling below a certain percentage remain underrepresented or get no seats at all, leading to their eventual disappearance. The psychological effect refers to "sophisticated" (or strategic) voting: Citizens over time vote not for their first preference overall, but for their first preference among parties that have a realistic chance of winning, making the party of second preference triumphant over the least-liked party. In other words, voters do not wish to "waste" their votes on parties with no chances of winning, even if these parties

TABLE 5—BHARATIYA JANATA PARTY
(BJP) AND INDIAN NATIONAL CONGRESS
(INC) IN NATIONAL ELECTIONS, 1952–98

ELECTION YEAR	PERCENTAGE OF NATIONAL VOTE		SEATS WON IN THE LOK SABHA		TOTAL SEATS
	INC	BJP	INC	BJP	
1952	45.0	3.1	364	3	489
1957	47.8	5.9	371	4	494
1962	44.7	6.4	361	14	494
1967	40.8	9.4	283	35	520
1971	43.7	7.4	352	22	518
1977	34.5		154		542
1980	42.7		353		542
1984	48.1	7.4	415	2	542
1989	39.5	11.5	197	86	543
1991	36.5	20.1	232	120	543
1996	28.8	20.3	140	161	543
1998	25.8	25.6	141	182	543
1999	28.3	23.8	111	182	543

Note: Until 1980, the BJP was known as Bharatiya Jan Sangh (BJS). The BJS merged with the Janata coalition in 1977 and 1980, making it impossible to derive good estimates of its popular vote.
Sources: See Table 4 on p. 211.

best represent their wishes and preferences. Over successive elections, according to Duverger, these two effects would lead to the gradual emergence of two-party systems in FPTP systems.

Some anomalies became evident soon after the law was proposed. Canada and India, for example, had more than three parties, despite FPTP. To explain the anomaly in Canada—a multiparty system that uses the FPTP electoral formula—Douglas Rae modified Duverger's theory by arguing that FPTP in the presence of federalism could result in a multiparty system nationally.[7] The capture of provincial-level political power, Rae suggested, was a sufficient incentive for the formation of regional parties. Once regional parties were in the electoral contest as one of the two leading parties in a state or province, the "sophisticated" voter would desert the weaker of the two national parties and vote for the regional party likely to defeat the stronger national party in the state or province. This process would thus keep regional parties alive, allowing them to become third parties nationally.

In an attempt to explain a second major anomaly—the one-party-dominant system of India until 1971—William Riker refined the argument further.[8] He introduced the concept of the Congress party as a Condorcet winner (a party able to defeat any other party in a pairwise contest because it occupies the median of voters on the ideological spectrum). Such a party's dominance is helped by "sophisticated" voting on the part of those who, on the other side of the ideological spectrum, would vote against its principal local opponent. Riker also argued that these effects are buttressed by "sophisticated" voting on the part of politicians and donors hoping to purchase influence with likely future governments.

However, as we know from the description above, the Congress-dominated multiparty system did not remain stable. In the five general elections from 1989 to 1999, a multiparty system in which no party won a majority in parliament emerged. Moreover, at the state level, two-party or two-alliance systems have gradually stabilized. How does one account for this? Several potential explanations are possible. One is to note that the Congress party was never, or gradually ceased to be, a Condorcet winner at the state and constituency (electoral district) level.[9] A second explanation, linked to our central theme of diversity, is to identify a misspecification in Riker's Condorcet winner argument: There is not one (typically left-to-right) ideological spectrum in India, but a multiplicity of social-cleavage–based political polarities, with complex state- and substate-level variations. A third explanation draws on Riker's category of "disillusioned" voting—that is, the larger and more ideologically diverse a party is, the more likely its voters are to desert it for other or new parties, since, employing coalition theory, such a party would generate more internal tensions over spoils and policy.

A fourth explanation, building upon the first three, would be that once rival and new parties have gained strength from such "disillusioned" voting, the federal system would strengthen state-based third parties as in Rae's argument, even as they generate two-party systems at the state level by the logic of the mechanical and psychological effects. These state-level two-party systems would tend to consist of the Congress party and a state-based party, which could vary widely from state to state. The net result would be a national multiparty system rather than a national two-party system. The beneficiaries of "disillusioned" voting are a multiplicity of state-based opponents, rather than a single national opposition party. In short, the effects of federalism and FPTP, in the presence of each other and of India's social diversity, can result in two-party (or two-alliance) systems at the state level, and, at the same time, in an undominated multiparty system nationally.

To summarize, the FPTP system tends to encourage strategies to aggregate votes, at least locally, as this is necessary to win seats. It also tends, for the same reasons, to encourage strategies to aggregate votes at the state and national levels. In a country where there is considerable heterogeneity at constituency levels as well as at the national and state levels, all parties are under pressure to adopt broad social-coalitional strategies and appeal, including even ideological parties of the right (like the BJP) and the left (like the communist parties). The growth of the BJP over the past decade has to a large extent been due to a conscious effort to cultivate new social bases among the OBCs, as well as new regional bases in the west, south, and east of the country.[10] Moreover, in 1998 and 1999, new coalition partners of the BJP have included parties that do not subscribe to some of the BJP's core ideological positions. India's diversity produces these pressures on all political parties, especially the more ideological ones.

What Kind of Party System?

That India does not have a one-party–dominant system any more is no longer in dispute. However, the question of how one should characterize

India's current party system remains unsettled. Is it, given the variety of parties, an example of extreme pluralism, or of what we would like to call moderate pluralism?[11] By extreme pluralism, we mean a system with highly centrifugal tendencies. By moderate pluralism, we mean a system that, despite many parties and multiple cleavages, has a primarily centripetal or centrist tendency. In such systems, only those parties that put together a coalition of social groups come to power, and extremist ethnic or religious politics are moderated by the coalitional requirements of power. Extreme pluralism, if present, either breaks down, leading to a violent overthrow of the democracy itself (as was the case in the German Weimar Republic), or tends to get politically stalemated (as occurred in Italy). Moderate pluralism, on the other hand, lacks such disintegrative or immobilizing tendencies.

Which category—extreme or moderate pluralism—best describes the developments in India since 1989? The governments formed in 1989, 1990, 1996, 1998, and 1999 have been minority governments or coalitions of multiple parties, the last two of more than ten. (Such coalitions are normally associated with a great deal of political instability.) India has also seen the rise of Hindu nationalist parties, which can be viewed as "antisystem" parties in that they question secularism, a fundamental doctrine of the national constitution. Finally, there has been a great deal of political violence in India since the early 1980s. Given these three factors— the number of parties constituting the governing coalition, the rise of antisystem parties, and the high levels of recent political violence—"extreme pluralism" would seem to be a more fitting description of the recent trends. Is there any one party that can successfully hold the center? Are the Hindu nationalists not pulling votes to the right wing, thereby undermining the well-known centrism of Indian politics? Though it may be tempting, on a quick analysis, to conclude that India is increasingly heading toward a potentially destructive and extreme pluralism, the logic of the country's party politics in fact indicates the emergence of moderate pluralism.

The best way to illustrate the centripetal character of Indian politics is to analyze in detail the electoral fortunes of the BJP. Indeed, the party's antiminority fervor has often been compared to the antisemitism of the German fascists. It was initially argued that the rise of such prejudicial attitudes and tendencies, if not arrested, would create the same problems for Indian democracy as the National Socialists did for the Weimar Republic in the 1930s. It is now widely accepted, however, that the BJP has moderated, at least outwardly, its ideological militancy of the early 1990s, when, among other such incidents, its supporters and cadres tore down a mosque in Ayodhya.[12] In contrast, for the 1998 and 1999 elections, the BJP sought many electoral allies, of which only one (the Shiv Sena) could be described as a right-wing party; the rest were middle-of-the-road parties. Moreover, the so-called National Agenda for Governance drawn to govern the functioning of the BJP-led government, dropped four major themes of Hindu nationalism: building a temple in Ayodhya; constructing a common civil code, which minorities have strongly resisted; abolishing the National Minorities Commission; and abrogating Article 370 of the constitution, which allows a greater degree of autonomy, at least in principle, to the Muslim-majority state Jammu and Kashmir.

Why has the BJP become more moderate? For one, Hindu nationalism has had a direct confrontation with three well-known constraints of Indian democracy—region, caste, and alliances. To come to power in Delhi, a party needs 272 out of the total 543 seats in the national parliament. The BJP has been popular primarily in India's north and west, which add up to a mere 320 seats in parliament. To make a serious bid for power on its own, the BJP must win 85 percent of the northern and western seats. This has turned out to be quite impossible, due to the fact that all of these states have significantly large anti-BJP parties. In particular, the lower-caste parties of Uttar Pradesh and Bihar have caused formidable difficulties for the BJP. Given these obstacles in the north and west, the BJP came to understand that it could not be a serious contender for power in Delhi unless it penetrated the south and the east. That, in turn, required constructing new coalitions, as the theme of Hindu-Muslim disunity has never had the same resonance in the east and the south as in the north and the west. It is therefore not surprising that instead of its earlier zeal to centralize India—which the south and east have always opposed—the BJP today favors "restructuring center-state relations," giving a "fairer share of central revenues."[13]

Secondly, as already explained, the lower castes add up to about 67 percent of India (see Table 3 on p. 210). After the awakening and mobilization of these castes, no party seeking power can make arguments for the revival of the caste hierarchy. In recent years, not only have the Hindu nationalists been doing a great deal of social work with the lower castes and tribes—running schools and hospitals, for example—but lower-caste politicians have also been among the fastest rising personnel in the BJP. Accommodating lower castes means allocating legislative, organizational, and cabinet seats partly on the basis of caste considerations, which the Hindu nationalist ideology, strictly speaking, does not permit. Those who are ideologically pure would rather build a united Hindu community without caste, for caste is widely viewed in Hindu nationalist circles as having been the biggest source, historically, of internal disunity within Hinduism. Paying attention to caste in electoral calculations, they argue, can only strengthen caste consciousness, not eradicate it. On the contrary, the moderates argue that without redressing caste inequities, Hindus cannot be united. The ideology of Hindu nationalism thus needs a modern-day, realistic modification.[14]

Finally, there is the vote-seats paradox of a first-past-the-post election system. Though one party can win a majority of seats in parliament with a mere 35–40 percent of the total vote, the same 35–40 percent vote can yield a substantially lower number of seats if: 1) the opposition gets together; 2) a polarization of votes takes place; and 3) the main political adversary concentrates on a critical minimum of constituencies rather than spreading thin, thus getting more votes in those targeted locales rather than more votes overall. It was just this phenomenon that caused the BJP's loss of power in three of the states it ruled after the 1993 state assembly elections.[15] In some states, several parties got together to defeat the BJP; in other states, BJP's destruction of the Babri mosque polarized the vote, increasing the BJP vote but also the anti-BJP vote. As already stated, the Congress party versus the rest used to be the principal electoral axis of Indian politics. Today, it is BJP versus the others.[16] This shift in axis can help the BJP, as it earlier benefited the Congress party, if and only if the anti-BJP vote splits, as was true of the anti-Congress vote prior to 1991.

   If polarization means that enough political parties are willing to come together, before or after elections, to prevent the BJP from coming to power, it stands only to hurt the BJP. This was the cause of the BJP's inability to stay in power after the 1996 parliamentary elections. Being the largest party, it was invited to form a government, but within 13 days, the BJP government fell because it could not persuade a majority of elected legislators to its side. The threat of BJP was not so alarming as to produce electoral coalitions, but it was strong enough to generate postelection coalitions to keep it out of power. Learning from this experience, the BJP put together electoral coalitions for the subsequent 1998 and 1999 elections. This strategy finally produced a BJP-led government, but an alliance for power also necessitated ideological moderation: Those ideologically pure postures that were unacceptable to alliance partners had to be dropped.

   To summarize, given the social diversity of India and the marginal relevance of the Hindu-Muslim cleavage in the politics of the south and the east, the BJP has had to make compromises and head toward a center-right position in order to come to power. The system required putting together regional, caste, and religious alliances. If the party had let the extreme right dominate, ideological purity might have been achieved, but the resulting polarization of party politics would have brought the non-BJP parties together, making it difficult if not impossible for the BJP to come to power. Despite the many changes in Indian politics since 1947, ideological centrism remains its center of gravity. There is a large enough space for a center-left or center-right coalition in Indian politics, but not for the extreme right or the extreme left. Only inconceivable exogenous shocks could effectively transform the centrist logic of India's party politics.

Change and Continuity

The Congress party.[17] Between 1947 and 1998, the Indian National Congress (previously and henceforth referred to as the Congress party, or simply Congress) has ruled India for all but seven years. With the exception of 1977, it was the largest party in India for more than four decades after independence, but in the 1996, 1998, and 1999 elections, it lost its leading position—in terms of seats, though not votes—to the BJP. It now holds a mere 28.3 percent of India's vote, whereas in earlier years, its vote share often exceeded 40 percent (see Table 5 on p. 213). The Congress party was founded in 1885 by a group of English-educated Indian lawyers, journalists, businessmen, and other members of the emerging intelligentsia. It gradually grew from a collection of urban-based notables pressing to improve the position of Indians under the colonial regime into a mass movement for independence. The leadership of Mahatma Gandhi was responsible for this transformation. Influenced by Gandhi's ideas, the Congress became both a party and a mass movement after the First World War, including peasants and workers. It also sought to include all religious communities, castes, linguistic and regional groups, and classes, as well as a variety of ideological strands ranging from soft Hindu nationalism, social conservatism, and pro-native business on the right to radical socialist and near-communist thinking on the left.

The Congress party developed an organizational machinery rooted in nearly all parts of the country. The local notables played a key role, as they controlled the major resources, especially land. Moreover, they were the educated people in a largely poor, illiterate society. Despite the party's encompassing and secular character and its accommodative politics, its major failure during the independence movement was to prevent the rise of alienation among the Muslims of the subcontinent, which led to the growth of the separatist Muslim League and eventually to India's Partition and the birth of Pakistan. It tried to incorporate the Muslims, but it succeeded only partially. In 1947, India had 100 million Muslims; 65 million of them became citizens of Pakistan.

With the partial exception of the Muslims, the Congress was indeed an all-encompassing umbrella party, with an elaborate organizational machinery at the provincial, district, and lower levels. The organization went all the way down to the village level in large parts of the country. It faced parties that were much narrower in social and geographical base, and hence unable to compete with it electorally. These parties at best offered localized challenges.

Internally, the Congress party was a grand coalition of the major political and social forces. What held it together was a set of significant factors: its image as the party that won India its independence; the name recognition and genuine popularity of its leaders, especially Gandhi and Jawarharlal Nehru; a host of competent provincial stalwarts who had participated in the national movement and managed the party organization at the state level; and an intraorganizational democracy that, however imperfect, allowed all significant voices to be heard, facilitated internal bargaining and conflict resolution, and accommodated the demands of various groups. Ideologically, the party was centrist, committed to democracy, minority rights, secularism, federalism, and a mixed economy. After independence, it received—and to some extent, won back—the support of the Muslims who had not gone to Pakistan. The Congress party as an internal grand coalition—confronted by a motley collection of smaller, narrower-based parties—was described in its ideal-typical phase (roughly the first two decades after independence) by Rajni Kothari as a "party of consensus" surrounded by "parties of pressure."[18]

At the grassroots level, party membership was open to all who paid nominal dues and were not members of any other political party. This rule opened the party to the masses as primary and active members; the latter category referred to those primary members who qualified by certain criteria of party activism. Above them was a hierarchy of local (subdistrict, or *panchayat,* block), district, state, and all-India Congress committees. The last three were called the District Congress Committees (DCCs), Pradesh Congress Committees (PCCs), and the All India Congress Committee (AICC). At the annual Congress session, held in a different part of the country every year, the delegates were the members of the PCCs. They elected one-eighth of their members to the AICC, to a two-year term. The AICC delegates elected a certain number of their members to the Congress Working Committee (CWC) and the president of the party. Thus at the apex were the party president and the CWC, collectively described as the "high command," which ran the party at the national level on a day-to-day basis. These structures and the periodic internal elections at all levels facilitated a two-way communication between the leadership and the grassroots level, and resolution of the factional conflict on personality, caste, and regional, ideological, and other lines of cleavage.

The organization gradually disintegrated over the issue of "bogus memberships," as party leaders at all levels—especially the local, DCC, and PCC levels—recruited large numbers of unverifiable members to swell their "vote banks" for party elections. In 1969, there was a big split in the Congress party between the faction led by then–prime minister Indira Gandhi and the leaders in control of the party organization, which led to an organizational crippling of the party from which it still has not recovered. The bulk of the party's office holders in most states stayed with the organizational faction. The organizational stalwarts were opposed to Mrs. Gandhi, but they were not electorally as popular; Mrs. Gandhi used her personal popularity to win national elections and defeat the organizational wing of the party. By the early 1970s, the organizational Congress was decimated in electoral politics, and Mrs. Gandhi's party gradually became recognized as the real Congress party. Charisma tripped organizational coherence.

Confident in her charismatic ability to keep wining elections, Mrs. Gandhi decided to suspend the decades-old organizational principles of the party, in particular the norm of intraorganizational elections. Between 1972 and 1992, the Congress party was progressively turned into what Richard Gunther and Larry Diamond in chapter 1 of this volume call a "catch-all party," in which office-bearers at all crucial levels were appointed rather than elected by the prime minister and Congress president, both the same person—Indira Gandhi, and later (between 1984 and 1989) Rajiv Gandhi. Party nominations for elections, and increasingly even for state assembly elections, had to be approved, if not decided, by the party high command, specifically Mrs. Gandhi (until her assassination in 1984). The criterion increasingly became one of personal loyalty to the leader above all other considerations. These centralizing tendencies served to weaken the party's leadership at the state and local levels.

In 1992, after a 20-year gap, organizational elections were finally held. In 1997, they were held again. The latest development in the Congress party is the rise of Sonia Gandhi, Rajiv Gandhi's Italian-born widow, now a naturalized Indian. In the 1998 campaign, she sidelined the formally elected party president, who simply could not lead the party organization and had to give in to her rising popularity. In retrospect, it is clear that Sonia Gandhi's election campaign energized the party organization and prevented a further drift of Congress voters to other parties. After the elections, she was installed by the CWC as both party president and leader of the Congress Parliamentary Party, leading to the ouster of the existing party president. In November 1998, her stature rose even further as the Congress party under her leadership and campaign fared extremely well, defeating the incumbent BJP state government in two states and winning the election for the incumbent Congress government in a third state. (There were four state elections in all in November 1998.) In the 1999 elections, however, despite a rise in its vote share to 28.3 percent from an unprecedented low of 25.8 percent in 1998, the Congress party finished with an all-time low of 114 seats. The 1999 elections clearly weakened her political stature.

Sonia Gandhi's role in the politics of the party is paradoxical. On the one hand, her becoming party president and leader of the Congress parliamentary party in 1998, despite not even having won an election until then, is in line with the long-term deinstitutionalization of the party. However, her declared goal, often stated as party president, has been to rebuild the party organization state by state and at the district levels. At this she has been only partly successful. The coming years will make it clear whether she can translate her remarkable and unexpected popular appeal into organizational rebuilding—and whether the Congress will cease to be a catch-all party. No long-term judgments are possible at this stage. The record in 1998 and 1999 has been mixed: Although the party plunged to an all-time low of 114 seats in the lower house, it increased its vote share in 1999 and won six state assembly elections in 1998 and 1999, including the important states of Madhya Pradesh, Rajasthan, Karnataka, and (in a postelection coalition) Maharashtra.

The Congress party's long-term trend toward organizational decay has been accompanied by a change in party finance and election campaigning styles.[19] Indian laws after 1969 banned company donations to political parties. Since then, there has been an increasing resort to illegal means of raising election funds. In the absence of state funding, the ban on company donations mandated by Mrs. Gandhi left no legal source of large-scale finance for elections, leading to an increasing reliance on kickbacks from licenses and state contracts in a highly regulated economy. The increasingly regulatory policy regime of the 1970s strengthened the political leadership's hands vis-à-vis the private sector. Mrs. Gandhi's plebiscitary style of campaigning increased the need for money, devaluing the tradition of door-to-door campaigning. It also led to the centralization of party finance, party-office appointments, and election nominations.[20] The increasing reliance on the electronic media, advertising, and whirlwind campaigning accentuated the neglect of the party organization and its year-round grassroots political activity by a multitude of party workers.

The re-legalization of company donations in 1985 made no difference to these trends; by then the system had become too deeply entrenched. Hardly any companies made donations via the legal route for fear of being publicly identified with particular parties and politicians—suicidal in an economy that is still highly regulated, with rapid turnover of the parties in power at the central and state governments. Election finance remains essentially unreformed, despite a reduction in the campaign period to 14 days since the 1996 elections, an increase in the expenditure ceiling for candidates, and the availability of free television and radio time in the 1998 and 1999 campaigns.

The Congress pattern of raising party funds—using the leverage of discretionary regulatory powers at the central and state levels—has been adopted by all of India's political parties. There have been only a few partial exceptions, especially the BJP and the communist parties. The BJP has historically depended on contributions in relatively small amounts from large numbers of small business supporters, typically raised and spent locally. However, with the rise of the BJP as a major party in the 1990s, its fundraising, though still disproportionately dependent on small business, has shifted toward the Congress pattern. The communist parties function on a relative shoestring budget, dependent on small contributions from party supporters and workers and, reportedly, business contributions mediated by leftist trade unions in states where the communists are in power. Their campaigning, on the whole, is labor-intensive.

The decline of the Congress party has also been due to several social factors. Key segments of the traditional Congress voter base have been moving to other parties. The first major social constituency to go over to the non-Congress opposition was the emerging rich farmer constituency, largely belonging to "lower castes" or the so-called "middle castes," in the Green Revolution belt of northwest India. The rising "lower" or "middle" caste peasantry resented the domination of the Congress organization by the "upper" castes.[21] The second major challenge to Congress dominance came from the regional parties, beginning with the victory of the DMK in the state of Tamil Nadu in 1967. Regional parties have focused on regional or linguistic identity and on demands for greater state autonomy in India's federal system, which gives extraordinary powers to the central government, including the right to suspend state governments and an overwhelming control over the tax revenue. As the Congress party centralized decision making under Mrs. Gandhi, regional parties gained strength.

The Scheduled Castes (ex-untouchables), constituting 16.5 percent of India's population, are the third major constituency to move away from the Congress party in several parts of India. Their growing assertiveness and organized political activity in northern India is identified with a new party, the Bahujan Samaj Party (BSP). Finally, the Muslims, comprising more than 12 percent of the total population, are the fourth major social constituency to part ways with the Congress party. The alienation of the Muslims began in the late 1980s, when the Congress did not resolutely challenge the rising Hindu nationalist movement, and culminated when the Congress government failed to prevent the demolition of the Babri mosque in 1992 by Hindu nationalists. The Muslim vote has gravitated to viable anti-BJP parties where they exist—like the Samajwadi Party and BSP in Uttar Pradesh and the Janata Dal party in Bihar—but has tended to remain with the Congress party in states where it is the only viable anti-BJP formation. Whether the Muslims will return to the Congress party under Sonia Gandhi remains to be seen.

Despite this erosion, the Congress party continues to have a broad, multiclass, multireligious, multicaste, multiregional, and both rural and urban appeal. Its residual base is still probably the broadest among India's political parties.[22] But it is also clear that the Congress failed to absorb and meet the aspirations of newly mobilized interests and identity groups in the way a grand-coalition, umbrella party in a heterogeneous society should ideally be able to do, leading to "disillusioned" voting for new and other parties by voters and a movement away by politicians affiliated with such newly mobilized groups. The Congress party, though much eroded since its heyday of 1947–67, still fits Gunther and Diamond's description of a "catch-all party" fairly well.

The Bharatiya Janata Party and Hindu nationalism. The BJP eclipsed the Congress as India's largest party in the 1996, 1998, and

1999 elections. It came to power in March of 1998, though in a coalition of 18 parties, and again in October of 1999, in a preelection coalition of 24 parties. At no point before 1989 did the BJP or its predecessor, the Bharatiya Jan Sangh (BJS), receive even one-tenth of the national vote; the average was 6.6 percent. In 1989, this share increased to 11.5 percent; in 1991, to 20.2 percent; in 1996, to 20.3 percent; in 1998, to 25.8 percent; and in 1999, to 23.8 percent (see Table 4 on p. 211). Equally important, support for Hindu nationalism has by now gone beyond the urban trading community, its customary base, to include villagers and the modernized (and modernizing) middle classes.[23] The turning point was in 1991: Hardly known for Hindu religiosity and Westernized in their daily life, nearly 30 retired generals, including a Jewish ex-general, joined the BJP that year, as did a number of former bureaucrats. For a party historically viewed as an obscurantist force, it was a moment of great symbolic significance. Since then, the BJP has enjoyed solid support in most of urban India, receiving 40 percent of the vote in urban areas in its stronghold states in northern and western India. Its support in rural India, though substantial, is not as high.

For any discussion of the BJP, its view of India has to be the starting point. It would be most accurate to describe it as an "ethno-nationalist" party, an example of what Gunther and Diamond call an ethnic party, with its parent organization, the RSS (Rashtriya Swayamsevak Sangh), sharing features of the fascist party type. It does not fit the description of another of Gunther and Diamond's categories—the denominational party—for three reasons:

First, Gunther and Diamond characterize the denominational party as not being in complete control of its fundamental ideological principles when it comes to religion: "Interpretation of basic religious beliefs and their applicability to the contemporary world is primarily the function of religious leaders. . . . This can lead to significant intraparty tensions, as when such issues as divorce are placed on the political agenda."[24] In other words, since the basis of the party's programs is a set of religious beliefs that are determined by a combination of tradition and interpretation by clerics or a religious institution outside of the party itself, the party is not fully in control of its core ideological precepts whenever they are directly linked to religious values. The difficulty with this category with regard to the BJP is that unlike Christianity, and Catholicism in particular, Hinduism has no organized church that is recognized as the authority for positions on such values as abortion, divorce, sexual preference, and artistic expression. Even Hindu personal law on marriage, divorce, property, and the like was codified not by the diversity of Hindu religious leaders themselves, but first by the British, then more fully after independence by Indian politicians in parliament (for example, via the Hindu Marriage Act of 1956). No clerical body has final authority on such matters for all Hindus. It is a religion rooted in doctrinal diversity.

Second, the beliefs of the BJP and RSS—since the mid-1920s for the RSS and since the early 1950s for the BJP (then called the BJS)—were never determined by tradition, by Hindu clerics, or by any outside religious institution. Indeed, the RSS-BJP can be considered a departure from traditional Hinduism. While many religious leaders are prominent in the affairs of the party, they are clearly not dominant. Even the Vishwa Hindu Parishad (VHP, or World Hindu Council), a BJP affiliate consisting of religious leaders, is led by nonreligious leaders at the national and local levels. Religious leaders are present in the organization, but it is not clear whether and to what extent they influence decision making, if at all. The VHP, having clerics but not an organized body of clerics, was created in the 1960s and became prominent only in the 1980s. Even after it became prominent, however, clerics have not taken it over; it is led by lay people, with the clerics thrown in here and there. It would be inaccurate, therefore, to say that "the party apparatus is not in complete control of its 'ideology.'" Instead, interpretation of basic religious beliefs and their applicability to the contemporary world is primarily the function of religious leaders."[25]

The third reason that the BJP is best classified as "ethno-nationalist" rather than denominational is that its parent organization, the RSS (although not the BJP itself), shares features of the fascist party types described by Gunther and Diamond. The RSS "detests minorities" that resist "assimilation" *(aikya),* and is not afraid to use violence against them—something that is not at all a necessary characteristic of denominational parties (Christian Democratic parties, for example). The RSS also shares fascist features such as the exaltation of "the nation or race above the individual, . . . intensive indoctrination of members, [and] strict internal discipline."[26] The RSS, however, is not a political party, and the party it is closest to, the BJP, cannot be described in these terms. Since many members of the BJP are also simultaneously members of the RSS, all one can say is that the danger of an antiminority streak is always present in the functioning of the BJP, and is checked primarily by the logic of coalition-building and electoral pragmatism.

For these reasons, the BJP does not fit the denominational party mold—a mold that itself is inappropriate within the context of an unorganized and decentralized religion like Hinduism. As noted above, it is more accurate to describe it as an "ethno-nationalist" party, if not actually yet, then perhaps potentially: To the extent that the BJP promotes a broad Hindu identity in a society where Hindus have always been split across language and caste lines, it resembles an ethnic party, ethnicity being defined in terms of religious-cultural markers. The BJP's ideological aim is to create a unified, pan-Indian—or even diasporic—Hindu ethnicity. It sees Hindus not primarily as a *religious* group—many BJP workers and supporters may not even be religious, and the founders of the RSS were definitely not—but as a *people/potential nation* with a

broadly common culture that must be molded, or unified, into a consciously Hindu nation by the politics of polarization. This view of the
nation is in contrast to the consciously and explicitly diverse, accommodative, and inclusive Indian nation that was created by the independence movement, the Congress party, and the constitution, where one
could be Muslim or Christian, for example, without being less Indian.
The latter view celebrated "unity-in-diversity," and never equated
"Indian" with "Hindu."

The two views can be compared to the contrast often drawn between
an *ethnic* nation, with fascism as its theoretically conceivable extreme,
and a *civic* nation. A telling example of this is the fact that diaspora
Hindus, including those holding foreign citizenships, are more acceptable
to many Hindu nationalists than are Muslims and Christians living in
India and holding Indian citizenship. Many of the BJP's stances and
actions fit the description of what Gunther and Diamond call the "electoral
logic of the ethnic party," that is, "to harden and mobilize its ethnic base
with exclusive and often polarizing appeals to ethnic group opportunity
and threat."[27] Such deliberately polarizing appeals have often marked
the history of the BJP, but not necessarily those of denominational parties.

The BJP is among the most ideologically inclined parties in India
and, as should be clear by now, its ideology—known as *Hindutva*
("Hindu-ness" is the closest translation; Hindu nationalism is the closest
description)—causes bitter controversy in India. The roots of Hindu
nationalism go back to the 1920s, when differences with India's national
movement prompted some to form a new organization and initiate an
ideological campaign. Since the rise of the Indian national movement
in the 1880s, three competing themes about India—geographical,
cultural, and religious—have fought for political hegemony.[28] The
geographical notion is simply that India has a "sacred geography,"
enclosed between the Indus river, the Himalayas, and the seas, and
emphasized for 2,500 years since the time of the epic Mahabharata. The
cultural notion is that tolerance, pluralism, and syncretism, which means
a merging of cultures, define Indian society. India has not only given
birth to several religions—Hinduism, Buddhism, Jainism, and Sikhism—
but throughout its history it has also regularly received, accommodated,
and absorbed "outsiders"—Parsis (Zoroastrians), Jews, and "Syrian Christians" (followers of St. Thomas, arriving apparently as early as the first
century; Christianity thus reached India before it reached Europe). In
the process, syncretistic forms of culture have emerged and become part
of India's cultural tapestry.[29] Apart from syncretism, pluralism and tolerance have also existed, with different communities finding their niche
in India and developing principles of coexistence. The religious notion
is that India is originally the land of the Hindus, and it is the only land
that the Hindus can call their own, a land that has the holy temples,
sites, and rivers of the Hindus. Most of India is, and has been, Hindu by

religion—anywhere between 65 to 70 percent in early twentieth-century India and more than 80 percent today. A great deal of internal diversity, both linguistic and caste-based, does exist within Hindu society, but a faith in Hinduism brings the different groups together. India thus viewed is a Hindu nation.

These three themes have yielded two principal attitudes about India's national identity—the secular nationalist and the Hindu nationalist. The former combines geography and culture; the latter, geography and religion. The Congress party has been the prime exponent of secular nationalism in this century, and the BJP (and its predecessor BJS) of Hindu nationalism. The former values India's religious, linguistic, and cultural pluralism, as it is embodied in laws (such as different personal laws of different religious communities and the protection of minority educational institutions) and in political institutions (such as federalism). The latter holds that finding a blending of territory and cultural pluralism is inadequate. The Hindu nationalists argue that emotions and loyalty make a nation rather than politics, laws, and institutions. Laws, they say, can always be politically manipulated. India's pro-minority laws, they contend, have not led to the building of a cohesive nation. Instead, "fissiparous tendencies" have regularly erupted.[30] A "salad bowl," as they put it, does not produce cohesion; a "melting pot" does. Rather than running away from Hinduism—the source of India's culture—one should explicitly ground politics in Hinduism rather than in laws and institutions.

The term "Hindu" is further specified by Hindu nationalists in the words of V.D. Savarkar, the ideological father of Hindu nationalism, who gave the following definition in *Hindutva,* the classic text of Hindu nationalism: "A Hindu means a person who regards this land . . . from the Indus to the Seas as his fatherland *(pitribhumi)* as well as his Holyland *(punyabhumi).*"[31] The definition is thus territorial (the land between the Indus and the seas), genealogical ("fatherland"), and religious ("Holyland"). Hindus, Sikhs, Jains, and Buddhists meet all three criteria, as all of these religions were born in India, and thus all can be included in this definition. Christians, Jews, Parsis, and Muslims meet only two, for India is not their holy land. Can non-Hindu groups be considered part of India? Yes, say the Hindu nationalists, by means of assimilation.[32] Of the groups whose "Holyland" is not India, Parsis and Jews are already assimilated, Hindu nationalists argue, having become part of the nation's mainstream. This leaves the Christians and Muslims, who, wrote Savarkar, "cannot be recognized as Hindus. For though Hindustan [India] to them is the Fatherland as to any other Hindu, yet it is not to them a Holyland too. Their Holyland is far off in Arabia or Palestine. Their mythology and Godmen, ideas and heroes are not the children of this soil. Consequently their names and their outlook smack of a foreign origin. Their love is divided."[33]

The Hindu nationalists, therefore, have identified Christians and Muslims as their adversaries. Historically, their anger has been principally directed at Muslims—partly because of their sheer numbers, and partly because a Muslim homeland in the form of Pakistan partitioned India in 1947. Muslims comprised 25 percent of pre-1947 India, and even after the formation of Pakistan, they have been the largest minority, constituting more than 12 percent of the country's population today. The Hindu nationalist claim is not that Muslims ought to be excluded from the Indian nation (although that may be the position of the extremists). Rather, *aikya* (assimilation) is the generic Hindu nationalist argument. That is, to become part of the Indian nation, Muslims must: 1) accept the centrality of Hinduism to Indian civilization; 2) acknowledge key Hindu figures, such as Rama (the mythological king from the 6th century epic Ramayana), as civilizational heroes, and not disown them as mere religious figures of Hinduism; 3) remorsefully accept that Muslim rulers of India between 1000 A.D. and 1757 A.D. destroyed pillars of Hindu civilization, Hindu temples in particular; 4) not claim special privileges, such as maintenance of religious personal laws; and 5) not demand special state grants for their educational institutions. To the Hindu nationalists, only via *aikya* can they prove their loyalty to the nation. Maintaining distinctiveness only serves to emphasize that "their love," as Savarkar put it, "is divided."

Of late, the Hindu nationalists have turned their attention toward India's Christians, targeting missionaries in India and attacking churches. This turn appears to be primarily strategic: For reasons identified earlier, the anti-Muslim rhetoric of Hindu nationalism has not worked electorally, having led to alliances between Muslims and the lower Hindu castes. Since the destruction of the Ayodhya mosque in December 1992, the BJP's vote share has not increased substantially, whereas the Hindu nationalists had expected that the destruction of the mosque—or at least the movement aimed at it—would polarize Hindus and Muslims, thereby giving the nationalists a solid majority of the Hindu vote and bringing them single-handedly to power. That did not happen. Eventually, the BJP had to make alliances with so many mainstream parties in order to come to power in 1998 that the coalition government could not give voice to the Hindu nationalist vision of India.

In contrast to the 110 million Indian Muslims, India has only about 20 million Christians, constituting 2.3 percent of the total population. They are electorally significant in only a few states, and can therefore be targeted without generating the same type of electoral backlash that anti-Muslim rhetoric triggered. This appears to be the rationale for an increase in anti-Christian arguments (and activity) in the Hindu nationalist camps. Whether this is true will become clear only when the next elections are held, and surveys can tell us if the larger Hindu society was offended by attacks on India's small and quietistic Christian minority.

One source of the BJP's strength is the RSS, the organizational centerpiece of the BJP. Born in 1925, the RSS is not an electoral body. It was founded as a cultural organization that would take the country in a Hindu direction. It recruits at a young age in India's urban neighborhoods. Meeting almost everyday in such neighborhoods, the cadres are trained in ideology, culture, and self-defense. Highly disciplined, the cadres tend typically to develop a lifelong commitment to the ideology. Most of BJP's leaders, though not all, come from an RSS background. The RSS cadres have often campaigned actively for the BJP during elections, and have provided committed manpower.

Another source of the BJP's strength is its base in the small business community. It has never lacked funds, even when it was not faring well. As its popularity has risen, its financial backing has come from leading industrialists as well as from small and medium-size businesses. An additional source of its funding has been the rich Indian diaspora in the United States and Britain. (Why India's diaspora has been so drawn to the Hindu nationalists has not been studied and remains unclear, but the support itself is beyond question.)

The BJP organization has many levels, starting from the village and district levels up to the state and national levels. Internal elections take place regularly, though elections are rarely contested. The emphasis is always on consensus, which the party has been able to maintain with considerable success. Intraorganizational battles did not surface for a long time, and have done so only after the party's growth in recent years. Intraparty differences were traditionally managed out of the glare of publicity, in contrast to the Congress and the Janata parties, in both of which factional fights have regularly erupted quite publicly, leading to splits and defections. As the BJP has grown, however, the latter afflictions have begun to mark its functioning as well. The extremists and the moderates in the Hindu nationalist camp have begun to fight openly.[34] As already indicated, most of BJP's state- and national-level leadership comes from an RSS background. But with the BJP's expansion, the gap between the extremist and moderate factions has been increasing. Earlier, all BJP or BJS leaders had an RSS background; today, many without an RSS background have been allowed to join the party and given fairly high positions. To convince the large middle class that it is an increasingly mainstream party, the BJP has recruited film stars, generals, bureaucrats, sports celebrities, and television personalities in large numbers. These high-profile recruits do not have an RSS background.

Will the BJP continue to grow and still maintain its historical cohesiveness? What will happen to its relationship with the RSS as its attempts to reach out to increasingly larger numbers of Indians recruit many more people with non-RSS backgrounds? The BJP is finding it extremely difficult to flatten India's many diversities into a Hindu-Muslim mold, and considerable intraparty dissidence can be easily predicted. The extremists would try not to give up ideological purity; the moderates know that they can ill afford ideological rectitude, electorally and politically, given the nature of Indian politics.

The Janata family of parties.[35] On grounds of personality rather than ideology, what was once the Janata party has by now split into so many parties that it is more accurate to describe the entire set as the Janata family—a family that is highly contentious but shares roughly the same ideology. In terms of vote share for the period between 1977 and 1989, the Janata family of parties was collectively the next largest to the Congress party. It lost that position to the BJP, however, in the 1991, 1996, 1998, and 1999 elections. The Janata party was formed by the merger of four leading non-Congress opposition parties at the time of the 1977 general elections, and it has undergone several splits since then. By now, in terms specified by Gunther and Diamond in this volume, all splinter organizations can be called ethnic parties, based essentially on caste, and mobilized through pre-existing clientelistic relations.

The ideological glue of the Janata family is the dual concept of lower caste unity and social justice. The Janata ideology speaks of the hierarchical and unjust nature of Hindu social order, an order in which upper castes have traditionally enjoyed many ritualistic privileges and superior social rank, and the lower castes have suffered many discriminations. An egalitarian restructuring of the Hindu social order is the chief goal of Janata politicians. Caste, they maintain, should not determine whether an individual is treated as an inferior or superior human being. Moreover, according to the Janata ideology, to make up for centuries of caste oppression, affirmative action favoring the lower castes in government jobs and education should be the primary vehicle of achieving social justice. The Janata ideology thus concentrates on India's religious majority, the Hindus. When it speaks of non-Hindu groups, it does so by arguing that both religious minorities and lower castes suffer from discrimination by the higher castes. A lower-caste–minorities alliance, therefore, can be constructed in politics.

The caste-based ideology of politics, by and large, has risen to national prominence only recently. It was successfully used to mobilize the masses in the first half of this century in southern India. In the 1980s and 1990s, it has spread to the north and the west. By focusing on—and reviling—the social hierarchy of Hinduism, the Janata ideology attacks Hindu nationalism. It does not believe in Hindu unity; it would place social justice at the heart of politics, and it seeks to pit the lower castes against the upper castes, whereas the Hindu nationalists would seek their cohesion. Since the lower castes add up to a large plurality, the potential power of lower-caste parties is significant—provided lower caste unity can be achieved.

The roots of the Janata ideology go back to the Congress Socialist

Party of the 1930s, which was a faction within the larger Congress-led national movement. It was village-oriented, favored land reform, and wanted to steer the middle-of-the-road Congress party toward its own ideological ends. After independence, some of the socialists split off from the Congress party to form socialist parties. They disliked the landlord- and upper-caste–dominated functioning of the Congress party at the district and state levels, as well as its promotion of big industry over agriculture. This ideology came to be known as "anti-Congressism" in the 1950s and 1960s. Ram Manohar Lohia was the leading ideologue of these parties.[36] He advocated the coming together of all non-Congress parties in a broad anti-Congress alliance, in order to avoid splitting of the non-Congress majority vote, which repeatedly turned the plurality vote of the Congress party into a seat majority. These developments led to the formation of non-Congress coalition governments in several major Indian states in the period between 1967 and 1971, when the Congress lost eight major states to such alliances in the state assembly elections. In the general elections held after the lifting of the Emergency—a 19-month period in 1975–77 in which democratic freedoms and civil liberties were suspended—four non-Congress parties came together to form the Janata party and confronted the Congress with a grand alliance of almost the entire opposition. The elections were a virtual referendum on the Emergency and were tailor-made for such an alliance. The Janata party won a thumping victory with 41.3 percent of the vote and 295 seats (out of 543) in parliament.

That victory notwithstanding, the Janata party was a fractious party composed of incompatible elements, ranging from the Hindu nationalist right to the socialist left. It failed to develop an organization, let alone to conduct party elections. In July of 1979, it split into two factions. In the 1980 elections, the two factions of the Janata party won 19.0 percent of the vote (31 seats) and 9.4 percent (41 seats), respectively, compared to the Congress's 42.7 percent and 353 seats. After this defeat, the Janata party disintegrated as the Congress party made a comeback under Mrs. Gandhi, and later under Rajiv Gandhi in 1985. In 1989, after an eight-year gap, the Janata party was reborn as Janata Dal, led by former finance minister (and later prime minister in 1989–90) V.P. Singh, and was given a lower-caste–based orientation once again. In the 1989 elections, Janata Dal won 17.7 percent of the vote and 142 of the 543 seats. Soon, however, personality clashes began to rock the party. In 1991, reduced by a split, the rump of the party that retained the name Janata Dal received 11.8 percent of the vote and 59 seats. In the 1996 elections, after another split, the rump that again retained the name Janata Dal won 8.1 percent of the vote and 46 seats. Prior to the 1998 elections, the party had two splits and was more or less was decimated. The rump that yet again retained the name Janata Dal got only six seats and 3.25 percent of the vote.

In the 1998 and 1999 elections, an apparent disintegration of the

Janata family of parties took place, with the virtual collapse of the United Front and with several Janata family splinters aligning with the BJP-led coalition of parties. This process had begun in 1996, when the Samata party, a Janata splinter group in Bihar, aligned with the BJP. This party represented a layer of the backward castes just below the uppermost of the backward castes (the *Yadavs*), the process representing fragmentation and infighting within the lower castes. In 1998 and 1999, only the Samajwadi party in Uttar Pradesh, the Rashtriya Janata Dal (RJD) in Bihar, and a Janata faction in Karnataka remained in the United Front of non-BJP, non-Congress parties. The Samata party in Bihar, the Biju Janata Dal (a Janata splinter in Orissa), the Lok Shakti (another Janata splinter in Karnataka), and the Haryana Lok Dal all allied with the BJP either before or after the elections. The lineup was similar in 1999, except that the remnants of the Janata Dal in Bihar and Karnataka split again, with the major factions allying themselves with the BJP.

Despite the recent fragmentation, though, it is still possible to speak of a loose Janata family of largely lower-caste, rural, and agrarian-oriented parties that are distinct from both the Congress and the BJP for two reasons: First, two of them (Samajwadi and RJD) are significant forces in India's two largest states, Uttar Pradesh and Bihar. Second, even the Janata family parties in the BJP-led coalition have maintained their distinct identity, rejected the *Hindutva* ideology of the BJP, and (with various regional parties) forced the BJP to shelve the more contentious Hindu nationalist policies in its agenda, acting as pressure groups for middle- and lower-caste interests that have clearly come to stay as a politically self-conscious and assertive (if highly fragmented) constituency, one that parties cannot ignore.

The support base of the Janata family of parties has consisted of small peasant proprietors of the lower castes, whose interests were not adequately represented in the caste coalitions that underpinned the Congress party, and whose demands for social justice, subsequently, were not recognized by the Hindu nationalists. This peasant proprietor base went in different directions in different states in the successive splits suffered by the party: to the Samajwadi party in Uttar Pradesh; to Rashtriya Janata Dal in Bihar; and to the splinter Biju Janata Dal and BJP in Orissa; as the BJP successfully coopted intermediate-caste–peasant proprietors, playing on their fears of job quotas for some castes and the mobilization of Scheduled Caste landless labor.

The main weakness of the Janata family of parties is and has always been organizational. They have been the most weakly organized of the major political parties in India, certainly compared to the cadre-based left parties and the BJP, but even compared to the mass-based Congress party during its worst periods of organizational decrepitude. Why has the Janata family of parties not been able to put together a cohesive organizational front? Their necessary and aspired-to unity has problems of both vertical and horizontal nature. The lower-caste platform has its own internal hierarchy, as it includes the lower castes as well as the SCs (the former untouchables). The lower castes were ritualistically higher on the social scale than the ex-untouchables, though both were traditionally below the upper castes. As a result, an internal differentiation within the presumed lower-caste unity has emerged. In some states like Uttar Pradesh, the SCs have openly rebelled against the lower castes, calling them the new oppressors.

There are also problems of horizontal aggregation. The lower-caste upsurge has been fairly effective in putting political parties in power at the state level, but it has had a great deal of difficulty in aggregating coalitions at the national level. Caste, as a concept, exists all over Hindu India, but, as an experience, caste is local or regional. There are "upper" and "lower" castes in all parts of the country, but the lower castes in one state may have little to do with the lower castes elsewhere. Their names, languages, and histories are different. They are all "lower castes," but they speak different languages, have different levels of education, different deprivations, and different oppressor castes. Similarly, *Brahmins* of the south may not be recognized as such by the *Brahmins* of the north and vice versa; each in their respective settings has traditionally enjoyed high status and ritual privileges, but each tradition may be different. As such, the lower-caste ideology of social justice has a nationwide resonance, but it has not been able to achieve a nationwide aggregation.

Can the lower-caste parties develop greater cohesion? In the best of circumstances, these horizontal and vertical problems would be hard to solve. Personality clashes and reliance on charismatic leaders make the disunity of lower-caste parties even worse, which is exactly why there are so many lower-caste–based parties in the Janata family. And, in conjunction with their being less institutionalized, the Janata family of parties is even less allied to formal civil-society organizations. Their fundraising strategies are very much like that of the Congress party at both the state and central levels, dependant on private contributions and kickbacks on public procurement exacted by the use of regulatory powers.

It may be premature to talk of the death of the Janata family of parties. Although individual parties and splinter groups within this family have gone through rise, decline, and extinction, and some are currently aligned with the BJP, some may still have reasonable prospects in several states. Parties belonging to this family can be said to represent a gradually awakening, country-wide, broad (if inchoate) social constituency, one that finds it extremely difficult to unite in the form of a cohesive organized party, due to state-level variations in agrarian relations and caste structures as well as to particularistic leadership. These stirrings from below are unlikely to fade away.

The Communist parties. The communist left has historically played a small but important role on the sidelines of Indian politics. The Communist Party of India (CPI), founded in 1920 by a small group of Marxist intellectuals influenced by the Russian Revolution, grew steadily in the years leading up to India's independence. It acquired localized bases among industrial workers and peasants in a few areas, and remained closely allied ideologically to the Soviet Union.

Immediately after independence—and after crushing a communist-led peasant insurrection in the Telangana region of Andhra Pradesh—the CPI turned to parliamentary politics and contested elections. It emerged as the single largest opposition party in the lower house in the 1952, 1957, and 1962 elections, with 16, 27, and 29 seats (about 3–6 percent of the seats). Its vote share was 3.3 percent, 8.9 percent, and 9.9 percent, respectively. Its principal regional bases were in the states of Kerala, Tripura, West Bengal, Andhra Pradesh, and Bihar. The first three of these states continue to be the principal strongholds of the communist left parties; the first two have seen the left parties alternating in power with Congress-led governments; the communist-dominated Left Front has ruled West Bengal continuously since 1977.

In 1964, in response to both domestic and international factors, the CPI split into two parties—the Communist Party of India–Marxist, or CPI(M), and the original CPI. The international factors were the Sino-Soviet split, the post-1956 Soviet line of peaceful coexistence with the West (in contrast to the then-militant Chinese line), Soviet improvement of relations with the Congress government in India, and the India-China border war of 1962. The domestic factors, which were probably more important, were the tensions within the party over its stance toward the ruling Congress party. As a result of the split, the pro-Soviet and relatively more pro-Congress CPI emerged over time as a smaller faction nationally than the initially more radical and more pro-Chinese CPI(M). The latter underwent further splits in 1967, as insurrectionary communist factions formed the CPI (Marxist-Leninist), which in turn broke up further into several factions, most of them electorally insignificant. The CPI tended to back the Congress party, viewing its left-leaning factions and its public-sector–led import-substitution policies as a bulwark against imperialism, representing the national bourgeoisie against U.S.-led transnational capital. The CPI(M) tended to be more strongly anti-Congress, to a large extent because in the states where it was strong and could also form governments, the Congress party was its immediate electoral adversary. Internationally, the CPI(M) assumed a posture of equidistance between the Soviet Union and China. In the late 1970s, the CPI and CPI(M) began to cooperate in left coalitions, along with some minor left parties, initially in West Bengal, subsequently in Kerala and then nationally. Today, the CPI and CPI(M) are organizationally distinct, but they increasingly cooperate for elections and government formation.

The communist left's electoral record since the split has been as follows. In 1967, the immediate post-split CPI still remained the larger party in votes and seats, but it yielded that position to the CPI(M) in every election thereafter. The combined seats of the CPI(M) and CPI ranged from a low of 28 (in 1984) to a high of 49 (in 1991), or about 5–10 percent of the total seats. Their combined vote percentages have not dropped below 6.9 percent (in 1998 and 1999) and have not risen above 9.8 percent (in 1971). Both seats and votes have been overwhelmingly concentrated in the stronghold states of West Bengal, Kerala, and Tripura. The social base of the communist left has been fairly stable: It is strong mainly in the rural areas of some states, among the middle and small peasantry and agricultural labor.

For all practical purposes, India's communist parties are left-of-center parties, following a broad, multiclass, social-democratic reformist strategy. This is especially evident in the past decade, when they unabashedly struck alliances with the Janata-led governments in 1989–90 and again between 1996–98.[37] Today, they are more important than ever before in national politics, precisely because hung parliaments and coalition politics magnify their clout in government formation and policy. This is so despite a stagnant (though stable) social base and vote share, and despite the marginalization of class issues in election campaigns, in which the main polarization has been on the issue of secularism between a rising BJP on the one hand and the centrist Congress and Janata family parties on the other.

Is Moderate Pluralism Sustainable?

Will India's moderate pluralism remain stable, or will the country's party system gravitate either toward a two-party system or two-alliance system on the one hand, or toward extreme pluralism on the other? More specifically, will the FPTP electoral system and federalism (and hence multiple bipolarities at the state level), combined with the multiple cross-cutting cleavages of India's social diversity, check the tendency toward a two-alliance and two-party system, nationally? And will the FPTP system's vote aggregation imperative check the tendency toward extreme pluralism inherent in India's remarkable heterogeneity? The answers to these questions will depend on which cleavages remain politically salient, and on whether social cleavages will remain cross-cutting or begin to coincide, resulting in less diversity and more polarity. If any one cleavage—for example, the ideological cleavage on attitudes toward secularism—becomes overwhelmingly salient compared to the others, it may lead to a secular versus *Hindutva* two-alliance polarization. Extreme political fragmentation, were it to emerge at all, is unlikely to be long-lasting, given the vote aggregation imperative of the FPTP system, even under federalism.

In our view, several cleavages will remain politically salient, varying regionally. Social cleavages will also by and large remain cross-cutting and not coincide. Hence, neither a two-party/two-alliance system nor extreme pluralism is likely to mark the Indian party system in the foreseeable future. Moderate pluralism is the most likely long-term scenario. All three major formations—the Congress, the BJP, and the Janata-left party cluster—will remain internally diverse on economic policy, on caste, and on regional bases. Due to the need to make alliances in electoral competition in a federal first-past-the-post system, it is unlikely that any of the three formations, even the BJP, will develop coherent policy positions on all major issues and a tightly knit, disciplined organization. Moderate pluralism and shifting electoral alliances and coalition governments, combined with moderate internal factionalism within parties, seems the most probable scenario in the foreseeable future.

NOTES

For comments on earlier drafts, the authors wish to thank Larry Diamond, Richard Gunther, and Yogendra Yadav.

1. For a discussion of why India's democracy has lasted so long, see Ashutosh Varshney, "India Defies the Odds: Why Democracy Survives," *Journal of Democracy* 9 (July 1998): 36–50.

2. Lloyd I. and Susanne Hoeber Rudolph, *In Pursuit of Lakshmi: The Political Economy of the Indian State* (Chicago: University of Chicago Press, 1987).

3. All population figures in this section are based on the 1991 Census, and all electoral data are derived from reports of the Election Commission of India. See Ashish Bose, *India's Basic Demographic Statistics: 177 Key Tables with Graphics* (Delhi: B.R. Publishing Corp. 1996), and *Election Commission of India, Statistical Report on General Elections, 1999 to the Thirteenth Lok Sabha*, Volume I, National and State Abstracts (New Delhi: Election Commission of India); see also previous versions of the same report, various years (1952–98).

4. Technically, the first-past-the-post system is the single-member district, single nontransferable vote plurality-rule system, but we use FPTP as a shorthand.

5. Maurice Duverger, *Political Parties: Their Organization and Activity in the Modern State*, Barbara and Robert North, trans. (New York: Wiley and Sons, 1963).

6. Bihar has become essentially bipolar, as the Congress party is currently in coalition with the ruling Rashtriya Janata Dal. This is only tactical, though, and the coalition could fall apart at any time. With the decimation of the Janata Dal in 1999, Karnataka too has become bipolarized between the Congress and the BJP-Lok Shakti alliance. A further complication has been the creation of three new states in November 2000—Uttaranchal, Jharkhand, and Chhattisgarh—carved out of the states of Uttar Pradesh, Bihar, and Madhya Pradesh, taking the number of states to 28. However, the party systems of these new states are bipolar: Uttaranchal and Chhattisgarh are Congress-BJP, and Jharkhand, although fluid, is NDA alliance versus RJD-Congress alliance.

7. Douglas W. Rae, *The Political Consequences of Electoral Laws* (New Haven: Yale University Press, 1971).

8. William Riker, "The Two-Party System and Duverger's Law," *American Political Science Review* 76 (December 1982): 753–65.

9. See Pradeep K. Chhibber and John R. Petrocik, "Social Cleavages, Elections and the Indian Party System," in Richard Sisson and Ramashray Roy, eds., *Diversity and Dominance in Indian Politics, Volume 1: Changing Bases of Congress Support* (New Delhi: Sage Publications, 1990). They have pointed out that the Congress party at the state level was not an encompassing umbrella party, but increasingly reflected local social cleavages and was based on particular social constituencies.

10. For a detailed analysis of the BJP's southward and eastward spread, and its "downward" expansion to the lower castes during the 1990s, see Oliver Heath, "The Anatomy of BJP's Rise to Power: Social, Regional, and Political Expansion," *Economic and Political Weekly* (Mumbai), 21–28 August 1999, 2511–17.

11. The term moderate pluralism has also been used by in Giovanni Sartori, *Parties and Party Systems: A Framework for Analysis,* vol. 1 (New York: Cambridge University Press, 1976). Our use of the term is different, however: Sartori has in mind a right-left ideological spectrum in the European sense, and moderate pluralism would reflect a left- or right-of-center focus. The European right-left distinction breaks down in India, given that Indian politics is driven less by class-based politics and more by caste, religious, and linguistic cleavages. For further details, see Myron Weiner, *The Indian Paradox: Essays in Indian Politics* (New Delhi: Sage Publications, 1989).

12. The evidence from the actions and stances of the party and its allied organizations on a while range of incidents and issues suggests that this outward moderation is something forced by the compulsions of the electoral and party systems, and not due to any change of heart or mind. However, for the purpose of our argument, this moderation, even if only tactical, is evidence enough of the nature of electoral and party-systemic compulsions.

13. *BJP Election Manifesto* (1996), 3–4.

14. For a detailed analysis of caste pressures within the BJP in northern India, see Christophe Jaffrelot, "The Rise of the Other Backward Castes in the Hindi Belt," *Journal of Asian Studies* 59 (February 2000): 86–108.

15. For more details, see Yogendra Yadav, "Political Change in North India," *Economic and Political Weekly* (Mumbai), 18 December 1993, 2767–74.

16. For elaboration, see Ashutosh Varshney, "Battling the Past, Forging a Future? Ayodhya and Beyond," in Philip Oldenburg, ed., *India Briefing 1993* (Boulder, Colo.: Westview Press, 1993).

17. This account of the Congress party draws on Rajni Kothari, *Politics in India* (Boston: Little, Brown and Co., 1970); Myron Weiner, *Party Building in a New Nation: The Indian National Congress* (Chicago: University of Chicago Press, 1967); Stanley Kochanek, *The Congress Party of India: Dynamics of One-Party Democracy* (Princeton, N.J.: Princeton University Press, 1968); Richard Sisson and Ramashray Roy, eds., *Diversity and Dominance in Indian Politics, Volume 1*; James Manor, "Parties and the Party System," in Atul Kohli, ed., *India's Democracy: An Analysis of Changing State-Society Relations* (Princeton: Princeton University Press, 1988); and Anthony Heath and Yogendra Yadav, "The United Colors of Congress: Social Profile of Congress Voters, 1996 and 1998," *Economic and Political Weekly* (Mumbai), 21–28 August 1999, 2518–28.

18. Rajni Kothari, *Politics in India,* 179.

19. Based on extensive interviews conducted by E. Sridharan; see his "Toward State Funding of Elections in India: A Comparative Perspective on Policy Options," *Journal of Policy Reform* 3 (October 1999), 229–54.

20. Further, the amendment of the law governing election expenditure limits in

1975—which effectively made party and supporter expenditure on behalf of a candidate not count toward the candidate's election spending ceiling—removed all effective checks on election expenditure.

21. Paul Brass, "The Politicisation of the Peasantry in a North Indian State" in Sudipta Kaviraj, ed., *Politics in India: Oxford in India Readings in Sociology and Social Anthropology* (New Delhi: Oxford University Press, 1998).

22. Yogendra Yadav and Alistair McMillan, "Results: How India Voted," *India Today*, 16 March 1998, especially pp. 49–50.

23. India now claims to have a 200 million–strong middle class. A fairly large segment of the new middle class is believed to support Hindu nationalism.

24. See Richard Gunther and Larry Diamond, "Types and Functions of Parties," pp. 3–39 of this volume.

25. Ibid.

26. Ibid.

27. Ibid.

28. The discussion of BJP's ideology in these paragraphs relies heavily upon Ashutosh Varshney, "Contested Meanings: Hindu Nationalism, India's National Identity and the Politics of Anxiety," *Daedalus* 122 (Summer 1993): 227–62.

29. Urdu—a language combining Persian and Hindi, written in Arabic script—is a typical syncretistic language, developed under the Muslim rule.

30. Nanaji Deshmukh, *Rethinking Secularism* (Delhi: Suruchi Prakashan, 1989); H.V. Sheshadri, K.S. Sudarshan, K. Surya Narain Rao, and Balraj Madhok, *Why Hindu Rashtra* (Delhi: Suruchi Prakashan, 1990).

31. V.D. Savarkar, *Hindutva*, 6th ed. (Bombay: Veer Savarkar Prakashan, 1989), title page; elaborated further between pp. 110–13.

32. M.S. Golwalkar, *We or Our Nationhood Defined* (Nagpur: Bharat Publications, 1939).

33. V.D. Savarkar, *Hindutva,* 113.

34. Following the controversial attacks on Christians and churches in December 1998 and January 1999, a cabinet minister of the BJP-led government, who has worked with the party throughout his life, resigned and openly accused the right-wing of Hindu nationalism of subverting the functioning of the BJP-led government. Such open confrontation at the highest levels of the party has been quite rare.

35. This account of the Janata family of parties draws on state-by-state accounts of Congress dominance and decline in Richard Sisson and Ramashray Roy, eds., *Diversity and Dominance in Indian Politics;* Francine R. Frankel, "Middle Castes and Classes," in Atul Kohli, ed., *India's Democracy;* and Francine Frankel and M.S.A. Rao, eds., *Dominance and State Power in Modern India: Decline of a Social Order,* vols. 1 and 2 (New Delhi: Oxford University Press, 1989).

36. See Ram Manohar Lohia, *The Caste System* (Hyderabad: Lohia Samta Vidyalaya Nyas, 1964).

37. The CPI participated in the United Front government of 1996–98, while the CPI(M) supported it from outside.

10

THE INSTITUTIONAL DECLINE OF PARTIES IN TURKEY

Ergun Özbudun

Ergun Özbudun is professor of political science at Bilkent University in Ankara. His publications include Social Change and Political Participation in Turkey *(1976) and* Contemporary Turkish Politics: Challenges to Democratic Consolidation *(2000).*

Commenting on Turkish politics in the 1950s, Frederick Frey argued that "Turkish politics are party politics. . . . Within the power structure of Turkish society, the political party is the main unofficial link between the government and the larger, extra-governmental groups of people. . . . It is perhaps in this respect above all—the existence of extensive, powerful, highly organized, grassroots parties—that Turkey differs institutionally from the other Middle Eastern nations with whom we frequently compare her."[1] Since the 1970s, however, Turkey's parties and party system have been undergoing a protracted process of institutional decay, as described in the first section. The party system has been beset by growing fragmentation, ideological polarization, and electoral volatility. Parties themselves have been dogged by declining organizational capacity and a lack of public support and identification. The next section will discuss the common organizational characteristics of Turkey's main political parties. I shall argue that, in general, Turkish parties are catch-all and cartel parties. In the following sections, I shall discuss the social, ideological, and organizational characteristics of the Welfare Party (now the Virtue party), the Motherland Party, the True Path Party, the Democratic Left Party, and the Republican People's Party, as well as a few minor parties.

Deinstitutionalization, Fragmentation, and Polarization

Turkey displayed the characteristics of a typical two-party system between 1946 and 1960, when the two main contenders for power were the Republican People's Party (RPP) and the Democratic Party (DP). In the 1961 elections that followed the military intervention of 1960, no

TABLE 1 —PERCENTAGE OF VOTES (AND SEATS) IN TURKISH
PARLIAMENTARY ELECTIONS (1950–77)

PARTY	1950	1954	1957	1961	1965	1969	1973	1977
DP/JP	53.3	56.6	447.7	34.8	52.9	46.5	29.8	36.9
	(83.8)	(93.0)	(69.5)	(35.1)	(53.3)	(56.9)	(33.1)	(42.0)
RPP	39.8	34.8	40.8	36.7	28.7	27.4	33.3	41.4
	(14.2)	(5.7)	(29.2)	(38.4)	(29.8)	(31.8)	(41.1)	(47.3)
NP	3.0	4.7	7.2	14.0	6.3	3.2	1.0	
	(0.2)	(0.9)	(0.7)	(12.0)	(6.9)	(1.3)	(0.0)	
FP			3.8					
			(0.7)					
NTP				13.7	3.7	2.2		
				(14.4)	(4.2)	(1.3)		
TLP					3.0	2.7		0.1
					(3.3)	(0.4)		(0.0)
NAP						2.2	3.0	3.4	6.4
						(2.4)	(0.2)	(0.7)	(3.6)
UP						2.8	1.1	0.4
						(1.8)	(0.2)	
RPP						6.6	5.3	1.9
						(3.3)	(2.9)	(0.7)
DEM. P.							11.9	1.9
							(10.0)	(0.2)
NSP							11.8	8.6
							(10.7)	(5.3)

Note: The first row of figures for each party represents percentages of the popular
vote, and the second row (in parentheses) presents the percentages of seats won.
Source: Official results of elections, State Institute of Statistics.
Abbreviations: DP: Democratic Party; JP: Justice Party; RPP: Republican People's
Party; NP: Nation Party; FP: Freedom Party; NTP: New Turkey party; TLP: Turkish
Labor Party; NAP: Nationalist Action Party; UP: Unity party; RRP: Republican Reliance
Party; Dem. P.: Democrat Party; NSP: National Salvation Party.

party obtained a parliamentary majority due to the fragmentation of the
DP votes among three parties (the DP had been banned by the military
regime), and the introduction of the D'Hondt version of proportional
representation. In the 1965 and 1969 elections, however, the Justice
Party (JP), having established itself as the main heir to the DP, was able
to gain comfortable parliamentary majorities, despite the growing
number of parties represented in parliament. The 1973 elections, which
followed the military intervention of 1971, produced another fragmented
parliament. So did the 1977 elections. No party enjoyed a majority in
either parliament, although the two major parties, the RPP and the JP,
were clearly stronger than others. Their combined share of the seats in
parliament was 63.1 percent in 1973 and 78.8 percent in 1977. According
to the D'Hondt version of proportional representation, which favors
larger parties, these figures corresponded to 74.2 percent of the seats in
1973 and 89.3 percent in 1977 (see Table 1 above).

The main characteristics—or "maladies"—of the Turkish party system
in the 1970s have been described as volatility, fragmentation, and
ideological polarization.[2] Volatility meant sudden and significant

TABLE 2—PERCENTAGE OF VOTES IN TURKISH PARLIAMENTARY AND LOCAL ELECTIONS (1983–95)

PARTIES	1983 (PARL.)	1984 (LOCAL)	1987 (PARL.)	1989 (LOCAL)	1991 (PARL.)	1994 (LOCAL)	1995 (PARL.)	1999 (PARL.)
MP	45.2 (52.9)	41.5	36.3 (64.9)	21.8	24.0 (25.6)	21.0	19.7 (24.0)	13.2 (15.6)
PP	30.5 (29.3)	8.8						
NDP	23.3 (17.8)	7.1						
SDPP		23.4	24.7 (22.0)	28.7	20.8 (19.6)	13.6		
TPP		13.3	19.1 (13.1)	25.1	27.0 (39.6)	21.4	19.2 (24.5)	12.0 (15.5)
WP/VP		4.4	7.2 (0)	9.8	16.9 (13.8)[1]	19.1	21.4 (28.7)	15.4 (20.2)
DLP			8.5 (0)	9.0	10.8 (1.6)	8.8	14.6 (13.8)	22.2 (24.7)
NAP			2.9 (0)	4.1		8.0	8.2 (0)	18.0 (23.5)
RPP						4.6	10.7 (8.9)	8.7 (0)
*	0.61		0.51		0.71		0.77	0.79

* Rae's Index of Fractionalization of Assembly seats.
Note: The figures in parentheses represent the percentages of parliamentary seats won by each party.
Source: Official results of elections, State Institute of Statistics.
Abbreviations: MP: Motherland Party; PP: Populist Party; NDP: Nationalist Democracy Party; SDPP: Social Democratic Populist Party; TPP: True Path Party; WP: Welfare Party; DLP: Democratic Left Party; NAP: Nationalist Action Party; RPP: Republican People's Party; VP: Virtue Party (contested in 1999).

changes in party votes from one election to the next. Fragmentation was observed in the increasing number of parties represented in parliament. As measured by Douglas Rae's index of fractionalization,[3] the fragmentation of seats in the National Assembly was 0.70 in 1961, 0.63 in 1965, 0.59 in 1969, 0.70 in 1973, and 0.60 in 1977. While such fragmentation was not too high, and the format of the party system was closer to limited or moderate multipartism, the rise of two highly ideological parties—the National Salvation Party representing political Islam and the ultranationalist Nationalist Action Party—in the 1970s increased ideological polarization and gave the system some of the properties of extreme or polarized multipartism.[4] Short-lived and ideologically incompatible coalition governments were unable to curb political violence and terror. The system finally broke down when the military intervened in September 1980.

The military regime attempted to overhaul the party system by manipulating the electoral laws. While maintaining proportional representation in principle, a new electoral law, passed in 1983, introduced a 10 percent national threshold and very high constituency thresholds (ranging between 14.2 percent and 50 percent, depending on

TABLE 3—VOLATILITY AND FRAGMENTATION IN THE PARTY SYSTEM

ELECTIONS	VOLATILITY[1]	FRAGMENTA-TION OF VOTES[2]	FRAGMENTA-TION OF SEATS[2]	DISPROPORTION-ALITY INDEX[3]	EFFECTIVE NUM-BER OF PARTIES[4]
1961		0.71	0.70	1.0	3.3
1965	24.5	0.63	0.63	0.75	2.6
1969	11.4	0.70	0.59	7.4	2.3
1973	28.4	0.77	0.70	5.6	3.3
1977	18.3	0.68	0.60	5.5	2.5
1983		0.66	0.61	4.5	2.5
1987		0.75	0.51	15.7	2.0
1991	16.6	0.79	0.71	7.1	3.5
1995	23.0	0.83	0.77	5.8	4.3
1999	19.9	0.85	0.79	4.1	4.9

[1] Total volatility is the sum of the absolute value of all changes in the percentages of votes cast for each party since the previous election divided by two. The 1961 elections are omitted since the DP was dissolved by the ruling military council (NUC) and the two entirely new parties (JP and NTP) competed for its votes. Likewise, the 1983 elections are omitted since the military government (NSC) closed down all existing parties and thus the three parties that competed in this election were new parties. Finally, the 1987 elections are omitted on the grounds that two of the three parties authorized by the NSC—PP and NDP—were relatively artificial parties that soon disappeared after the return to competitive politics. Had these three elections been included, the average volatility score would certainly have been much higher. In calculating the volatility scores, only those parties that have gained representation in parliament in at least one of the two consecutive elections are taken into account. For the 1991 elections, which the WP contested in an alliance with the NAP and small RDP (Reformist Democracy Party), their percentage of votes in the 1989 local elections were taken as a close approximation.
[2] Based on Douglas W. Rae's index of fractionalization in Douglas W. Rae, *The Political Consequences of Electoral Laws* (New Haven: Yale University Press, 1967), 56.
[3] Based on Arend Lijphart's index of disproportionality, which is "the average vote-seat deviation of the two largest parties in each election." Arend Lijphart, Democracies: Patterns of Majoritarian and Consensus Government in Twenty-One Countries (New Haven: Yale University Press, 1984), 163.
[4] Based on Markku Laakso and Rein Taagepera's formula which is as follows: $P_e = \sum_{i=1}^{n} \dfrac{1}{P_i^2}$ Markku Laakso and Rein Taagepera, "Effective Number of Parties: A Measure with Application to West Europe," *Comparative Political Studies* 12 (April 1979): 3–27.

the size of the constituency) in the hope that this would eliminate the more ideological minor parties and transform the party system into a more manageable two- or three-party system. The 1983 elections, in which competition was limited to three parties licensed by the ruling military authorities, indeed produced the expected result. The Motherland Party (MP) of Turgut Özal won an absolute majority of seats with 45.2 percent of the vote. Aided by the electoral changes that favored the larger parties to an even greater extent, the MP actually increased its parliamentary majority in the 1987 elections, even though it obtained a lower percentage of the overall vote (36.3 percent). By that time, however, the signs of refragmentation were already in the air. This became increasingly clear in the local elections of 1989 and 1994, and the parliamentary elections of 1991 and 1995 (see Table 2 on the facing page).

At present, the Turkish party system is more fragmented than ever. The largest party that emerged in the December 1995 elections (the Welfare Party, or WP, which was the heir to the National Salvation Party of the 1970s) received only 21.4 percent of the vote. The fragmentation of the Assembly seats as measured by the index of fractionalization is as follows: 0.61 in 1983, 0.51 in 1987, 0.71 in 1991, and 0.77 in 1995. Due to the electoral system's high national and constituency thresholds, the fragmentation of party votes has been much higher than the fragmentation of seats (see Table 3 on the previous page). Furthermore, the relatively greater weight of the two major parties in the 1960s and the 1970s (the center-right JP and the center-left RPP), which had given some degree of stability to the party system, has also disappeared over the years. Both major tendencies are now divided into two parties each: The center-right tendency is represented by the Motherland (MP) and the True Path (TPP) parties, and the center-left by the Democratic Left Party (DLP) and the Republican People's Party (RPP), with little hope of reunification in the near future.

Table 3 also demonstrates a high degree of volatility in the Turkish party system, which suggests an almost continuous process of realignment. Although such high volatility scores are to be expected given the frequency of military interventions that wreaked havoc in the party system (the 1960 intervention banned the DP, and the 1980 intervention closed down all political parties), 13 years after the most recent retransition to democracy, volatility is still high and rising. This presents a sharp contrast with Southern European party systems (that is, those of Italy, Spain, Portugal, and Greece) where, "following a critical election, volatility declined and voting behavior became more stable and predictable."[5] High Turkish volatility scores stem partly from the destructive effects of military interventions, as mentioned above, and partly from the fact that Turkish political parties are not strongly rooted in civil society, as will be spelled out below. To the extent that the stabilization of electoral behavior is an element of democratic consolidation, the current trend in Turkey seems to be detracting from it.

Another worrisome change in the party system is the increasing weakening of the moderate center-right and center-left tendencies. The 1995 elections marked the lowest points ever for both tendencies that so far have dominated Turkish politics: The combined vote of the two center-right parties was 38.9 percent, while that of the two center-left parties was 25.4 percent. This represented a sharp decrease from previous years and a corresponding rise in the votes of noncentrist parties. In addition to the 21.4 percent of the vote won by the Islamic WP, the ultranationalist NAP obtained 8.18 percent, and the Kurdish nationalist People's Democracy Party (HADEP) won 4.17 percent. Although the latter two parties could not send any representatives to parliament because they failed to meet the 10 percent national threshold, the combined vote of the three extremist parties reached 33.8 percent, or more than one-third, of the entire electorate. The increasing salience of religious and ethnic issues represents an overall increase in ideological polarization, especially since such issues are more difficult to resolve and less amenable to rational bargainings than socioeconomic ones. Increasing polarization is also substantiated by recent public-opinion research. A survey carried out in 1991 within the framework of the "World Values Survey" demonstrated that 50 percent of Turkish voters placed themselves at the center on a left-right continuum, 5 percent at the extreme left, 20 percent at center-left, 18 percent at center-right, and 8 percent at the extreme right. A follow-up survey carried out in 1997 gave the following figures: 7 percent extreme left, 14 percent center-left, 35 percent center, 23 percent center-right, and 20 percent extreme right. A comparison of the two survey's findings clearly demonstrates an erosion of the center and the rapid rise of the extreme right.[6] Thus all three maladies of the Turkish party system in the 1970s (volatility, fragmentation, and polarization) have reappeared, if anything in worse form. The pivotal position of the WP (and its successor, the Virtue Party) has made coalition alternatives limited in number and difficult to accomplish. For some years, the only possible minimum-winning coalitions have been the right-left (MP, TPP, and one of the leftist parties), the WP-right (either with the TPP or the MP), and the WP-left (together with both leftist parties) coalitions. The last one is most unlikely because of the strong secularist views of the leftist parties. At any rate, the rise of the WP, no doubt, increased polarization along the religious dimension, since the party's views on the role of Islam in state and society sharply differentiated it from all other parties.

A fourth malaise in the party system is the organizational weakening of parties and party-identification ties. This seems to be part of the more general problem of "disillusionment" *(el desencanto)* typical of many new democracies.[7] The seemingly intractable nature of problems— increasing economic difficulties, very high inflation, a huge foreign and domestic public debt, growing inequalities in wealth, a sharp deterioration of social policies, and pervasive political corruption— have created a deep sense of pessimism and disappointment among voters, many of whom vote for parties not with any degree of enthusiasm but with the intention of choosing "the least evil" among them.

In this rather bleak picture, the only notable positive change compared to the 1970s is the seemingly stronger elite and mass commitment to democracy. Although all major political parties remained committed to democracy even during the profound crisis of the late 1970s, some significant groups on the left and on the right challenged its legitimacy. The radical left was not represented in parliament, but it found many supporters among students, teachers, the industrial working class. The radical right, on the other hand, was represented in parliament, even in government, by the NAP, whose commitment to liberal democracy was at best dubious. There were indications that this party was involved in right-wing political violence. Finally, in the eyes of many ordinary citizens, including some civilian politicians, it was quite legitimate for the armed forces to intervene in such a crisis to end the violence and chaos. In other words, democracy was not seen by all as "the only game in town."

Today, the situation seems to have changed considerably. The collapse of the communist regimes in Eastern Europe and the Soviet Union truly marginalized the groups on the extreme left. The NAP underwent a silent transformation, becoming a more moderate, pro-system, nationalist party. Calls for a military intervention subsided significantly. The sense of disillusionment among many voters did not turn into an ideological challenge to the democratic system itself. "Increased valorization" of democracy as an end in itself is operative in Turkey, as in many other new democracies.[8] As Guillermo O'Donnell observes, "the current prestige of democratic discourses, and conversely, the weakness of openly authoritarian political discourses" is a major factor working to the advantage of democratic actors. He is also right in his words of warning, however, that this factor "is subject to withering by the passage of time. . . . [T]he influence of democratic discourses depends . . . in part on their capacity to be translated into concrete meanings for the majority of the population."[9]

Organizational Characteristics of Political Parties

Since the beginnings of multiparty politics in the mid-1940s, Turkish political parties have generally been described as "cadre" or "catch-all" parties with strong clientelistic features. If mass parties are defined as parties based on a carefully maintained membership registration system and the mass membership of card-carrying, dues-paying members, with emphasis on political indoctrination,[10] no major Turkish political party qualifies as a mass party with the possible exception of the WP (during its later years), as will be spelled out below.[11] Although a 1996 survey showed 12.1 percent of all voters as party members,[12] the irregular nature of party registers and the loose link between the party and the member suggest that what is meant by party "member" in Turkey is often little more than a party "supporter." Many local party organizations, particularly in the relatively less developed regions, remain inactive in periods between elections[13] and engage in limited, if any efforts to give their members a political education or indoctrination. Membership participation in party activities other than voting was found to be highest in the two strongly nationalistic parties, the NAP and the HADEP, and lowest in the two center-right parties (MP and TPP). The WP (somewhat surprisingly) and the two center-left parties (DLP and RPP) obtained scores between these two extremes.[14]

The loose link between the party and the party members also implies that membership dues are not paid regularly and do not therefore constitute a significant portion of party income. Instead, parties have been financed by state subsidies since the constitutional amendment of 1971. The present law provides state subsidies to parties that obtained more than 7 percent of the votes in the most recent general parliamentary elections in proportion to the votes received. Private donations also provide an important source of income for parties.

Such organizational characteristics are to be explained by the circumstances in which Turkey made a transition to multiparty politics in the mid-1940s. The opposition Democratic Party (DP) successfully used the longstanding center-periphery cleavage by appealing to peripheral grievances against the RPP's centralist, bureaucratic single-party rule. Most students of Turkish politics agree that the origins of the Turkish party system lie in such a center-periphery conflict, which pitted a nationalist, centralist, secularist, and cohesive state elite against "a culturally heterogeneous, complex, and even hostile periphery" with religious and antistatist overtones.[15] Whether the center-periphery cleavage is still the dominant one in Turkey is open to debate. In the 1980s and the 1990s, no single party has emerged to stand for the "values and interests of the center" or received the kind of electoral support that the RPP had received in the past. With the fragmentation of the vote described above, there is no leading party of the periphery either. "To complicate the picture further, the center is no longer what it used to be: Turkey lacks a coherent and compact elite group occupying the center and defending the collective interests of the center."[16] These circumstances were not conducive to the development of mass parties. The RPP remained what it was during the single-party period, namely a party of the state elites, and the DP found it more convenient to base its appeal on broad populist, antistatist slogans rather than trying to anchor itself in a particular social group.

Another factor that shaped the Turkish party system was "factionalism," prevalent in many rural communities and small towns. Such factionalism gave the DP ready "vote banks" with one faction supporting the DP and the other supporting the RPP. Factionalism contributed to the rapid rise of the DP, but at the same time made it a socially heterogeneous alliance united only in its opposition to the RPP. Later on, when the DP came to power in 1950, it built an effective rural machine based on the distribution of patronage and pork-barrel benefits. Thus the original two-party system was based on vertical rather than horizontal loyalties. "Parties concentrated their efforts in securing the allegiance of faction leaders and local patrons who were then entrusted with the task of mobilizing electoral support. In either case, vertical networks of personal followings proved to be a major base of political loyalties."[17] Later, with increasing rural to urban migration, similar party machines appeared in the larger cities and were used effectively by the

DP and its successor, JP. The prevalence of vertical clientelistic networks and the machine-type politics help explain the failure of political parties to develop organizations based on horizontal loyalties such as common class or group interests. In the 1970s and the 1980s, the increasing complexity of the society and the growing salience of ideological issues led to a fragmentation of the party system, but without changing the clientelistic nature of political parties. A leading student of Turkish politics describes the present political system of Turkey as a "party-centered polity," meaning a "party system largely autonomous from social groups" in the absence of a strong bourgeoisie in the historical development of the Ottoman-Turkish state.[18]

The last point is related to the overall weakness of linkages between political parties and other civil society institutions, again with the partial exception of the WP. If we exclude the 12.1 percent of voters who are members of political parties and the 9.8 percent who are affiliated with a trade union, we are left with only 6.2 percent of voters who are members of all other associations. The overwhelming majority of the latter category are members of public professional organizations, where membership is legally obligatory.[19] All organizational links and all kinds of cooperation among political parties and civil-society institutions were explicitly forbidden by the Constitution of 1982 and other laws, until the constitutional amendments of 1995. But even when such links were not forbidden, as in the period between 1961 and 1980, they were extremely weak or nonexistent. Turkish parties, due to their organizational characteristics described above, do not establish or maintain close ties with organized interests or specific sectors of society. Rather, they maintain autonomy from social groups, shifting from one potential base of electoral support to another, or abandoning the interests of their electoral clientele once elected to office.[20]

Organizationally, all Turkish parties display similar characteristics since the Political Parties Laws of 1965 and 1983 imposed upon them a more or less standard organizational model. This model consists of party congresses (conventions) and elected executive committees at the national and local (provincial and sub-provincial) levels. The smallest organizational unit is the sub-province organization (ilçe). Parties are not allowed to organize below that level. Thus the party "branches" (ocak) that existed in villages and urban neighborhoods prior to 1960 were banned by the military government in 1960–61, a ban that was continued under the 1965 and the 1983 laws on political parties. The organizational model imposed by these laws seems consistent with democratic principles since party leaders and executive committees at all levels are elected by appropriate party congresses which, in turn, are supposed to represent the entire body of party members. Nevertheless, historically and at present, all parties display strong oligarchical tendencies.[21] All are overly centralized, and the central executive committees have the power to dismiss recalcitrant local committees. Changes in the top leadership are very rare. Indeed, Bülent Ecevit (DLP), Necmeddin Erbakan (WP), and Alparslan Türkeş (NAP) have led their parties for more than a quarter of a century, and Süleyman Demirel remained the leader of the JP and the TPP from 1964 to 1993, when he was elected president of the republic.

Perhaps the most important function of political parties is elite recruitment or candidate selection. As E. Schattschneider observed, "the nature of the nominating procedure determines the nature of the party; he who can make the nominations is the owner of the party. This is therefore one of the best points at which to observe the distribution of power within the party."[22] The current Political Parties Law leaves the choice of the candidate-selection procedure to party constitutions. If parties choose to hold party primaries, in which either all registered party members or their elected delegates in that constituency can participate, such primaries are conducted under judicial supervision. This method, however, has rarely been used in recent elections, and the tendency is for all parties to have candidates nominated by their central executive committees. These committees are, in turn, strongly controlled by party leaders. Therefore, the candidate-selection procedure has turned out to be one of the most centralized and oligarchical methods used in Western democracies.[23] Central control over candidate selection is both a cause and a consequence of the oligarchical tendencies alluded to above. In addition, such central control allows party leaders to nominate a relatively large number of political novices (usually former prominent bureaucrats) who have no grassroots support and are therefore completely dependent on party leaders. There are no special procedures for socializing party candidates into their respective sets of norms, values, or issue stands either prior to nomination or after election to office.

Turkish parties have traditionally played an important role in electoral mobilization through local branches, door-to-door canvassing by party activists, and other grassroots activities to get out the votes. In recent elections, however, they have increasingly neglected such old-style organizational work and concentrated their efforts on media appeals and image-building with the help of professional public relations experts. The abolition of the state monopoly over radio and television broadcasts in 1993 and the consequent proliferation of private television and radio networks is an important contributing factor in this regard. Television appeals that necessarily center around party leaders have also contributed to the strengthening of their authority and to the oligarchical tendencies within parties. Another factor in the organizational decline of political parties is the slowing down of economic growth and the lessening of the state's role in economy. These changes mean that there is a limit to the spoils parties can distribute to their followers, and, in the absence of strong ideological motivations, this is an important factor that saps their organizational strength.

The only party that managed to avoid this decline was the WP, until it was found to be in violation of provisions of the constitution and banned by the Constitutional Court on 22 February 1998. Just days before that decision, a new party, the Virtue Party (VP), was formed and then quickly attracted some 135 MPs from the proscribed WP, making the Virtue Party the main opposition party in parliament. Thus the VP is essentially a continuation of the WP, led by Recai Kutan, who has been one of the closest associates of Necmeddin Erbakan, the leader of the proscribed WP. Most of the elected WP mayors and the leaders of their local organizations also joined the VP. Therefore, the analysis offered for the WP here also holds true for the VP. It was the only party that appreciated the importance of classical door-to-door canvassing with the help of hundreds of thousands of highly motivated, devoted, and disciplined party workers. Besides, such activities were not limited to campaign periods but continued all year round. Interestingly, the WP's workers included many women activists, but the party did not nominate a single woman even for the most modest elected office. This practice continued until the WP was shut down. The VP, however, nominated several women candidates in the 1999 parliamentary elections, three of whom were elected. One of them was not permitted to take her parliamentary oath since she refused to take her head scarf off. She eventually lost her membership.

The organizational decline of parties is also reflected in public attitudes toward parties. A 1996 national survey showed that more than half of Turkish voters (50.7 percent) thought that there were no parties defending the rights of the "oppressed," as opposed to 30.6 percent who answered this question affirmatively. The percentage of those who saw "their own" party as defending the rights of the oppressed was 85.6 for the WP, 88.4 for the DLP, 82.1 for the RPP, and 85.3 for the HADEP. The two center-right parties, the TPP and MP, ranked lowest, with 45.3 and 37.8 percent, respectively.[24] Another survey showed that political parties were among the least trusted public institutions. The confidence score (computed by subtracting the total of those who had no or little trust in the institutions from the total of those who had much or some trust) was – 40 for political parties in 1997. Interestingly the armed forces ranked first with a confidence score of 88, followed by the police (44 percent), the courts (43 percent), religious institutions (40 percent), and the public bureaucracy (36 percent). Furthermore, a comparison of the two parallel surveys of 1991 and 1997 indicate a marked erosion of trust in "political" institutions such as the government and the parliament.[25]

The role played by parties in "issue structuration" became less prominent in the 1980s and the 1990s, following the collapse of the communist regimes and the decline of the socialist ideology in general.

Consequently, the left-right division over economic issues has lost its relative importance, since all parties now support, to varying degrees, a free-market economy and the private ownership of the means of production. Conversely, the rise of political Islam as represented by the WP meant that issues related to a religious-secular cleavage rose in prominence. Nevertheless the WP, walking on a tightrope in a constitutional system where secularism is strongly safeguarded, generally refrained from structuring issues in overtly religious forms, as the Virtue Party has also done since its founding. Rather, the WP intentionally couched its appeals in such vague concepts as the "just order" and the "national and moral values." In general, parties have emphasized "valence issues" such as clean government and economic prosperity, rather than "position issues."[26] The relatively low salience of issues is both a cause and a reflection of another general characteristic of Turkish parties, namely personalism. In election campaigns the trustworthiness and other personal qualities of party leaders loom much larger than the parties' positions on issues. This high degree of personalism is also responsible for the division of the center-right and the center-left tendencies into two separate parties each. The personal rivalries between Yilmaz and Çiller on the center-right, and between Ecevit and Baykal on the center-left make a merger highly unlikely in the foreseeable future.

Finally, Turkish parties have been characterized since the beginnings of the multiparty politics by a high degree of party discipline particularly in parliamentary voting. Deviation from the party line is very rare and, if it happens, usually leads to the expulsion of the recalcitrant MP. This appears to be an outcome of the high degree of centralization of authority within parties, and particularly the strong position of leaders. The parliamentary system of government has also contributed to high party cohesion, since the fate of the government depends on party unity in parliament. In other words, party discipline and cohesion are necessary virtues in a parliamentary system, whereas their role is much less significant in a presidential one. Thus parties can normally be expected to produce and maintain relatively stable and efficacious governments, even though the fragmentation of the party system makes coalition politics a necessary and rather difficult game. Such party unity in parliament is all the more remarkable in view of the fact that most Turkish parties suffer from a marked tendency toward factionalism.[27]

Given the organizational characteristics mentioned above, one may wonder about the place of Turkish parties in the overall classification of political parties. A recent study has distinguished among four sequential models of party: elite (cadre) party, mass party, catch-all party, and cartel party.[28] Most Turkish parties combine certain characteristics of cadre and catch-all parties, with some elements of cartel parties. In a number of respects, they approach the model of the cartel party. First, the principal goals of politics seem to have become politics as profession, in which party competition takes place on the basis of competing claims to efficient management. Second, party work and party campaigning have become capital intensive. Third, parties have become increasingly dependent on state subsidies and state-regulated channels of communication. And fourth, as a result, parties have shown a tendency to become part of the state and act as agents of the state. In the change from a cadre party model to a catch-all or cartel party model, Turkish parties have never gone through a mass party phase. To some extent the WP was an exception to this rule, as I will discuss below.

The Rise of Political Islam: The Welfare Party

One of the most important events in Turkish politics in the last decade has been the rise of political Islam as represented by the WP. Although the party's origins go back to 1970, its predecessor, the National Salvation Party (NSP), remained a medium-sized party between 1973 and 1980, with its national vote share never exceeding 12 percent.[29] After a modest restart in 1984 under the name of the WP, its vote share rose steadily, climbing to just over 19 percent in the local elections of 1994, which gave the party control over Turkey's two largest cities and many other provincial centers. The 21.4 percent of the vote (158 parliamentary seats) that it won in the December 1995 elections represented political Islam's best national showing ever. The VP received 15.4 percent of the vote in the April 1999 elections.

Opinions vary as to the nature of the challenge that the WP represented (and which the VP now poses). The WP combined religious appeals with nonreligious ones, such as its emphases on industrialization, social justice, honest government, and the restoration of Turkey's former grandeur. It is unclear whether the WP seriously intended to establish an "Islamic state" based on the *shari'a* (sacred law) or whether it would have been satisfied by certain, mostly symbolic acts of Islamization in some areas of social life. The creation of an Islamic state is a remote possibility that would require the support of a two-thirds majority in parliament to pass an amendment to the present constitution. The party's statements on these questions were vague and contradictory enough to lend themselves to more than a single interpretation, and they ultimately led to the Constitutional Court ruling that the WP's actions were not compatible with the secular character of the state, as enshrined in the Constitution.

Ambivalence also marked the WP's views on democracy. The party's 1995 campaign platform called the present system in Turkey a "fraud," a "guided democracy," and a "dark-room regime" and announced the WP's intention to establish "real pluralistic democracy." Apart from promising to enhance freedom of conscience and make greater use of referenda and "popular councils," however, the WP never actually defined "real democracy." In the party's view, freedom of conscience implies the "right to live accordingly to one's beliefs," a concept that is bound to create conflicts with Turkey's secular legal system. The WP prudently refrained from challenging the basic premises of democracy and declares elections the only route to political power. One gets the impression, however, that the version of democracy it envisaged is more majoritarian than liberal or pluralistic. In a 1996 newspaper interview, Tayyip Erdoğan, the former mayor of Istanbul and one of the strongest candidates for party leadership after Erbakan, admitted that the WP considered democracy not so much an aim as an instrument.[30] Erbakan himself stated in the same vein that democracy is an instrument, not an aim. The aim is the establishment of an "order of happiness" *(saadet nizami)*, an apparent reference to the era of Prophet Mohammed, which is usually referred to as the "age of happiness" *(asr-i Saadet)* in Islamic writings. A leading Turkish student of the WP concluded that "the WP is neither pro-*shari'a* . . . nor democratic, because it is both pro-*shari'a* and democratic in its own way."[31] Erbakan and other party leaders often stated that there were only two groups in Turkey, the WP supporters and the potential WP supporters, a notion that is hardly compatible with a truly pluralistic conception of society.

As for the economy, the WP proposed an Islamic-inspired "just order" that it viewed as a "third way" different from and superior to both capitalism and socialism. Although the party claimed that the "just order" is the "true private-enterprise regime," its implementation, if possible at all, would require a heavy dose of state control. Many observers would agree that Islamists in Turkey have undergone a significant change in the last decades. Thus, while the NSP in the 1970s appeared as the party of the small Anatolian merchants and businessmen, the rise of an important "Muslim" bourgeoisie in the 1980s made the party much more open to the interests of the big business. Indeed, "since the 1980s, the Islamist sector in the economy has expanded, with large-scale holding companies, chain stores, investment houses, banks, and insurance companies. Particularly noteworthy are the joint businesses and investments that Islamist organizations have with international companies based in the Gulf countries."[32] Thus the WP moved away from statist, protectionist concerns to a position much more in favor of a free-market economy and Turkey's integration into the global economy.[33]

Whether the WP should be considered in retrospect an antisystem party is an open question. Certainly, it took pride in its claims to be different from all other parties. It accused them of being "mimics" that seek to ape the West and make Turkey its "satellite." The WP denounced current economic arrangements as a "slave system" that is based on the

International Monetary Fund, interest payments, taxes, corruption, and waste and is maintained by a repressive "guardian state" that contravenes the history and beliefs of its own people. The ideological chasm between the WP and the secular parties appeared quite wide. We will never know whether, if the party had not been banned by the Constitutional Court, the chasm could have been bridged in time by gradual elite convergence. Behind its radical rhetoric, the WP often showed signs of pragmatism and flexibility. For the most part, the WP mayors elected in 1994 in about 400 cities and towns, including Istanbul and Ankara, acted not like wild-eyed radicals but like reasonably honest and efficient managers. Similarly, the WP ministers in the WP-TPP coalition government, which lasted from June 1996 until June 1997, vacillated between moderate and responsible positions and highly controversial symbolic acts intended to keep radical Islamists loyal to the party.

An analysis of the attitudes and social characteristics of the WP voters also provides clues about the ambivalence of party policies and positions. Earlier research had indicated that religiosity (as defined by faith and practice of Islam and participation in religious rituals) was a major factor in determining the party preferences of Turkish voters. Thus, according to a 1990 survey, low levels of religiosity are associated with the left vote (although the DLP vote does not show a strong correlation with religiosity), while high levels of religiosity are correlated with electoral support for the MP, TPP, WP, and NAP.[34] More specifically, with regard to the association between political Islam and support for the WP, surveys show that the WP combined a religious appeal with a class appeal. According to a 1995 survey, 61.3 percent of WP voters were in favor of an Islamic political order *(şeriat düzeni),* as opposed to a minority among the supporters of other parties (31.1 percent in the NAP, 16.1 percent in the MP, 14.9 percent in the TPP, 8.3 percent in the DLP, and 4.6 percent in the RPP). On the other hand, 23.7 percent of the WP voters did not subscribe to an Islamic political order, and 15 percent had no opinion. Of all voters, 26.7 percent were in favor of an Islamic political order, as opposed to 58.1 percent who were against, and 15.2 percent who had no opinion. About 50 percent of those who were in favor of an Islamic political order saw it as an indispensable element of their religious beliefs. There are strong correlations between adherence to political Islam and the class position of the respondents: 14.3 percent of the upper and upper-middle class, 18.6 percent of the middle class, 22.9 percent of the lower-middle class, and 27.9 percent of the lower-class respondents were found to be in favor of an Islamic political order.[35]

Similarly, a December 1996 survey demonstrated that 60.6 percent of the WP voters favored the inclusion of some Islamic principles in the constitution. When voters were asked why they voted for the WP, however, only about half gave ideological reasons, such as the WP's defense of religious values (20.9 percent), its promise of a "just order" (13.4 percent), and its respect for "national and moral values" (12.5 percent). About one-third (29.6 percent) stated that they voted for the WP because they perceived it as an honest and reliable party. Also, 79.3 percent were of the opinion that the WP was the most honest party of all. About half of the WP voters seemed to follow the party line on most ideological issues. For example, 56 percent believed that the government should oblige or encourage women to wear head scarves; 49 percent were in favor of separate education for men and women; 45 percent favored separation of the sexes in public transportation; and 59.5 percent saw the Organization of Islamic Conference as the international organization best serving Turkey's interests (as opposed to a total of one-fourth for NATO, the EU, and the UN).[36]

These findings suggest that a good part of the WP's appeal was indeed founded on religious grounds. The same findings also demonstrate, however, that between one-third and one-half of the WP voters seemed to vote for it for nonideological reasons. The WP vote also correlates with the class variable. The party's call for a "just order" apparently appealed to the small farmers and the low-income groups in the cities, even though the content of the just order was never made explicit. This appeal was particularly strong in an economic environment marked by high inflation, unemployment, urban migration, deteriorating income distribution, and widespread corruption. Thus economic problems were cited by a substantial number of the WP voters as Turkey's most important problem: inflation (8.4 percent), economic growth (6.9 percent), unemployment (6.2 percent), and the deterioration of income distribution (3.2 percent). The largest group of WP voters (27.2 percent), however, saw "anarchy and terror" as Turkey's most important problem. Among the country's most urgent economic problems, unemployment ranked first (43.2 percent), followed by inflation (33.3 percent). About one-third (33.1 percent) of WP voters saw their party as the party of the poor and the oppressed, as opposed to the 53.5 percent who saw it as a party appealing to all sectors of society.[37]

Prior to the local elections of 1994, the left had won most of the municipalities in the low-income immigrant neighborhoods along the peripheries of the large cities. By the latter half of the 1990s, however, the same neighborhoods had become strongholds of the WP, evidence of the extent to which the WP had sunk strong roots among the urban poor. "WP support in metropolitan areas [was] overwhelmingly peripheral and provincial, in the sense that it rest[ed] on a politically active 'secondary elite' highly effective in mobilizing the urban, lower-middle and lower-income groups, and Kurds."[38]

The WP was stronger in rural areas (more than half of its voters were rural), and the WP vote was inversely related to years of schooling. Electoral support for the WP came disproportionately from small farmers,

blue-collar workers, small traders, and artisans, and from among the
lower and lower-middle classes.[39]
These findings go a very long way in explaining the vagueness and
ambivalence in the party's positions on issues. To appeal to the more
centrist voters who have no desire to see an Islamic state in Turkey, the
WP had to moderate its positions and move to the center, in the process
becoming a party much like the Christian Democrats in Europe. Some
observers perceived that the WP had already completed this transformation. Others noted the WP's efforts to maintain its support among
the more radical Islamists and to emphasize its differences with the
other parties along a religious-secular dimension, which risked
polarizing the conflict and even threatening democracy. The VP faces
the same dilemma, although its leaders have been much more careful
than their predecessors in using explicitly religious themes.
Organizationally, the WP was the only Turkish party that has come
close to the model of a mass party, or a party of social integration.[40] The
Islamists constitute the most organized sector of Turkish society, as
evidenced in their numerous associations, foundations, newspapers,
periodicals, publishing houses, television networks, Quran courses,
student dormitories, university preparation courses, a pro-WP trade
union (HAK-İŞ), a pro-WP businessmen's association (MÜSÁD), holding
companies, as well as such informal groups as various *sufi* orders and
other religious communities. Even though most of these groups and
organizations had no formal or direct link with the WP, they provided
a comprehensive network effectively encapsulating the individual
member and creating a distinct political subculture. Members and
opponents of the WP recognized it as representative of the Islamist
segment of civil society.
On the other hand, the WP seemed to lack the intraparty democracy
usually associated with mass parties. Membership entailed obligations
(such as taking part in the party work) rather than rights. Party policy
was made top down by a small group of leaders (Erbakan and his close
associates) who dominated the WP and its predecessors for more than a
quarter of a century, with little input from rank and file members.
(However, Erbakan and some other WP founders were barred from party
politics for five years when the WP was proscribed by the Constitutional
Court in February 1998.) There was almost no genuine intraparty debate
or competition at the party congresses, which invariably endorsed the
leadership by acclamation. In parliamentary votes, the WP deputies
displayed perfect discipline. The party had effective women's and youth
organizations that campaigned for the party not only during elections
but throughout the year. A new member was immediately introduced to
party work and given responsibilities in any of a number of committees,
including those for women, youth, workers, or polling booths. In fact,
the party's organization was based on polling-booth districts, and within

such districts, each street, sometimes even each apartment building, was
assigned to a particular member, who, among other things, had to get out
the vote on election day. Political education or indoctrination within
the party was strongly emphasized and carried out by party members
called "teachers." Each subprovince *(ilçe)* was assigned to the
responsibility of a "headmaster," and there were "inspectors" at the
provincial or regional level to supervise political education.[41]

Among its many activities, the WP organization also provided some
welfare services for its supporters. According to one report, the WP
mayor of a poor district in Istanbul distributed 1,500 tons of coal in one
winter and gave out packages of food (250 kilos each) to 3,500 families
during the holy month of Ramadan.[42] In fact, providing such welfare
services was a characteristic not only of the WP but of Islamist
organizations in general. A student of these organizations concluded
that "following the example of similar movements in other Islamic
countries, the *sufi* organizations have, in the past few years, tended to
concentrate their efforts on welfare services, of which education is one.
The economic reformist policies of the 1980s limited government
expenditure on social services and on the welfare state in general. This
in a country in which these services were only at a rudimentary state and
at a time when the rapid rural-urban exodus created widespread poverty
in cities. The religious organizations have jumped to organize relief for
the poor, medical centers, and hospitals that offer treatment schemes
and child-care programs."[43] In the final analysis, however, the rising
electoral fortunes of the WP were due more to the failure of the centrist
parties to fulfill their promises and to provide benefits to the voters and
less to the organizational prowess of the WP.[44]

The Center-Right

Since the first free multiparty elections of 1950, Turkey has been
ruled by the center-right parties, except for the periods of military rule
and the brief spells when their chief rival, the RPP, led coalition
governments. The center-right was represented by the DP in the 1950s
and by the JP in the 1960s and the 1970s. The TPP claims descent from
the JP. When the DP was closed down by the military government in
1960, three parties competed for its votes in the 1961 elections: the
Justice Party (JP), the New Turkey Party (NTP), and the Republican
Peasant Nation Party (RPNP). As a result, the former DP votes were split
among these three parties. The JP eventually established itself as the
principal heir to the DP, and in the 1965 elections won the absolute
majority of the votes and of the National Assembly seats. Following the
1971 military intervention, the center-right vote was again fragmented
among the JP, the Democrat Party (Dem. P, which was a conservative
offshoot of the JP), and the Islamist National Salvation Party (NSP).

Consequently, in the 1973 elections, the JP vote fell to 29 percent while the Dem. P and the NSP gained about 12 percent apiece. Most of the Dem. P leaders and voters returned to the fold in the 1977 elections. The NSP persisted, however, as the representative of a distinct segment of voters. Thus, toward the end of the 1970s, the Turkish party system displayed an essentially four-party format: the center-right JP, the center-left RPP, the Islamist NSP, and the ultranationalist NAP.[45]

The military regime (NSC) that ruled Turkey between 1980 and 1983 outlawed all existing parties and permitted the establishment of new ones just prior to the November 1983 elections. This was a carefully controlled process that led to a "limited choice election" that only three parties approved or licensed by the military were allowed to contest. To the surprise of many, the Motherland Party (MP) led by Turgut Özal won the elections with 45 percent of the vote and an absolute majority of the Assembly seats. The MP also won the 1987 elections with a reduced percentage of votes (36.3 percent) but an increased majority of the seats due to the favorable changes it introduced into the electoral system. The 1987 elections were held after the military-imposed ban on former political leaders and members of parliament was removed by a popular referendum, and were thus contested by the four former political leaders (Ecevit, Demirel, Erbakan, and Türkeş) at the head of their own parties.

The most noteworthy feature of party politics in the 1980s was the predominance of the MP, which gave Turkey eight years of uninterrupted single-party government, the first since 1971. The MP did not claim descent from any of the old parties. In fact, Özal always proudly asserted that he brought together all four preexisting political tendencies under the MP roof, although a majority of its votes seems to have come from former JP supporters. Statistical analysis of the party votes in the 1983 elections did not show strong correlations between the MP vote and the votes for former parties in previous elections, thereby lending support to Özal's argument that the MP was not the continuation of any of the old parties but was a new actor in Turkish politics.[46] In other words, of all the Turkish parties of the 1980s, "only . . . the Motherland Party is based on new societal cleavages and mobilization of a relatively new ideological concept known as the new right."[47] While some scholars view the MP "as an extension of the 1980 coup government," others see it as "the initiator of liberal revolutions, antibureaucratic, pluralist, modern, and able to bring together a coalition including a wide range of ideological groups," and thus a "genuine catch-all party."[48]

In the 1983 elections, the MP fared better in urban areas and in the most developed regions. It appears that it "gained support from the upwardly mobile, entrepreneurially minded, pragmatic, modernist groups that were predominantly urban and living in the developed areas of Turkey. This included considerable support from such occupational groups as the urban self-employed, businessmen and upwardly mobile urban workers."[49] The MP's urban accent continued in the subsequent elections, albeit to a more limited degree.

The coalition brought together by the MP did not prove to be enduring. The erosion of the MP support was due to increasing economic difficulties (particularly high inflation) on the one hand, and to the competition of the other right parties on the other. With the reactivation of the WP and the NAP, some of their former supporters who voted for the MP in 1983 returned to the fold. But the most dangerous competitor for the MP was the TPP. With the removal of the ban on the political activities of former politicians, Demirel became the leader of the TPP in 1987. Under his energetic leadership the party became the leading party on the center-right in the 1989 local and the 1991 parliamentary elections, thereby bringing the MP's predominance to an end. In this race the TPP, as the direct heir to the JP, had the advantage of being based on an older, more powerful, and closely knit network of local party organizations with strong clientelistic ties. By comparison, the MP was closer to a cadre party or caucus party model with relatively weak local organizations.[50]

As for the ideological differences between the two main contenders on the center-right, as opposed to the new right, free-market ideology of the MP, the TPP represented a more conservative, populist, and egalitarian ideology in the tradition of the DP and the JP. Both parties tried to appeal to the conservative voters by making references to nationalist and religious symbols. However, the MP's propaganda in the 1980s gave much more prominence to the themes of change and modernization, as was evident in Özal's slogans of "transformation" and "leaping to a new age" *(çağ atlamak)*. In contrast, the TPP engaged in a more populist discourse based on the notions of economic justice, egalitarianism, distributive policies, and a paternalistic protective state.[51] The ideological differences between the two parties have tended to disappear in recent years, however. The TPP under Tansu Çiller moved closer to Özal's free-market oriented, antipopulist, and antiwelfare policies, while the MP under Mesut Yilmaz moved closer to a Demirel-style egalitarian populism.

Public-opinion data demonstrate that the urban-rural factor is still an important variable differentiating between the MP and the TPP supporters. As of 1996, 54 percent of MP supporters (as opposed to 49 percent of TPP supporters) were urban residents. With regard to occupational categories, the TPP seems to be more popular among farmers (35 percent as opposed to 30 percent for the MP), and the MP slightly more popular among blue-collar workers and small traders and artisans. As far as the respondents' class positions are concerned, the MP seems to be doing slightly better among the lower classes, while the TPP performs better among the upper and upper-middle classes. Nevertheless, these differences are generally too small to suggest that the two center-right parties are indeed based on clearly distinguishable social bases, leading to the conclusion that the fragmentation of the center-right is due less to deep-seated sociological differences than to historical events and the clash of personalities.[52]

The Center-Left

The center-left position on the political spectrum has been occupied in recent years by two parties, the DLP of Bülent Ecevit and the RPP of Deniz Baykal, and for a while it was represented by three parties (the DLP, the RPP, and the SDPP) until the merger of the latter two. Thus the divisive effects of the 1980 military intervention can also be observed on the center-left. In the limited-choice elections of 1983, the center-left was represented by the Populist Party (PP), which the military viewed as a loyal and moderate opposition party to its first choice for winning a parliamentary majority, the Nationalist Democracy Party (NDP). On the other hand, the National Security Council did not permit the Social Democratic Party (SDP), founded by a number of former RPP politicians and headed by Erdal İnönü, the son of former president and RPP leader Ismet İnönü, which looked like a more credible heir to the RPP. The PP received 30.5 percent of the vote in the 1983 elections, but soon afterwards it decided to merge with the SDP to become the Social Democratic Populist Party (SDPP). In the meantime, Mr. Ecevit, who had strong reservations about the factional conflicts within the old RPP prior to 1980, formed his own party, the DLP. Since Ecevit, like all former political leaders, was banned from political activity, the party was headed by his wife, Rahzan Ecevit, until the ban was removed by the constitutional referendum of 1987.

The ideological differences between the DLP and the SDPP (now the RPP) are not substantial, although they are much more strongly emphasized by the DLP leaders than by the RPP leaders. A fairly important difference is that the DLP does not claim to represent the legacy of the old RPP, while the elements of continuity are much more marked between the old and new RPP. Ecevit characterizes the old RPP as too elitist, representing a notion of reform from above, "for the people but against the wishes of the people." Another difference is that while the SDPP (RPP) program gives a more prominent role to the state in economic affairs, the DLP is more inclined to diversify the economic structure by encouraging the establishment of cooperatives and produc-ers' unions in order to prevent both state and private monopolies.[53] On most other issues, however, the two parties' positions are rather similar. A 1990 survey found that the mean left-right score for SDPP supporters was 3.94, and for DLP supporters it was 4.28, putting the DLP very slightly to the right of the SDPP.[54] Similarly, a 1996 survey demon-strated that differences between the socioeconomic characteristics of the DLP and the RPP supporters were small. The RPP was stronger among the white-collar and upper and upper-middle class voters and the DLP did somewhat better in all other social categories. Although both parties draw disproportionate support from urban areas, the urban character of the DLP supporters was stronger than that of the RPP (67.9 percent urban for the DLP as opposed to 58.0 percent for the RPP).[55]

As a result of the April 1999 elections, the DLP emerged as the strongest party in the country, with 22.2 percent of the vote, while its rival RPP remained below the 10 percent threshold, with 8.7 percent of the vote. A new tripartite coalition government was formed between the DLP, the Nationalist Action Party (NAP), and the MP under the premiership of Ecevit. This unlikely coalition has turned out to be surprisingly long-lasting.

Minor Parties

Since Turkish electoral law does not permit parliamentary representation to parties that receive less than 10 percent of the total national votes cast, at present no minor party is represented in the National Assembly. The only exception is the Grand Unity Party (a religiously oriented conservative offshoot from the NAP) as it was allied with the MP in the 1995 elections and presented its candidates on MP lists. After the elections, seven deputies elected on the MP lists resigned from the MP and rejoined their old party.

The other two parties that obtained a fairly high percentage of votes but were barred from representation for failing to meet the 10 percent threshold were the NAP and the People's Democracy Party (PDP, HADEP in Turkish). The origins of the NAP go back to the mid-1960s when the party became an ultranationalist (to its opponents, a fascist) political force under the leadership of ex-colonel Alparslan Türkeş, one of the leading figures in the 1960 military intervention. The NAP played a highly polarizing role in the 1970s in the violent clashes between the extreme left and extreme right-wing groups. It appears, however, that the NAP moved to a more centrist position in the 1980s and particularly in the 1990s, although it is arguable whether the NAP moved to the center or the center moved closer to the NAP's nationalist and statist lines.[56] The NAP contested the 1991 elections in alliance with the WP and consequently was able to send some representatives to parliament. In the 1995 elections, it received 8.2 percent of the vote, barely below the national threshold. It still represents an ultranationalist position, especially with regard to the Kurdish issue, but its commitment to democratic processes is more explicit today than it was in the 1970s.[57] The NAP emerged as the second largest party with 18 percent of the vote in the 1999 elections, and it joined in the coalition government led by Ecevit.

Another fairly important minor party that was not able to pass the electoral threshold in 1995 and 1999 is the PDP (People's Democracy Party, HADEP), representing the Kurdish minority. Since both the Constitution and the Political Parties Law proscribe ethnic parties, the two predecessors of the PDP (People's Labor Party and the Democracy Party) were banned by the Constitutional Court. The PDP contested the December 1995 elections and won slightly more than 4 percent of the national vote. Most of its support came from the southeast, where the Kurdish minority is concentrated. The PDP received more than 40 percent of the vote in two southeastern provinces and more than 20 percent in six others. As long as the relevant articles of the constitution and the Political Parties Law remain unchanged, however, the PDP is likely to share the fate of its predecessors. The PDP also participated in the 1999 elections and received 4.75 percent of the vote, its support again concentrated mostly in the southeast.

Deinstitutionalization

The historical overview of Turkey's political parties and party system suggests that Turkey represents a case of deinstitutionalization. The Turkish party system until the end of 1970s was essentially a bipolar (if not a two-party) system, in which two highly organized, well-established parties with strong historical and social roots (the RPP and the DP/JP) dominated the political scene. The tendencies toward electoral volatility, party fragmentation, and ideological polarization, which had already started to affect politics adversely in the 1970s, have now reappeared in worse form after a stable, one-party MP government for a period of eight years (1983–91). These three maladies in the party system no doubt constitute an important obstacle to further democratic consolidation.

Together with these tendencies in the party *system,* there appears to be an overall decline in the organizational capabilities of political *parties* (particularly in regard to their candidate selection, electoral mobilization, and issue structuration functions) and a fall in the public esteem in which they are held. While in much of Europe organizational change in parties is generally from a mass-party to a catch-all or cartel party model, in Turkey there has been a direct leap from the cadre party to a catch-all or cartel party without having gone through a mass-party phase. To some extent, the WP provided an exception to both generalizations. It was the only Turkish party that avoided organizational decline and the only party that approximated the mass-party model. Parallel to organizational decline, there has been a sharp drop in the public's confidence in political parties, which seems to be at the lowest point ever. Parties are generally perceived as corrupt and highly oligarchical institutions run dictatorially by narrow-minded and uncompromising leaders who are unable to produce solutions to the country's pressing problems.

And yet, Turkish politics are still, by and large, party politics. Most people realize that in a democracy there is no alternative to political parties. Therefore, much of the current debate in Turkey centers around new policies aimed at making parties more democratic and responsive. It is hoped, for example, that the adoption of a single-member, double-ballot majority system will make deputies less dependent on their leaders and more responsive to their voters. Such a system may also reduce party fragmentation by forcing similar-minded parties to forge electoral alliances. Another proposed reform is to limit the leaders' influence on candidate selection by, for example, making it compulsory for all parties to hold primary elections. Finally it is hoped that by reducing the state's role in the economy, the spoils of politics would be limited and party work would be based more on idealistic motives than those of personal material gains.

The trends described above were not significantly altered by Turkey's April 1999 parliamentary elections (although they did produce some surprising results). Once again, the elections produced, as expected, a fragmented parliament with five parties passing the 10 percent national threshold. The two big winners of the elections were the DLP of Ecevit, with 22.2 percent of the vote, and the NAP of Devlet Bahçeli (who became the leader of the party upon the death of Alparslan Türkeş), with 18.0 percent. The two main losers were the two center-right parties, the MP and the TPP, whose votes fell from about 19 percent apiece, to 13.2 and 12.0 percent, respectively. Also among the losers were the Virtue Party (from 21.4 percent for the WP in 1995 to 15.4 percent) and the RPP (from 10.7 percent to 8.7 percent). Thus the RPP, the oldest party of the Republic, remained below the 10 percent threshold and was unable to send any representatives to the parliament. Neither was the Kurdish nationalist HADEP (PDP), which only slightly increased its votes to 4.75 percent. In terms of electoral volatility, the 1999 elections were the most volatile in the last decade.

Issues played a relatively unimportant role in the campaign. The DLP's and the NAP's gains owed to their "clean" images. Conversely, the MP and the TPP apparently suffered from charges of corruption, as well as from the bitter feud between the two parties. The VP's significant loss of support was another important feature of the elections. It seems that the protest votes that went to the WP in 1995 this time switched mainly to the NAP.

Perhaps even more importantly, the 1999 elections confirmed the trend toward identity politics in Turkey. Three parties that define themselves mainly in terms of identity-oriented issues (the NAP representing Turkish nationalist identity, the VP representing Islamic identity, and the HADEP representing Kurdish ethnic identity) together received a total of 38 percent of the vote. To this must be added the growing identity consciousness among the Alevis (Turkish Shi'ites), even though their votes were split among different parties. The rising importance of identity-oriented issues can be considered another source of difficulty in the development of Turkey's party system in a more consensual and pragmatic direction.

NOTES

1. Frederick W. Frey, *The Turkish Political Elite* (Cambridge, Mass.: The M.I.T. Press, 1965), 301–3. On the importance of party-system institutionalization for democratic consolidation, see also Larry Diamond, "Democracy in Latin America: Degrees, Illusions, and Directions for Consolidation," in Tom Farer, ed., *Beyond Sovereignty: Collectively Defending Democracy in the Americas* (Baltimore: Johns Hopkins University Press, 1995), 78–81.

2. Üstün Ergüder and Richard I. Hofferbert, "The 1983 General Elections in Turkey: Continuity or Change in Voting Patterns?" in Metin Heper and Ahmet Evin, eds., *State, Democracy, and Military: Turkey in the 1980s* (Berlin: Walter de Gruyter, 1988), 81–102. Ergun Özbudun, "The Turkish Party System: Institutionalization, Polarization, and Fragmentation," *Middle Eastern Studies* 17 (April 1981): 228–40.

3. Douglas W. Rae, *The Political Consequences of Electoral Laws* (New Haven: Yale University Press, 1967), 56.

4. For this distinction, see Giovanni Sartori, *Parties and Party Systems: A Framework for Analysis* (Cambridge University Press, 1976), 131–45.

5. Leonardo Morlino, "Political Parties and Democratic Consolidation in Southern Europe," in Richard Gunther, P. Nikiforos Diamandouros, and Hans-Jürgen Puhle, eds., *The Politics of Democratic Consolidation: Southern Europe in Comparative Perspective* (Baltimore: John Hopkins University Press, 1995), 321.

6. Yilmaz Esmer, "Dini Değerler Yükselişte" (Religious values on the rise), *Milliyet,* 9 April 1997.

7. Samuel P. Huntington, *The Third Wave: Democratization in the Late Twentieth Century* (Norman: University of Oklahoma Press, 1991), 255–58.

8. Larry Diamond, "Democracy in Latin America," 77; Juan Linz and Alfred Stepan, "Political Crafting of Democratic Consolidation or Destruction: European and South American Comparisons," in Robert A. Pastor, ed., *Democracy in the Americas: Stopping the Pendulum* (New York: Holmes and Meier, 1989), 47.

9. Guillermo O'Donnell, "Transitions, Continuities, and Paradoxes," in Scott Mainwaring, Guillermo O'Donnell, and J. Samuel Valenzuela, eds., *Issues in Democratic Consolidation: The New South American Democracies in Comparative Perspective* (Notre Dame: University of Notre Dame Press, 1992), 21. See also Scott Mainwaring, "Transitions to Democracy and Democratic Consolidation: Theoretical and Comparative Issues," *idem,* 311.

10. Maurice Duverger, *Political Parties: Their Organization and Activity in the Modern State* (London: Methuen, 1959), 61–79.

11. Arsev Bektaş, *Demokratikleşme Sürecinde Liderler Oligarşisi, CHP ve AP (1961–1980)* (Leadership oligarchy in the process of democratization), (Istanbul: Bağlam, 1993), 39–52, 133–37; Sabri Sayari, "Aspects of Party Organization in Turkey," *The Middle East Journal* 30 (Spring 1976): 188–89.

12. TÜSES Veri Araştirma A.Ş., *Türkiye'de Siyasî Parti Seçmenlerinin Nitelikleri, Kimlikleri ve Eğilimleri* (Characteristics, identities, and tendencies of party voters in Turkey) (Ankara: TÜSES, 1996), 95.

13. Sabri Sayari, 197–99.

14. TÜSES, 132–33.

15. Ersin Kalaycioğlu, "Elections and Party Preferences in Turkey: Changes and Continuities in the 1990s," *Comparative Political Studies* 27 (October 1994): 403. See also Şerif Mardin, "Center-Periphery Relations: A Key to Turkish Politics," *Daedalus* (Winter 1972): 169–90; Metin Heper, *The State Tradition in Turkey* (Walkington, England: Eothen, 1985); Ergun Özbudun, *Social Change and Political Participation in Turkey* (Princeton, N.J.: Princeton University Press, 1976), ch.2.

16. Ersin Kalaycioğlu, 407.

17. Sabri Sayari, "Some Notes on the Beginnings of Mass Political Participation in Turkey," in Engin D. Akarli with Gabriel Ben-Dor, eds., *Political Participation in Turkey: Historical Background and Present Problems* (Istanbul: Boğaziçi University Publications, 1975), 123–25. See also Paul Stirling, *Turkish Village* (New York: Wiley, 1965), 281–82.

18. Metin Heper, *The State Tradition in Turkey,* 100–1.

19. TÜSES, 93–94. Obviously, these figures do not include informal groups such as religious communities and *sufi* orders.

20. A typical example is a frank admission by Abdullah Gül, a former minister of state and a leading figure in the WP that "what counts is our performance in the government, not what the voters were told." *Milliyet,* 20 February 1997.

21. Arsev Bektaş, *passim.*

22. E. Shattschneider, *Party Government* (New York: Holt, Rinehart and Winston, 1942), 64.

23. For comparisons, see Michael Gallagher, "Conclusion," in Michael Gallagher and Michael Marsh, eds., *Candidate Selection in Comparative Perspective; The Secret Garden of Politics* (London: Sage Publications, 1988), 236–45.

24. TÜSES, 121–22, 127–28.

25. Yilmaz Esmer, "Birbirimize Güvenmiyoruz" (We don't trust each other), *Milliyet,* 8 April 1997. See also TÜSIAD (Association of Turkish Industrialists and Businessmen), *Türk Toplumunun Değerleri* (Values of Turkish society) (Istanbul, 1991), 22–23.

26. For the distinction between valence issues and position issues, see William Schneider, "Electoral Behavior and Political Development," mimeo., Harvard University, Center for International Affairs, 1972. Valence issues "are characterized by only *one* body of opinion on values or goals. They define a condition or a situation which is highly valued by the electorate, and political leaders do not take one side or the other. Valence issues are exemplified by peace and prosperity."

27. Huri Türsan, "Pernicious Party Factionalism as a Constant of Transitions to Democracy in Turkey," *Democratization* 2 (Spring 1995): 169–84.

28. Richard S. Katz and Peter Mair, "Changing Models of Party Organization and Party Democracy: The Emergence of the Cartel Party," *Party Politics* 1 (January

1995): 5–28. For a slightly modified version of this scheme, see Klaus Von Beyme, "Party Leadership and Change in Party Systems: Towards a Postmodern Party State," *Government and Opposition* 31 (Spring 1996): 135–59.

29. On the NSP period, see Binnaz Toprak, *Islam and Political Development in Turkey* (Leiden: E.J. Brill, 1981); Jacob M. Landau, "The National Salvation Party in Turkey," *Asian and African Studies* 11 (1976): 1–57; Ergun Özbudun, "Islam and Politics in Modern Turkey: The Case of the National Salvation Party," in Barbara Freyer Stowasser, ed., *The Islamic Impulse* (London: Croom Helm, 1987), 142–56; Ali Yaşar Saribay, *Türkiye'de Modernleşme, Din ve Parti Politikasi: MSP Örnek Olayi* (Modernization, religion and party politics in Turkey: A case study on the NSP), (Istanbul: Alan, 1985).

30. *Milliyet,* 14 July 1996.

31. Ruşen Çakir, *Ne Şeriat, Ne Demokrasi: Refah Partisini Anlamak* (Neither the *shar'ia* nor democracy: Understanding the Welfare Party), (Istanbul: Metis, 1994), 128–29.

32. Sencer Ayata, "Patronage, Party and State: The Politicization of Islam in Turkey," *Middle East Journal* 50 (Winter 1996), 51.

33. Serdar Şen, *Refah Partisinin Teori ve Pratiği* (Theory and practice of the Welfare Party), (Istanbul: Sarmal, 1995).

34. Ersin Kalaycioğlu, 420–21.

35. TÜSES, 67–76, 118–19.

36. PIAR, "Siyasal Islamin Ayak Sesleri" (Footsteps of political Islam), unpubl. ms., 1997, 4, 14, 16, 19, 31.

37. PIAR, 9, 12, 21.

38. Sencer Ayata, 54.

39. TÜSES, 106–16.

40. For parties of social integration, see Sigmund Neumann, "Toward a Comparative Study of Political Parties," in Sigmund Neumann, ed., *Modern Political Parties: Approaches to Comparative Politics* (Chicago: The University of Chicago Press, 1956), 404–5.

41. Ruşen Çakir, 51–52, 71–73. See also Serdar Şen, 79–101 and Sencer Ayata, 52.

42. Ruşen Çakir, 185.

43. Sencer Ayata, 50–51.

44. Morton Abramowitz, quoted by Ilkay Sunar, "State, Society, and Democracy in Turkey," in Wojtech Mastny and R. Craig Nation, eds., *Turkey between East and West: New Challenges for a Rising Regional Power* (Boulder, Colo.: Westview Press, 1996), 151.

45. On the dynamics of the party system in the late 1970s, see Ergun Özbudun, "The Turkish Party System: Institutionalization, Polarization and Fragmentation," *Middle Eastern Studies* 17 (April 1981): 228–40; on the RPP for the 1945–1980 period, see Frank Tachau, "The Republican People's Party, 1945–1980," in Metin Heper and Jacob M. Landau, eds., *Political Parties and Democracy in Turkey*

(London: I.B. Tauris. 1991), 99–118; for the JP, see Avner Levi, "The Justice Party, 1961–1980," in ibid., 134–51.

46. Üstün Ergüder and Richard I. Hofferbert, 81, 102. See also Üstün Ergüder, "The Motherland Party, 1983–1989," in Metin Heper and Jacob M. Landau, eds., *Political Parties and Democracy in Turkey*, 152–69.

47. Ayşe Ayata, "Ideology, Social Bases, and Organizational Structure of the Post-1980 Political Parties," in Atila Eralp, Muharrem Tünay, and Birol Yeşilada, eds., *The Political and Socioeconomic Transformation of Turkey* (Westport, Conn.: Praeger, 1993), 32.

48. Ibid., 33, 37.

49. Ibid., 35.

50. Ibid., 38, 40. Feride Acar reports that as of October 1988, about 70 percent of the local heads of the TPP were former JP members: "The True Path Party, 1983–1989," in Heper and Landau, eds., *Political Parties and Democracy in Turkey*, 190.

51. Feride Acar, 193–97. Ümit Cizre Sakallioğlu, "Liberalism, Democracy and the Turkish Centre-Right: The Identity Crisis of the True Path Party," *Middle Eastern Studies* 32 (April 1996): 142–61.

52. TÜSES, 107, 113, 115.

53. Andrew Mango, "The Social Democratic Populist Party, 1983–1989," in Metin Heper and Jacob M. Landau, eds., *Political Parties and Democracy in Turkey*, 170–87; Şahin Alpay and Seyfettin Gürsel, *DSP-SHP: Nerede Birleşiyorlar, Nerede Ayriliyorlar?* (DLP-SDPP: Where do they agree, where do they differ?), (Istanbul: Afa, 1986).

54. Ersin Kalaycioğlu, 415. See also Yilmaz Esmer, "Parties and the Electorate: A Comparative Analysis of Voter Profiles of Turkish Political Parties," in Çiğdem Balim et al., eds., *Turkey: Political, Social and Economic Challenges in the 1990s* (Leiden: E. J. Brill, 1995), 84–85.

55. TÜSES, 107, 113, 115.

56. Ayşe Kadioğlu, "Samurai Sendromu ve MHP" (The Samurai syndrome and the NAP), *Yeni Yüzyil* (daily), 12 April 1997.

57. For the NAP, see Jacob M. Landau, "The Nationalist Action Party in Turkey," *Journal of Contemporary History* 17 (1982): 587–606; Mustafa Çalik, *Siyasî Kültür ve Sosyolojinin Bazi Kavramlari Açisindan MHP Hareketi: Kaynaklari ve Gelişimi* (The NAP movement, its sources and development in terms of political culture and certain sociological concepts), (Ankara: Cedit, 1995).

11

THE LEGACY OF ONE-PARTY HEGEMONY IN TAIWAN

Yun-han Chu

Yun-han Chu is professor of political science at National Taiwan University, and he serves concurrently as president of the Chiang Ching-kuo Foundation for International Scholarly Exchange. He is the author, coauthor, editor, or coeditor of ten books. Among his recent English publications are Crafting Democracy in Taiwan *(1992),* Consolidating the Third Wave Democracies *(1997), and* China Under Jiang Zemin *(2000).*

Among the third-wave democracies, Taiwan (the Republic of China, or ROC) is the only case where a quasi-Leninist party not only survived an authoritarian breakdown but capitalized on the crisis to its advantage, at least for a long while.[1] The Kuomintang (KMT, or Nationalist Party), an intrinsic part of the old regime, managed to engineer a transition from a one-party authoritarian regime to what T.J. Pempel termed "a one-party dominant regime."[2] In the process, it stretched its undisrupted rule on the island for another 15 years, from the beginning of democratic transition around 1985–86 until its stunning defeat in the March 2000 presidential election. Altogether, the KMT ruled continuously in Taiwan for more than 50 years and enjoyed eight decades of undisrupted rule dating back to its heyday on the Chinese mainland.

The particular mode and outcome of Taiwan's regime transition provides us with a rare opportunity to examine the various ways in which a hegemonic party can determine the characteristics of its emerging competitors, the parameters of electoral competition, the institutionalization of the party system, and the quality of the new representative democracy, as well as the prospect for its consolidation.[3] For the KMT has not been just a political party in the normal sense. For five decades, it organized the society that it governed, structured the political arena, and articulated a worldview, grounded in historically specific socio-political conditions, that lent substance and coherence to its political domination.

From a comparative perspective, the Taiwan case exemplifies a possible evolutionary trajectory by which a former Leninist party may transform itself into a mass-based party with a pluralistic rather than proto-hegemonic orientation. The old KMT conformed to many of the organizational and operational characteristics of Leninist parties as defined by Richard Gunther and Larry Diamond in chapter 1 of this volume. In particular, there was a symbiosis between the party and the state, and the party-state organized and penetrated the society. The KMT's Leninist legacy stemmed from its close cooperation with the Soviet Union around the mid-1920s. Unlike the Leninist regimes of the Soviet bloc, however, the KMT had a long and firm association with the West; permitted private property rights, markets, and at least a partial rule of law; and enjoyed the support of a distinctive development coalition. Another feature that set the KMT apart from other Leninist parties was its early implementation of limited electoral competition at the local level. Over time, the competitive logic of local elections compelled the KMT to open its closed structure, relax the selection criteria of party membership, and actively recruit members from the native Taiwanese elite stratum less on the basis of ideological commitment than on the demonstrated capacity to mobilize votes. In addition, the export-oriented industrialization strategy implemented under KMT rule delivered rapid growth with equity. Thus, on the eve of democratic transition, the KMT inherited from its one-party authoritarian rule not only an established pattern of electoral dominance but also a development strategy with extensive social support.

The Taiwan case also demonstrates the critical and problematic role of a quasi-Leninist party in shaping the democratic transition and structuring the new representative democracy. The process of democratic transition necessitates a complete overhaul of a Leninist party's structural relationships with the state, political society, and civil society.[4] Democratization required the KMT to release its partisan grip on the state bureaucracy, the military, the judiciary, and agents of political socialization (such as schools and mass media), to put its governing position at risk in a democratic contest, to renounce its manipulation over basic rules of political contestation, and to relinquish its monopoly on political recruitment and on interest representation and aggregation. However, none of these transformations can be completed without struggles. The KMT had every incentive to contain the scope of democratic reform. This risked preserving certain residual authoritarian elements in the new regime. Thus, from the perspective of consolidating Taiwan's new democracy, the historic power rotation that occurred in 2000 was long overdue.

As a longstanding hegemonic party, the KMT shaped the emerging party system through its power of institution making. In particular, the electoral system for representative bodies reinforced a decentralized and spatially segmented power structure. The electoral system also obstructed the KMT's competitors from developing strong organizational ties with emerging groups in civil society. As a hegemonic party, the KMT also shaped the party system with its power of political caging, that is, containment of political actors behind clear, fixed, and confined social and ideological boundaries.[5] And it severely constrained the growth of party opposition by filling up most of the organizational space in the society and locking in the support of key constituencies.

Taiwan's case illustrates why the political legacy of persistent hegemony by a quasi-Leninist party is at best a mixed blessing for democracy. In Taiwan, this legacy generated a very uneven development of the competitive party system from the very beginning. The new competitive party system was instantly endowed with established patterns of ubiquitous presence of partisan politics in all organized sectors of the society, all-encompassing social mobilization in electoral contests, and a monopoly by political parties in elite recruitment and organizing the political process. As a consequence, the party system manifested many superficial signs of maturity—a high overall level of party enrollment, a high density of networks between parties and organized sectors of the society, and a rather high degree of crystallization in the formation of partisan allegiance. Thus electoral volatility has been surprisingly low for a new democracy. Yet in some important respects, the party system is democratically shallow and politically unstable. The organizational integrity of the hegemonic party remained heavily dependent on its control of the state. Yet this long grip on power had given it structural, financial, and political advantages that (in conjunction with an impressive adaptability) kept the electoral field tilted. Finally, the omnipresent political parties severely compressed the space for an autonomous civil society. Thus while most maturing democracies are mourning over the decline of political parties, Taiwan's new democracy may be burdened not only with an excess of power and penetration of political parties but also a deficiency of elec-toral competitiveness and uncertainty.

As such, when the Democratic Progressive Party (DPP), the major opposition party that emerged with democratization, won governing responsibility for the first time in 2000, it encountered all kinds of difficulties adapting to the existing institutional arrangements that were mainly crafted by the KMT for the purpose of its own continued dominance. The historic power rotation opened up possibilities for cleansing the system of its residual authoritarian elements and deepening democracy. It did this in several ways: by undermining the state corporatist arrangements, loosening the KMT's grip on organized interests, dissolving the partisan allegiance of state bureaucrats and military officers, and redressing the gross asymmetry in resources between the KMT and other parties. At the same time, Taiwan's new democracy remains burdened with the multifaceted legacies of the KMT's five decades of rule, and the turbulent disintegration of one-party-dominant rule into a much more competitive and fluid system complicates the task of democratic governance.

The Authoritarian Legacies

The KMT regime entered the 1970s with a proven formula for maintaining the political dominance of the (minority) mainlander elite at the national level and for controlling limited popular elections at the local level.[6] The KMT's core commitment to Chinese nationalism formed the legitimating pillar of its one-party authoritarian rule on Taiwan. The KMT maintained a stable political order through an elaborate ideology akin to socialism, a cohesive and highly penetrating party apparatus organized along Leninist democratic-centralist lines, and a powerful and pervasive but less visible security apparatus reinforced by martial law. The party apparatus consisted of crosscutting functional units organized along both geographical and corporatist (sectoral) lines.[7] Layers of encompassing associations or federations were created by the state under the party stewardship. Beginning in 1950, native Taiwanese were allowed to elect their representatives up to the provincial level and executive heads up to the county/city level.[8] To consolidate its political dominance on a new social soil, the KMT adopted an inclusive recruitment policy beginning in the mid-1950s. Party membership jumped dramatically during the 1960s and 1970s, peaking at almost one-sixth of the entire adult male population.[9] During these early decades, the party accumulated tremendous financial, organizational, and ideological resources, including a complex web of party-run or party-invested enterprises, a major television network,[10] newspapers, and leading radio stations.[11]

At the grassroots level, the KMT incorporated existing patron-client networks into the party structure. Within each administrative district below the provincial level, the KMT nurtured and kept at least two competing local factions striving for public offices and for a share of region-based economic rents.[12] Sitting on top of this, the central leadership could claim the overall electoral victory delivered by disparate local factions. All factions were geographically bound. The party effectively blocked any attempts to form an island-wide political alliance among local factions. Thus the party effectively turned the competitive logic and screening mechanism of local elections into an instrument of legitimation, political control, and selective incorporation. On the eve of the democratic opening, the KMT, as a political organization, had already undergone significant transformation, moving further away from the classic Leninist model and closer to a mass-based party supplemented by a clientelistic structure in the rural area.

The Emergence of a Competitive Party System

The political system installed by the KMT was never a full-fledged Leninist regime, which denies the validity of dissent and open

contestation in principle. The official ideology of the KMT did not
challenge democratic norms in principle. Rather, it defended the
authoritarian arrangements on the ground that the country was under
imminent military threat from the rival communist regime on the mainland. Thus authoritarian rule was based on extraconstitutional legal
arrangements and emergency decrees that replaced or superseded many
important provisions of the ROC Constitution.[13]

Under the ROC Constitution, the Executive Yuan (the cabinet) and
the Legislative Yuan (the parliament) constitute the principal axes of a
complicated five-branch (yuan) national government. The other three
independent branches in this system are the Control Yuan (an
ombudsman agency), the Judicial Yuan, and the Examination Yuan
(responsible for the civil-service system). On top of the five Yuans is the
National Assembly, which was bestowed with the power to elect the
president and amend the constitution. The KMT regime also intentionally
retained a cumbersome four-tier administrative system designed for all
of China (with national, provincial/municipal, county/city, and town/
borough levels).

To contain limited political pluralism, the KMT employed the singular
nontransferable vote (SNTV)[14] system for election of representative
bodies at all levels. The SNTV system places a premium on organized,
reliable votes. This electoral design enabled the KMT to implement a
strategy of divide-and-rule. The fierce competition among KMT-
sanctioned factions left little space for non-KMT candidates. At the same
time, in each district, the party secretariat made sure that no faction
could establish political dominance in a given county by controlling
the "iron votes" of key constituencies (loyalist mainlanders, state
employees, and military personnel).

By the beginning of the 1970s, drastic changes in the external
environment compelled the ruling elite to respond to the rising popular
demand for political opening. Limited electoral opening of national
representative bodies was first instituted in 1972, expanded in 1980 and
again in 1989. Each time a greater percentage of the seats in the
Legislative Yuan (LY) as well as the National Assembly was subject to
popular reelection, known as supplementary election. This gradual
expansion of national electoral competition gave rise to a loose anti-
KMT coalition of independent candidates with national political aims,
known as *Tangwai* (literally "outside-the-party"). *Tangwai* candidates
used the electoral process to fan popular aspirations for democratic reform
and a separate identity for Taiwan. Emboldened by their electoral success,
Tangwai candidates steadily moved closer to forming a quasi-party
during the early 1980s. On the eve of the December 1986 supplemental
LY election, *Tangwai* leaders formally founded the Democratic
Progressive Party (DPP) in open defiance of the official ban on new
parties.[15]

The decision by President Chiang Ching-kuo (CCK) to tolerate the formation of the DPP and the subsequent announcement (one week later) of his intention to lift martial law and terminate many long-time political bans pushed the process of authoritarian breakdown past the point of no return. To maintain control over the transition outcome, the KMT leadership favored a formula of "democratization by installment" that lasted almost a decade. Through a multistage constitutional reform, the KMT managed to ensure an orderly sequencing of democratic opening. The first reelection of the National Assembly in December 1991 was followed by the first reelection of the LY in December 1992, then by the first popular elections for the executives of Taiwan Province and the two municipalities (Taipei and Kaohsiung) in 1994. Thus the decisiveness normally associated with a "founding election" was diluted and the risk dispersed among a series of national elections.

The KMT's landslide victory in the 1991 National Assembly election gave the incumbent elite a virtual blank check for revising the constitution over the next four years. However, the natural tendency of the incumbent elite to limit the scope of democratic reform was partially arrested by a succession crisis following the death of CCK in January 1988. Lee Teng-hui, a native Taiwanese who (as vice-president) succeeded to the presidency, initially enjoyed a very limited power base within the party-state apparatus. In attempting to consolidate power, Lee and his allies, dubbed "the Mainstream Faction" (MF) by local media, clashed with entrenched old-timers, the so-called "Non-Mainstream Faction" (NMF), over control of the party, the scope of democratic reform, and, most fundamentally, national identity.[16] The MF persistently pushed for the removal of all legal restrictions on the advocacy of independence, popular election of the president, and a redefinition of the ROC's sovereign status.

The intraparty power struggle provided a strategic opening for the DPP, which sided with Lee at all crucial junctures of the power struggle between the MF and NMF. This tacit grand coalition between the DPP and the MF culminated in their joint effort to oust Premier Hau Pei-tsun, the leader of the NMF. The downfall of Hau after the December 1992 LY election triggered a formal split in the KMT. Some leading figures of the NMF broke away from the KMT to establish the New Party (NP) in August 1993. The marginalization of the NMF cleared a major obstacle for the MF to negotiate in a pact-making spirit with the DPP over further constitutional changes.

Although the KMT made some concessions to the DPP, the dynamics of constitutional change were largely driven by the KMT's internal politics. Before the NMF was pushed out of the ring, the overriding concern of the MF was to consolidate the power of President Lee by transforming the system from parliamentary to semipresidential. Subsequently, the MF shifted its concern to restoring the party's directive authority over the legislature as the party leadership's grip on executive power was threatened by a shrinking parliamentary majority and a more assertive KMT parliamentary caucus. Toward the end of 1996, Lee Teng-hui became alarmed by the political ambition of James Soong, the first popularly elected governor of Taiwan Province, whose meteoric surge in popularity began to threaten the presidential prospect of Lee's heir apparent, Vice-President Lien Chan. To deal with these institutional and political challenges, Lee and his inner circle pressed two major initiatives during the fourth round of constitutional change in 1997. To give the president a free hand in shaping the cabinet, they sought to remove the requirement of parliamentary confirmation of the premier. To undercut the rising Soong, they sought to scale down the provincial government and suspend all elections at the provincial level.

The DPP agreed to these constitutional changes in exchange for a realignment of power relations among the president, the premier, and the parliament. The resulting constitutional order now resembles the semipresidentialism of the French Fifth Republic except for four important differences: The president is elected by a plurality; the president can dissolve the parliament only when the legislature votes no confidence against a sitting cabinet; the parliament cannot initiate another vote of no confidence against the same premier within one year of its last failed attempt; and neither the president nor the cabinet is empowered with any lever to steer the legislative agenda. The revised constitution, however, is not adequately designed to cope with divided government. There is no built-in mechanism to break a deadlock between the president and the assembly during a period of *cohabitation*. The president cannot improve his position in the parliament through an early election as long as the majority party in the parliament refuses to force a resolution through a vote of no confidence.

While the DPP has played second fiddle in the game of institutional change, it has nailed down better statutory protection for its coveted status as the principal opposition. Over the years, the KMT yielded to the DPP's demands for free media time for major parties during the official campaign period for national elections, a public-funded subsidy to qualified parties and candidates, and (to discourage splinter parties) a 5 percent threshold for the one-fifth of parliamentary seats elected by proportional representation.[17] Over the short run, the KMT's Mainstream Faction seemed to be the major beneficiary of the four-stage constitutional revision. It accomplished at least four political objectives—to marginalize rival factions within the KMT, to buttress the executive's authority over the legislature, to reconsolidate the party's governing position under a competitive regime, and to harness the antisystem propensity of the DPP. Little did the MF know, however, that its constitutional tinkering was planting the seed for the party's stunning defeat a few years later. The attempt to disarm James Soong politically

TABLE 1—OUTCOMES OF RECENT PARLIAMENTARY ELECTIONS

	DECEMBER 1992			DECEMBER 1995			DECEMBER 1998		
	SEATS	SEAT RATIO	POPULAR VOTE	SEATS	SEAT RATIO	POPULAR VOTE	SEATS	SEAT RATIO	POPULAR VOTE
KMT	101	62.7%	52.5%	85	51.8%	46.1%	123	54.7%	46.4%
DPP	51	31.7%	30.8%	54	32.9%	33.2%	70	31.1%	29.6%
NEW PARTY	--	--	--	21	12.8%	13.0%	11	4.9%	7.1%
OTHERS*	9	5.6%	16.7%	4	2.4%	7.8%	21	9.3%	17.0%
TOTAL	161			164			225		

* Including independent and smaller parties' candidates
Source: Central Election Commission, Executive Yuan.

caused irreparable damage to the party's coherence and eventually drove Soong and his numerous followers to leave the party and launch their independent presidential bid.

Emerging Patterns of Electoral Competition

Before the founding of the DPP in 1986, the KMT-affiliated local factions and the party apparatus had together consistently delivered majorities of more than two-thirds in popular votes and more than three-quarters in seats in elections for representative bodies at all levels. As democratization unfolded, however, the KMT became increasingly hard-pressed to maintain a solid majority in parliament and dominance over subnational elective offices through its traditional means of electoral mobilization (patron-client networks, lineage and communal ties, and vote buying). In the LY election of December 1992—the first time the KMT formally staked its governing position in a democratic contest—the DPP expanded from 28.2 percent to almost a third of the popular vote, while the KMT slipped from 60.6 percent to only 52.5 percent. Still, the KMT managed to win more than 60 percent of the seats due to its superior organizational ability to equalize votes among its candidates (a key determinant of success in the SNTV system). From this point on, the KMT suffered visible erosion of its electoral support and its vote-equalizing ability. In the December 1995 LY election, the KMT's popular vote sunk to an all-time low of 46 percent, reducing the KMT's majority in the LY to a razor-thin margin of three seats. Three years later, with the same percentage of the popular vote, the KMT expanded its parliamentary seat majority to a more comfortable margin (see Table 1 above).

The eclipse of the KMT's electoral dominance was inevitable. First, the social transformation brought about by rapid industrialization and the accompanying demographic changes tended to erode the mobilizing capacity of the local factions. Next, the mobilization by various social movements of the 1980s loosened the firm grip of the party-state on civil society. In addition, the KMT's monopoly control of the electronic media waned over time with the rise of independent radio and cable TV news

FIGURE—CHANGE OF ELECTORATE'S PARTY ID (1984–99)

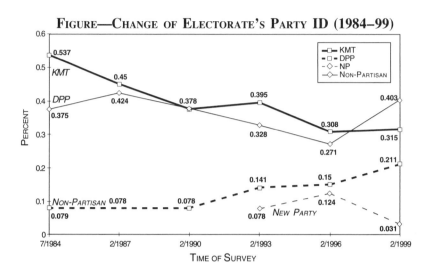

channels. Last but not least, the KMT could no longer resort to repressive measures to constrain the opposition.

At the same time, democratization triggered a process of party dealignment. A large portion of the adult male population that had joined the KMT involuntarily during the authoritarian years chose to withdraw or abstain. The active dues-paying members declined from a peak of 2.1 million in the early 1980s to less than a million by the late 1990s. As the KMT grew increasingly arrogant, complacent, and corrupt after several decades of rule, its base of committed supporters also shrank precipitously. The proportion of voters with a psychological attachment to the KMT dropped from 53 percent before the political opening to less than 40 percent around the early 1990s and to barely over 30 percent after the NP broke off (see the Figure above). On the other hand, as the direct successor to the anti-KMT coalition during the democratic struggle, the DPP was endowed at its birth with a sizable "natural constituency" of people who had developed strong anti-KMT sentiments under authoritarian rule.

Another immediate factor explaining the KMT's electoral decline was its strained relationship with local factions. In the past, the nominating authority of the KMT had been built upon its ability to construct long-term, multifaceted bargains among competing factions. With intensified electoral competition, however, both the ability of the party to deliver on long-term promises and the willingness of local factions to stay within binding agreements deteriorated. Also, the defection of the traditional loyalists, who became alienated by the swift Taiwanization of the party leadership and the marginalization of the NMF, deprived the local party secretariat of important leverage over the local factions. This diminished leverage, in turn, hampered the party's

TABLE 2—ELECTORAL OUTCOMES OF TOP EXECUTIVE OFFICES
(1994–2000)

	KMT	DPP	NEW PARTY	PFP	OTHERS
1994 GUBERNATORIAL ELECTION	56.22%	38.72%	4.31%	--	0.75%
1996 PRESIDENTIAL ELECTION[1]	54.00%	21.13%	14.90%	--	9.98%
2000 PRESIDENTIAL ELECTION[2]	23.10%	39.30%	0.13%	36.80%	0.63%
TAIPEI MAYOR RACE					
1994	25.89%	43.67%	30.17%	--	0.28%
1998	51.13%	45.91%	2.97%	--	--
KAOHSIUNG MAYOR RACE					
1994	54.46%	39.29%	3.45%	--	2.79%
1998	48.13%	48.71%	0.81%	--	2.53%

[1] The New Party did not nominate its own candidates; instead, it endorsed the Lin-Hau ticket.
[2] James Soong actually ran as an independent in the 2000 presidential election, and he founded the PFP only afterward.
Source: Central Election Commission.

ability to limit candidate nominations, distribute the party vote, and so optimize the party's showing under the SNTV rule. Increasingly, disgruntled factions defied the party nomination decisions and threw their political weight behind candidates without party endorsement. Popular election of the president and provincial governor turned out to be a double-edged design. On the one hand, it offered the KMT's top leaders a chance to redefine the parameters of electoral competitiveness and to move the center of electoral gravity away from representative bodies to executive offices. It enabled the KMT leadership to develop new and direct mobilization mechanisms, bypassing the local factions, and to translate the national acceptance of its platform, the popularity of its national leadership (especially Lee Teng-hui), and its incumbency advantage into tangible electoral gains. On the other hand, direct popular election for the top executive offices posed a strong challenge to the party's organizational coherence. The aggrandizement of the presidential office turned the political succession within the party increasingly into a "winner-take-all" game, leaving losers much less incentive to remain within the party. It became more difficult to construct a power-sharing scheme among major contenders for the party nomination and even more difficult to sustain a collective leadership afterward. At the same time, the penetrating power of the modern media enables a charismatic politician to build up a potent candidate-centered campaign apparatus as a substitute for the party's elaborate political machine. As it turned out, intraparty power struggles and the resulting breakaway of splinter factions provided a more immediate and powerful explanation for the KMT's electoral misfortunes in key executive races. The KMT paid its first heavy toll in the 1994 election for Taipei mayor, in which the DPP candidate, Chen Shui-bian, carried the race with 43.7 percent as the KMT and NP candidates divided up the traditional KMT constituents. Next, the electoral surge of the NP accounted for much of the KMT's setback in the 1995 LY election. In the 1997 elections for city and county executives, the breakdown of discipline within the KMT was so rampant that the party lost two-thirds of the seats, with the DPP winning a narrow majority of seats. In the 1998 LY election, however, the disarray within the New Party helped the KMT to reverse its electoral slide slightly (see Table 1 on p. 273). And in the concurrent race for mayor of Taipei, Chen Shui-bian was defeated in his bid for reelection by the KMT's Ma Ying-jeou, who, as a popular mainlander candidate, was able to woo back most NP supporters to the KMT (see Table 2 on the previous page).

Prior to 2000, the DPP had never won more than 35 percent of the vote in a national election. This led most observers to figure that the DPP could only win a presidential election if the KMT split and two contenders divided the other 65 percent of the vote fairly evenly. To prevent such a calamity in the 2000 presidential election, many supporters of Lien Chan and other pragmatists within the KMT sought early on to bring Lien and James Soong together into a "dream ticket." But there was no getting past the absolute opposition of President Lee, the KMT chairman, who was obsessed with stopping Soong and mistakenly believed that his personal popularity could carry over to his vice-president. This and other miscalculations dealt the KMT its most shattering defeat since its fall from power on the mainland in 1949. Running as an independent, Soong almost won the presidency with 37 percent, while Lien Chan won only 23 percent of the vote and Chen Shui-bian emerged victorious with 39 percent (see Table 2).

Despite its historic victory in 2000, the DPP was unable during its first year in the presidency to convert independent voters or former KMT supporters. Much of the KMT's electoral eclipse was caused by challenges from KMT breakaway candidates and splinter factions, rather than the DPP's own electoral rise. In fact, in the 1998 LY election, the DPP declined somewhat both in popular vote and seats.

Moreover, the underlying distribution of partisan attachments, as measured by public-opinion polls, revealed a surprising degree of stability following the electoral tumult of 2000. When voters were asked the usual measure of party attachment—which party, if any, they feel closest to—a TVBS poll found that the main changes were the sudden evaporation of support for the KMT and the meteoric rise of the People's First Party (PFP), founded by James Soong a few weeks after the election. However, this could happen only because a great many of the KMT's long-time supporters, who viewed James Soong as the "true" leader of the KMT and the PFP a "real" KMT in spirit if not in name, defected to the PFP en masse. At the same time, the bandwagon effect that Chen's victory brought the DPP turned out to be ephemeral. Partisan support for the DPP, as gauged by the closeness measure, escalated from about 22 percent throughout the campaign to 31 percent three months after Chen was inaugurated, making the DPP the most popular party on the island. After nine months in office, Chen's governance problems and sagging popularity brought the DPP's support back down to 24 percent. If we look not at the KMT alone but at the so-called "Pan-KMT" camp—the KMT plus its splinter parties—this support remained virtually unchanged. A year before the 2000 presidential election, the combined strength of the "Pan-KMT" camp stood at 34.8 percent. A year after the presidential race, the figure was virtually identical, though now the PFP was at 23 percent and the KMT at 12 percent. To unveil the sources of the DPP's sluggish growth in partisan support, we need to delve deeper into its ideological rigidity, its organizational weakness, and the ways in which it has been overwhelmed by the KMT's superior ability to restructure the issue dimensions.

Social Cleavages and Issue Structuration

Unlike most Latin American and East European cases, the political opening in Taiwan was not triggered by socioeconomic crisis. Rather, regime transition followed a quarter-century of remarkable economic growth with equity through export-oriented industrialization. Beneath Taiwan's long-running economic prosperity and full employment was a very fluid class structure. The private sector was highly decentralized with a large number of owner-operators as well as a sizable temporary working class. A large portion of the male population has experienced upward class mobility personally or within the family. The economic structure has greatly inhibited the growth of independent trade unions. This open and fluid class structure made it intrinsically difficult for the opposition to capture any major social groups with a distinctive socioeconomic program.

Also, carefully crafted political engineering has complicated the politics of subethnic cleavage since the early 1970s. Long before CCK initiated political liberalization in 1986, he accelerated the Taiwanization of the KMT power structure.[18] The process of indigenization culminated in his decision to nominate Lee Teng-hui as his vice-president (and official successor) in 1984. As a result, many coopted native Taiwanese elites acquired a high stake in preserving the political dominance of the KMT. Radical changes in the political institutions posed a grave risk to most native Taiwanese KMT politicians, whose gradual ascendance in national politics was better assured by the KMT-sponsored reforms.

At the start of the regime transition, however, the KMT was still politically vulnerable on a number of scores. The DPP challenged the KMT on the issues of power distribution between mainlanders and native Taiwanese, democratic reform, and national identity as well as Taiwan's sovereign status. All three issues had the potential to arouse widespread popular support and deal the KMT a fatal electoral blow. On the other hand, from early on, the DPP leaders had built up their electoral support by highlighting the shared sense of suffering and deprivation among the native Taiwanese. The DPP leadership played up the issue because it was considered an effective strategy to counter the KMT's success in socioeconomic development and a common cause that could unite DPP supporters of diverse social and economic interests.

The post-CCK succession crisis provided the necessary impetus for a redirection of the KMT's core commitments. Within eight years of CCK's passing, Lee Teng-hui transformed the KMT from an instrument of mainlander dominance into a vehicle of majoritarian politics, and from a bastion of Chinese nationalism into an incubator of Taiwanese identity.[19] During the power struggle, Lee skillfully shifted the burden of defending orthodox interests to his rival—the Non-Mainstream Faction—while projecting his program of ideological redirection and power consolidation as imperative for the political survival of the KMT.

With the marginalization of the NMF, Lee was able to absorb the DPP's political demands into the KMT's own platform. These absorbed demands included removing legal restrictions on the advocacy of Taiwan independence, reinstating the civic rights of former political prisoners and dissidents in exile, alleviating historical grievances such as the February 28 incident,[20] and instituting direct popular election for the presidency. Consequently, it became difficult for the DPP to define new democratic-reform issues that could arouse widespread popular support. The appeals to democratic ideals and Taiwanese identity had simply exhausted their electoral utility.

Furthermore, Lee's "pragmatic diplomacy" considerably narrowed the ideological distance between the KMT and DPP over national identity. Although the DPP's formal position on the statehood of Taiwan was still in stark contrast to the KMT's reunification rhetoric, the DPP found it increasingly difficult to put forward a truly distinctive mainland policy and foreign policy. Lee's steadfast opposition to direct air and sea links between Taiwan and mainland China and concerted diplomatic effort to join the United Nations ran embarrassingly close to the DPP's own platform.

On the other hand, the DPP had been long handicapped by its official endorsement of Taiwan independence and its antisystem claims, for example, rejecting the name of the ROC and advocating a complete overhaul of the constitution. The KMT's propaganda effectively characterized the DPP's independence clause as dangerous and irresponsible and the NP's pro-reunification platform as disloyal to the Taiwanese people. The DPP had tried to break out of this dilemma by shifting its emphasis from democratic reform and Taiwan independence to issues of the environment and socioeconomic justice since the 1992 LY election.

Two parallel developments in the early 1990s sharpened the DPP's competitive edge on the socioeconomic agenda. First, with the rapid ascent of elected politicians in both the KMT power structure and the formal policy making process, corruption—which had existed for a long time in local politics—was transmitted into the national arena. Next, as indigenization of the top party and state personnel accelerated, the old institutional insulation between the central leadership and the business sector began to melt down. The Mainstream Faction vigorously reached out to the business community and local factions because it started from a weaker power base within the party-state apparatus. The KMT was transformed by Lee from a political coalition of the dominant mainlander state elite and collateral native politicians to one of conservative state elites, local factions, and big businesses. It thus became increasingly difficult to uphold the pretense that the KMT was still the embodiment of an all-class political alliance. These parallel developments enabled the DPP to define for the electorate a new line of party cleavage.[21]

However, the DPP's new platform, centered around social welfare and "clean politics," only marginally improved its electoral fortune. Strategically, it proved impossible for the DPP to monopolize the social welfare and clean politics issues. The KMT leadership had responded to the rising demand for entitlement programs with its own social welfare platform. In 1995, the KMT government formally introduced universal health insurance and pledged to install a national pension scheme by 2001. Assistance to veterans, the elderly, farmers, the unemployed, and families below the poverty line increased dramatically, from 16.5 percent of government expenditures in 1991 to 25.8 percent in 1999. At the same time, as the NP and PFP tried to expand their electoral bases beyond the traditional KMT strongholds, they also emphasized the anticorruption issue to appeal to the urban middle class.

During the second half of 1990s, cross-Strait relations became the overriding concern of Taiwan's electorate. The PRC's demonstrated resolve to use military means during the Taiwan Strait crisis of 1995–96 seriously discredited the independence option among stability-minded business elites and middle-class voters. The deterioration of cross-Strait relations since the mid-1990s helped the KMT to maximize its competitive advantage on this most salient issue. First, the tension with mainland China virtually shut out all other policy concerns, such as the environment, corruption, and deterioration in law and order. Second, it pushed more and more voters into a centrist position, where preserving the status quo and resisting the PRC's hostile reunification campaign are favored over either independence or reunification. This explains why the DPP's new emphasis on social welfare and clean politics substantially improved its electoral fortune at the subnational level, where DPP candidates could effectively avoid the issue of national identity, but not at the national level.

The Strait crisis of 1995–96 also brought the DPP leadership to a sobering awareness that the KMT under Lee Teng-hui had already run the strategy of "creeping independence" to its realistic limits. A growing number of DPP leaders became convinced that they could not hold off a reexamination of the party's Taiwan independence platform any longer. Yet few DPP leaders dared to initiate the debate, which has long been preempted by the sizable bloc of pro-independence zealots (estimated at around 12–15 percent of regular voters and almost two-fifths of the DPP's traditional supporters). These activists have been the major source of campaign financing and continue to wield considerable influence in party primaries.

Most fundamentally, the KMT under Lee Teng-hui was able to consolidate its centrist position on the national identity issue through state-orchestrated resocialization programs in the schools and mass media, with the aim of fostering a new sense of common national identity.[22] As soon as the NMF was pushed out of the party, Lee wasted no time pressing the state bureaucracy to promote the burgeoning Taiwanese consciousness while deemphasizing Chinese culture and history. In particular, Lee vigorously promoted the concept of "New Taiwanese" as a cultural vehicle for a new, assimilative identity. At the same time, Lee tried to harness the independence zeal by channeling the rising popular sentiment for a separate identity in the international community into a national drive to consolidate the status quo, that is, the de facto sovereign status of the Republic of China.

Since the inception of democratization, the proportion of the public identifying exclusively as Taiwanese has risen sharply from 16 percent in 1989 to 35.6 percent in 1996, then leveling off at 32.9 percent in 1999. The greatest growth, however, has been in the proportion of the population that considers itself both Taiwanese and Chinese (26 percent in 1989, 40.5 percent in 1996, and 51.7 percent in 1999). Exclusive Chinese identity has sharply declined from 52 percent in 1989 to 20.9 percent in 1996 and to a mere 11.8 in 1999. There is also a trend of increasing support for Taiwan independence (from 6 percent in 1989 to 18.2 percent in 1996 and 22.3 percent in 1999) and a sharp drop in support for reunification (from 55 percent in 1989 to 16.9 percent in 1999). Most significantly, those who prefer the status quo have risen sharply, from 10.8 percent in 1993 to 43.8 percent in 1999. While the surge in Taiwanese identity and declining support for reunification occurred within all three subethnic groups—mainlanders, Minnan-speaking native Taiwanese, and Hakka-speaking native Taiwanese—it was most striking among the dominant group, the Minnan-speaking Taiwanese.[23] A large majority of mainlanders remained staunch supporters of reunification, although increasingly their second generation began to acquire a dual identity.[24]

The surge in Taiwanese identity and the growing consensus on consolidating the status quo was so compelling that both the DPP and NP were forced to soften their respective nationalist stances. Since the mid-1990s, the NP has reformulated its Chinese nationalist appeal by giving priority to consolidation of the new democracy and normalization of cross-Strait exchange before the pursuit of reunification. Meanwhile, some pragmatic DPP leaders, notably party chairmen Shih Ming-teh (1994–96) and Hsu Hsin-liang (1996–98), also began to soft-peddle the Taiwan independence claim through a reinterpretation of the status quo. These adjustments suggest that the KMT's formidable electoral strength was built on its capacity not only to coopt the popular platform of the opposition but also to contain the opposition ideologically. By taking an ambiguous centrist position on the predominant cleavage dimension and an eclectic, pragmatic posture on socioeconomic issues, the KMT was able to retain its broad appeal to all classes and social groups. Throughout the 1990s, it received majority support among both Minnan-speaking and Hakka-speaking Taiwanese, while competing with the NP for mainlander voters with equal effectiveness. At the same time, the KMT also enjoyed broad-based socioeconomic support, albeit less effectively over time.

Thus when Chen Shui-bian entered the 2000 presidential race, his campaign inevitably encountered two formidable obstacles. The first was the deep-seated worry among middle-class voters and the business elite over the risk of giving the untested and historically pro-independence DPP control of the presidency, and thus of cross-Strait relations. The second was the lingering doubt about the DPP's ability to manage the national economy, which had performed consistently well under KMT stewardship, even during the difficult period of the East Asian financial crash of 1997–98.

Public opinion on the performance of Lee Teng-hui and the KMT, however, had undergone a dialectic shift toward the end of Lee's 12-year tenure. His reform agenda and many of his policies had run out of steam and exhausted their utility. First, many voters were appalled by the rising tide of "black gold" politics: the power of organized crime and its penetration into party politics and electoral representative bodies, as well as the incestuous links between wealthy corporate interests and the party-state. They blamed the outgoing president and his party for the government's failure to confront these challenges.

Next, there was growing anxiety among the populace over the protracted political stalemate and escalating military tension across the Strait. While Lee was widely praised for his perseverance in resisting the PRC's hostile reunification campaign, his approach was increasingly viewed as adventurous. In particular, his announcement in July 1999 of a "special state-to-state" relationship between Taiwan and the PRC stunned Taiwan's political allies in Washington, sparked a major controversy at home, and prompted intense scrutiny of his policy legacy on national identity and cross-Strait relations. Even the business community openly voiced concern over the protracted political stalemate and criticism of the heavy restrictions on cross-Strait economic exchange.

The shift in popular sentiment motivated the next-generation leaders to answer the call to correct some of Lee's excesses. Chen Shui-bian's presidential campaign put the emphasis on "black and gold" to address the popular demand for comprehensive political reform. The widespread aspiration for an improvement in cross-Strait relations gave James Soong a chance to distance himself from Lien Chan, who felt obligated to defend Lee's policy legacy. The renewed debate on cross-Strait relations also offered Chen Shui-bian a chance to reposition himself. Chen proposed to normalize cross-Strait economic relations upon WTO accession to sooth the business community at large and the Taiwanese business expatriates on the mainland in particular. Chen's pragmatic platform might not have won over many businessmen and middle-class voters, but it at least neutralized some of the long-held suspicion about his pro-independence credentials.

As the country entered the post–Lee Teng-hui era, a new centrist, crosspartisan position emerged out of the presidential campaign, emphasizing the need to reverse the deterioration in cross-Strait relations and to scrap restrictions on cross-Strait economic exchange that had outlived their usefulness. Thus, upon his inauguration, Chen Shui-bian was in a good position to transform the popular perception about the DPP and substantially broaden the party's electoral base by advancing this centrist line. He was also well placed to reshape the political landscape by brokering a coalition government or a majority coalition in the parliament.

In his first year in office, however, Chen Shui-bian failed to chart a new course for his party. Instead, his presidency stumbled into a deep political quagmire. Believing that he could bypass brokering by political parties and govern through direct appeals to popular sentiment, Chen rejected a proposal to form a coalition government with either the KMT or PFP.[25] Instead, he established a "government of national unity" by drawing into the cabinet independents and KMT members individually rather than through party-to-party negotiations. But his government was soon crippled by deadlock between the president and the opposition-controlled parliament. Then, the DPP government failed to act on the deteriorating economy, which had not fully recovered from the regional financial contagion and was vulnerable to a downturn in the U.S. economy. The business community was particularly annoyed that he gave priority to the environment and social welfare just as Taiwan's export sector was increasingly feeling the pinch of shrinking U.S. demand. Less than two months after the May 20 inauguration, a perception of a deteriorating business climate began to take hold, precipitating a long slide in Taiwan's stock market. Chen's abrupt decision to scrap the ongoing construction of the country's fourth nuclear power plant further depressed business confidence and stirred a wave of capital outflow into China. Furthermore, obstruction from within the DPP hampered his ability to steer cross-Strait relations on to a more stable course. His efforts in sending conciliatory messages to Beijing leaders were repeatedly nullified by contradictory remarks of the pro-independence elders of his own party.

In his first seven months in office, Chen's approval rate plunged from 77 percent upon inauguration to 35 percent at the end of the year,[26] while the stock market lost half of its value. As the hope of riding on Chen's coattails in the forthcoming LY election diminished, the DPP had to pursue a conservative nominating strategy, counting on its reliable base of 35 percent of the electorate. This figured to constrain Chen's ability to redefine the party's stance on cross-Strait relations and so broaden its national appeal. As the majority of DPP candidates for parliament were trying to consolidate their traditional constituencies, they were left vulnerable to the scrutiny of the vocal and sizable pro-independence hardliners.

As Chen's government floundered, the KMT and the PFP effectively claimed back the strategic higher ground by redefining the centrist line. The KMT and PFP soon mended their fences and formed a loose alliance along with the NP on the legislative floor. Controlling virtually two-thirds of the LY, this "Pan-KMT" alliance forced Chen Shui-bian to swallow his decision to scrap the fourth nuclear power plant by threatening a recall election as well as impeachment. They also put the DPP government on the defensive over its management of cross-Strait relations, pressuring President Chen to loosen up restrictions on investment, speed up the "three direct links" (trade, shipping, and air flights), recognize the oral agreement on the "one China principle" struck between Taipei and Beijing in 1992, and reactivate the symbolic National Unification Council. Seeing Chen's weakness, China decided to sit on the fence and wait for Taiwan's party realignment to unfold.

Organizational Evolution of the Three Major Parties

Punctuated changes in the evolution of the KMT. During its several decades in power, the KMT was a hierarchical constellation of entrenched state and party elites. Even the process of national democratization during the 1990s barely touched the KMT's power structure at the core. In contrast to the rapid Taiwanization of its power structure and the swift redirection of its ideology, organizational reform of the KMT was slow to come during Lee Teng-hui's tenure. Lee inherited a highly centralized arrangement that concentrated both decision making and appointment power in the epicenter of the party, the chairman. The party chairman appointed all senior party officials, most importantly the secretary general of the Secretariat of the Central Committee (SCC), and ran the party bureaucracy without any meaningful accountability. This put a vast party bureaucracy and an annual budget up to NT$7 billion (approximately US$220 million) at the chairman's disposal. Theoretically, the chairman was directly elected by the Party Congress. However, the SCC had the power to designate up to one-third of the delegates and always influenced vigorously the election for the remaining two-thirds. The incumbent chairman was by tradition reelected unopposed. Theoretically, power flows upward from the party base, but in reality, control comes downward through the party hierarchy. Lee Teng-hui had little incentive to change the structure. In fact, the intraparty power struggle during 1988–93 only reinforced Lee's resolve to resist any major change to the party's decision-making process.

With Lee at the helm, the party's 31-member Central Standing Committee (CSC) exercised final authority over all significant candidate nominations—for county magistrates, city mayors, and members of the National Assembly, Legislative Yuan, Provincial Assembly, and municipal councils.[27] The presidential nomination was only slightly more open. In 1991, when President Lee ran for his first full term unopposed, the 300-member Central Committee formally ratified the only candidate recommended by the CSC. In 1995, the presence of a popular incumbent, Lee Teng-hui, discouraged other leaders from actively seeking nomination, although potential opponents argued for a primary election among party members. As a token of legitimation, the formal power to select the presidential candidate was transferred from the CSC to the Party Congress. In 1999, Lee opposed any changes to this procedure to make sure that Soong would not grab the nomination from Lien Chan.

Starting with the second LY (elected in 1992), however, the central party leadership had to wrestle with a more assertive legislative branch. Under the SNTV system, virtually all members elected in geographical districts had to raise their own campaign finances and fight to establish their own name recognition and support base. This made it difficult to impose strict party discipline. In response to KMT legislators' demand for a stronger presence in the central leadership, the party introduced a cosmetic reorganization in March 1993. The Central Policy Committee (CPC) was expanded and elevated to formal parity with the SCC. Under the CPC, four new departments were created for policy research and for coordination with the LY caucus, the National Assembly caucus, and the opposition. The party felt compelled to select the heads of the CPC and of three of its four departments from KMT members of the LY. The CPC was entrusted with a dual function—coordination between the KMT cabinet and the KMT LY caucus and negotiation with the opposition on the legislative floor. In addition, the CPC supervises the KMT LY caucus with the assistance of the party whip (elected annually since 1993 by the KMT LY caucus).

To maintain control over the legislative agenda, the KMT cabinet had to use a mixture of particularistic payoffs and political sanctions in dealing with KMT legislators. The executive branch officials enjoyed the upper hand in this relationship because they exercised wide

discretionary authority over government spending, patronage appointments, and especially economic favors. Furthermore, they commanded
the allegiance of the sizable number of lawmakers who got elected on
the party's PR list or who received the orchestrated electoral support of
state employees and military personnel. Third, the top party leaders
enjoyed the final say over candidate nominations. Repeatedly, the central
party leadership obstructed attempts to form durable subgroups among
KMT LY members, while also warding off demands by the KMT caucus
for some meaningful input in the selection of the premier and cabinet
members.

During the 1990s, the party's top leaders continued to enjoy a high
degree of autonomy from all organized sectors of the society. The top
KMT leaders used their diffuse power to construct an unequal partnership
with the local factions, business elites, and other social groups, making
long-term policy commitments while setting limits on influence-buying
and policy contestation. The party controlled the organizational bases
of interest mediation in most of the strategic sectors, such as business
and labor. With its huge financial empire, composed of party businesses
and investments worth an estimated US$7 billion, the KMT was relatively
free of dependence on external resources.

Another important reason for the continued preeminence of the KMT
top leadership was that—until the 2000 electoral debacle—the same
person held the two most powerful offices: party chairman and president
of the country. The shift to semipresidentialism enabled the top party
leaders to maintain the KMT's long-running tradition of keeping the
recruitment of technocrats and elected politicians on two separate tracks,
with the former consistently outranking the latter in the power hierarchy.
The drift toward an imperial presidency and then omnipotent party
chairmanship reinforced each other.

Toward the end of President Lee's political tenure, the KMT seemingly
acquired most of the characteristics of an institutionalized political party
in terms of adaptability, organizational complexity, and stability in
electoral support. But the party was deficient in two critical aspects.
First, there was no institutionalized conflict-resolution mechanism to
facilitate an ordered succession or to sustain a collective leadership. The
legacy of the overconcentration of power in the party chairman was
perilous for the party's cohesion during leadership transition because it
turned political succession into a winner-take-all game. When James
Soong emerged as a strong contender for the party's presidential
nomination in early 1999, the only institutional device that could have
resolved the competition between Soong and Lien without a party split
was a primary election, a device totally alien to the party's quasi-Leninist
tradition of democratic centralism. Second, the party leadership's
commanding authority over local factions and the party caucuses in
representative bodies rested heavily on its sustained control over the

state apparatus. A loss of governing power for any extended period of time thus threatened to deal a fatal blow to the party's organizational integrity.

With Lien Chan's humiliating defeat on 18 March 2000 came the moment of truth: The defeat touched off a backlash against Lee Teng-hui from the party's rank-and-file members, leading to his abrupt departure from the party chairmanship. In a state of crisis, the party elected the only consensual figure available, Lien Chan, to the chairmanship and adopted unprecedented organizational reforms. These reforms opened up the party chairmanship to direct election by all party members and gave the Central Committee the power to elect all 31 members of the Central Standing Committee. They granted the CPC more authority in coordinating the legislative agenda, in recognition of the much greater importance of the KMT LY caucus now that the party no longer controlled the presidency or the cabinet. Its abundant wealth enabled the KMT to retain many talented former government officials in a newly created party think tank and to maintain its organizational links with many social groups by creating several grantmaking mechanisms. Most significantly, it turned over a new leaf, putting an anti-black-gold clause into its party charter.

Since its defeat, the former ruling party has demonstrated unexpected resilience. Its elaborate party apparatus, stalwart financial position, and prospect of returning to government (through a strengthened pan-KMT alliance) after the December 2001 election has helped the KMT hold itself together. It retained its majority in the LY despite the defection of some KMT legislators to James Soong's camp. While the KMT seemed certain to lose its majority in the approaching parliamentary election, its electoral strength remained formidable. Thus, much like the LDP in Japan after the 1993 debacle, the KMT is temporarily down but hardly out.

The transformation of the DPP. In stark contrast to the KMT, the DPP had to build up its party organization, national leadership, and central coordinating mechanism from scratch. From the very beginning, the founding members of the DPP created a peculiar set of decision-making rules and organizational structures that were designed to preserve the principles of collective leadership and democratic accountability. Inadvertently, these institutional arrangements have also tended to breed factionalism and suppress the supply of collective resources. By the initial design, the supreme decision-making body was the 30-member Central Executive Committee (CEC), which is elected by the Party Convention. The CEC then elected the ten-member Central Standing Executive Committee (CSEC), which is in charge of running party affairs. Presiding over the CSEC, the party chairman is only "first among equals," even though he is directly elected by the rank-and-file members.[28] The party chairman nominates the secretary general, whose appointment required the confirmation of the CEC until 1994. The party chairman has typically had to nominate a secretary general from a different faction to meet the expectation that no one faction should dominate party affairs. The aversion to a strong central figure was so intense among the founding members that the party charter initially stipulated a one-year, nonrenewable term for the party chairman. This folly of "musical chairs" was only slightly corrected later on, first by allowing one renewable term and then in 1988 by extending the term to two years. As a result, the chairmanship has rotated among a half-dozen leading figures, changing hands from one faction to another. No chairman has been able to exercise strong leadership and give the party clear direction. The fundamental reason for a weak party center has been the constraining effect of the larger institutional setting. During the authoritarian years there was no electoral avenue for the rise of a few leading opposition figures that could claim island-wide popularity. Most of the founding members enjoyed nothing more than a limited electoral base. Not until the initiation of direct elections for municipal mayor, provincial governor, and president did a few leading candidates get a chance to break out of the dense pack.

A weaker center also meant that there were few tangible collective resources at the disposal of the national party headquarters. Also, under SNTV, most DPP politicians were interested only in soliciting political donations for their own campaign coffers. Party chairmen muddled through from one fiscal crisis to another until the introduction of the government subsidy scheme in 1997. Before Chen Shui-bian came to power, the most valuable things the national headquarters could offer its candidates during the campaign were the party label, moral support, and a few well-known, eloquent speakers to attract audiences to rallies.

The DPP's decision-making process is also thoroughly decentralized. The national headquarters has no say in the choice of local party officials, who are elected by the local party members. All local party subunits are expected to be self-financed. The DPP LY caucus, to which the bulk of weighty DPP factional leaders and prominent founding members belong, has been highly independent. It elects its own leader on an annual basis and enjoys full authority in negotiating with other parties over legislative proposals.

The party was saddled with factionalism from the very beginning. Between 1986 and 1991, two competing factions, Formosa and New Tide, emerged out of a cleavage over strategies for democratic struggle. The Formosa faction emphasized building up popular aspirations for democratic reform through electoral mobilization and political maneuver in the representative bodies, while the New Tide faction placed equal emphasis on within-system struggle and antisystem strategies, for example, social movements and political demonstrations.[29]

The competition for party nominations under SNTV reinforced

factionalism. In many districts with magnitudes of four, five, and six seats, the two factions always argued over the optimal number of nominees wherever the potential electoral support looked substantial enough to elect more than one DPP candidate to the LY. But with the extension of the LY from 130 to 161 and eventually to 225 seats and the corresponding enlargement of district magnitude, there was room for new factions to emerge. Three new factions were formed from among DPP independents, the Justice Alliance, the Welfare Alliance, and the Taiwan Independence Alliance. Most factions were bound together by personal and generational ties more than by a common ideological stand. There were no meaningful ideological distinctions among the Formosa, Justice Alliance, and Welfare Alliance factions. The New Tide faction is slightly more coherent in its ideological claim as some leading figures, such as Chiu I-ren, advocate social democratic ideals and are more sympathetic to the labor movement. (The Taiwan Independence Alliance, the smallest of the five factions, typically takes a hard-line position on the Taiwan independence issue.) From 1992 on, the two major factions and three minor factions competed vigorously for party nominations, for control of local party secretariats, and for National Convention delegates through enlisting new party members.

Regardless of their factional affiliation, all DPP politicians rely on their personalized campaign organization and financing to sustain their political life. Most DPP LY members have developed a vested interest in the existing electoral arrangements. The SNTV rule prompts them to develop an insatiable appetite for campaign resources (making them liable to money politics), but it helps them to build up political autonomy and electoral predictability.

Without a strong central authority, DPP leaders and members from all factions have favored party primaries to select among competing candidates. Only when there were too few candidates to make nominations contestable did party officials skip primaries and rely on the CEC to ratify nominations. The small size of the dues-paying party membership in each district unfortunately gave DPP politicians a strong incentive to engage in all kinds of unsavory practices. These included bribing party members with cash or gifts, or bringing in "phantom" party members (who are paid to join the party and vote for a certain candidate in the primary election). The rampant practice of transporting busloads of captive "phantom" party members to the polling stations soon ran amok, prompting the DPP to reform its nomination procedure. Since 1996, party nominations have been decided by a weighted average of the vote by party members and the level of support in an opinion poll of the electorate at large.[30] The use of opinion polls was acceptable to all factions because the polls tend to favor incumbents and thus preserve the existing political equilibrium. This, however, only further suppressed the influence of the party center over nominations.

Coupled with SNTV, this decentralized nomination procedure thus perpetuated a weak party center and reinforced factionalism. Despite vigorous factional strife and the breakaway of some hard-line supporters of Taiwan independence in 1996, the DPP has managed to hold together. Entering the second half of 1990s, three new elements began to serve as adhesive forces: crystallization of partisan identity in the electorate, institutionalization of the rules of conflict resolution, and the prospect of power alternation at the national level. Over the years, anti-KMT sentiment has been successfully converted into DPP party identification. By the late 1990s, the DPP identifiers had risen to more than 20 percent of eligible voters (see the Figure on p. 274) and more than one-quarter of regular voters. The party label brought party nominees sizable and dependable electoral support, which, in turn, bolstered their ability to mobilize campaign resources.

Chen's historic presidential election victory gave the DPP its first opportunity to reorganize its debilitating factional structure. To strengthen Chen's position in the party, his own faction, the Justice Alliance, tried to forge a mainstream alliance with the Welfare and two smaller factions (the New Era Institute and New Dynamics) that emerged after the collapse of the Formosa faction. Chen himself established a "government of national unity" by appointing Tang Fei, the KMT Defense Minister, the premier and recruiting individual ministers from different political backgrounds. These moves temporarily freed Chen of the constraints of factional politics, as DPP factional leaders were largely excluded from the government formation process.

Tthe DPP's factional structure, however, has refused to go away. First, Chen's long-time competitor Frank Hsieh, the leader of the Welfare faction and mayor of Kaohsiung, and the New Tide outmaneuvered him and grabbed the steering wheel of party affairs with the election of party delegates and of Frank Hsieh to the party chairmanship in July 2000. To ward off the opposition campaign for recall or impeachment during the political storm over the fourth nuclear power plant, Chen felt compelled to share decision-making power with DPP factional leaders through the creation of an ad hoc nine-member policy circle. With his dwindling approval rate, Chen fell further away from establishing himself and the presidency as the epicenter of the DPP.

As long as party hardliners enjoy an independent political base, it remains a daunting task for Chen Shui-bian to forge a new consensus on how the DPP should adjust its core ideological commitments. Thus factional politics and the holdover of ideological baggage dampened the party's prospects in the December 2001 LY election, hampering its goal of forming a DPP-led majority coalition. Facing an uncertain electoral prospect, the DPP has had a hard time recruiting new talent from the civil service, academia, and the private sector to fill policy-making posts and run the elaborate state bureaucracy. After the joy of electoral triumph in 2000, the party was visibly overwhelmed by the challenge of governing as minority. Many DPP leaders began to realize that their party, too long in opposition, lacked the administrative experience, mentality, ideological adaptability, and organizational capability to govern effectively.

KMT splinter parties: The struggle for political survival. Both the New Party and the People's First Party emerged out of power struggles within the KMT, stemming from Lee Teng-hui's leadership and policies. In both cases, the splinter party acquired its initial political momentum from the better-than-expected electoral performance of its founding members running as maverick KMT candidates. During 1990–92, as the issues of political reform and national identity drove a wedge between the Mainstream and Non-Mainstream factions of the KMT, NMF followers in the LY formed the New-KMT Alliance, which began to question Lee's commitment to Chinese nationalism. Many key figures in the New-KMT Alliance entered the 1992 LY elections without party endorsement, but they won their reelection bids with impressive margins. This success convinced them that there would be space for a third party, as the MF was abandoning Chinese nationalism and seeking ideological accommodation with the DPP. Seven years later, the PFP grew out of the power struggle between Lee Teng-hui and James Soong, who established the party to consolidate his electoral base and sustain his political momentum after nearly winning the 2000 presidential race as an independent.

While the historical conditions in which the two splinter parties were created looked strikingly similar, they differed in some significant respects. First, while the NP and the PFP both established their political identities in opposition to Lee Teng-hui's leadership and policies, the NP had fought an uphill battle and was destined to become a marginal political force. At the time, Lee Teng-hui was establishing himself as a popular, charismatic leader with a historical mission to indigenize the KMT's power structure, strengthen Taiwanese identity, reform the constitution, and expand the island's international space. In contrast, when James Soong launched his challenge, Lee's popularity was much deflated and his political agenda had run out of steam and was encountering burgeoning criticism.

Second, while the leaders of both parties faced the daunting task of overcoming the subethnic divide, the PFP was in a much better position than the NP to defy the derogatory label of "a party of mainlanders." The leading figures of the NP had little contact with grassroots Taiwanese society. They built their electoral base primarily upon mainlander state employees and middle-class voters in the metropolitan area of northern Taiwan. In contrast, Soong was the first mainlander to build a truly national political following since Lee Teng-hui had "Taiwanized" the

KMT and the entire political system. During his four years as governor
of Taiwan Province (1994–98), Soong worked brilliantly to cultivate
ties to grassroots constituencies and to cement patron-client bonds with
local political bosses. His performance and persona as governor gave
him a base of sympathy and support that cut across the traditional divides
of party and ethnicity, and in the 2000 election he won a plurality in 15
of the 23 cities and counties.[31]

Without the prospect of joining the government, it was virtually
impossible for the NP to compete with the major parties for executive
offices. In contrast, the PFP instantly emerged as a strong contender for
executive offices at both national and county levels. As the December
2001 elections approached, the PFP seemed in a good position to
capitalize on popular disenchantment with the discredited KMT and
growing disillusionment with the DPP government. Finally, the rise of
the PFP has left the NP with little breathing space as it has annexed
virtually all the NP's core constituencies.

Much like the NP, however, the PFP remains organizationally thin
and institutionally weak. It lacks strong organizational links with its
core constituents and clear decision-making procedures; all important
decisions are left to its paramount leader. The PFP has not yet articulated
a clear and compelling vision of its purpose, other than presenting the
electorate with a viable alternative to the KMT and the DPP. While the
PFP was endowed with James Soong's impressive political capital, it is
unclear how long traditional KMT loyalists will sustain their allegiance
to the PFP. New Party voters (the most politically conscious and
sophisticated) would probably vote strategically (as they did in the 1998
Taipei mayor's race), shifting their support to any politically promising
KMT candidates who shared their ideology. It is also unclear how long
James Soong, without control of the tangible political resources that
derive from holding major office, can sustain his bonds with local
factional leaders. For the time being, the party's political fate remains
intimately bound up with Soong's personal popularity and his electoral
prospect in the year 2004 presidential race. Thus the PFP is best
characterized as a personalistic party within the Gunther and Diamond
framework presented in chapter 1 of this volume.

The Reach of Political Parties into Civil Society

During Taiwan's regime transition in the 1980s and early 1990s, there
was a reciprocal dynamic between opposition forces in politics and civil
society. With the political opposition in the forefront of challenging the
authoritarian order, social-movement leaders found a strategic opening
to exert their claims. In turn, the social movements provided a mobilized
soil for the opposition party to take root. As a result, the intellectuals,
feminist groups, middle-class public interest groups, professional

associations, and college students gradually won a relatively unrestrained public space outside the organizational purview of the KMT. In response to this increasingly assertive civil society, the KMT reorganized the state administrative apparatus and revitalized the existing corporatist arrangements. New ministry-level state agencies, notably the Commission on Labor Affairs and the Environmental Protection Agency, were created to respond to the growing demands on emerging social issues. Moderate movement leaders were coopted into various advisory committees under state agencies, while autonomous union movements were preempted by state-sanctioned union organizations under the exclusive representation rule.

More importantly, the KMT managed to control many strategic organized sectors such as business, state employees, labor, and farmers. The KMT's Social Affairs Department routinely promoted the "party nominees" in elections for the leadership of all peak organizations, in particular the presidents of the three peak business associations.[32] More significantly, the policy of selective incorporation was replaced by a more inclusive approach. Starting in 1989, young business executives, especially heirs to the business groups, have been vigorously recruited by the KMT. Furthermore, since the late 1980s, the party has expanded its business empire into high-growth sectors, such as banking, leasing, insurance, and high-tech, mostly in joint ventures with leading business groups. Thus the party has built up a seamless web of business partnerships and interlocking interests throughout the private sector.

Confronted with the issue of political neutrality of the military, the security apparatus, the judiciary, and the civil servants, the KMT grudgingly made some adjustments. The judicial branch experienced the most extensive changes, mainly due to the revolt of independent-minded prosecutors and judges. However, the KMT made little concession toward political neutrality of the civil service as it maintained party cells in the state bureaucracy and state-owned enterprises. During the 1990s, the KMT also closely guarded its coveted control of the existing three television networks. To quell DPP protests and signify media deregulation, the KMT government awarded the license for the fourth broadcast television network to a DPP politician. (Subsequently, much more media pluralism has emerged with the growth of cable television). In response to the opposition's demand for a "nationalization of the military," the KMT took some cosmetic measures. Instead of abolishing party cells in the military, the KMT moved them under-ground and away from the barracks. In the name of national security, however, the security apparatus still routinely conducted surveillance on the opposition and whomever it suspected of posing a threat to the KMT top leaders, without much consideration for due process. Thus there was some lingering doubt as to whether the still highly politicized military and security apparatus would ever volunteer allegiance to a democratically elected non-KMT government, especially one with pro-independence credentials.

Before coming to power, the DPP had a hard time developing organizational ties with social movements and autonomous social sectors. The expectation of continued KMT incumbency loaded the political dice in favor of the ruling party. As long as the KMT could make credible policy commitments, new social groups were inclined to look to it rather than to the opposition for solutions. The highly decentralized and spatially segmented power structure of the DPP also hampered its ability to integrate the individual mandates of its candidates into a coherent national socioeconomic program.

The historic power rotation in 2000 gave the DPP its first opportunity to break the KMT's iron grip on organized sectors and to address the politicization of the civil service and military-security apparatus. The power handover did trigger a meltdown of the entrenched corporatist arrangements that had chained many organized sectors to the state and ruling party. Even before Chen Shui-bian was inaugurated, the KMT had lost control of some state-sanctioned peak organizations, notably the Chinese Federation of Labor. Once in power, the DPP amended the Labor Union Law to remove the provision for singular representation. At the same time, the DPP government has pressured peak business organizations to sever their ties with the KMT if they want to retain their governmental subsidies, coveted status, and privileged access to the policy-making process.

During the KMT's reigning years, a prevailing pattern of all-encompassing electoral mobilization had put the DPP at a clear disadvantage. This ubiquitous mobilization—a key reason for Taiwan's exceptionally high voter-turnout rate—drew upon every form of social capital (lineage, communal bond, school ties, religious affiliation), most social organizations (trade associations, professional organizations, family-owned firms, social clubs, mass media, etc.), vast fiscal and administrative resources of the public sector, and incredible private financial resources.[33] The logic of electoral competition has driven DPP candidates to rely more on their own vote-mobilization mechanisms and name recognition than the party because they were increasingly competing among themselves under the SNTV rule. Yet as the democratic transition ended, their followers' enthusiasm also gradually waned. To sustain their electoral strength, most DPP politicians had to compete with their KMT rivals in a down-to-earth manner, through pork-barrel projects, district services, and large campaign war chests. This marked shift in the nature of electoral competition clearly worked to the DPP's disadvantage, as evidenced in the disappointing results of the 1998 LY election.

While the DPP leaders had vowed to curtail the reach of the KMT, in many instances they have been prone to become the mirror image of the

KMT. Since its inauguration, the Chen Shui-bian government has been keen to prop up pro-DPP labor unions, environmentalist groups, grassroots organizations, and organized intellectual circles. The DPP ministers as well as country magistrates also indulged in partisan use of public-sector resources. Chen Shui-bian negated his campaign promise to turn the government-controlled television networks into public TV stations. Instead, the DPP government asked Chen's campaign advisors and speechwriters to run these powerful media. And in its first six months, the Chen administration revamped virtually all the boards of state-owned enterprises, banks, electronic media, government-funded research organizations, semipublic institutions, and foundations, replacing the incumbents with DPP-affiliated politicians or professionals. Thus, as the DPP has moved to create a "level playing field" for itself, few branches of the state and organized social sectors have been truly able to free themselves from partisan politics.

Implications for Taiwan's New Democracy

The ability of a former quasi-Leninist party to maintain a streak of electoral successes long after the transition to democracy was no small achievement. During the KMT's reigning years, its partisan grip on the state was an important ingredient of its electoral fortune, but it was no longer the decisive element. During the 1990s, the KMT reinvigorated its electoral strength in much the same way as other dominant parties do in advanced industrial democracies. It built a winning majority on a rare combination of flexibility and continuity and a unique blend of symbols and payoffs, redefining itself as a catch-all party (albeit one still exhibiting significant Leninist organizational legacies). Expecting a protracted incumbency, few major social groups during the 1990s chose to break free of their ties with the KMT. The power to shape and reshape institutional designs enabled the KMT to redefine the center of electoral gravity away from elections for representative bodies to the contests for major executive offices. Furthermore, it had demonstrated that its ability to achieve its historical projects—security, development, and international legitimacy—was not hampered by the transition to democracy. None of the above, however, protected the KMT from its political debacle in the post-Lee Teng-hui era. While the KMT had acquired most of the characteristics of an institutionalized political party, in terms of adaptability, organizational complexity, and stability in electoral support, it had two fatal institutional flaws: First, it lacked mechanisms of accountability to prevent its top leadership from pursuing ill-conceived strategies. Second, it lacked institutionalized mechanisms for resolving intraparty conflicts and sustaining collective leadership. These were the institutional legacies of the party's long quasi-Leninist history.

The KMT's role in shaping the democratic transition and structuring the new representative democracy was critical and problematic. The incumbent-initiated constitutional change was too much the result of unilateral imposition and short-term partisan calculation to give the new democratic institutions the kind of broad-based legitimacy that a constitution in a consolidated democracy should enjoy. Parties in a sense remained too strong. The ubiquitous presence of partisan politics in all organized sectors of society produced a hyperactivated political society, which has in turn compressed the sphere for open public discourse and an autonomous civil society. Even after the rotation of power to the DPP, the creation of nonpartisan mass media and a politically neutral civil service and military remains a daunting task.

Under a largely regime-initiated democratic reform, the DPP came into being in conditions not of its own choice. Its organizational character has been shaped not by abstract considerations of how to achieve the optimal internal coherence and scope of social representation so much as by the exigencies of the competitive environment and institutional setting. Factional politics and the holdover of ideological baggage (particularly on the issue of Taiwanese independence) have complicated its transformation into a party representing the mainstream views of the society, thus hampering Chen Shui-bian's efforts to enlarge its electoral base. If the DPP is today a programmatic party, it is too factionalized and too ideological to become a majority party without significant further internal evolution.

Due to the uniqueness in the mode and outcomes of its democratic transition, Taiwan had for a long while been immune to the global trend of declining significance of political parties in structuring issues, aggregating interests, and organizing government. However, Taiwan may not defy the global trend much longer. Disenchantment with the KMT and widespread popular discontent with the performance of the DPP government will stir more and more voters to detach themselves from political parties. The semipresidential system might also undermine the organizational coherence of the KMT as well as the DPP in the near future. James Soong demonstrated in 2000 how direct popular election of the president enables a charismatic national figure to take a mobilizational shortcut, bypassing the party apparatus to reach voters directly through the mass media and personal campaigning.

Taiwan's days of one-party dominance—not to mention one-party hegemony—are over. But the lingering legacies of this regime complicate the tasks of democratic governance and consolidation. Societal actors have lost their political moorings while the state bureaucracy is searching for new political anchorage. The frozen clarity of one-party dominance has been replaced by the confusion of a multiparty system with divided and frequently deadlocked government. Gone is the centralized power structure that gave coherence to the state apparatus and predictability to policy making for five decades. Gone is the elite political structure that was capable of mediating social conflict, fostering social consensus, and imposing its agenda on societal actors. Left to fill the void, for the time being, is an inexperienced and factionalized former opposition party, one that is painfully discovering that the political vacuum created by its defeat of the hegemonic party is too vast for it—or any other single party—to fill up. On top of the political challenges are those of governance: Memories of the KMT governing as a dominant party created an unreasonably high performance benchmark for the DPP governing as minority. It may take a long while for Taiwan's electorate to adjust itself to the posthegemonic era.

NOTES

1. For the Leninist features of the KMT, see Tun-jen Cheng, "Democratizing the Quasi-Leninist Regime in Taiwan." *World Politics* 42 (July 1989): 471–99.

2. A one-party dominant regime refers to a democracy characterized by a ruling party with a large and seemingly permanent majority. See T.J. Pempel, ed., *Uncommon Democracies: The One-Party Dominant Regimes* (Ithaca, N.Y.: Cornell University Press, 1990), introduction.

3. In contrast to a dominant party, which could potentially be defeated in an election, a hegemonic party does not allow for any effective electoral challenge to its rule. Giovanni Sartori, *Parties and Party Systems: A Framework for Analysis* (Cambridge: Cambridge University Press, 1976), 230–38.

4. For the distinction of three domains, see Alfred Stepan, *Rethinking Military Politics: Brazil and the Southern Cone* (Princeton, N.J.: Princeton University Press, 1988).

5. I borrow the "caging" metaphor from Michael Mann, *The Sources of Social Power: Volume II, The Rise of Classes and Nation-State, 1760–1914* (Cambridge: Cambridge University Press, 1993), 39–40.

6. Overall, mainlanders (people who were born on the Chinese mainland and their offspring) account for about 15 percent of the population of Taiwan, but there is growing intermarriage between mainlanders and native Taiwanese.

7. Yun-han Chu, *Crafting Democracy in Taiwan* (Taipei: Institute for National Policy Research, 1992), ch. 2.

8. The native Taiwanese, whose ancestors migrated from Fujian and Guangdong Provinces of China to Taiwan between the 17th and 19th centuries, accounted for about three-quarters of the population around the early 1950s. Their numerical dominance has steadily increased to about 83 percent around the early 1990s due to a lower reproduction rate of the mainlander group.

9. Ping-lung Jiagn and Wen-cheng Wu, "The Changing Role of the KMT in Taiwan's Political System," in Tun-jen Cheng and Stephan Haggard, eds., *Political Change in Taiwan* (Boulder, Colo.: Lynne Rienner, 1992).

10. For several decades, the KMT also indirectly controlled the remaining two broadcast television networks, nominally under the Taiwan provincial government and the Ministry of Defense.

11. Bruce Dickson, "The Kuomintang before Democratization: Organizational Change and the Role of Elections," in Hung-mao Tien, ed., *Taiwan's Electoral Politics and Democratic Transition: Riding the Third Wave* (Armonk, N.Y.: M.E. Sharpe, 1996), 42–78.

12. Joseph Bosco, "Taiwan Factions: *Guanxi,* Patronage and the State in Local Politics," in Murray Rubinstein, ed., *The Other Taiwan: 1945 to the Present* (Armonk, N.Y.: M.E. Sharpe, 1994), 114–44.

13. For the evolution of these extraconstitutional arrangements, see Hung-mao Tien, *The Great Transition: Political and Social Change in the Republic of China* (Stanford, Calif.: Hoover Institution Press, 1989).

14. Under SNTV, voters are allowed to vote for only a single candidate in a multiseat district, and the excess votes of popular candidates cannot be transferred to other candidates on the same party ticket in the district. Thus, since the personality towers above the party in electoral significance, all candidates are compelled to invest heavily in building up their personal networks, identities, and vote-getting mechanisms.

15. For the formation of the *Tangwai,* see Chia-lung Lin, "Paths to Democracy: Taiwan in Comparative Perspective," unpubl. diss., Department of Political Science, Yale University, 1998, especially ch. 7.

16. The formation of two competing power blocs was triggered by President Lee's new foreign policy initiatives. The factionalism became crystallized after Lee's nomination (over the objection of many senior KMT leaders) of Lee Yuan-tsu as his running mate. See Hung-mao Tien and Yun-han Chu, "Taiwan's Domestic Political Reforms, Institutional Change and Power Realignment," in Gary Klintworth, ed., *Taiwan in the Asia-Pacific in the 1990s* (Sidney: Allen & Unwin Publishers, 1994); and Yun-han Chu and Tse-min Lin, "The Process of Democratic Consolidation in Taiwan: Social Cleavage, Electoral Competition, and the Emerging Party System," in Hung-mao Tien, ed., *Taiwan's Electoral Politics and Democratic Transition,* 79–104.

17. PR in Taiwan is not conducted with a separate ballot. Rather, the seats are distributed on the basis of the national aggregate vote each party wins in the geographical districts.

18. See Edwin Winckler, "Taiwan Transition?" in Tun-jen Cheng and Stephan Haggard, eds., *Political Change in Taiwan* (Boulder, Colo.: Lynne Rienner, 1992).

19. Yun-han Chu and Chia-lung Lin, "Democratization and Growth of Taiwanism: Competing Nationalisms and National (In)Security," paper delivered at the Second Annual Conference of the EU-China Academic Network (ECAN), Centro de Estudios de Asia Oriental, Universidad Autonoma de Madrid, Spain, 21–22 January 1999.

20. In this tragic incident in early 1947, thousands of native Taiwanese were shot dead during a military crackdown on an island-wide mass revolt against the corruption of the Nationalist carpetbeggars. See George Kerr, *Formosa Betrayed* (Boston: Houghton Mifflin, 1965).

21. Yun-han Chu and Chia-lung Lin, "The Process of Democratic Consolidation in Taiwan."

22. Most recent literature suggests that national identities are not inborn but are socially and politically constructed sentiments subject to political mobilization and manipulation. For empirical evidence on how Taiwanese identity grew under the intensive mobilization of political elites, see Yun-han Chu and Chia-lung Lin, "Democratization and Growth of Taiwanism."

23. The Minnan group, which accounts for about 72 percent of the population, is the single largest subethnic group among native Taiwanese. Minnan, literally Southern Fujian, refers to the Taiwanese who originally came from the southern part of Fujian province and speak southern Fujianese. Hakka, which accounts for about 12 percent of the population, came originally from both Fujian and Guangdong provinces and speak Hakka.

24. See Yun-han Chu and Chia-lung Lin, "Democratization and Growth of Taiwanism."

25. Chen eschewed a coalition with the KMT because he was convinced that the former ruling party might never put its act together again after its humiliating defeat.

26. Based on TVBS Polls.

27. Starting in 1983, the KMT selectively experimented with party primaries. However, the party primary was never institutionalized. Typically, the chairman appointed a seven-member Central Nomination Sub-Committee, which made the nominating decision with only partial reference to the results of a primary election or public-opinion polls. Julian Baum and James Robinson, "Party Primaries in Taiwan: Continuing Appraisal," *Asian Affairs* 24 (Spring 1997): 3–13.

28. Between 1986 and 1988, the party chairman, like other members of the Central Standing Committee, was elected by the Central Executive Committee. Between 1989 and 1997, the position was elected directly by the delegates of the Party Convention. After 1998, the party chairman has been elected directly by all party members.

29. The factional divide was also generational. Most leading figures of the Formosa faction were founding members of *Tangwai* movement of the late 1970s and imprisoned after the Kaohsiung incident of 1979. Leaders of the New Tide faction, who are at least half a generation younger, emerged out of the resurgence of the opposition movement during the early 1980s.

30. In the 1998 LY election, the popular vote and opinion poll each counted 50 percent. For the 2001 LY election, the weight of the opinion poll was increased to 70 percent. For the 1995 local election, the party substituted evaluations by party officials for the public-opinion polls, but that experiment was not repeated.

31. Larry Diamond, "Anatomy of a Political Earthquake: How the KMT Lost—and the DPP Won—the 2000 Presidential Election in Taiwan," in Muthiah Alaggapa, ed., *Taiwan's Presidential Election: Democratic Consolidation and Cross-Strait Relations* (Armonk, N.Y.: M.E. Sharpe, 2001, forthcoming).

32. The Federation of Industry, the Federation of Commerce, and National Council of Industry and Commerce.

33. Campaign spending per capita is extremely high in Taiwan. It is estimated that in two recent parliamentary elections, most KMT candidates spent between US$3 million to US$9 million individually and most DPP candidates between US$1 to US$1.5 million in order to win only about 30,000 to 40,000 votes each.

12

DIVERGENT PATHS OF POSTCOMMUNIST DEMOCRACIES

Herbert Kitschelt

Herbert Kitschelt is professor of political science at Duke University. His extensive work on the changing West European party systems includes The Transformation of European Social Democracy *(1994) and* The Radical Right in Western Europe *(1995). His study of the transformation of clientelist politics, "Linkages between Citizens and Politicians in Democratic Politics" appeared in* Comparative Political Studies *(2000).*

After the collapse of communist rule across Eastern Europe, the initial hunch of many comparative political theorists, including this author, was that *all* postcommunist party systems in the emerging democracies would share essential properties that derived from their common experience of state-socialist economics and the "Leninist legacy" of communist party rule.[1] By 1998, it was obvious that, aside from a few common underlying patterns of interest mobilization, *diversity* across the former communist countries was much more impressive than *commonality* of democratic development and party-system formation. For a start, some communist regimes never became democracies, including Belarus, Serbia, and most of the Central Asian republics of the former Soviet Union. Other countries, particularly Croatia and Slovakia, were backtracking on their democratic commitments under the tutelage of semiauthoritarian rulers who had emerged from the old communist party establishment, even though their current parties might not directly trace their origins to the communist parties of the past. Also, among those former communist countries that had become democracies, the diversity of parties' programmatic appeals and abilities to build electoral coalitions often overwhelmed crossnational common-alities. In this chapter, I submit that crossnational diversity among postcommunist democracies is not random but derives from both historical legacies and current institutions.[2] Moreover, the linkage between legacies, institutions, and party systems is not accidental and chaotic but mediated by deliberate strategies of rational, power-seeking

actors, even though miscalculations, variations in the sequencing of
interactions, and unique bargaining opportunities may dilute the causal
connection between these aspects of the postcommunist democratic
transition.

I will sketch a set of hypotheses to account for diversity in postcommunist democracies in two respects. First, why do individual parties
mobilize in different ways in the new democracies? Second, why do
national party systems, as aggregate phenomena, vary across Eastern
Europe? My concern will primarily be with the *modes of linkage
building between citizens and parties and the resulting strategies of
party competition.* Political entrepreneurs may attract voters with one
of three linkages: personal charisma, direct selective inducements to
and exchanges with constituents (clientelism), and the programmatic
promise of public policy, if elected to office. The thrust of my argument
is that no single model of party or party system is likely to characterize
East European polities. Moreover, a standard model of party mobilization
in Western Europe after World War II—mass parties with primarily
programmatic appeals—is unlikely to dominate Eastern Europe. In the
new democratic polities, parties often remain organizationally small
framework parties. Where mass parties appear, they are more typically
associated with clientelist linkage patterns.

In the first section, I elaborate these distinctions and identify
organizational correlates of different tactics of linkage building. The
subsequent three sections are devoted to developing hypotheses
accounting for the variability of East European parties and party systems
and illustrating, but not rigorously testing, their validity. In the final
section, I speculate about the consequences of different linkage
strategies. My analysis draws on an in-depth empirical study of party
formation in four East Central European countries[3] and exploratory
research on the relation between trade openness, democratic institutions,
and party systems in the region.[4]

Why Parties in Democracies?

If democratic governance is about establishing linkages of
accountability and responsiveness between citizens and competing
political elites, democracies must create organizational vehicles that
overcome problems of *collective action* and problems of *social choice.*
Parties are the devices that can, but not always do, address these
challenges.[5] Problems of collective action occur in citizens' demand
for and politicians' supply of candidates for representative office. By
pooling resources in a party, candidates can more effectively address
electoral constituencies and advertise their purpose of running.
Conversely, parties have the means to lower the voters' costs of gathering
information about alternatives and even to assist them in turning out to

the polls. Efforts to overcome collective-action problems thus warrant *investments in organizational infrastructures* that coordinate politicians and voters.

Social-choice problems result from the complexity of political agendas. Modern democracies build on the principle of territorial representation through electoral districts, not the functional representation of policy areas and sectional interests. In legislatures, representatives are asked to take policy positions on an uncertain and indefinitely variable set of issues legislators place on the agenda. With great probability, the variance of the representatives' preference schedules over each issue and over the entire set of issues on the agenda at any time is great. As a consequence, no set of policies may be uniquely preferred according to simple criteria of democratic choice, for example that the ultimately winning alternative in a democratic choice process has to beat all the other contending alternatives when pitted against each of them in a pairwise contest ("Condorcet winner"). To prevent cycles of decision making in which each victorious bill is displaced by a new alternative, politicians make *investments in consensus building* to bundle policy choices and establish common preference orderings. In the short run, they accomplish this through *log-rolling*. In the long-run, politicians reduce transaction costs of preference aggregation by a *legislative committee system* and especially by *programmatic party formation*. Politicians here commit themselves to the entire bundle of issue positions offered by a party, which are advertised to the electorate through simple cues, such as the location of a party program on the left-right dimension.

The distinction between investments in organizational infrastructure and consensus building permits us to typologize alternative forms of political interest articulation and aggregation in the arena of electoral competition.[6] If politicians make investments *neither* in organizational infrastructure *nor* in modes of consensus building, all they can hope for is that people rally to their cause based on some unique quality of their personality ("charismatic linkage"). They neither hold out material incentives for their following nor commit themselves to a policy program that results from investments in political consensus building. Charismatic authority tends to be unresponsive and unaccountable to the electorate, something Guillermo O'Donnell captured in the notion of "delegative democracies."[7] But over time, followers of charismatic politicians demand accountability and responsiveness. Then charisma has to give way to politicians' accomplishments, which manifest themselves in the capacity to disburse direct favors to electoral constituencies (clientelism) or to propose and implement public policies.

If politicians invest in consensus building, but not at all in organizational infrastructure, they may come up with joint preference schedules—such as in a legislative caucus—but with no effective vehicle to advertise their politics to voters. Most of the time such strategies of legislative coordination, by themselves, are insufficient to get politicians elected in a mass democracy. What does not follow from this, however, is the inverse conclusion that the more investments a party makes in organizational infrastructure and encapsulation of the electorate, the better its electoral performance.

Where politicians care above all about organizational infrastructure but do not invest in modes of consensus building around common policy programs, they create *clientelist parties*. They approach constituents with requests for funds and votes. Some of the funds that they receive from capital-rich, vote-poor constituencies they hand over to vote-rich, capital-poor constituencies in the form of direct material inducements to surrender their vote (personal gifts). Both vote-rich and capital-rich constituents also expect direct compensation for their support, once party politicians have been elected and can disburse favors to their clients out of public funds (jobs, housing, business contracts, regulatory rulings). Because direct exchanges and side-payments get politicians elected and constituencies compensated, neither side might bother about the existence of a general program of party policies.

Finally, politicians may invest in organizational infrastructure and modes of consensus building to create *programmatic parties*. Politicians compensate voters and activists for their support indirectly, via policies whose impact is not confined to party supporters. Programmatic parties require some organizational infrastructure in addition to investments in consensus building in order to build vehicles that can effectively advertise policy positions in electoral campaigns. These investments, however, are likely to be less costly than in parties crafting direct material exchange (clientelist) relations with voters and financial donors.

In the comparative analysis of party organization, a party's investment in organizational infrastructure is often captured by its *membership size in relation to the size of its electoral constituency,* that is, its capacity to "encapsulate" the vote-rich electorate. No party achieves encompassing membership without offering material incentives. Investments in mechanisms of consensus building are harder to measure at the process level. They manifest themselves in the formalization of binding internal collective-choice procedures—for example by party conventions and elected leaders—and also in the informal investment of time and effort activists and party leaders make to ensure the convergence of most party faithful on key programmatic issues. While concern with programs is likely to fuel internal conflict, if not factionalism, on average programmatic parties are likely to be more *cohesive* in their policy outlook than clientelist parties in which consensus building about policies is irrelevant and may not even be attempted. Thus procedural codification of decision making and programmatic cohesion may be suitable indicators of investments in consensus building.

Approximations of the different models of party organization tend to cluster around different regions. In Latin America, for example, the major parties tended to follow the clientelist model until recently. In Western Europe, the programmatic-party model prevailed, but particularly large mass parties, such as the Christian Democratic and socialist parties, always needed to rely on a significant dosage of selective incentives and clientelist linkage. In the interwar years, social democrats, for example, were hegemonic in Berlin and Vienna not just because of their programmatic appeal to blue-collar constituencies but also because they ran city governments that engaged in large public-housing projects and controlled access to city-owned flats.[8] Material incentives thus played a rather large role in the construction of mass parties, and it is only with the growing affluence and individualism of European societies that the attractiveness of party-controlled incentives has declined and become politically controversial. Where parties never provide direct material compensation for members, they rarely become mass parties but typically stay closer to the model of legislative-framework parties with limited investments in organizational infrastructure. This applies to most European liberal parties and more recently to the cohort of "left-libertarian" Green parties.[9] My illustrations of different party types around the world suggest two potential causes for diverging modes of party formation: the basic ideological orientation of parties and the institutional and cultural contexts of the democratic polities in which they thrive. Let us now turn to Eastern Europe and explore how we may account for more clientelist or more programmatic parties and party systems in light of these determinants.

The Effects of Party Ideology

The types of citizen-politician linkages that prevail in a democratic polity may vary from party to party. In Colombia and Uruguay, for example, the major liberal and conservative parties are highly clientelist with far-flung organizations but little programmatic cohesiveness. Since the 1970s, they have been challenged in both countries by leftist competitors who explicitly reject clientelist organization. In a similar vein, clientelism and factionalism in Italian and Japanese parties is much more pronounced in the large ruling center-right Christian and Liberal Democratic parties than in the leftist opposition. More generally, quantitative crossnational research has found a rather robust linkage between party ideology and organizational structure.[10]

What are the theoretical arguments that might lead us to expect that, in postcommunist Eastern Europe as well, the modes of citizen-party linkage in a given country might vary across parties? *Ideology* and *opportunity* are the two critical variables that deserve close attention. Ideologies that claim a *universalist* representation of societal interests are much more likely to yield programmatic parties than ideologies that highlight *particularist* group claims. Thus liberalism and socialism propose universalist programs for a viable societal organization that are explicitly aimed at eradicating unfair advantages accruing to individuals and rent-seeking groups. They rely on universalist standards of fairness either as equal rights to participate in the marketplace of voluntary exchange (liberalism) or as equal entitlement to basic societal goods (socialism). Both liberals and socialists thus have a basic revulsion against rent-seeking special interests that get their way through direct exchanges with clientelist party politicians.

Thus in postcommunist societies, market-liberal parties are least disposed to build mass party organizations based on material exchanges with contributors. With regard to the communist-successor parties, the circumstances of the communist collapse may create some complications. Politicians fight not only for an ideology but also for survival. In the immediate aftermath of the communist collapse, *socialist ideology is so widely discredited that communist-successor parties cannot possibly rely on it to appeal to voters.* In this circumstance, communist-successor politicians may tone down their universalist conception of social order and attempt to maintain linkages to electoral constituencies through direct material exchange. Moreover, in electoral campaigns they will highlight the local popularity of individual party candidates rather than their ideological affiliation.

Whether the tactics to replace programmatic appeals with clientelism and the personal charisma of politicians work for communist-successor parties depends on *opportunity.* Where communist-successor parties remain entrenched in the state apparatus even after the collapse of the old order, they most likely opt for clientelist network building. Here, their old universalist ideology is useless because the party presides over a gradual economic decline, as long as it fights against market-liberalizing reforms and the associated severe economic dislocations. At the same time, the party has control over resources to serve select constituencies. *Nomenklatura* privatization, cheap credits to party-affiliated enterprises, and subsidies (particularly to the countryside where communists remain strong) are typical phenomena associated with this process. Among countries with moderately fair elections, the reign of quasi-communist parties and local politicians in Bulgaria, Romania, and Ukraine in the 1990s illustrates such developments. Opportunities for clientelist linkage building are even greater in all those authoritarian and semiauthoritarian regimes where communists were never displaced from power, such as Belarus, Macedonia, Serbia, and most of the former Soviet republics of Central Asia.[11]

In some other countries, however, several forces may eventually drive communist-successor parties back to a more programmatic orientation. First, where they lose the founding elections, change their labels, credibly dissociate themselves from the old regime, and embrace democracy and market capitalism, they reconstitute their universalist ideology on a reformist, social-democratic programmatic basis. This process has taken place most unambiguously in Hungary, Poland, and the Baltic countries. Not by accident is it in these countries that the communist-successor parties have shed upwards of 95 percent of their pre-1989 members, whereas in countries with communist parties more firmly rooted in the old ways, and consequently equipped with a stronger penchant to cultivate clientelist linkages, their organizational decline has been much less steep.

Second, where communist parties are cut off from access to the material resources necessary to construct and maintain clientelist networks, they are likely to revert to a universalist ideological appeal, particularly once anticommunist governments have inflicted serious economic pain on the electorate—such as unemployment and declining standards of living—in the course of market-liberalizing reforms. The resurgence of the Russian communists may become an example of this trajectory.

Postcommunist party systems are not confined to party families relying in principle on universalist ideologies. There are a number of parties that appeal to "sectional" constituencies and explicitly seek to draw boundaries between "friends" and "foes" in a *particularist sociocultural* fashion. These parties run under religious, peasant, nationalist, and ethnocultural (minority or majority) labels. In each case, at least two mechanisms often, but not always, favor clientelist linkage building between politicians and voters rather than programmatic politics. First, because the favored constituencies are clearly identifiable, it is easier for such parties to organize and monitor direct exchanges between voters and politicians in clientelist networks. Parties with a universalist appeal face a more amorphous electorate and encounter greater problems in monitoring contracts. For this reason, Donald Horowitz concludes with regard to ethnic politics that "the ethnic party is the interest group."[12] Second, sociocultural and sectional parties *lack a theoretical conceptualization of the imperatives of economic reform, the most important item on the postcommunist legislative agenda.* They shun firm commitments on economic policy making for fear of dividing their sociocultural constituencies. Because they cannot build comprehensive programs that address the most important economic policy issues of the day, they attempt to resort to clientelist linkages.

The importance of clientelist constituency encapsulation for many sociocultural, peasant, and national parties shows up in their member/ voter ratios, which tend to be higher than those of their liberal or social-democratic counterparts. Again, in addition to ideology, opportunity (that is, access to state resources) is a critical issue. Thus member/voter ratios tend to be comparatively high in Czech and Hungarian Christian Democratic parties, which have participated in government, and in the

Polish Peasant Party, which has built effective clientelist networks in its time in office since 1993.[13] The extreme case of a nationalist government party building a far-flung clientelist network is Vladimir Mečiar's Movement for Democratic Slovakia.

Where sectional parties are excluded from power, they encounter greater difficulties obtaining resources to build clientelist networks successfully. In these instances, the charismatic authority of the leader must often substitute for investments in organizational infrastructure. Examples are Ganchev's Bulgarian Business Bloc, Torgyan's Independent Smallholders in Hungary, Sladek's Republicans in the Czech Republic, and Zhirinovsky's Liberal Democrats in Russia.[14] I have little doubt that these parties would build clientelist machines if they were to participate in government. The record of Hungary's Independent Smallholders since its entry into the government in May 1998 suggests that this hypothesis may be correct.

To summarize my propositions, ideology does affect the techniques politicians employ to build citizen-party linkages. Liberal-democratic parties emphasize investments in consensus building to promote their programmatic agenda more than investments in organizational infrastructure, although a modicum of the latter is unavoidable. They are likely to remain "framework parties" with a limited encapsulation of the electorate. Basic ideological dispositions by themselves are not sufficient to predict the nature of organizational investments made by communist-successor parties. Here my discussion has already invoked systemic contingencies. Under some circumstances, they become democratic reformists and tend to develop framework parties with limited encapsulation of the electorate; under other circumstances, they remain more intransigent in their views of liberal democracy and aim at a more encompassing encapsulation of the electorate and typically employ clientelist linkage techniques.

So far, I have advanced hypotheses about the variability of party formation *among parties within the same party system.* Only in the case of communist-successor parties have I made party structure contingent upon the systemic context. In order to advance from individual parties to the characterization of crossnational divergence among entire party systems, we must examine the variable systemic context of postcommunist politics more closely to show why certain types of parties and linkage strategies dominate in different East European polities.

Historical Legacies in Eastern Europe

Democratic party systems do not come into being overnight but typically require extensive periods of *learning* on the part of electorates and politicians. Moreover, where the introduction of democracy coincides with momentous economic changes, as in all postcommunist democracies, the trial-and-error period—during which parties and voters learn to take advantage of the new rules of democratic competition without achieving stable modes of operation ("equilibria")—is prolonged. During this learning period, institutionalized rules, such as electoral laws, are unlikely to constrain the conduct of actors in the same way as in established democracies. For example, whereas single-member districts restrict the effective number of parties in established democracies, in newly emerging polities large crowds of competitors may enter the electoral market, all hoping to become the lucky contenders to survive the selection process.[15]

Although institutions constrain political conduct less in emerging postcommunist democracies than in consolidated polities, the former are far from chaotic. Politicians' and voters' learning processes are guided by the communist regime's legacies, which provide powerful mechanisms that allow parties to create political resources, images, and orientations shaping the dynamic of the new parties and party systems. In a stylized fashion, one might therefore distinguish "early" postcommunist parties and party systems that can be empirically observed now from whatever party systems solidify in "later" periods of learning, when institutions gain more independent weight in shaping actor strategies. Even then, however, the legacies of the precommunist and communist past "lock in" power relations that congeal around democratic institutions shaping political actors' strategies for a long time to come. In accounting for divergence among parties and party systems in contemporary Eastern Europe, we must examine how these historical legacies systematically vary across countries.

In Eastern Europe, history did not begin with communist rule. Communist regimes were themselves a passing phase in a longer trajectory of economic, institutional, and cultural development that left its imprint on communist party governance. The variability of communist rule influenced the transition process to democracy, the democratic institutions, and the early patterns of party system formation.

Precommunist rule. I distinguish three configurations of rule in this period.[16] First, there are regions of Central Europe where both the working class and the urban middle strata mobilized politically before the advent of communism around liberal, religious, social-democratic, and communist parties (Eastern Germany, Bohemia/Moravia). In these regions, liberal democracy successfully worked for some or all of the interwar era. In a second area, the working class remained comparatively small and insignificant, but urban middle-class and rural peasant constituencies mobilized around a variety of parties (the Baltic countries, Hungary, Poland, Slovenia, possibly Croatia). This second region had less luck with liberal democracy in the interwar period and was primarily governed by semiauthoritarian

Divergent Paths of Postcommunist Democracies

dictators who manipulated elections and legislative representation, but did not suffocate civic pluralism entirely. In a third area, middle-class politics was confined to a thin urban stratum of administrators servile to authoritarian rulers, and the working class was all but nonexistent as a socioeconomic entity and an associational voice. These countries experience mass mobilization only around the poor peasantry (Southeastern Europe, Russia, Slovakia).

Communist rule. Building on these initial conditions, after 1917 in the Soviet Union and after World War II elsewhere in Eastern Europe, communist parties were able to draw on different resources and bargaining capacities to shape their apparatus of rule. Where both the working class and the middle class had a strong political voice, the new ruling parties could mobilize working-class constituencies within a formidable organizational weapon that allowed them to institute strictly *bureaucratic-authoritarian communism* and repress other potential political contenders rooted in the peasantry, the urban middle class, or associated religious and sociocultural causes. Where the middle class and the peasantry had been mobilized but working-class organizations had been weak in the interwar period, the entrenchment of communist rule remained sufficiently feeble that party leaders were motivated to seek at least tacit accommodation with potential opponents after direct Soviet control of domestic politics began to wane after 1955–56. In subtle ways, the local communist rulers invoked the preservation of national autonomy from the Soviet Union as an argument to request compliance and restraint from a sometimes visible, sometimes virtual opposition camp. The implicit exchange between rulers and their antagonists eventually yielded a less repressive form of *national-accommodative communism,* with economic market reforms or a modicum of civil rights. Gomulka and Gierek in Poland, as well as Kadar's "goulash communism" in Hungary, highlight this strategy.

Third, where both working-class and middle-class mobilization had been weak before World War II, the new communist rulers neither en-joyed the benefits of a politically disciplined working class or a bureau-cratic party machine nor experienced the constraints of urban middle-class opposition when building the new regimes. In this vacuum, the new rulers drew on patrimonial-statist methods of repressive and clientelist political rule and engaged in a rapid forced industrialization that destroyed the peasantry and created new, politically inexperienced and compliant working-class and middle-class sectors whose members could easily be coopted through material favors. Thus, while in the Soviet Union in the late 1920s and in Bulgaria, Romania, and even Slovakia after World War II more than 80 percent of the gainfully employed were peasants, communist rule transformed these countries into industrial societies in the span of a single generation.

Transition process. Once the structural economic crisis of communist regimes set in, the repressiveness of communist rulers and the (virtual) resourcefulness of the opposition shaped the transitions to democracy in the late 1980s. Under bureaucratic-authoritarian communism the ruling parties were intransigent to reform and clung on to power until the bitter end, but an urban middle-class opposition was potentially resourceful against the backdrop of historical memories and practical experiences in the interwar period. Communism here disappeared at a late stage by *implosion* when the ruling parties could no longer contain demands for fundamental change. The collapse of East Germany and of the Czechoslovak regime in November 1989 exemplify this case.

Under national-accommodative communism, where the incumbent party was more flexible in granting reforms and limited civil rights and thus allowed opposition groups to become comparatively resourceful, democracy evolved through a *negotiated transition* between rulers and representatives of the opposition. Prolonged bargaining characterized the transitions in Hungary, Poland, Slovenia, and possibly in Croatia and the Baltic countries, where the communist party leaderships began to accept oppositional representation before the communist regimes collapsed.

Under patrimonial communism, by contrast, rulers had relied on repression and cooptation and opposition forces remained weak and isolated, thus never creating a serious threat to the political incumbents. When communism was crumbling in one country after the other, elements of the ruling communist parties themselves chose *preemptive reform* to salvage as much of their power as possible into a new postcommunist era in which they expected to continue their domination over a passive civil society. Preemptive reform was the idea behind Gorbachev's initial innovations, as well as the regime changes in Bulgaria, Romania, some of the Yugoslav republics, and many of the Soviet republics in 1990–91.

Institutional choice. The new institutions of democracy and capitalism resulted from the traits of the old regimes and the strategic bargaining power of the emerging actors in the transition process. Path-dependency appeared but was diluted by contingencies of the situation: Timing and sequence, for example, mattered in the construction of new democracies. In the moment of transition, communist ideology was discredited, and liberal-democratic politics became the most attractive programmatic alternative. Because politicians in communist-successor parties therefore wished to deemphasize programmatic competition and adopt personalist or communitarian-nationalist appeals with little programmatic content, they advocated democratic governance structures that would put a premium on personality and direct exchange between voters and clients rather than on programmatic party competition:

candidate-oriented electoral systems and a strong, directly elected executive presidency. As a rule of thumb, the stronger the leverage of former
communists and nationalists in the choice of democratic institutions,
the more such institutions emphasized the personal character of competition between candidates as well as direct relations between voters
and representatives, to the detriment of programmatic competition
among parties.[17] Conversely, the stronger and more self-confident
liberal-democratic forces were, the greater were their chances to press
for democratic institutions emphasizing competition among ideas
rather than personalities. Since multi-member districts with closed
party lists depersonalize electoral competition, politicians who wished
to personalize the electoral system embraced single-member districts
with first-past-the-post winners or multimember districts that permitted
preference voting, gave parties limited or no influence over the nomination of candidates, and prohibited vote pooling among candidates
running under the same party label.[18] Only where liberal politicians
had weak anchors in mass electorates and faced strong communist parties
did they tend to opt for personalizing political institutions in the hope
of electing a popular liberal politician to the executive presidency,
which could then become the stronghold of liberal reforms.

As a consequence, former bureaucratic-authoritarian rule and
transition by implosion are associated with parliamentary rule and
closed-list proportional representation. Here communists had little
bargaining power and the diverse liberal-democratic protoparties agreed
on depersonalizing democratic competition. In democracies emerging
from national-accommodative communism, where reformist communists
and oppositional groups tended to balance each other's power in negotiated transitions, democratic institutions often combined both personalist and programmatic principles of interest aggregation. For example,
if the communists wanted an executive presidency, the opposition forces
got proportional representation (Poland, 1989–91). If parliamentarism
prevailed, the communists received a mixed electoral system with some
single member districts (Hungary, Lithuania).

Most democracies emerging from patrimonial communism have rather
powerful executive presidents or electoral systems that highlight a
personal relation between voters and politicians. Here, former communists who engineered the preemptive reform typically attempted to
impose their preferred institutional design but did not always succeed.
In Bulgaria, the anticommunist opposition managed to discredit the
sitting communist president and force the ruling party to accept a
democratic constitution with depersonalizing political competition. In
the all-important case of Russia, the anticommunists captured the office
of the presidency in 1991, but the liberal-democratic party structure was
too weak for them to opt for a democratic design with depersonalizing
competition. Here, an anticommunist president imposed a strongly

personalist democratic constitutional design over the opposition of communists and elements of the liberal-democratic opposition.

Historical Legacies and Party Systems

The relative strengths of different types of parties and their access to power in the divergent postcommunist regimes determine whether the new polities adopt more programmatic or more clientelist party competition. After *patrimonial communism,* communist parties tend to remain dominant and face weak, divided liberal opponents who are not able to put forth a clear, coherent, and popular programmatic alternative. Whereas communist-successor parties rely on patronage, as long as they can hold on to office, their liberal opponents engage in individual representation and charismatic appeals with only limited investments in consensus building and party infrastructure. In Russia, communists were cut off from such networks, but they have begun to reappear around the presidential office, for want of effective liberal-democratic parties that could organize a presidential coalition.

After national-accommodative or bureaucratic-authoritarian communism, chances for programmatic party competition are more favorable where the old communist party loses most of its grip on valuable economic and administrative resources. Here noncommunist liberal-democratic parties have more popular support, practical skills, and political capacities to develop programmatic appeals. At the same time, communist-successor parties can make a comeback only once they adopt a new social-democratic outlook. Programmatic competition takes hold early, as my empirical research in the Czech Republic, Hungary, and Poland demonstrates.

In the longer run, the new democratic institutions reinforce the divergence between postcommunist party systems that rely on programmatic competition and those that emphasize clientelist and personalist linkages. Strong presidentialism and personalist electoral laws promote programmatically amorphous parties that loosely hold together constituency-serving representatives who are constantly exposed to the temptations of clientelism in their direct dealings with local voters. This particularly applies to communist-successor and nationalist parties, for the reasons elaborated in the previous section. Conversely, closed-list proportional representation and parliamentary government centralize political power in the national party organization and force individual politicians to become team players supporting a common programmatic appeal.

In a variety of ways, the legacies of the three types of communist rule also influence the *political divisions around which programmatic competition unfolds* in the years after the adoption of democracy. This applies foremost to the division between supporters and opponents of the new democratic regime. The regime divide is likely to subside most rapidly in the former national-accommodative communist countries, where communist parties made a credible commitment to democracy and capitalism in the negotiated transition. In Hungary, the government coalition between the communist-successor party and the party that rallied the most prominent dissidents under communism, the Alliance of Free Democrats, symbolizes the bridging of the regime divide. This divide is also likely to subside after bureaucratic-authoritarian communism, because the communist-successor forces are too weak and marginalized to stage a significant challenge. A deep regime divide, however, is likely to remain after patrimonial communism, where a strong communist-successor party continues to confront a weak and divided democratic camp. The deep hatred between those who happen to belong to communist or anticommunist social networks reinforces the personalist and clientelist character of democratic competition in these countries. Even when parties do emphasize programmatic issues, often they are actually highlighting the struggle of warring camps for control of the state apparatus rather than stating sincere and effective commitments to policy programs.

All former communist countries have a common line of political division and competition between parties: the economic divide between winners and losers of market liberalization. Depending on historical legacies of communism, however, these economic divides are combined with sociocultural divisions in the arena of party competition. How such sociocultural divisions relate to economic conflict, however, varies across postcommunist polities according to their unique pathways and legacies.

After *bureaucratic-authoritarian communism,* the sharp polarization between a strong liberal-democratic party camp and a weak but intransigent communist-successor party—which may gradually be displaced by social-democratic alternatives—focuses the competition on economic issues, while secondary issues of religion, civil rights, ethnicity, and nationality attract voters only to minor niche parties.[19] In contrast, after *national-accommodative communism,* the economic policy divide between communist-successor and anticommunist parties is much narrower and sociocultural conflicts are likely to crosscut the economic divide. The precommunist political mobilization of the middle class typically relied on societal divisions that are now being revived by new parties (religion, urban-rural divisions). Given the limited interparty competition on economics, politicians in multiparty systems gladly seize upon secondary cultural, religious, or ethnic political divides to distinguish their programmatic message from those of other parties. In this vein, Hungary, Poland, Slovenia, and the Baltic countries have two dimensions of competition.

After *patrimonial communism,* finally, chances are greatest for mutually reinforcing and polarizing economic, political, cultural, and ethnic divisions. Still powerful and often unreconstructed communist-successor parties engage in populist appeals to rally the losers of the economic liberalization and reinforce their campaigns by invoking national closure and authoritarian law-and-order policies to set themselves apart from a fragmented field of liberal-democratic opponents depicted as rootless cosmopolitans with criminal connections. The insistence on national identity, compliance with collective norms, and ethnic status provides ascriptive criteria to undercut open, universalistic competition for resources among all members of society. For this reason, the losers of market liberalization seek protection under the umbrella of group categories that justify principles of economic distribution outside the realm of the competitive market. In addition to communist-successor parties, nationalist and ethnic-particularist parties stand to benefit from such voter demands.

The differentiation of types of communist rule and their antecedents and consequences brings Robert Putnam's "social capital" approach to bear on the problem of postcommunist party formation.[20] Citizens' and politicians' cognitive skills, resources, moral-political dispositions, and associational networks shape their capacity to build new democratic institutions and processes. In contrast to Putnam, however, whose Italian case study of social-capital differentiation relies on "long-distance causality" over a span of more than seven hundred years, the theoretical model of communist legacies identifies plausible "intermediate-term" mechanisms and rational-actor strategies that build bridges from precommunist regimes to communist rule and from there, via modes of transition, to current postcommunist democracies.

The Table on page 315 summarizes the argument. Of course, the hypothesized correlations and causations have a statistical character, implying that there are always exceptions where historical contingencies not accounted for in a parsimonious framework create outliers. From the perspective of political actors, it may be a relief that history is not destiny and that path-dependency at times will be broken, a critical observation we have to keep in mind when making predictions about individual postcommunist countries.

My discussion of systemic conditions has built a bridge between individual parties and entire party systems. In formerly bureaucratic-authoritarian communist states, clientelism tends to be weak because ideological party families and institutional rules of democratic party competition prevail that foster programmatic competition. Here politicians focus most of their energy on consensus-building inside parties and legislative caucuses and relatively less on the construction of extensive organizational infrastructures, such as mass parties. The reverse applies in former patrimonial communist polities, where communist and nationalist parties tend to be dominant. Party ideology and systemic opportunity here support, on balance, more clientelist linkage strategies. In particular, the more-or-less unreconstructed former communist ruling parties, which often remain entrenched in the state apparatus, seize the opportunity to bind voters to the party through clientelist networks. In a similar vein, sociocultural particularist parties tend to be prominent, yet unable to coordinate supporters around synthesizing political programs, especially around issues pertaining to economic reform. After patrimonial communism, market-liberal parties have the greatest incentive to appeal to voters around cohesive programs, but they remain weak and divided and thus cannot give the party system much momentum to crystallize around programmatic competition.

Former national-accommodative communist countries have intermediate historical conditions and new democratic institutions for programmatic or clientelist party competition, but they generally tilt toward the liberal-democratic variant. Here, both liberal-democratic parties and social-democratized communist-successor parties refrain from heavy organizational investment and clientelist linkage-building. Such strategies are more typical of sociocultural parties that tend to have rather diffuse programmatic appeals.

Rival Hypotheses

The sociological and political science literature yields a wealth of hypotheses about the conditions under which parties and party systems develop more programmatic or more clientelist features. I will briefly review the applicability of these arguments to Eastern Europe, drawing on as yet uncompleted macro-comparative quantitative research on all postcommunist democracies.[21] For reasons of space, I cannot introduce the operationalization of all variables and report estimations of different statistical models. The most contentious aspect of this work may be the operationalization of clientelism, a concept inherently difficult to measure. I rely on the judgment of country risk analysts evaluating the severity of problems of corruption in each postcommunist polity. Corruption involves the exchange of money for political favors. In democracies at least, this exchange is most often mediated through party channels. Where corruption is a standard, institutionalized form of linkage between politicians, administrators, and electoral constituencies, it tends to congeal around clientelist networks.

The most common theory relates clientelist or programmatic competition to conditions of development.[22] Poor, uneducated voters have short time horizons and weak capacities to conceptualize causal chains leading from the election of politicians to public-policy outcomes years later. They opt for quick and certain material gratifications derived from direct clientelist exchanges rather than the indirect and uncertain benefits resulting from politicians' policy commitments. At the same time, facing poor clients, political entrepreneurs are more likely to be

TABLE—ANTECEDENTS AND CONSEQUENCES OF THREE TYPES OF COMMUNIST RULE

	BUREAUCRATIC-AUTHORITARIAN COMMUNISM	NATIONAL-ACCOMMODATIVE COMMUNISM	PATRIMONIAL COMMUNISM
1. PRECOMMUNIST RULE			
MOBILIZATION OF POLITICAL FORCES	1. highly mobilized urban middle strata 2. highly mobilized working class 3.agrarian pressure groups	1. highly mobilized urban middle strata 2. unmobilized working class 3. strong agrarian mobilization	1. demobilized urban middle strata 2. unmobilized working class 3. strong agrarian mobilization
PRECOMMUNIST POLITICAL REGIME	competitive representative democracy	semi-authoritarian rule with "managed" party competition	traditional authoritarian or absolutist rule
2. COMMUNIST RULE			
FORMAL BUREAUCRATIZATION OF THE STATE APPARATUS	high levels of formal professional bureaucratization low corruption	intermediate levels of of formal professional bureaucratization low-medium corruption	low levels of formal professional bureaucratization high corruption
METHODS TO INDUCE POPULAR COMPLIANCE WITH PARTY AUTHORITY	repression: intense cooptation: secondary	repression: secondary cooptation: intense	repression: intense cooptation: intense
3. MODES OF TRANSITION FROM COMMUNISM			
INCUMBENTS	united, intransigent to offer concessions	predominantly ready cliques	divided, personalist
CHALLENGERS	strong liberal democrats weak nationalist groups	strong liberal democrats and nationalists	weak liberal democrats strong nationalists
TRANSITION PROCESS	implosion of regime short, sharp protest wave	protracted negotiations between challenger and incumbent elites	preemptive reform by incumbent elite faction
4. INSTITUTIONAL CHOICE			
ELECTORAL LAWS	proportional representation, closed list features	mixed PR/plurality systems, open list features in PR systems	plurality/majoritarian rules, open list
EXECUTIVE-LEGISLATIVE DESIGN	parliamentary system with weak presidential powers	cabinet with parliamentary responsibility medium presidential	strong presidential powers, weak parliaments
5. CONSEQUENCES FOR THE PARTY SYSTEMS			
CITIZEN-ELITE LINKAGE	stronger programmatic than clientelist	more programmatic than clientelist	stronger clientelist than programmatic
DOMINANT DIVISIONS OF PARTY COMPETITION	weak regime divide strong economic divide weak sociocultural divides	weak regime divide weak economic divide crosscutting sociocultural divides	strong regime divide strong economic divide reinforcing sociocultural divides

able to raise the funds necessary to satisfy their material demands than those of an educated middle class. Hence, clientelist parties prevail in poor countries (system level) and primarily appeal to poor voters (party level). Increasing affluence and education stirs up "progressive" movements, led by urban middle strata, that undercut clientelist networks.

A second theory of clientelism, proposed by Martin Shefter, argues that political structure is key for clientelism.[23] It evolves only if, at the time of suffrage expansion, no rational-bureaucratic civil service exists. This allows self-interested, calculating politicians who already have a foothold in oligarchic assemblies to employ the state apparatus as a resource for political deal-making and attracting a mass electorate. By contrast, parties faced with an absolutist state apparatus—built on a professionalized civil service—and those excluded from oligarchic assemblies build programmatic parties.

My threefold typology of precommunist and communist regime types essentially blends developmentalist and state-structuralist arguments together. Bureaucratic-authoritarian communism relies on early industrialization and bureaucratization and thus makes it difficult to form clientelist parties. Patrimonial communism, by contrast, emerges from agrarian societies with little rational bureaucratization, such as in Bulgaria, Romania, Russia, or Ukraine. In fact, the statistical association between communist regime type and level of political corruption, as scored by business risk analysts in 1996, is almost perfect.

A further argument on citizen-party linkages associates clientelism with ethnocultural pluralism in the polity.[24] At the present time, however, East European countries do not exhibit a pronounced correlation between cultural pluralism and corruption. This does not rule out that in a broader sample of countries the postulated relationship would emerge.

A fourth argument relates a country's trade dependence to programmatic competition.[25] In open economies, politicians rally strong public support for measures that prevent less competitive sectors from obtaining rents from the government and that endanger trade relations and undercut national competitiveness (in forms such as tariffs or trade restrictions). Less economically "efficient" institutions that provide more opportunities for rent-seekers, such as first-past-the-post plurality electoral rules or strong executive presidencies, prevail only in more closed economies. In fact, in Eastern Europe, trade openness, "efficient" democratic institutions, and levels of corruption are rather strongly associated. Once we control for communist regime type and other domestic polity variables, however, the independent effect of trade on democratic institutions and on levels of corruption all but disappears.

If corruption is a valid measure of the propensity toward clientelism in the new postcommunist democracies, then communist regime type, democratic institutions, and a dummy variable for a country's origin in the former Soviet Union explain the bulk of the variance in national levels of clientelism. Former bureaucratic-authoritarian communist countries now have democratic institutions that are less conducive to clientelism (parliamentary government, proportional representation). Moreover, they have always been located outside the borders of the Soviet Union. In these countries, market-liberal reform has progressed swiftly, and the state sector has shrunk dramatically, thus removing potential resources for building clientelist networks. At the other extreme, former patrimonial-communist countries mostly have political institutions that facilitate direct clientelist exchange networks and undercut programmatic party structures (personalist voting systems, strong presidential authority). These countries maintain a large, non-competitive state or quasi-state sector offering politicians resources to act on this propensity. The former national-accommodative communist countries now exhibit intermediate conditions for clientelist or programmatic competition, although most are closer to the institutional arrangements and political-economic reforms of democratic polities emerging from bureaucratic-authoritarian communism.

The Consequences of Parties and Party Systems

Does this structural divergence—postcommunist countries with stronger market-liberal parties, more depersonalizing political institutions, and more programmatic citizen-party linkage, on the one hand, versus countries with weaker market-liberal parties, democratic institutions of representation that emphasize personality, and more clientelist citizen-party linkage, on the other—actually matter? In fact, in postcommunist Eastern Europe, parties and party systems are elements of alternative political configurations that exercise considerable impact both on public satisfaction with and trust in the new political institutions, as well as on economic performance, mediated by a country's propensity to engage in economic reform and its attractiveness for business investors. Technically it is difficult, however, to isolate the independent causal contribution of parties and party systems to the economic performance and legitimacy of the new democracies because the former are strongly multicollinear with other correlates of regime structure and development, such as the nature of preceding communist regime or geographic proximity to the European Union (EU).

In the immediate aftermath of communism's collapse, the assertion of market-liberal, anticommunist parties in government led to distinctly better economic performance by the mid-1990s. But this success took place against the backdrop of diverse democratic transitions, communist regime patterns, and precommunist institutions of economy and polity. These can be traced back even further to the predominant religious denominations and types of rule prevailing in the seventeenth through nineteenth centuries.[26]

Resistance to reform, organized by the tenacious obstruction of strong communist parties, locks in a pattern of gradual but accelerating economic decline with a simultaneous pilfering of public assets by former *nomenklatura* members,[27] whereas dramatic economic restructuring leads to a sharp but short economic crisis and an ensuing economic recovery. Power relations blocking economic reform are most likely in new polities that build on patrimonial-communist foundations, that preserve the power of communist politicians, and that offer them opportunities to steal public resources or to divert them to rent-seeking groups that are incorporated into clientelist networks. Thus, by 1995–98, countries emerging from bureaucratic-authoritarian or national-accommodative communism (with comparatively strong market-liberal parties and communist-successor parties that had essentially adopted social democracy) showed, on average, more robust economic performance over the entire restructuration cycle since 1989 than those emerging from patrimonial communism. The most efficient predictors of economic recovery, however, are not our master variables, such as former communist regime form or corruption, but phenomena rather closely associated with them, such as distance of a country's capital from the EU, the implementation of economic reform measures in 1990–95, and the strength of legal safeguards in 1995.[28]

Democratic institutions and economic performance leave their mark on public trust in democracy and optimism that one's country is heading in the right direction. At the macro-level, a crossnational comparison of levels of popular regime satisfaction is quite hazardous in postcommunist democracies, however, because different countries' mass publics have different anchor points for their evaluations. Thus asking Romanians about their evaluation of the new democratic order may yield a more positive response than that of Hungarians. This is not because Hungarians are intrinsically less supportive of democracy but because the anchor point for Hungarians is the "good old days" of national-accommodative goulash communism in the 1970s, whereas for Romanians it is the repressive and economically deteriorating late Ceausescu regime.

Nevertheless, taking these difficulties of crossnational analysis into account, where patrimonial-communist party elites have continued to wield a great deal of power, mass publics appear generally less happy with the direction of their country's pathway and express much less trust in democracy than in other East European countries.[29] Moreover, a better business climate is directly related to more democratic trust and optimism about a country's future. Both of these measures, in turn, are also associated with the nature of democratic institutions. Where these institutions depersonalize political competition, democratic trust and business optimism tend to be substantially greater than in countries with more personalized democratic rules.

Because of the multicollinearity of communist regime features, current institutions, levels of corruption, and economic achievements, it is at this time statistically impossible to sort out the independent effect that each of these variables has on democratic trust, public optimism, and the business climate in a precise and reliable macro-quantitative comparison. But the sharp contrast between alternative clusters of countries is impressive. In one cluster of countries, proximity to the EU, former bureaucratic-authoritarian or national-accommodative communism, depersonalizing democratic institutions, low levels of corruption in politics, strong legal safeguards, and advanced market reforms coincide. Outside this cluster, countries that lack one of these elements typically also lack most of the others. Political parties and party systems are unlikely to have caused these starkly diverging patterns, but they are indicators and catalysts of policy processes that reproduce diversity among the former communist countries.

Advantages of Backwardness?

My analysis has emphasized the diversity of postcommunist pathways of regime transformation with regard to the emergence of political parties and party systems. New democracies in Southern Europe and other parts of the world may display important features of diversity scholars have also accounted for in terms of path dependency.[30] But path dependency as a theoretical framework, mediated by rational actor strategies, must not be reified into historical determinism. Fundamental crises that shake the basic institutions of a country, together with external political and economic pressures and the demonstration effects of successful reform elsewhere, may at times dislodge polities from their paths. From the normative perspective of advocating democracy and economic efficiency, one might very much hope for a rupture with path dependency in much of Southeastern Europe and the former Soviet Union. But at the time of this writing, I remain skeptical. It appears that mechanisms of path-dependency have configured postcommunist polities around highly diverse institutions and power relations that are likely to last for some time to come. Even in countries that may be most responsive to West European influences, particularly the lure of joining NATO and the EU, the power of path dependency is undeniable at this time. Against the backdrop of deep economic crisis precipitated by the half-hearted reforms and corrupt practices of communist-successor party governments, two formerly patrimonial-communist countries, Romania in 1996 and Bulgaria in 1997, voted for new liberal party governments that promised to catch up with the economic and political reforms of East Central Europe and lead their countries toward Western Europe. While both governments managed the easy part of reform, imposing a tight fiscal and monetary macroeconomic policy, they subsequently proved much less capable of delivering structural microeconomic and administrative reform that would have helped to lay the foundations for democratic political parties no longer enjoying the option of clientelist linkage-building.

Inspired by the path dependency claim, my analysis does not suggest a simple imitation of Western experiences anywhere in Eastern Europe. From the vantage point of West European experiences, the surprising result of my inquiry is that the new postcommunist democratic polities that have the least chance of building encompassing mass parties appear to have the best chance of consolidating around strong liberal-democratic and social-democratic parties and of experiencing the best relative economic performances. Skeptics might point out that in these countries, the volatility of party support is also still very high compared to established democracies. This volatility, however, is not associated with the rapid appearance of new parties but takes place within rather well defined blocs and ideological sectors of the political issue space.

It thus appears that democracies need not "encapsulate" electorates with heavy investments in party infrastructure, particularly via the construction of mass parties employing at least some material selective incentives built into direct clientelist exchanges. In Western Europe, the era of mass parties came to an end because political professionals tended to displace amateur activists in the task of mobilizing the vote and because the traditional clientelist incentives and exchange mechanisms became increasingly ineffective and illegitimate when faced with an electorate that responded to policy positions. In the face of changing voter demands, large party apparatuses may in fact reduce the strategic mobility of parties—and thus their democratic accountability and responsiveness—by infusing considerations of patronage and political network politics.[31]

Compared to Western Europe, at least some East European countries enjoy the "advantages of backwardness" of never having made investments in mass parties and of facing political demand structures and institutional opportunities that make the construction of mass parties unlikely. At least after bureaucratic-authoritarian and national-accommodative communism, most parties tend to remain small cadre parties with politicians who routinely must construct and reconstruct their electorates based on updated programmatic appeals on salient competitive issue dimensions. It is unreasonable to measure the future of party democracy in these East European polities against the past of West European party formation. In some postcommunist countries, however, the formation of mass parties with rather pronounced clientelist linkages is more plausible. But the extension of such structures may be detrimental to their economic performance and, as a consequence, to their democratic procedures and popular legitimacy as well.

NOTES

1. See Kenneth Jowitt, *New World Disorder: The Leninist Extinction* (Berkeley: University of California Press, 1992), and Herbert Kitschelt, "The Formation of Party Systems in East Central Europe," *Politics and Society* 20 (March 1992): 7–50.

2. Compare Beverly Crawford and Arend Lijphart, "Explaining Political and Economic Change in Post-communist Eastern Europe: Old Legacies, New Institutions, Hegemonic Norms, and International Pressures," *Comparative Political Studies* 28 (July 1995): 171–99.

3. See Herbert Kitschelt, Zdenka Mansfeldova, Radek Markowski, and Gábor Tóka, *Post-Communist Party Systems: Competition, Representation, and Inter-Party Cooperation* (New York: Cambridge University Press, 1999). For an extension of this framework to the study of Russian party formation, see Herbert Kitschelt and Regina Smyth, "Issues, Identities, and Programmatic Parties: The Emerging Russian Party System in Comparative Perspective," paper prepared for presentation at the 1997 Annual Meeting of the American Political Science Association, Washington, D.C.

4. Readers of my earlier work will notice that this essay and the book on East Central Europe build on but modify previous theoretical statements and initial empirical analyses. See Herbert Kitschelt, "Patterns of Competition in East Central European Party Systems," paper prepared for the 1995 Annual Meeting of the American Political Science Association, Chicago; Herbert Kitschelt, "Party Systems in East Central Europe? Consolidation or Fluidity?" *Studies in Public Policy* 241 (Glasgow: University of Strathclyde, Centre for the Study of Public Policy, 1995); Herbert Kitschelt, "The Formation of Party Cleavages in Post-Communist Democracies," *Party Politics* 1 (October 1995): 447–72.

5. John Aldrich, *Why Parties?* (Chicago: University of Chicago Press, 1995).

6. Of course, also outside electoral politics, vehicles of interest articulation and aggregation differ in terms of their investment strategies. Social movements, for example, invest neither in organizational infrastructure nor in modes of consensus building and therefore have only an intermittent existence. When their activists attempt to pursue their causes in a durable fashion they make investments in organizational infrastructure and become interest groups.

7. See Guillermo O'Donnell, "Delegative Democracy," *Journal of Democracy* 5 (January 1994): 55–69.

8. In other Christian Democratic and social-democratic mass parties, the close association between unions and parties—often combined with the administration of unemployment, pension, or health insurance by party or union—provided the material incentives for mass membership. This applies to the Scandinavian countries as well as to Belgium and the Netherlands.

9. On the organization of these parties, see Herbert Kitschelt, *The Logics of Party Formation* (Ithaca, N.Y.: Cornell University Press, 1989).

10. See Kenneth Janda and Desmond King, "Formalizing and Testing Duverger's Theories on Political Parties," *Comparative Political Studies* 18 (July 1995): 139–69. As I have argued above, this does not rule out that social democrats also employ some techniques of material citizen-party linkage.

11. Clientelist practices result in a halfway house of economic reforms where beneficiaries of privatization closely tied to the old elites entrench themselves and block further moves toward a more efficient set of economic institutions. See Joel

S. Hellman, "Winners Take All: The Politics of Partial Reform in Postcommunist Transitions," *World Politics* 50 (January 1998): 203–34.

12. Donald Horowitz, *Ethnic Groups in Conflict* (Berkeley: University of California Press, 1985), 344.

13. For a description of the Hungarian Christian Democratic People's Party, see Zsolt Enyedi, "Organizing a Subcultural Party in Eastern Europe: The Case of the Hungarian Christian Democrats," *Party Politics* 2 (July 1996): 377–96.

14. Zhirinovsky's party, however, has developed the most comprehensive organizational structure.

15. On non-equilibrium strategies of politicians under the condition of new institutions, see Mikhail Filippov and Olga V. Shvetsova, "Political Institutions and Party Systems in New Democracies of Eastern Europe," paper delivered at the 1995 Annual Meeting of the American Political Science Association, Chicago; and Robert G. Moser, "The Impact of the Electoral System on Post-Communist Party Development: The Case of the 1993 Russian Parliamentary Elections," *Electoral Studies* 14 (October 1995): 377–98.

16. For the historical reconstruction of divergence in Eastern Europe, see Daniel Chirot, ed., *The Origins of Backwardness in Eastern Europe* (Berkeley: University of California Press, 1986); Andrew C. Janos, "The Politics of Backwardness in Continental Europe, 1780–1945," *World Politics* 41 (April 1989): 325–58; and George Schöpflin, *Politics in Eastern Europe* (Oxford: Blackwell, 1993).

17. Exceptions confirm the rule. In Bulgaria, in a moment of weakness, the communist-successor party had to give up on its preferred personalist institutional design, that is, a rather powerful presidency together with a first-past-the-post electoral system.

18. See John M. Carey and Matthew Soberg Shugart, "Incentives to Cultivate a Personal Vote: A Rank Ordering of Electoral Formulas," *Electoral Studies* 14 (October 1995): 417–39.

19. On the territory of the former German Democratic Republic, the decline of the communist-successor party has been halted by the party's success in presenting itself as the voice of East Germans against the dominant Western part of the country. See Gero Neugebauer and Richard Stöss, *Die PDS. Geschichte. Organisation. Wähler. Konkurrenten* (Opladen: Leske and Budrich, 1996).

20. Robert Putnam (with Robert Leonardi and Rafaella Y. Nanetti), *Making Democracy Work: Civic Traditions in Modern Italy* (Princeton, N.J.: Princeton University Press, 1993).

21. Elements of this research are included in Herbert Kitschelt, "Accounting for Outcomes of Postcommunist Regime Change. Causal Depth or Shallowness in Rival Explanations," paper prepared for the 1999 Annual Meeting of the American Political Science Association, Atlanta, September 3–6. Also, Herbert Kitschelt and Edmund J. Malesky, "Constitutional Design and Postcommunist Economic Reform," prepared for presentation at the Midwest Political Science Conference in Chicago, 28 April 2000.

22. For a summary of the literature, see Shmuel Eisenstadt and Luis Roniger, *Patrons, Clients and Friends: Interpersonal Relations and the Structure of Trust in Society* (Cambridge: Cambridge University Press, 1984).

23. Martin Shefter, *Political Parties and the State: The American Historical Experience* (Princeton, N.J.: Princeton University Press, 1994).

24. See Donald Horowitz, *Ethnic Groups in Conflict,* ch. 8.

25. Ronald Rogowski, "Trade and the Variety of Democratic Institutions," *International Organization* 41 (Spring 1987): 203–23.

26. See M. Steven Fish, "The Determinants of Economic Reform in the Post-Communist World," *East European Politics and Societies* 12 (Winter 1998): 30–78. He finds that the countries' economic-reform trajectories are determined by the victory of noncommunist parties in the first democratic election, not by the historical properties of path dependency (such as the dominant religious denomination of a country), which also capture the development of state structure and political economy. In a multivariate regression, religion washes out when initial election results are entered as an additional predictor of postcommunist countries' economic reform efforts (p. 55). Given that Fish's coding of the religion variable (p. 41) is very strongly correlated (r = +.80) with the initial election results (p. 49), high multicollinearity should have prevented Fish from entering both items as independent predictors of economic reform effort. It is more reasonable to claim that historical legacies, of which religion may be an indicator, affect initial election outcomes which, in turn, affect postcommunist polities' economic-reform efforts.

27. Anders Åslund, Peter Boone, and Simon Johnson, "How To Stabilize: Lessons from Post-Communist Countries," paper prepared for the Brookings Institution Panel on Economic Activity, Washington, D.C., 28–29 March 1996.

28. Our operational measures of these concepts are correlated with former communist regime form at the level of .75 to .87.

29. I am relying here on survey data reported in Richard Rose and Christian Haerpfer, "New Democracies Barometer III: Learning from What is Happening," *Studies in Public Policy* 230 (Glasgow: University of Strathclyde, Centre for the Study of Public Policy, 1995); and data from Anders Åslund, Peter Boone, and Simon Johnson, "How To Stabilize," Table 15.

30. See most recently Richard Gunther and José R. Montero, "The Anchors of Partisanship: A Comparative Analysis of Voting Behavior in Four Southern European Democracies," in Nikiforos Diamandouros and Richard Gunther, eds., *Parties, Politics, and Democracy in the New Southern Europe* (Baltimore: Johns Hopkins University Press, forthcoming 2001).

31. I have argued in a comparison of West European social-democratic parties that voter encapsulation or "organizational entrenchment" reduced parties' strategic flexibility in the 1970s and 1980s. See Herbert Kitschelt, *The Transformation of European Social Democracy* (Cambridge: Cambridge University Press, 1994), ch. 5.

IV

Conclusion

13
CHALLENGES TO CONTEMPORARY POLITICAL PARTIES

Stefano Bartolini and Peter Mair

Stefano Bartolini is a professor in the department of political and social sciences at the European University Institute in Florence and author of The Political Mobilization of the European Left, 1860–1980: The Class Cleavage *(2000) and* Parties and Party Systems: A Bibliographic Guide to the Literature on Parties and Party Systems in Europe Since 1945 *(1998). Peter Mair is a professor of comparative politics at Leiden University in the Netherlands and coauthor (with Michael Gallagher and Michael Laver) of* Representative Government in Modern Europe: Institutions, Parties, and Governments *(2000).*

One of the central issues raised by the editors in chapter 1 of this volume, and addressed in a variety of ways by the authors of the ensuing chapters, is whether political parties are ceasing—or even failing—to perform functions that are key to the performance of healthy democracies and newly democratizing polities. In confronting this issue, the earlier chapters have assessed the role and performance of parties in a range of diverse settings, including Western Europe, the United States, the new postcommunist democracies, Latin America, Japan, Turkey, India, and Taiwan. Crucially, in none of these areas is the diagnosis clearly benign; problems of performance and legitimacy appear to impact parties in all of these settings with varying degrees of intensity. While far from innocuous, the diagnosis is still unclear as to whether these problems reflect a long-term and perhaps structural change in the role of parties as they adapt to new environments, or whether they are symptomatic of a secular and irreversible decline. On this question, as is the case with the contemporary literature on parties more generally, the jury is still out.

It goes almost without saying that any discussion of the role and importance of political parties in new or developing democracies is unlikely to ensue without reference to their role and importance in the more established democracies, particularly those in Western Europe. There are two principal reasons for this. First, as is more than evident to

even the most casual observer, political parties in the established
democracies have grown to acquire substantial status and legitimacy,
and they have long operated as the key mechanism for political
representation, the organization of government, and the maintenance
of democratic accountability. Even when it is argued that many of the
parties in these established democracies are now experiencing a period
of crisis or decline, this does not deny their importance for the long-
term development and stabilization of these democracies. Hence, what
these parties do or have done will always remain a crucial reference
point. Second, much of the scholarly literature that informs our
understanding of the role and importance of political parties in modern
democracy takes its terms of reference primarily from the Western
experience. This is the source of our models and our paradigms. Thus,
even if it emerges that parties in new democracies are somehow
different (a point emphasized in this volume by Herbert Kitschelt in
particular), the difference would likely be defined by reference to the
standards set by parties in the established democracies.

Comparison between parties—both those in the new and developing
democracies and those in the established democracies (especially in
Western Europe)—is not always easy, however, and different
expectations of possible parallels and similarities can be entertained.[1]
First, it might be argued that, regardless of the era or context, the role
and importance of parties in all democracies will tend to develop in
more or less the same evolutionary fashion. That is, to a greater or
lesser extent, all parties will tend to go through the same evolutionary
stages of development, notwithstanding the specific timing or staging
of the wider process of democratization. Whether we are dealing with
parties that first emerged to compete in the democracies of Western
Europe in the 1920s, in Southern Europe in the 1970s, or in
postcommunist Europe in the 1990s, we will tend to witness more or
less the same trajectory running from elite party to mass party, to catch-
all party, to electoral-professional party, and so on. Following this
argument, party forms and roles will be seen to be conditioned by the
particular stage of democratic development a system is in, with the
early stages encouraging the formation of mass parties, which later
develop into catch-all parties as democracy becomes more institutionalized and routinized. In fact, what evidence we have on the character
and style of parties in third-wave democracies in particular suggests
this is a highly implausible approach, a point that both Kitschelt and
Philippe Schmitter agree on in these pages. At the same time, the
argument does have a certain heuristic value and can serve as a useful
reference point.

Second, it might be argued that the role and importance of parties
in all democracies will tend to reflect the prevailing—and also
increasingly standardized—social, economic, and governmental

circumstances in which these parties compete. These common circumstances include the availability of technological and other resources
and the impact of globalization, individualization, and mass communication. In this view, we can expect to find substantial similarities
among parties competing in contemporary democracies regardless of
their location or stage of democratization. Echoes of this perspective
may be seen in the emphasis placed by Michael Coppedge on the
dynamics of "political Darwinism" in Latin America. Moreover, whether
operating in democracies first established in the 1920s, the 1970s, or
the 1990s, the governments that parties currently occupy are all subject
to similar policy constraints, and this in itself obliges parties to pursue
similar strategies, both politically and electorally. Therefore, apart from
inevitable "teething" difficulties, the role and importance of parties
are expected to develop in a common pattern, whether the democracies
are emerging or established, Eastern or Western. Looking at the content
of the various chapters in this volume, there is clearly much to be said
for this argument. Problems of electoral fragmentation, of low or
declining grip on electoral identities and choices, of loosening ties
with interest groups, and of coping with governmental tenure seem to
be similar in such widely diverging contexts as those of Italy, India,
Japan, and Turkey. Seymour Martin Lipset's argument in chapter 3
about the end of American exceptionalism can also be read from this
perspective, with the pressure of shared external circumstances leading European socialist and denominational parties to de-emphasize
their original social and ideological identities and to follow a path not
too far removed from that which helps to define the American party
landscape.

Third, it can be argued that the role and importance of political
parties in contemporary democracies will tend to vary according to the
circumstances of their initial formation and development. Following
this approach, which emphasizes the lasting impact of largely genetic
factors, we would expect marked and potentially enduring differences
between the parties and the party systems that first emerged in Western
Europe during the early part of the century and those that emerged
during the more recent third-wave transitions. If the mainstream West
European parties have grown to be reasonably similar to one another, it
is because they were all formed and later developed in similar
circumstances, as a result of the politicization of similar cleavage
structures.[2] This would further imply that there is no good reason to
expect that the parties that began to emerge in new democracies in the
1970s and 1990s would follow a similar path, since, as both Kitschelt
and Schmitter underline, the circumstances of their initial formation
and development were quite different from those of their West European
counterparts.[3] Nor would we expect any convergence of party styles
across different global regions. Thus Latin American parties will appear

quite different from those in Asia, while each set will also differ substantially from those in Europe or the Middle East.

The Functions of Political Parties

Although parties and party systems can be compared and contrasted
along a variety of different dimensions, as Hans Daalder emphasizes in
chapter 2, a concern with party roles and importance inevitably requires
a particular focus on *the functions* that parties perform, or that they may
be expected to perform. This focus is also useful for comparing parties
across different regions and time periods, since it offers a more abstract
set of terms of reference that may be applied to democracies in very
different social settings and levels of political development.[4] In
assessing and comparing the functions of parties in different settings,
however, it is important to recognize that we are not dealing with
something that is necessarily intrinsic to parties, or that necessarily
defines the nature of parties as such. To begin with, it is obvious that
parties may actually be defined in quite a wide variety of ways. According
to Giovanni Sartori's minimal definition, for example, a party is "any
political group that presents at elections, and is capable of placing
through elections, candidates for public office."[5] It follows, therefore,
that to define a party is not necessarily to specify its various functions,
and to identify the functions that parties perform is not necessarily to
specify the character of these parties. These are two quite separate
inquiries, and it is perfectly reasonable to conceive of a set of actors, all
of which merit being defined as parties, yet each of which in practice
performs very different functions in their respective polities. Indeed,
this is already implicit in the earlier chapters, where the very wide variety
of party categories presented suggests an equally wide variety of
functions performed. According to Richard Gunther and Larry Diamond
in chapter 1, for example, parties may be categorized as "elite parties,"
"mass-based parties," "ethnicity-based parties," or "electoral parties."
In detailing the contemporary Italian case in chapter 6, Leonardo Morlino
speaks of "modern cadre parties" and "movement-parties." In
postcommunist Europe, one of Kitschelt's key distinctions is that between
"clientelist parties" and "programmatic parties." In Japan, according to
Bradley Richardson in chapter 7, we see evidence of a "mass personalized
network party," while in parts of Latin America, according to Coppedge,
we see a "national revolutionary or 'Aprista' party." Nor is this
differentiation of party types and functions simply a matter of different
contexts. In the Latin American case, for example, as in Italy and Turkey,
we see the coexistence of a variety of different party categories, and
hence, we must assume, the coexistence also of different party functions.

One of the problems involved here is the inevitable and quite com-
monplace confusion between what a party *is*, on the one hand, and what

it *does,* on the other. More specifically, in determining what a party is, it seems to us that too much weight is accorded to what a party does. There are two extreme positions that can be adopted here. On the one hand, we can hold on to the minimum definition of party, and hence we can see parties, however fragmented, in every polity in which elections are freely contested. Once candidates are nominated for election, we can assume the existence of parties as the nominees of these candidates even if, at its most extreme, the "parties" in question are simply groups of supporters loosely cohering behind the nomination of individual candidates. By this very minimal definition, a case could be made that the United States is composed of at least 100 distinct parties competing in 50 state-level party systems. On the other hand, by conflating functions and definition, and by insisting that parties exist only when they enjoy an effective monopoly on a number of key functions within the polity (as Schmitter implies), we risk developing a set of criteria by which it becomes increasingly difficult, if not impossible, to find any parties whatsoever. Part of the difficulty here is that the functions classically ascribed to political parties (which we detail later in this chapter) are in fact those that were most readily associated with a particular type of party—the classic mass party, as described by Maurice Duverger, Sigmund Neumann, and Otto Kirchheimer.[6] And given that the age of the mass party has now passed within the established democracies, and (as many of the earlier chapters testify) that there is very little evidence that genuine mass parties can or have emerged in more newly democratized polities, we then risk being left with a situation in which no party remains that properly fulfills our expectations. At the one extreme, therefore, parties proliferate and are unavoidable; at the other, they are scarcely to be found. Neither alternative is satisfactory.

It might also be argued that in assessing the role and importance of parties in a given polity, we should not be so concerned with whether a particular function is performed by parties as such, but rather with the extent to which that function remains a monopoly of parties, as opposed to being shared with other nonparty organizations or agencies. In other words, what matters is the extent to which parties enjoy more or less *exclusive* control with respect to certain functions, and the extent to which their role is now challenged or supplanted. Ever since the initial mapping by Gabriel Almond in 1960, and the more critical evaluation by Anthony King in 1969, an effective agreement exists on the range of potential functions that may be associated with the role of political parties in democratic polities.[7] These include the integration and mobilization of the citizenry; the articulation and aggregation of interests; the formulation of public policy; and the recruitment of political leaders. To these can also be added the function of organizing parliament and government, since this is an especially important role for parties in parliamentary democracies in particular. These are the

tasks that parties perform—the things they do—although obviously
their capacity to do them, and the extent to which they enjoy a monopoly
in their performance, will vary from polity to polity and from period to
period.

Representation and Institutions

These various functions can easily be grouped under two main
headings. On the one hand, parties may be seen to perform a variety of
representative functions, including interest articulation, aggregation,
and policy formulation. On the other hand, they also perform a variety
of *procedural* or *institutional* functions, including the recruitment of
political leaders and the organization of parliament and government.[8]
Seen in this way, moreover, we have an analytic distinction that may be
assimilated to an older historical and genetic distinction regarding the
forces that originally shaped the nature and the role of parties—social
inputs, or cleavages, on the one hand, and institutional organization on
the other. From the social inputs perspective (that is, through the
mobilization and politicization of social cleavages), parties could be
seen to have structured polities politically, linking individuals, groups,
and interest associations into a specific pattern of organizational
membership and voting. Within this perspective, and regardless of any
signs of crisis in the relationship between parties and citizens, new
cleavages find difficulty in being articulated, in that the alignment and
alliances of the "ins" strongly determine the chances and the alliance
opportunities of the "outs." Once a system is structured in this way, it
becomes resistant to change, with parties learning to adapt their ideologies and policy positions to incorporate new issues and new demands.
Should the system fail to be structured in this sense, however, we are
likely to find the situation depicted by Coppedge, in which existing
actors are replaced by those who develop a more appropriate strategy
for dealing with new challenges. Conversely, from the institutional
perspective, the role of parties may be seen in terms of institutional
performance and harmonization. Parties are shaped by, and themselves
shape, the work of institutions, whether electoral systems,[9] parliament,
or executive office.

What is perhaps more important, however, is that each of these perspectives on how parties originated can lead to quite opposing
expectations regarding their present and future roles. To stress, for
example, the importance of social inputs in the origins of parties is to
underline the uniqueness of party formation in the West, particularly
Europe, as well as the enduring linkages that parties need to maintain
with civil society in order to qualify as parties. This, in turn, reminds
us that the modern "mass party" was not only the historical product
of the coincidence of specific processes of social mobilization,

industrialization, and urbanization with those of political mobilization, suffrage expansion, and political organization, but was also typical of certain historical periods and moments that tend naturally to decay as politics itself becomes more routinized. The modern mass party, in other words, was both a temporary and context-specific phenomenon.

Thus, following the last wave of collective mobilization in the wake of World War II, different models than those that had determined their initial formation and development have inevitably begun to shape the trajectory of the original mass parties. It was no longer necessary to integrate new masses entering the political system. Interests and demands grew to become more fragmented, more particularistic, and, in the end, more transient. The capacity of parties to aggregate demands inevitably declined. Meanwhile, increasing state intervention rendered daily political activity more complex and technical, with the result that the political class tended either to emphasize its professionalism or to project ever-more-simplifying charismatic or populist images. Mass communication increasingly facilitated a more immediate perception of the protagonists of politics and a greater centralization of the management of political socialization and the mobilization of consensus. In such circumstances, it became increasingly difficult, costly, and even unnecessary to allocate resources to grassroots political participation.[10]

This transformation went far beyond the early signs noted by Kirchheimer in his influential essay on the catch-all party.[11] A political market that had once been dominated by the supply side became increasingly demand-oriented. The citizen as subject became the citizen as consumer, and the laws of the consumer society, after quite a long delay, finally began to enter politics. Competing channels of representation began to open up, with the emergence of "alternative" organizations or movements that were seen to offer a more effective or satisfactory means of linking citizens to decision-making processes. At the same time, the revolution in communications quickly spelled an end to differentiated publics and differentiated political languages. Coupled with a growing individualization—in which it became legitimate for each citizen to seek to fulfill his or her own private desires and motives in politics—the result has been the progressive weakening of those networks of organizations and collective identities that formerly constituted the principal framework for political involvement and participation, as well as the increasing demand and search for new units of identification (such as through regions, localities, and ethnicity). Above all, citizens began to acquire an apparent capacity for direct action, and no longer seemed reliant on political mediation.[12] Not only has political aggregation in such circumstances become difficult and unrewarding, but political intermediaries are also increasingly regarded as having only an instrumental legitimacy.

It is almost self-evident that, within such a context, the social roots of political parties will tend to fade. Indeed, it is striking to note how such a diversity of party settings as is examined in this volume tells such a similar story about the erosion—or even, in the more recently democratized polities, the non-appearance—of "societal partyness." The one exception might be the case of Taiwan, as noted by Yun-han Chu in chapter 11 of this volume, but even he notes that this is a case unlikely to continue to challenge the global trend. Moreover, it is not surprising that this process should be seen as reflecting party decline, since by focusing attention on changes in the relationships between parties and citizens, it is easy to conclude that the parties of today are no longer those of the past, or that even the parties that have newly emerged look very different from those that once dominated the Western political stage.

In addition, and beyond these immediate chapters, there is an ample and growing literature testifying that we now live in an age characterized by increasing popular disenchantment with political parties, and by growing distrust with the political class more generally.[13] The evidence here is wide-ranging but also fairly consistent: a declining sense of party attachment and partisan identification; diminishing public confidence in parties in general; falling party memberships; reduced electoral turnout; increasing support for new parties, small parties, and "antiparty" parties—and, more generally, for anti-establishment organizations of the extreme left and the extreme right—as well as for autonomist, regionalist, and populist movements. All of this evidence clearly points to a declining capacity on the part of traditional parties to maintain solid linkages with voters, and to engage these voters and to win their commitment. Above all, the evidence points increasingly and unequivocally to the decline of parties as representative agencies.

Furthermore, no longer do parties enjoy such a privileged position in this regard—as was the case during the so-called "golden age" of the mass party—in that other means have increasingly become available through the emergence of alternative channels of interest articulation, and possibly even aggregation. These include interest groups themselves, which have burgeoned in recent years and which now operate increasingly independently of party, as well as social movements, civic action groups, and so on. Other channels through which political leaders may learn of popular concerns also exist, including polling agencies and the mass media. In this respect, as has rightly been pointed out by students of the new social movements in particular (and as Schmitter also emphasizes), parties can no longer claim anything even approaching a monopoly in the function of interest representation. In this sense also, their role is challenged.

It is also important, however, to recognize a crucial distinction here, in that this particular development may not necessarily constitute a chal-lenge to the party as such; rather, and perhaps even at most, it constitutes a challenge to party *organizations,* at least insofar as these organizations once served as the principal means of communicating popular concern upward to political leaders, and of communicating leadership decisions down to the population or constituency at large. It follows from this that the emergence of new and alternative channels of representation need not make parties as such redundant, even if they do undermine the classic role associated with the party as mass organization in particular. What this latter distinction may also imply, of course, is that parties could quite easily learn to live with these parallel agencies, and to take advantage of their presence in order to learn of new interests and demands as they are articulated. Indeed, in one reading, these parallel agencies may be regarded as proving quite functional for parties. In the past, parties were helped in their representative function by being able to make certain *assumptions* about where interests lay. Formalized communication was not that important. Socialist leaders could assume knowledge of working-class interests; confessional political leaders could assume that they knew what was best for confessional voters; farmers' leaders knew what farmers wanted. But this is hardly feasible now, and hence communication—via interest groups, social movements, the media, and public-opinion polling—becomes much more important. To speak of a potential conflict of interest between party and nonparty channels of representation, and to set one off against the other, may therefore be misleading. In contemporary democracies, both channels may well feed off one another.

Moreover, the nonparty channels of communication, if closely examined as mechanisms of representation, present their own weaknesses and problems, and can at best be depicted as a limited complement to political parties' activities rather than as a substitute for them. If corporate interests and social movements were advocated as a comprehensive principle for organizing the representation within the political system, the problems of systemic rationality would be completely overlooked. One should also not underestimate the fact that some corporate organizations and social movements might reflect political difficulties as deep (if not deeper) than those of the parties themselves. In short, although they challenge the "monopoly" of the input function of political parties as representative agencies, and sometimes even their output function as "policy makers," these alternative channels should not necessarily be seen as wholesale functional alternatives.

There is one further important qualification that needs to be under-lined here: While the representative functions of the party—at least in-sofar as these were channeled directly though the party—may well have declined within the established democracies, and while they may also be poorly developed in many of the newer democracies, the same cannot be said for the procedural or institutional functions. Indeed, these latter functions are effectively unchallenged—whether by alternative agencies

or the media. This is a crucial point, for despite an increasingly volumi-
nous literature dealing with the supposed decline of the party, there is
scarcely anything to suggest that a viable democratic alternative can be
found to substitute for the role of parties in the recruitment of leaders or
in the organization of government. At this level, it can even be argued
that the functions of parties have become enhanced. Thus we see that
recruitment to government posts (including cabinet posts) and to key
posts in the public sector, for example, now often appears more party-
based than before. In addition, government formation processes in parliamentary democracies have now become more open and less predictable, with coalitions becoming both more innovative and promiscuous.
All of this suggests that parties are obliged to devote more and more
attention to and become more and more central in the organization and
maintenance of executive and parliamentary offices. The importance of
the procedural role played by parties has also won increasing recognition
in the form of growing state subventions and extended party laws, all of
which lends parties an increasingly "official" status within the various
polities.[14]

What we witness, therefore, is a shift in the balance of party functions
from the combined representative and procedural roles that were
characteristic of the mass party in the so-called golden age to a more
exclusively procedural function. What we have also witnessed, of course,
is the rapid endowment of such a procedural role on the fledgling parties
in the new democracies, many of which have taken on the creation and
legitimation of the newly democratized institutions as their primary
task.

Decline or Adaptation?

Given this historic shift, an emphasis on the role of parties within
democratic institutions and procedures will likely lead us to a very different conclusion from one deriving from a focus on their representative
role alone. Policy decisions, the organization of elections, running
parliamentary life, the formation of executives, and the like will always
and everywhere require a certain amount of group behavioral conformity,
and such conformity is normally and perhaps most effectively achieved
by party alignments within these institutions. Seen from the perspective
of the actual functioning of key political institutions and how they
relate to the state, parties may therefore appear more "central" than
even half a century ago. From the perspective of the parties themselves,
this shift from an emphasis on channeling representation to an emphasis
on organizing procedures—the shift of parties from society to the state—
can also be interpreted as a strategy of survival. Among other benefits,
it cements parties within decision-making loci, through which they can
create circumstances and sponsor laws favorable to their own situation.

In other words, they can afford to avail themselves of public privilege in a way that enhances their own resources and position.

At the same time, however, this development poses two further problems, both with long-term implications. On the one hand, although increasing public privileges at a time of declining representativeness may serve to sustain the parties in the short term, it may also undermine their legitimacy in the longer term.[15] This may well be one of the keys to understanding the present malaise that grips parties and the institutions they inhabit throughout the established democracies, in that their enhanced and increasingly well-protected institutional role has been accompanied by a seeming erosion of their relevance within the wider society. On the other hand, this new division of functions also begs the question of how long it can actually be maintained in practice, and whether the parties that seek to sustain themselves by retreating into the institutions can actually survive as parties. We return to this question later. If the distinctive and defining feature of parties is the creation of a minimum behavioral conformity in institutional arenas by a group of people united by common instrumental power interests, then of course it can be easily concluded that parties will always exist, just as it can be easily concluded that they also always existed among the factions of medieval communes, in the time-honored Vatican assemblies, and even in the Roman senate. However, it is equally true that what was historically new about "modern" political parties, as they emerged in the historical phase inaugurated by both the industrial (British) and political (French) revolutions, was something more than this, involving something other than simply an exclusively institutional role. Hence, if we now see these parties being reduced more or less exclusively to the role of public-office holders, we may simply be assimilating them to the electioneering and parliamentary groupings of like-minded people that preceded mass politics. In this sense, and echoing Ruud Koole's depiction of the "modern cadre party," we may see parties coming back full circle.[16] The question then becomes whether they have a meaningful future at all.

Students of parties, together with many party activists and political observers, have long regarded the historically specific mass party as a norm. In many respects, the mass party represented the high point of party development, with its particular combination of representative and institutional roles legitimizing both the party itself and the wider polity within which it functioned. The ever-more pronounced separation of the representative and institutional roles (and especially the evidence of a shedding of the party's representative capacities) may in this sense signal decline. Yet it is not difficult to argue that what we observe here is adaptation rather than degeneration, and that what are emerging in the new politics are simply "different" parties, no better and no worse, perhaps, than the mass party that preceded them, but certainly better

suited to the needs and constraints of contemporary democracies. Echoing Coppedge, this is political Darwinism writ larger. Moreover, and
returning to the threefold distinction at the beginning of this chapter,
this view could also be read as sustaining the second, more "generational" approach, in which the conditions prevailing in primarily postindustrial and globalized economies call forth a new style of party,
almost regardless of where these parties are to be found or at what stage
in the democratization process they compete. We might therefore be
witnessing evidence of convergence across different polities, in which
the evolutionary trajectory of parties in established democracies as they
move from mass parties to catch-all parties and beyond meets with that
of the parties in new democracies as they begin to settle into roles that,
at least initially, were forged almost exclusively by the exigencies of
public office.

Here again, as elsewhere in this volume, it seems that we are still left
with uncertainty as to whether we are witnessing degeneration or regen-
eration, decline or adaptation. But this uncertainty is itself important,
in that the sheer difficulty involved in trying to make sense of this
changing party universe may itself be read as an indication of a historical
"crisis" of political parties. On the one hand, any discussion of the role
of parties in present and future democracies involves strong normative
overtones and combines different and not necessarily complementary
hypotheses. On the other hand, the very concept of party "crisis" or
"decline" is itself elusive. Short of bankruptcy and disappearance, as
Daalder reminds us, no other symptom may be regarded as sufficient or
insufficient to test the hypothesis.[17] So how do we find our way out of
this puzzle? There are two problems that need to be addressed here.
First, we need to establish a clearer understanding of how the historic
role of parties in processes of democratization differs from that seen in
more contemporary settings. Second, in light of this contrast, we need
to ask whether an exclusively institutional role—or what we shall refer
to as the capacity for institutional integration—is sufficient to sustain
parties that seem increasingly unable to perform a representative role,
or that no longer enjoy the capacity for *political* integration. For if
political integration fails, how then can institutional integration be
sustained?

Three Challenges Parties Confront

The key historical role parties have played in the various democratization processes that have now extended from the middle of the
nineteenth century to the beginning of the twenty-first century has been
the effort to harmonize different *institutional orders* and *political
processes* within the nation-state. To be sure, parties were not always
and everywhere equally successful in performing this role. Yet, when

compared to the other principal means by which modern democracies became politically structured—through territorial division and corporate interest representation—parties were the only institution that deliberately aimed at integrating and making compatible the various processes and institutions of the democratic polity. These included: 1) the electoral process, in which noncorporate or unorganized interests, aspirations, movements, and public opinion could be taken into account; 2) the process by which corporate or organized interests were channeled, in which the regulative orders were agreed upon by strong interests, and state bureaucratic agencies were checked for mutual compatibility and system compatibility by the counterbalancing effect of the electoral channel; 3) the parliamentary legislative process, in which majorities were required for consistent institutional life and legislative output; 4) the process of executive formation; and 5) the process of policy making. Simply put, there has been no other modern political institution that has extended its role through such a wide-ranging set of processes and institutions, and at the same time attempted their systemic integration.

There are thus two factors involved here: *political* integration and *institutional* integration. Political integration requires control of individual and group behavior, with parties seeking to organize, shape, influence, and eventually control the behavior of voters, interest groups, social movements, and parliamentary groups through systems of loyalty and partisan identification, through political linkage, material reward, and clientelistic networks. Institutional integration, on the contrary, requires the overall harmonization of the institutional order, including the selection and socialization of the political personnel, the formation of parliamentary majorities, the organization of support for executives, and the accommodation of conflicts and tensions among different institutional, territorial, and functional subsystems. These political and institutional integration capacities have been far from uniform, however, and clear contrasts can be seen between the genetic phase of democratization and the more mature phase, between the recently democratized and the more established and stable polities, and between periods of transition and periods of consolidation.

The various chapters in this volume, as well as much of the wider literature, reinforce the view that the political integration capacity of parties has considerably eroded. The ability of contemporary parties to discipline individual and group political behavior, and to control the demands of social movements and the claims of substate territorial units, is now far more limited than that of their predecessors in the long-established democracies, while within many of the new democracies, this capacity has developed only within quite narrow limits. If this diagnosis is valid, then the question as to whether parties have a future can be reformulated by asking whether they will continue to be able to provide institutional integration—that is, to harmonize the working of different institutional arenas—in a context in which their capacity for political integration is clearly in decline. In this regard, there are three particular challenges that parties now face.

First, in order to integrate different institutional arenas (such as is involved in the relationship between parliamentary alignments and cabinet formation, for example), political parties need to be able to produce a relatively coherent internal hierarchy and to be in a position to "duplicate" or "export" such a hierarchy into the arenas they intend to organize and discipline. This task obviously becomes increasingly difficult if the internal hierarchy is progressively diluted into a less authoritative environment. If the internal life and external activities of parties are regulated excessively by public law, for example, this will lead to their being redefined as public service agencies, with a corresponding weakening of their own internal organizational hierarchical order. Indeed, if the "party rules" become "legal rules"!—if internal party processes become externally regulated, and if, eventually, every member, sympathizer, or even ordinary citizen who does not even take part in the life of the organization becomes empowered with respect to internal decision making and personnel selection—then the hierarchical order of the party organization progressively weakens and loses the capacity to duplicate itself and to expand.

Second, parties need to recover their autonomy and coherence, which are key dimensions of their institutional integrity. The increasingly extensive resort in contemporary democracies to the principle of "competence" or expert legitimacy as opposed to *political* legitimacy (as in the increasing reliance on decision making by nonpolitical central banks, expert commissions, technical bodies, and so on), along with the extensive use of referenda and the referral to institutional solutions that dilute political responsibility (such as regulatory agencies and the judiciary), effectively reduces the autonomy of parties by encouraging their external takeover by other institutions and actors. A similar outcome may result from the growing phenomenon of "lateral entry" within parties, such as occurs when parties incorporate actors endowed with particular personal or private resources (money, social prestige, notoriety, stardom, clienteles, and interest-group support); this accentuates their loss of autonomy.[18] In the long run, parties therefore become penetrated by the hierarchies and the resources available in the external environment rather than exporting and duplicating their own internal hierarchies.

A challenge to the autonomy and coherence of parties emanates from those areas in which supranational institutions and governance add a new layer of decision making. Historically, parties were devices for the centralization of national conflicts, identities, and demands. The multiplication of layers of government—local, regional, national, and supranational—now makes it that much more difficult for parties to exercise control and coordination. In playing these multilevel territorial games, parties are likely to experience a decline in their organizational coherence and political autonomy. As such, the same party may find it increasingly difficult to adopt similar policy positions in the various arenas, while party legislators group or regroup in different ways in different arenas. In addition, the opportunity to promote the salience of particular issue dimensions that are favorable in one arena may well be affected by the need to consider their compatibility with other arenas.[19] Multilevel governance also implies that, while parties may remain effectively responsible and accountable at the domestic level, this can involve policy decisions on which they enjoy only limited or even nonexistent leverage.

The third challenge facing the institutional role of parties derives from their potential loss of legitimacy in the eyes of the citizenry. Three elements are involved here: The first is legal and is reflected in the declining conformity to legal rules and in the growing discrepancy between legal or even moral standards, on the one hand, and political standards on the other. Evidence of corruption and a lack of transparency in decision making are obviously key indicators of this source of strain. The second element is attitudinal, and is reflected in the increasingly widespread awareness of a fundamental discrepancy between party actions and how their historical functions in democracies are understood. Evidence of representative failures is obviously important here, as is the sense of the growing "insulation" of the political class from popular concerns and grievances. The third element is behavioral, and is reflected in the declining popular support for traditional parties, as well as in the declining expressions of consent for party action and party rule. Evidence of popular disengagement from party politics is relevant here, both at the electoral and party organizational levels, as is the increasing tendency for voters to opt for anti-establishment—or sometimes even explicitly antiparty—alternatives.

The Future of Political Parties

Most analyses share the view that parties and the democratic institutions they articulate are expressions of the consolidation and the boundary control of the modern state. Seen in this perspective, parties are a crucial device for internal political articulation within what has been an externally closed political entity—that is, within a polity that has enjoyed relatively pronounced control over its external economic, cultural, and politico-administrative boundaries. One of the steepest challenges parties confront today stems from the final loosening of this historical capsule, the nation-state. Put very briefly, territorial units that tend to become more and more softly bounded economically, administratively, and culturally may undermine not only the political integration capacity of parties but also their institutional integration capacity.

Yet even when recent analyses emphasize that parties now face a number of competing actors and challenging new processes, they nevertheless also recognize that in both old and newly established democracies, no real alternatives have emerged. Parties may face an increasing number of *competitors,* but as yet they seem to have faced no real *alternative.* Strikingly, in none of the many and varied experiences that are evaluated in this volume is a credible alternative institution cited that could adequately control political behavior and harmonize different institutional orders.

To be sure, the lack of alternatives to the political party is not any guarantee of its future success or even survival. Parties could become reduced to mere labels reflecting factionalized, clientelistic struggles among more or less independent political entrepreneurs, each of whom seeks to win the support of voters by using methods and resources outside the reach and control of party organizations as such.[20] But while this might represent one possible future for parties, it leaves open new questions regarding the wider political systems in which these parties compete. For if parties no longer do the job, who will then act as the agent for political and institutional integration? More to the point: What happens to democracy if neither political nor institutional integration proves possible any longer?

NOTES

1. See Ingrid van Biezen, "The Development of Party Organizations in New Democracies: Southern and Eastern Europe Compared," Ph.D. diss. (Leiden: Leiden University, 2001).

2. See Hans Daalder, "The Rise of Parties in Western Democracies," pp. 40–51 in this volume; see also Stein Rokkan, "Nation Building, Cleavage Formation and the Structuring of Mass Politics," in Stein Rokkan, *Citizens, Elections, Parties: Approaches to the Comparative Study of the Processes of Development* (Oslo: Universitetsforlaget, 1970), 72–144.

3. See Herbert Kitschelt, "Divergent Paths of Postcommunist Democracies," pp. 299–323 in this volume; see also Peter Mair, *Party System Change: Approaches and Interpretation* (Oxford: Oxford University Press, 1997), 175–98.

4. See Richard Gunther and Larry Diamond, "Types and Functions of Parties," pp. 3–39 in this volume.

5. Giovanni Sartori, *Parties and Party Systems: A Framework for Analysis* (Cambridge: Cambridge University Press, 1976), 64.

6. Maurice Duverger, *Political Parties: Their Organization and Activity in the Modern State,* Barbara and Robert North, trans. (New York: Wiley and Sons, 1963); Sigmund Neumann, "Towards a Comparative Study of Political Parties," in Sigmund Neumann, ed., *Modern Political Parties: Approaches to Comparative Politics* (Chicago: University of Chicago Press, 1956), 395–421; and Otto Kirchheimer, "The Transformation of Western European Party Systems," in Joseph LaPalombara and Myron Weiner, eds., *Political Parties and Political Development* (Princeton, N.J.: Princeton University Press, 1966), 177–200.

7. Gabriel A. Almond, "A Functional Approach to Comparative Politics," in Gabriel A. Almond and James S. Coleman, eds., *The Politics of the Developing Areas* (Princeton, N.J.: Princeton University Press, 1960), 3–64; and Anthony King, "Political Parties in Western Democracies: Some Sceptical Reflections," *Polity* 2 (December 1969): 111–41. See also Richard Gunther and Larry Diamond, "Types and Functions of Parties," pp. 3–39 in this volume.

8. Peter Mair, "De toekomstmogelijkheden van politieke partijen, links, en de democratie," *Socialisme & Democratie* 57 (December 2000): 544–53.

9. See Giovanni Sartori, "The Party Effects of Electoral Systems," pp. 90–105 in this volume.

10. Alessandro Pizzorno, "Elementi di uno schema teorico con riferimento ai partiti politici in Italia," in Giordano Sivini, ed., *Partiti e partecipazione politica in Italia* (Milan: A. Giuffré, 1969), 4–40.

11. Otto Kirchheimer, "The Transformation of the Western European Party Systems."

12. Stefano Bartolini, "Collusion, Competition, and Democracy, Part I," *Journal of Theoretical Politics* 11 (1 October 1999): 435–70, and Stefano Bartolini, "Collusion, Competition, and Democracy, Part II," *Journal of Theoretical Politics* 12 (1 January 2000): 33–65.

13. For example, see Pippa Norris, ed., *Critical Citizens: Global Support for Democratic Governance* (Oxford: Oxford University Press, 1999); and Susan J. Pharr and Robert D. Putnam, eds., *Disaffected Democracies: What's Troubling the Trilateral Countries?* (Princeton, N.J.: Princeton University Press, 2000).

14. Richard S. Katz and Peter Mair, "Changing Models of Party Organization and Party Democracy: The Emergence of the Cartel Party," *Party Politics* 1 (January 1995): 5–28.

15. Peter Mair, *Party System Change*, 120–54.

16. Ruud A. Koole, "The Vulnerability of the Modern Cadre Party in the Netherlands," in Richard S. Katz and Peter Mair, eds., *How Parties Organize: Change and Adaptation in Party Organizations in Western Democracies* (London: Sage Publications, 1994), 278–303.

17. See Hans Daalder, "The Rise of Parties in Western Democracies," pp. 40–51 in this volume; see also Hans Daalder, "A Crisis of Party?" *Scandinavian Political Studies* 15 (December 1992): 269–88.

18. For a good example of this in the structure of Forza Italia, see Leonardo Morlino, "The Three Phases of Italian Parties," pp. 109–42 in this volume.

19. For example, see Michael Laver, "Party Competition and Party System Change: The Interaction of Coalition Bargaining and Electoral Competition," *Journal of Theoretical Politics* 1 (July 1989): 301–24.

20. See, for example, Kitschelt's distinction in this volume between personal and infrastructural investments.

INDEX

352

Index